THE ENGLISH
UTILITARIANS
AND INDIA

Oxford University Press, Amen House, London E.C.4

GLASGOW   NEW YORK   TORONTO   MELBOURNE   WELLINGTON
BOMBAY   CALCUTTA   MADRAS   KARACHI   KUALA LUMPUR
CAPE TOWN   IBADAN   NAIROBI   ACCRA

THE ENGLISH
UTILITARIANS
AND INDIA

BY

ERIC STOKES

PROFESSOR OF HISTORY IN THE
UNIVERSITY COLLEGE OF
RHODESIA AND NYASALAND

OXFORD
AT THE CLARENDON PRESS
1959

> *'Mill will be the living executive—I shall be the dead legislative of British India.'*
>
> BENTHAM

PRINTED IN GREAT BRITAIN

TO THE MEMORY OF
IAN ALISTAIR MACGREGOR

PREFACE

THIS book is a study of the English political mind in the nineteenth century as it was to be found at work in the administration of India. I would like to think, therefore, that the work serves a twofold purpose, making a modest contribution both to the history of India and to the history of English political ideas. It has been my conviction that British rule in India was not a disconnected and meaningless fragment of English history, but that even from the most insular standpoint it holds a mirror up to nature, reflecting the English character and mind in a way that often escapes the Englishman confined within his domestic setting. I hope that my examination of the Utilitarian influence on India will help to throw the Utilitarian movement as a whole into new perspective, and in particular I would like to think that it counters the prevalent tendency to be interested in the Utilitarians solely as abstract moral and political theorists, to the neglect of their practical aims and influence. I have sought to show that the nature of these practical aims was deduced logically from their abstract theory, and that both fall into a system whose completeness is more obvious in Indian than in English history.

Some surprise may be occasioned by the small figure which John Stuart Mill makes in these pages, despite the thirty-five years he spent as an official at the India House. But, as I have pointed out, his official work was almost entirely confined to handling political relations with the Indian states, and neither by temperament nor belief was he fitted to take over the leadership of the doctrinaire programme laid down by his father and Bentham. Undoubtedly his authority did much for the general acceptance of his father's notion of the Indian land revenue and for upholding the cause of peasant proprietorship, but his true importance lay in the very much broader field of political theory. It is significant that the most powerful challenge to his attempt to lead the Utilitarian tradition within the fold of popular liberalism came from one whose whole faith and argument rested upon

Indian experience. It was India which most clearly exposed the paradox in utilitarianism between the principle of liberty and the principle of authority, and it was Fitzjames Stephen, on his return from India, who challenged the intellectual basis of J. S. Mill's political doctrine and sought to rally the Utilitarian tradition to the principle of authority and the maintenance of empire. I have dealt with this question in the concluding chapter. Similarly, I have dealt briefly with the other broad movement of intellectual qualification affecting the standing of the Utilitarian dogmas—that prompted by the historical and comparative method of Sir Henry Maine. I have suggested that this current of ideas also found practical expression in a school of Indian policy.

It should perhaps be explained that the word 'India' is used throughout the book either to describe the former British Indian Empire or as a geographical expression.

I should like to acknowledge the sympathetic help and encouragement I have received from Dr. Percival Spear of Selwyn College, Cambridge, and from Professor C. H. Philips of the School of Oriental and African Studies, University of London. I am particularly indebted to my friend Charles Parkin, Fellow of Clare College, Cambridge, whose suggestions have done much to improve the book; and to another dear friend, the late Ian Macgregor, whose death on the Gold Coast in 1956 deprived Portuguese colonial history of a most promising scholar. Dr. K. A. Ballhatchet of the School of Oriental and African Studies has most kindly looked up a number of important references for me. Mr. S. C. Sutton and his staff at the India Office Library have also been of great service, especially in lending books to me while in Malaya and Africa—surely a unique library service. Finally, for all the tedious work of typing and indexing, I would like to record my gratitude to Mrs. J. A. Hallett of Salisbury.

E. T. S.

University College of Rhodesia and Nyasaland
Salisbury

CONTENTS

INTRODUCTION   *page* xi

I. THE DOCTRINE AND ITS SETTING
    1. The Battle of the Two Philosophies   1
    2. Liberalism and the Policy of Assimilation   25
    3. The Utilitarians and India   47

II. POLITICAL ECONOMY AND THE LAND REVENUE
    1. The Doctrine of Rent and the Land Tax   81
    2. The Effect of the Rent Doctrine on Indian Land Tenures   110

III. LAW AND GOVERNMENT
    1. The Reform of the Administration   140
    2. The Reform of the Superior Government   168
    3. Macaulay as Law Member   184
    4. The Penal Code   219

IV. THE UTILITARIAN LEGACY
    1. The End of the First Age of Reform   234
    2. 'The Dead Legislative of British India'   243
    3. Utilitarianism and Late-nineteenth-century Imperialism   287

NOTES   323

BIOGRAPHICAL NOTES   331

BIBLIOGRAPHY   334

INDEX   339

INTRODUCTION

IT has been customary to regard the activities of the British in India as a separate and isolated portion of their history, a dim, half-fabulous tale of ferocious greed and valour, succeeded by the rule of a bureaucracy as monotonous, dusty, and sun-dried, as the Indian plains in the long hot weather. The former Indian Empire was always looked upon as something unnatural and alien; 'the strangest of all political anomalies' Macaulay described it. It was a common conviction that east of Suez the Englishman's character underwent a mysterious transformation, so that in the minds of his countrymen he was set apart as some distinct species, to be treated either with awed bewilderment or humorous ridicule. The popular notion is not, of course, without its grain of truth, although one would perhaps ascribe it more to the English mentality itself, with its curious inability to assimilate anything outside its fixed circle of experience. Certainly India played no central part in fashioning the distinctive qualities of English civilization. In many ways it acted as a disturbing force, a magnetic power placed at the periphery tending to distort the natural development of Britain's character as a great commercial power. It was a military empire in an unimperial age, a vast commitment dubiously balanced by its actual commercial value to English industry, a possession which generated that artificial rivalry with Russia which preoccupied British foreign policy throughout the nineteenth century. Mentally it reacted upon the English middle class by infusing an authoritarian counter-current into the main tide of Liberal opinion, so that serious men from Chatham onwards wondered whether the possession of a despotically-ruled empire might not prove fatal to the cause of liberty in England. Yet this aspect of India's influence on the British outlook is more true of the later phases of the relationship, when the growth of European rivalries after 1870 led to a preoccupation with power. It should not mask the more formative role which India played in English history throughout the greater part of the nineteenth century. Particularly in the earlier decades, India provided that element of scale and expansiveness to the new middle-class mind, so essential for the deployment of its political and moral ideas. Indeed, considering the general public indifference to Indian affairs, it is remarkable how many of the movements of English life tested their strength and fought their early battles upon the Indian question. To Adam Smith the hated 'mercantile system' found its embodiment in the East India Company, which he attacked in an unusual furore of denunciation. The cause of Free Trade was to a large extent fought out in the struggle for the abolition of the Company's commercial functions. It was the same with other contemporary movements of ideas. Evangelicalism, the rock upon which the character of the nineteenth-century Englishman was founded, owed much of its impetus to the Indian connexion. Two of the founder members of the Clapham Sect, Charles Grant and John Shore (Lord Teignmouth), were Company's servants who had been Cornwallis's advisers on the question of the Bengal Permanent Settlement; and the militant, aggressive Christianity of Clapham became a force in public life as much through the cause of Indian missions as through the campaign against the slave-trade. Because of this family tie with India enjoyed by the Grants, the Stephens, the Thorntons, and others, Clapham and its offshoots were to send forth generations of Indian civil servants stamped with the Evangelical assurance and earnestness of purpose, if not always the old religious conviction.

The family connexion with India was repeated in the case of the Utilitarians. What led James Mill to undertake the labour of his *History of British India* is uncertain, but the work resulted in the employment of him and his son after 1819 in the East India House and firmly fixed Utilitarian influence in Indian affairs.

The relation of such movements to India was not merely personal and fortuitous. British policy moved within an orbit of ideas primarily determined in Europe, although it lost nothing, of course, of its clothing of expediency and its habit of waiting upon events. The loose, tolerant attitude of Clive and Hastings, their readiness to admire and work through

Indian institutions, their practical grasp of the British position, unclouded by sentiments of racial superiority or a sense
of mission, were ultimately the reflection of eighteenth-
century England." The transformation of the Englishman
from nabob to sahib was also fundamentally an English and
not an Indian transformation, however much events assisted
the process. Indian experience undoubtedly hardened certain traits in the English character, but for their origin one
needs to penetrate to the genesis of the nineteenth-century
English middle class, and to the hidden springs setting its
type. The fierce, downright exterior, the instinct for his own
caste and race, the consciousness of religion, the sense of a
moral code and a constant dwelling under an unwritten law
of duty, the eager and crude intellectual appetite—all the
images the imagination must summon to picture the Englishman of the early Victorian age in India, are really drawn
from English social history.

This determining influence of English history extends
beyond character to the broad fashioning of British policy.
However confused the surface of events, the tide of British
policy in India moved in the direction set by the development of the British economy. The Industrial Revolution
and the reversal it brought about in the economic relation of India with Britain were the primary phenomena. A
transformation in the purpose of political dominion was the
main result. Instead of providing a flow of tribute—a conception which survived at least until the end of the eighteenth
century—the British power in India came to be regarded
after 1800 as no more than an accessory, an instrument for
ensuring the necessary conditions of law and order by which
the potentially vast Indian market could be conquered for
British industry. This transformation of economic purpose
carried with it a new, expansive, and aggressive attitude,
which the French, who were its later masters, termed that
of *la mission civilisatrice*. The missionaries of English civilization in India stood openly for a policy of 'assimilation'. Britain
was to stamp her image upon India. The physical and mental
distance separating East and West was to be annihilated by
the discoveries of science, by commercial intercourse, and
by transplanting the genius of English laws and English

education. It was the attitude of English liberalism in its
clear, untroubled dawn, and its most representative figure in
both England and in India was Macaulay. The material and
intellectual elements of which it was composed were the
three movements which have already been described as
possessing a special and particular connexion with India.
Free Trade was its solid foundation. Evangelicalism provided its programme of social reform, its force of character,
and its missionary zeal. Philosophic radicalism gave it an
intellectual basis and supplied it with the sciences of political
economy, law, and government. These three movements
were its constituent elements, but liberalism in the first age
of reform could hardly be each of these things in turn.
Macaulay again was the true representative. Of a middle-
class merchant family, brought up among the Clapham Sect,
and falling under the spell of Utilitarian doctrines at Cambridge in 1818, he found the confines of each creed too
constrictive. Purging them of dogma and blending their practical aims and spirit, he voiced the trenchant, generous,
empirical liberalism of the eighteen-twenties and thirties.
Doubtless local circumstances and the changing economic
relationship between England and India opened the path for
Indian reform, but the opportunity was seized by a movement of much more than local significance. The whole
transformation of English mind and society, as it expressed
itself in liberalism, was brought to bear on the Indian connexion. And it was brought to bear—it is this which makes
Indian history important for the most insular of English
historians—by its most distinguished representatives, James
and John Stuart Mill, Bentham and Macaulay. One has only
to add Maine, Fitzjames Stephen, and Morley for later
Indian history, to enumerate most of the important figures in
the intellectual history of English liberalism in the nineteenth century.

The Liberal current began to assert itself in India at the
same time as it did in English political life. It was from about
1818 that the cause of reform gathered momentum. There
had indeed been earlier, isolated victories. In the parliamentary battle of 1813 the free-traders had stripped the Company
of its commercial monopoly over India, and separately,

Wilberforce and Charles Grant had gained freedom for
Indian missions. But the movement was not homogeneous,
and was prevented from exploiting its gains by Indian conditions. From 1798 until 1818 the British power was preoccupied with internal war and political problems. For it was
during this period that the political map of India was given
a recognizably modern shape, and the British territorial
possessions, scarcely changed from the time of Clive, were
expanded until they bestrode the Peninsula. Madras and
Bombay rose from small coastal settlements to be the administrative capitals of two great new Presidencies; the one
absorbing—apart from the puppet states of Mysore and
Travancore—the whole of India south of the Kistna, the
other taking in a broad belt of territory in western India
running from Surat in the north to join with the Madras
territories in the south. In the Bengal Presidency the British
frontier was advanced from the centre of the Ganges valley
to its headwaters, and a new dependent province (later to be
known as the North-Western Provinces), stretching from
Allahabad to beyond Delhi, was set up as the fruits of
Wellesley's conquests and annexations.[1] With the exception
of the Indus delta the whole coastline of India was now in
British hands, and the native states within the circle were
reduced to dependent powers.

This expansion had its own logic, but again in a sense it
owed its impulse and sanction to the martial epoch through
which Britain passed in the Napoleonic Wars. By 1818 the
Mahratta power had been extinguished, and the political
problem ceased to be of the first importance. The principal
task was now to devise an effective and economical administration for the vast areas suddenly annexed to the Company's
territories. It was the same task which Grey was later to
announce as the programme of his Ministry—'Peace, Retrenchment, and Reform'. However favoured by local circumstances, the reform movement in India depended upon

---

[1] In reading this work it is necessary to keep in mind the numerous changes of
title which these Provinces underwent. Known at first as the Ceded and Conquered Provinces, or more popularly as the Upper Provinces, in 1822 they became
the Western Provinces, in 1834 the Presidency of Agra, in 1836 the North-
Western Provinces, in 1902 the United Provinces (of Agra and Oudh), and
finally in 1950 Uttar Pradesh.

the influence of contemporary England, for it was in England that liberalism as a name and a force was emerging in 1818. As Shelley wrote in that year in his preface to *Prometheus Unbound*, the cloud of mind was discharging its collected lightning, and the equilibrium between institutions and opinions was about to be restored. It was in that year that the orator of the new liberalism, the young Macaulay, shook off his father's toryism and avowed himself a Radical. It was in the same year that James Mill published his great *History of British India*, and became a candidate for high office in the Company's Home Government.

The resistance which liberalism encountered in India was not the ordinary inertia of the existing order. It encountered what in a more intellectualized political tradition would be called a rival political philosophy. It encountered the spirit of Burke. The Liberal attempt to assimilate, to anglicize, was met by a generation of administrators, founded by Sir Thomas Munro, who possessed all Burke's horror at the wanton uprooting on speculative principles of an immemorial system of society, and shared all his emotional kinship with the spirit of feudalism and the heritage of the past. In the shaping of Indian policy this form of conservatism was to have a much stronger hold than in England, where the progress towards an industrial society was rapidly to empty it of content. In India, as the attitude of paternalism, it was able to make strong head against the reforming tides and to divide its opponents. It succeeded so far as to shift the emphasis of liberalism, by drawing out the latent authoritarianism that resided in its doctrine. In doing this it tended to divide and confuse the Liberal aims. Particularly did it draw off the influence of the Utilitarians. It will therefore be necessary to examine all these currents of thought, and to observe their Indian context, before the special influence of utilitarianism can be studied.

I

THE DOCTRINE AND ITS SETTING

1. *The Battle of the Two Philosophies*

THE setting of British administrative policy was laid at the foundations of the British dominion in India. In the early period after Plassey expediency predominated. The immediate problem at that time was the manner in which the British should exercise their controlling power in the Bengal territories. At first they felt too inexperienced and unready to contemplate taking the government of the country into their own hands, and had resort to the expedient of a puppet Indian government. Even when this system broke down, and Clive obtained from the titular Mughal authority the grant of the formal right to collect the land revenue and administer civil justice (the grant of the *Diwani* in 1765), he was determined that the native administration and its officers should be continued, and the Company's power still held in the background. The result was Clive's famous 'double government'. The first point in his politics, as he told the Bengal Council on his departure in 1765, was that the Company's sovereignty should be masked.[1] In this way as little interference as possible was to be made with the indigenous political system. The attitude persisted when the considerations of expediency which had prompted it were no longer so strong. As the indigenous system withered, the British were compelled increasingly to intervene in the revenue and judicial spheres, and to fashion administrative machinery of their own. But they continued to regard themselves as inheritors rather than innovators, as the revivers of a decayed system and not the vanguard of a new. Social conditions favoured this attitude. A handful of eighteenth-century Englishmen, scattered throughout the Bengal

[1] Clive to Verelst and Select Committee, 16 Jan. 1767: *Second Report on East India Company, 1772*; also Clive to Court of Directors, 30 Sept. 1765, *Third Report on East India Company, 1773*.

territories, without English wives, or prospects of furlough, and with no rigid moral or religious code, soon adapted themselves to Indian ways of living. Set on making their fortune before the climate or disease carried them off, they were zealots for no cause or political principle, and were content to conduct the public business according to its traditional Indian forms and in the traditional hybrid Persian. Yet their very presence betokened a change in the character of government, however long its effects might be delayed. The breach had been made, and the pressure of the Directors for patronage steadily widened it until the English element in the government of Bengal predominated. Although a product of circumstance rather than design, the principle of anglicization had taken root. Warren Hastings attempted to resist its implications. He was the first to recognize the necessity of abandoning the sham of Clive's 'double government' and openly to assert British sovereignty and responsibility. Yet he feared not only the immediate effects of releasing a horde of plundering English officials into the interior, but also the more lasting consequences of loosing English ideas and methods on the weakened fabric of Indian society. He tried, unsuccessfully as it proved, to confine the British element in the administration to the Supreme Government at Calcutta, and to leave the ordinary provincial administration in the hands of the old Indian official class.

The first conscious movement to introduce English principles into the British possessions arose out of the attempt of Parliament to control the excesses of the Company's servants in India. Lord North's Regulating Act of 1773 instituted the Calcutta Supreme Court, 'the chief purpose of which', in Burke's words, 'was to form a strong and solid security for the natives against the wrongs and oppressions of British subjects resident in Bengal'.[1] The Supreme Court was made independent of the Governor-General and Council, and administered English law. With its powers of jurisdiction defined in only the vaguest manner it was possible for the Court by legal construction to extend

[1] *Ninth Report of Select Committee on the Affairs of India, 1783*; Burke, *Works*, 1852 edn., vol. vi, p. 384.

its authority over the larger part of the civil justice administered in the Bengal territories. The threat that English law would displace the indigenous Hindu and Muslim system aroused in Hastings the first conscious reaction in favour of preserving Indian society and its institutions against the anglicizing danger. For the first time such an attitude did not rest upon reasons of expediency but was grounded on an emotional prejudice. As he protested, 'the people of this country do not require our aid to furnish them with a rule for their conduct, or a standard for their property'. Hastings's encouragement of oriental scholarship and, in particular, of Halhed's translation of Hindu laws were part of this attitude. When he interfered to reorganize the whole judicial system, he claimed that 'no essential change was made in the ancient constitution of the province. It was only brought back to its original principles.'[1] Thus while Clive's 'double government' was abandoned and all effective administrative authority taken into English hands, the dual principle remained. Hastings refused to recognize the legal fiction of the grant of the *Diwani* as giving the Company any power or right it did not already possess; but undoubtedly the conception of the dual origin of the Company's authority, the grant from the Crown and the grant from the Mughal emperor, continued to colour English thinking. As the legatee of Mughal rule the Company was regarded as bound to respect the religion and habits of the people and to preserve to them their special laws.

The second wave in the gathering tide of anglicization came with Cornwallis, the Governor-General from 1786 to 1793. But it still came in what might be called a defensive form. The institution of the Supreme Court, exercising the jurisdiction of English law over the acts of the Company's servants in their individual capacity, had failed to extinguish open abuse and corruption. Cornwallis's outlook still moved in accordance with the motives which had inspired its establishment. He inherited the belief that the Company's financial difficulties and the troubles and miseries besetting the Company's territories sprang from the failure to control

[1] Hastings to Lord Mansfield, 25 Aug. 1774: G. R. Gleig, *Life of Warren Hastings*, vol. i, p. 401.

4 THE DOCTRINE AND ITS SETTING

its own European servants; and he proposed to subject them
not merely as individuals but as a system of government to
the rule of English constitutional principles. Despite Francis's
urging, there was now no question, even if Cornwallis had
wished, of a return to the indigenous system under Indian
officials; but in any case it was oriental principles of
government which in Cornwallis's eyes were fundamentally
at fault. He saw in the Company's adoption of Asian despotism the source of every ill. To him the essence of the problem
was to limit governmental power and so prevent its abuse.
Thus while he confirmed and extended the English administration, taking over criminal justice from the control of
the Nawab and firmly establishing the system of district
administration, he was all the time concerned to limit its
power. He consciously broke with the personal, authoritarian tradition of Indian government, and based his work
explicitly on the principles of the English political tradition.
The authors of the *Fifth Report* of 1812 saw this point quite
clearly. According to them Cornwallis had the choice of
consolidating British rule on the basis of the Mughal system
or of adopting an entirely new and foreign foundation. A
case for attempting to preserve the Mughal institutions
could be argued; it was, that

when brought back to their original state of utility, and improved by
such regulations as might be superadded by the British government,
[they] would, under a just and vigilant administration, unite the
liberal policy of an European state with the strength and energy of an
Asiatic monarchy, and altogether be better suited to the genius,
experience, and understanding of the natives, than institutions founded
on principles, to them wholly new, derived from a state of society
with which they were unacquainted. . . .

Cornwallis's decision was, however, for

the introduction of a new order of things, which should have for its
foundation, the security of individual property, and the administration
of justice, criminal and civil, by rules which were to disregard all
conditions of persons, and in their operation, be free of influence or
control from the government itself.[1]

1 *The Fifth Report from the Select Committee on the Affairs of the East India
Company. Ordered by the House of Commons to be printed, 28 July, 1812*, p. 18.

The Permanent Settlement of Bengal (1793) was a frank attempt to apply the English Whig philosophy of government. It had as its central belief the Whig conviction that political power is essentially corrupting and inevitably abused; that power, to be exercised with safety, must be reduced to a minimum, and even then kept divided and counterbalanced. Cornwallis sought to reduce the function of government to the bare task of ensuring the security of person and property. He believed this could be achieved by permanently limiting the State revenue demand on the land; for he was convinced that the executive arm of the Government would always abuse its power so long as the State demand was variable from year to year.[1] Once the settlement was fixed in perpetuity, the Boards of Revenue and the collectors could be deprived of all judicial powers, and their functions confined 'to the mere collection of the public dues'.[2] The executive would thus be divested of all discretionary authority, and would be subject to the rule of law as framed into formal legislative enactments by the Supreme Government and enforced by a judiciary entirely independent of the ordinary executive authorities. The permanent limitation of the revenue demand, and the curbing of executive power which it made possible, were not, however, the most decisive feature of the Permanent Settlement. This was rather the determination to introduce private property rights in land and uphold them through a Western type of law system. Cornwallis believed that everything hinged upon the recognition of the proprietary rights of the zemindars, the great landholders; and indeed landed property is the kernel of the Whig conception of political society. To the Whig mind landed property appeared as the agency which affected the reconciliation of freedom with order. Itself almost a part of the law of nature, there flowed from a system of landed property a natural ordering of society into ranks and classes, 'nowhere more necessary than in this country', maintained Cornwallis, 'for preserving order in civil society'.[3] In the

[1] Minute of Cornwallis, 10 Feb. 1790: G. W. Forrest, *Selections from the State Papers of the Governors-General of India: Lord Cornwallis*, vol. ii, p. 113.
[2] Despatch to Court of Directors, 6 March 1793: Forrest, *Cornwallis*, vol. ii, p. 124.
[3] Despatch to Court of Directors, 2 Aug. 1789: *Correspondence of Marquis Cornwallis*, ed. Charles Ross, vol. i, p. 554.

Whig outlook society was thus naturally self-ordered without the direct interference of government. So far from meaning the exercise of arbitrary or discretionary authority, the true function of government was simply the administration of justice. Its task was no more than the impartial administration of fixed and equal laws for the maintenance of private property rights. Once these latter were secured, all else followed. Political authority, in the form of the subjection of one man to the will of another, was reduced to its lowest point; and the happy marriage of liberty and security provided the most favourable conditions for the production of wealth. Throughout Cornwallis's Minutes there resound unconscious echoes of Locke's classic statement of the Whig theory. He sought to give concrete form to the rule of law in the Bengal Code of Regulations of 1793, and the preamble to Regulation II stated the general principle:

Government must divest itself of the power of infringing, in its executive capacity, the rights and privileges, which, as exercising the legislative authority, it has conferred on the landholders. The revenue officers must be deprived of their judicial powers. All financial claims of the public when disputed under the regulations, must be subjected to the cognisance of the courts of judicature, superintended by judges, who from their official situations, and the nature of their trusts, shall not only be wholly uninterested in the results of their decisions, but bound to decide impartially between the public and the proprietors of land, and also between the latter and their tenants. The collectors of the revenue must not only be divested of the power of deciding upon their own acts, but rendered amenable for them to the courts of judicature; and collect the public dues, subject to a personal prosecution for every exaction exceeding the amount which they are authorized to demand on behalf of the public, and for every deviation from the regulations prescribed for the collection of it. No power will then exist in the country by which the rights vested in the landholders by the regulations can be infringed or the value of landed property affected. Land must in consequence become the most desirable of all property; and the industry of the people will be directed to these improvements in agriculture which are as essential to their own welfare as to the prosperity of the state.

In this spirit Cornwallis carried through a sweeping anglicization of the British power, removing Indians from all but the petty offices, and taking away from the great

Bengal landholders their last quasi-political power, the right to keep armed retainers and to police their districts. He sought by his reforms to erect an impersonal government of law, 'a system upheld by its inherent principles, and not by the men who are to have the occasional conduct of it'; and he resorted to the classic Whig division of the powers, with its separation of the judiciary and executive. In each district of the Bengal territory a Collector was established, who was designed to be merely what his name implied, not an all-powerful discretionary official, but a mere collector of fixed public dues. He was given no political or magisterial authority, and was not even entrusted with the control of the district police. The great figure in the district, the true representative of the British system, was meant to be the District Judge and Magistrate; it was he who was empowered to administer the impersonal law system of the Cornwallis Code of Regulations, even, if need be, against the collector himself in his official capacity. The district judge was given the control of the police, and a status and salary superior to that of the collector.

Wellesley, the next important figure among the Governor-Generals (1798–1805), saw and admired these English principles. He asserted that the British constitution had supplied the model of Cornwallis's work, and believed he was carrying this work to its proper completion by divesting the Governor-General's Council of its function as the high court of the Company's judicial system, and instituting instead a separate Court of *Sadr Diwani* and *Nizamat Adalat*.

The early administration of the Company succeeded to the despotic power of the native princes. Those princes, as in other despotic governments, united in their own persons, the whole legislative, executive, and judicial powers of the State, and exercised them according to the dictates of their own discretion. No form of Government could be so ill-adapted to these countries when they became dependent possessions of the British Empire, subject to be governed by persons occasionally deputed from the Mother Country. Experience of the evils attendant on this form of Government conducted by a delegated British administration, led to the modelling of the Government of Bengal, on principles drawn from the British constitution. A distribution of the legislative, executive, and judicial powers of the state, analogous to that which forms the basis of the British constitution was made the foundation of the new constitution of the Government of Bengal.

In his enthusiasm for these constitutional principles and his anxiety to see them adopted in the Madras territories, Wellesley maintained that the question of a permanent settlement of the land revenue was altogether separate, and formed no necessary part of the 'fundamental principle of the new constitution'. Even at this time, when a marked improvement in the quality and probity of the British official was noticeable, Wellesley still defended the abandonment of the native tradition and the separation of the judicial from the executive authorities by the Whig argument that all power was inherently liable to abuse.[1]

Although based on frankly English principles and on a conscious abandonment of what was held to be native tradition, the movement of anglicization was still defensive in outlook. It was not designed to effect a wholesale revolution of Indian society; its purpose was rather to limit the interference of government. Wellesley still mirrors this outlook, claiming as he did, that the indigenous form and institutions of government were no essential part of Indian society. In fact, he declared, the British system of public law, administered by an independent judiciary, was the best guarantee of toleration and protection for those interests to which the great mass of the people were truly attached. For these interests embraced no system of political principles or form of government, but consisted of the religion of the people, their ancient customs, and the pursuit of their domestic concerns. The 'new constitution' pivoted, however, on the definition and enforcement of private property rights in the Western sense; and whatever the original intention, this was to prove an innovation that ultimately was to play the most decisive role in the overthrow and transformation of the old society.

The resistance to this policy of applying British constitutional principles to the Indian administration came some-

---

[1] Letter of Governor-General in Council to Madras, 19 July 1804, para. 25. Wellesley was sufficiently proud of this despatch to have it published in London in 1812 (see India Office Library Tracts, vol. 465).

what surprisingly from the brilliant group of subordinates which served Wellesley: from Munro, Malcolm, Elphinstone, and Metcalfe.[1] Out of their thought and work emerged a new and conscious alternative to an anglicized form of administration. They deserve a close study because they were the dominant school in the formation of Indian policy when liberalism first began to exercise an influence on internal administration after 1818. Despite a disparity of age and temperament, there is a unity of thought in this knot of men which makes it possible to speak of them as the founders of a political tradition. Their great work was in various forms to counter the spirit of the Cornwallis system. Although most of them spent the main part of their careers in military and diplomatic activities, their concrete and visible achievement was the *ryotwar* system of land settlement and general administration, first developed by Munro, and extended by him throughout the Madras Presidency in the period of his governorship from 1819 until 1827. Mountstuart Elphinstone, who was rewarded in 1819 for his diplomatic achievements against the Mahrattas with the governorship of the Bombay Presidency, adopted the *ryotwar* system for the large area of western India that was annexed to the Bombay Presidency as a result of the Mahratta defeat; and his work was maintained by his successor, John Malcolm, Governor from 1827 until 1830. In the north, Metcalfe, the youngest and the last to leave India, threw all the weight of his influence (as Resident of the Delhi Territory and later as member of the Governor-General's Council) against the extension of the Cornwallis system to the Ceded and Conquered (afterwards North-Western) Provinces. He lived to see the 'village communities' there made the basis of the revenue settlement, and the executive and magisterial functions permanently reunited in the person of the collector.

Except for Munro, these men owed their early advancement to Wellesley, to whom they had also been attracted imaginatively by the scale of his imperial vision. Wellesley had brought to India a mind and ambition inflamed with the world-struggle for empire against Napoleonic France. He deliberately set out, as none of his predecessors had

[1] See Biographical Notes, pp. 331–2.

deemed practicable or desirable, to reduce the whole Indian peninsula to subjection to the British power, and he poured open scorn on the narrow counting-house mentality of the Court of Directors and their anxiety over the financial un-profitability of such a dominion. His *grande manière*, his majestic conception of Indian affairs, fired the enthusiasm of his subordinates, to whom he was always the 'glorious little man'. All of them were kindled with his imperialist ambition—to raise up, as Malcolm said, 'a monument of glory' in the form of a great eastern empire. Their constant awareness of the historical significance of their work gives to all their writing a largeness of outlook and a certain majesty of statement, never again to be recaptured in British Indian annals. From the glimpses which the records of their private thoughts permit, they possessed what might be termed the Romantic temperament; combining a strong introspective bent, a sensibility for natural beauty and for historical associations, with an imaginative urge for release in action and adventure. Charles Metcalfe, even as a youth, was the morose and solitary being he was to remain through-out his life. His early journal records a fervent belief in the heroic nature of politics, 'the most noble of professions', and his faith in the superiority of 'active talents' over expert scientific knowledge contrasts strongly with the cult of expertise and administrative technique which tended to set in after 1818.[1] This superior comprehensiveness of outlook, which Metcalfe as a young man was seeking, is evident in the other figures. It is true that Munro was able to combine such an outlook with an expert and detailed knowledge of revenue affairs, and that Malcolm insisted upon a thorough know-ledge of details as the only basis for a true grasp of the art of Indian administration. But in his final advice to his assistants in central India, it was this catholicity of attitude to which Malcolm returned. Nothing could keep them right in detailed questions of policy, he said, but accustoming their minds to dwell upon the character of British power in India, and that of the empire over which it was established.[2] The width

[1] J. W. Kaye, *Life of Metcalfe*, vol. i, p. 88.
[2] Sir John Malcolm, *The Political History of India*, 2nd edn., 1826, vol. ii, p. 159. Id., *Memoir of Central India*, vol. ii, p. 474.

of vision which these men exhibit, and the heroic manner in which they regarded political activity, is a reflection of the great Napoleonic struggle in Europe, and of that conscious sense of fashioning history which prevailed in the Romantic age.

Malcolm had little of a brooding, melancholic nature, but his aim at self-completeness is characteristic of his world. That impulse for completion, which made every great Romantic poet a politician, worked in him to transform the roughly educated soldier into a finished statesman and writer. For a busy man of affairs his literary achievement was remarkable; it included his *History of Persia* (still regarded as a standard work), *The Political History of India*, *Central India*, *The Government of India*, the *Life of Clive* (upon which Macaulay wrote his famous *Edinburgh Review* article), as well as various occasional verse. With Munro there was the same intellectual eagerness, continuing far into life and prompting him at the age of sixty to go painstakingly through Ricardo.[1] Of this group Mountstuart Elphinstone was the scholar-statesman *par excellence*. Taking a text from *Cymbeline* as his motto:

> What pleasure, sir, find we in life, to lock
> it from action and adventure?

he wedded the life of court, camp, and chase, with a passion for intellectual pursuits—for the Latin, Greek, and Persian classics, and for history, philosophy, and jurisprudence. The laconic entry in his diary after the storming of Gawilgarh during the Assaye campaign indicates his ideal: 'I breakfasted with Kennedy and talked about Hafiz, Saadi, Horace, and Anacreon. At nine I left him and went to the trenches.' But the Byronic melancholia, to which his acute sensibility was subject, and the introspectiveness, so unusual in a man of action, link him clearly with the Romantic temperament. Elphinstone would have scorned such a thought as affectation, and on this ground he reserved his judgement on the Lake poets, though reading Byron avidly. He had, however, all the Romantics' worship of nature; there is no mistaking

---

[1] For an account of Munro's intellectual pursuits, cf. Gleig, *Munro*, vol. i, p. 9. Cf. vol. ii, pp. 282–305, for his notes on Ricardo's *Political Economy*.

its note in his description of the falls of Gokauk by moon-
light, when he 'felt as in the presence of a superior being and
was filled with a reverential and almost superstitious awe'.[1]

Metcalfe also shared this feeling for Nature,[2] and it was
also to be found in the more rough-hewn and simpler
character of Munro, who had few of the trappings of the
eighteenth-century cultivated gentleman. Elphinstone was
himself surprised at the poetic sensibility which Munro hid
beneath his bluff soldier's exterior.[3] Indeed, in Munro we
come nearer to the elemental emotion which Wordsworth
experienced in the face of Nature. In a letter to his sister, he
wrote:

I spend many of my leisure hours on the highest summit of the
rock on which the fort stands, under the shady bastion, built by Hyder.
The spot has for me a certain charm, which I always strongly feel, but
cannot easily describe. . . . While seated on the rock, I am, or fancy
that I am more thoughtful than when below. The extent and gran-
deur of the scene raises my mind, and the solitude and silence make
me think that 'I am conversing with Nature here'. To the east, I see
a romantic, well-cultivated valley, leading to the wide plains of the
Carnatic. To the south, a continuation of the same valley, running as
far as the eye can reach, into Mysore. All the rest, on every side, is a
vast assemblage of hills and naked rocks, wildly heaped one above the
other.[4]

It was these wild and desolate scenes of Nature which he
believed to be 'sublimer subjects of poetry than all the fic-
tions of Greece and Rome'. There is the same insistence, as
with Wordsworth, on natural simplicity, the same contempt
for the artifices of civilized society, and for mere book-
learning and abstract philosophy, and the same reverence
for the accumulated wisdom of the past.[5] Above all, the aura

---

[1] For Elphinstone's character, cf. T. E. Colebrooke, *Life of Mountstuart Elphinstone*, vol. i, pp. 166, 351–3, vol. ii, pp. 145–8.
[2] Cf. a passage from one of Metcalfe's letters in 1827, cited Percival Spear,
Twilight of the Mughuls, pp. 167–8.
[3] Journal, 28 May 1820: Colebrooke, *Elphinstone*, vol. ii, p. 110.
[4] Munro to his sister, Ambore, 1 March 1795: Gleig, *Munro*, vol. i, pp. 86–87.
[5] Munro to his sister, 15 Sept. 1795: ibid., p. 170: 'It is distressing that we should
persevere in the absurd practice of stifling the young ideas of boys of fourteen or
fifteen with logic. A few pages of history give more insight into the human mind,
in a more agreeable manner, than all the metaphysical volumes that ever were published.' Cf. Wordsworth, *The Prelude*, Book XIII.

of sentiment with which Wordsworth and the Romantics invested the noble peasant was fully shared by Munro; and it is not idle to see in this the emotional and mental background to the *ryotwar* system of land settlement, which is Munro's particular title to greatness.[1] To take the peasant in all his simplicity, to secure him in the possession of his land, to rule him with a paternal and simple government, and so to avoid all the artificialities of a sophisticated European form of rule—these political aims surely spring directly from that current of contemporary thought in Europe which literary historians have called the Romantic movement.

It was ironic that this group of men should attain to the fullness of power at the moment when the world of diplomatic and military action, in which their ideas were nurtured, had come to its end.[2] With the termination of the final Mahratta war in 1818, and the crushing of the last independent power which could oppose the British, the political problem in India was transformed. 'The task of conquest was slight', reflected Malcolm, 'in comparison with that which awaits us, the preservation of the empire acquired.'[3]

The age of chivalry had gone; that of sophisters, economists, and calculators was to succeed. The sword was to be exchanged for the pen, and the soldier-diplomat to give way before the administrator and judge. The change in itself meant a new temper. The large discretion permitted to individuals, in the early days of conquering and settling a country, was bound to be replaced by a more regular and centralized form of administration. In writing to Metcalfe in 1821, Malcolm was referring to a fast-fading past when he said that neither of them were 'exactly at the disposal of what Captain Clutterbuck calls a clattering piece of parchment, and can halt or move as the clouds indicate'.[4] In practice, he knew that even men in the highest position were being placed 'as much under minute check and control as a collector of a

[1] Munro to Col. Read, 16 June 1801: Gleig, *Munro*, vol. iii, p. 162.
[2] In 1819 Munro became Governor of Madras, and Elphinstone Governor of Bombay. In 1827 Metcalfe became a member of the Supreme Council, and Malcolm succeeded Elphinstone as Governor of Bombay.
[3] Malcolm, *Political History*, vol. ii, p. 64.
[4] Malcolm to Metcalfe, April 1821: Kaye, *Malcolm*, vol. ii, p. 337.

small district'; and he feared that this, and the absence of stirring political events, would result in a deterioration of the Company's civil servants.[1] Although he and his companions in ideas recognized such a change, from the excitement of military and diplomatic activity to the humdrum of day-to-day administration, as a natural process in the growth of British rule, they accepted its implications with foreboding. They were aware that the new age of peace, retrenchment, and reform, would bring forth a generation of administrators, purposeful and earnest, but with ideas alien to their own. None of them, not even Munro, the oldest of them, was hostile to reform; indeed they all prided themselves on their liberal opinion. But their political instincts were traditional and sentimental. They distrusted the chilly dogmatics of the reforming spirit, which was to eradicate in the name of utility all the historical associations connected with the rise of British power; and in the cause of efficiency, simplicity, and economy, sought to reduce the historical modes of government to one centralized, uniform practice. Against the tendency that would transform British rule from a personal, paternal government, to an impersonal, mechanical administration, they took their stand.

In the history of British India they are the true conservative element; but the term needs definition. It is not to be confused with a desire to return to the pre-Cornwallis era, to the ambiguities and deceits of 'dual rule', and the tradition of the nabobs. The men whom we are discussing were far removed in outlook from that world whose traces had until recently survived at the Residencies in the native states, where a Kirkpatrick at Hyderabad, a 'King' Collins at Ujjain, or an Ochterlony at Delhi, had lately reigned with their harems and fabulous retinues of elephants and guns. That reform of morals by which Burke sought to sanctify public life, and the Evangelicals to purify private and social life, had left its mark in the austerity of their lives and their commanding sense of public duty. Nor is their tradition to be confused with that of Cornwallis, the inherent passivity of which had grown with its ageing. Mere *vis inertiae*, mere partiality for the existing order, is not properly conservatism;

[1] Malcolm, *Political History*, vol. ii, p. 82.

and it was, indeed, against the Cornwallis system that these
men spent their lives contending.

It is true that by 1810 the Bengal system had established
itself as the orthodox pattern of British rule, and was already
loaded with the dead weight of a tradition. The efforts of
Munro and his contemporaries to upset this system were
therefore often regarded as innovation, when in fact, as
Malcolm insisted, it was theirs that was the true conservative attitude.[1] The outlook of Munro, Malcolm, Metcalfe,
and Elphinstone towards the Cornwallis school is of particular importance, because it blends almost imperceptibly
into their attitude to the movement of reform, which gathered
pace in the eighteen-twenties.

As the 'Romantic' generation in British-Indian history,
they revolted against what they considered to be the cold,
lifeless, mechanical principles informing the Cornwallis
system,[2] its *a priori*, unhistorical attitude, which would impose English ideas and institutions on Indian society, and
its facile optimism in the virtue of human nature when left
untrammelled by government. They could not renounce the
entire philosophy of the Cornwallis system, because in the
end it represented the permanent English political instinct;
but they sought to modify that philosophy in the manner in
which Burke had redeemed whiggism from its superficiality
and crudeness. They brought to the Indian problem Burke's
notion of history, that conception which regards human
society as a continuous community of the past, present, and
future. The Bengal system they saw as the denial of this
touchstone of history and experience; it was the ignorant
application of *a priori* political ideas without regard to the
history and circumstances of Indian society. It rested on the
fallacy that a political society could be constructed anew, on
the basis of abstract principles wrung from an alien tradition.
They did not deny the theoretic virtue of the rule of law
and division of the powers, but they denied that these could
be introduced unmodified into India.

[1] Malcolm to Wynne (President of Board of Control), 19 April 1828: Bentinck
MSS.: '. . . to hear them speak of changes *we have introduced within the last ten years*
you would suppose that an effort to revert to usages sanctioned by as many centuries evinced a spirit of innovation! ! !'
[2] Cf. Sir John Malcolm, *Government of India*, Appendix, p. 21.

There was a deeper emotional objection, going beyond
mere considerations of political expedience. They shared
neither the Whig enthusiasm for the original virtue of man
in a state of nature, nor its pessimism as to the exercise of
political power. They had no hopes of sudden and miraculous
changes in the progress of human society, and there lingered
in their thinking, particularly in Munro's, something of that
older tradition, which saw the division of society into rulers
and ruled as a natural ordering, and which envisaged submission to authority as necessary to the anarchic nature of
man. Power to them was not a delegation of natural rights
from the people, but rather a trust imposed by an inscrutable
Providence.

There were, of course, important differences of opinion
among this group, but in broad terms these general features
marked the attitude of them all. The sharpest difference was
between Malcolm and Metcalfe over the policy towards the
Indian states and the old aristocracy. Malcolm, with the
others, had no illusion that British rule could ever rest on
the affection of the people; its security depended on the
impression of its invincibility.[1] But he believed that it was
politic and right to try to conciliate the displaced aristocracy
by generous treatment; to cushion the impact of a foreign
dominion by an attempt to preserve something of the
methods and institutions of Indian society; and to palliate
the undesirable effects of direct rule at the hands of a foreign
race by encouraging the survival of the Indian states.[2]
Metcalfe, on the contrary, was pessimistic about the feasibility of conciliating the old ruling classes. He believed that,
within certain rigidly defined external frontiers, the soundest
policy was to use every just occasion to annex native states,
and to resume pensions and revenue alienations made to
privileged classes before the British conquest. The revenue

[1] Malcolm, *Government of India*, Appendix, p. 157.
[2] Cf. Malcolm to Wynne, (Copy) 19 April 1828: Bentinck MSS.: 'With respect
to raising natives both in the fiscal and judicial line, I am of the same sentiments as
Sir Thomas Munro. I desire not only to maintain Princes and Chiefs, whom we
find existing over the lands ruled by their forefathers and to encourage cultivators
to become proprietors, but I desire to share the Aristocracy of Office with the natives
of India. There may be some hazard in their admission but there is much more in
their exclusion. . . .'

thus acquired would make provision for an invincible armed force, instead of being dissipated by fainéant Indian rulers, whose loyalty must always be doubtful.[1] He had no sympathy with Malcolm's fear that, once the British had absorbed the whole of India under their direct rule, turbulence would be denied its natural outlets, and all discontent would gather to a single head against the British power.

Malcolm's compassion for fallen greatness is immediately reminiscent of, if not inspired by, Burke. Metcalfe had spurned as a contemptible sham the perpetuation of the Mughal emperor's suzerainty; for he believed that power could not be shirked, and must be made to stand forth openly and unequivocally. Malcolm, however, thought that the arrangement:

. . . had its root in a wise conformance to usage, in a generous consideration of the feelings of fallen greatness. It was the veneration of a great power that had passed away; and the superstition that continued to give homage to the shrine which we had addressed to propitiate our rise, was sanctioned by the example of the wisest among nations. There was little except goodness in it.

And then he passes to the heart of Burke's teaching, that illusion is necessary to life, that the pomp and circumstance with which men clothe political power is a vital succedaneum, 'necessary', as Burke says, 'to cover the defects of our naked shivering nature'.

Bacon has told us what shrunken things the minds of most men would be if stripped of their vanities and pretensions; but where would you leave states, if you were to knock away the thousand props, seen and unseen, by which they were supported?—many and some of the strongest of which, have their foundation in what one of your *mere* general politicians or authors would pronounce, justly enough, folly, prejudice, ignorance or absurdity.[2]

Despite this difference in their attitude towards the conquered ruling classes, it implies no sundering of the fundamental unity of their thought. This domestic difference was to be repeated later in the Punjab, between John and Henry Lawrence, but it was merely a tension within the same world

---

[1] Paper, dated 7 Sept. 1820: Kaye, *Papers of Metcalfe*, pp. 151–2.
[2] Malcolm to Gerald Wellesley: Kaye, *Malcolm*, vol. ii, p. 378.

of ideas. Indeed Metcalfe, while favouring direct rule and an unsentimental policy towards the Indian aristocracy, and priding himself on his political liberalism, was at heart the most conservative of his group. His liberalism consisted, in fact, of a few superficial measures, such as freedom of the press and the unrestricted immigration of Europeans. When asked in 1829, in connexion with the renewal of the Company's Charter, for his views on future policy, he penned a minute filled with the deepest pessimism. At a time when Bentham was feeling 'as if the golden age of British India were lying before me', when Charles Trevelyan thought that it could not 'be concealed that India is on the eve of a great moral change',[1] Metcalfe was meditating on the mortality of empire. 'Empires grow old, decay, and perish. Ours in India can hardly be called old, but seems destined to be short-lived. We appear to have passed the brilliancy and vigor of our youth, and it may be that we have reached a premature old age.'[2] In the age of reform after Bentinck's arrival, when Metcalfe was a member of the Supreme Council at Calcutta, he found himself in an alien world. Although personally on good terms with his colleagues, he confessed that in his official views he stood quite alone among them, and every day tended to widen the separation.[3]

The common aim of the paternalist school was to conserve the original institutions of Indian society rather than to construct that society anew. Metcalfe had been schooled in Wellesley's haughtiness towards the Indian aristocracy, and scorned sharing with it 'the aristocracy of office'. But his vision was of a benevolent paternalism founded on the unchanging 'village republics', and he never contemplated a system of direct rule that would remould India in the image of the West. He never ceased to acknowledge Munro as master, and to pursue Munro's ideal of a prosperous society of yeoman farmers enjoying a freehold property

---

[1] Draft letter, Bentham to Bentinck, 19 Nov. 1829 (original not in Bentinck MSS.): Bentham MSS., Box X, f. 179. C. E. Trevelyan to Bentinck, 9 April 1834: Bentinck MSS.

[2] Minute on future government of India, 11 Oct. 1829. Kaye gives extracts, *Papers of Metcalfe*, pp. 161–77. The original is in the Bentinck MSS., dated 11 Oct. 1829, and with Bentinck's comments given marginally.

[3] A private letter, dated 8 March 1828: Kaye, *Papers of Metcalfe*, p. 170.

right.[1] Malcolm and Elphinstone disliked the notion of sacrificing the aristocracy in the interests of the peasantry, and wanted to preserve Indian society in all its rich variety. Apart from this difference of emphasis, the group was drawn together by the feeling of having to wage a common struggle against alien forces which were bent on sweeping away the old India they loved.

The spirit which they fought they termed 'regulation' or 'innovation'; and they made little attempt to analyse its manifestations. They knew it most clearly in the form of the Cornwallis settlement, and in the eighteen-twenties they recognized its presence in a new aggressive shape. All spoke against it.

The ruling vice of our government is innovation . . . it is time that we should learn that neither the face of the country, its property, nor its society, are things that can be suddenly improved by any contrivance of ours, though they may be greatly injured by what we mean for their good; that we should take every country as we find it, and not rashly attempt to regulate its landed property either in accumulation or division.[2]

This was the first lesson according to Munro, and it followed for him that the task of government was paternal protection and little more.

It is too much regulation that ruins everything. Englishmen are as great fanatics in politics as Mahomedans in religion. They suppose that no country can be saved without English institutions. The natives of this country have enough of their own to answer every useful object of internal administration, and if we maintain and protect them, the country will in a very few months settle itself.[3]

To Munro politics were essentially experimental and pragmatic. The brief period the British had spent on problems of government in India was far too short for any permanent solution to be found.[4] The result of precipitancy and 'the zeal for permanency' had been the social upheaval in Bengal,

[1] Metcalfe's Minute on Revenue Administration of Delhi Territory, 1815: Kaye, *Papers of Metcalfe*, pp. 43–44. Cf. also Percival Spear, *Twilight of the Mughuls*, chap. v.
[2] Minute of Munro 'On the state of the country', 31 Dec. 1824: Gleig, *Munro*, vol. iii, p. 381.
[3] Munro to Elphinstone (on future administration of conquered Mahratta country), 12 May 1818: ibid., p. 252.   [4] Ibid., pp. 319–20.

consequent on Cornwallis's misreading of the problem. By recognizing a proprietary right in the great *zemindars*, a revolution had been effected in Bengal which had grievously weakened the whole structure, and made the task of administration infinitely more difficult.

Against the Cornwallis system the four men spoke with one voice.[1] They saw it as a system of abstract principles inapplicable to India, as an impersonal bureaucracy instead of a personal, human, and tangible form of government. Government conducted from the office, rather than from the tent and the saddle, necessarily proceeded by forms and precedents; and when its functions were kept confined to the operation of courts of justice and to the mere realization of the revenue, its criterion of success was similarly limited to superficialities—to the speed with which judicial business was dispatched, and the volume and promptitude of revenue payments. Malcolm said he dreaded no

human being (certainly no Nabob or Maharajah) . . . half so much as an able Calcutta civilian, whose travels are limited to two or three hundred miles, with a hookah in his mouth, some good but abstract maxims in his head, the Regulations in his right hand, the Company's Charter in his left, and a quire of wire-woven foolscap before him.[2]

And Munro, as Governor of Madras, wrote to Canning in 1823, that he had not credited that the records of government 'contained such useless trash'.

Every man writes as much as he can, and quotes Montesquieu, and Hume, and Adam Smith, and speaks as if he were living in a country where people were free and governed themselves. Most of their papers might have been written by men who were never out of England, and their projects are nearly as applicable to that country as to India.[3]

In contrast to the abstractions of the rule of law, and the blind, automatic operation of an impersonal bureaucracy, Munro's school looked to a continuation of the Indian tradition of personal government. Apart from the reserva-

---

[1] Cf. Malcolm to Malony, 'Correspondence 1817–21': Kaye, *Malcolm*, vol. ii, p. 391. Metcalfe's paper of 29 June 1820: Kaye, *Papers of Metcalfe*, pp. 150–1. Elphinstone to Strachey, 3 Sept. 1820, and 21 April 1821: Colebrooke, *Elphinstone*, vol. ii, pp. 115 et seq., 124 et seq.

[2] Malcolm to Malony, 8 April 1821: Kaye, *Malcolm*, vol. ii, pp. 335–6.

[3] Munro to Canning, 1 May 1823: Gleig, *Munro*, vol. ii, p. 66.

tions of Metcalfe, they saw in the preservation of the Indian states one method of pursuing their aim, and, at the same time, of providing a possible haven for the culture and higher graces of Indian life. While aware of the irregularity and frequent oppressiveness of princely governments, they recognized that ultimately these were closer to their own ideal. Devoid of the artificial legalism of the Presidencies, where the race went to the quick-witted, the Indian states maintained a rough, natural simplicity and personal character. They provided a focus for the ordinary instincts of loyalty and racial sentiment, and satisfied, as British rule never could, the need of a peasant society for paternal direction and an easily intelligible form of law and government. This tradition Munro and his contemporaries wished to adapt for the territories under direct British rule. To the *ryot*, government must be represented simply; not by a multiplicity of officers and a multiplicity of written forms, but by a single officer, who had powers to inquire, to judge, and to punish, without the delay and intricacies of the Western legal process.[1] This officer was not to be a distant and awful figure, presiding in his cutchery like a deity in his temple, but a familiar lord, visiting and speaking with them of their quarrels and their crops, and looked up to as *ma-bap*, father and mother. In practical terms this meant a union of powers, at least at the district level. None but Metcalfe had the logical temerity to propose their absolute union and the abolition of a separate judiciary; but they all agreed that the collector should be accorded magisterial powers, which would give him control of the district police and a power of summary punishment. The collector's office was to be the great executive office of local government, controlling in firm subordination the whole inferior executive arm.

The extent of his command was greatly magnified in all territories, other than Bengal, by the form of land revenue settlement. By circumstance and deliberate choice, Munro's *ryotwar* system eschewed all intermediaries and settled directly with each peasant for his individual holding. This fact, and the detailed work which an annual settlement

[1] Cf. Munro, Minute 'On the state of the country', 31 Dec. 1824: Gleig, *Munro*, vol. iii, p. 379.

imposed, necessitated a much larger staff of subordinates and a much more active type of government. The State consciously assumed an administrative responsibility for the mass of the people which it had just as consciously abdicated in Bengal. In the new Bombay territories Munro's system was adopted, and also in a modified form in the Ceded and Conquered Provinces after 1819.

Such a policy was founded on the contrary assumption to that of Cornwallis; the end was the protection of the community by government and not against it. The whole apparatus for checking and counterbalancing political power, by which Cornwallis sought to prevent its abuse, was rejected. Metcalfe had stated the plea for a new unity of government in its extreme form:

> Revenue, and judicial, and when practicable, military powers also, should be exercised by the same person; union, not division, should be the order of our rule. Confidence [in the Company's civil servants], not distrust, should be the engine to work with.[1]

This plea for unity is to be carefully distinguished, however, from that for uniformity, with which it was to be confounded in a reforming age. Malcolm was the foremost to recognize the need for a more unified system of government, once the peninsula was bestridden. He was alive to the requirements of economy, efficiency, and a greater consistency of principle. But he believed these objects should be attained by the delegation of full powers to trusted individuals, and not through a deadening centralized administration.[2] To reform, as such, none of Munro's school was hostile. With varying degrees of enthusiasm they favoured liberal measures, whether it was the admission of Indians to higher posts in the civil service, or a broad-based educational scheme. But they had no sympathy with the intellectual foundation of the new reforming creeds and the attitude these engendered. It was not easy for them to distinguish readily the forces of the age. The passion for uniformity, for mechanistic administration and legislative regulation, which possessed the Utilitarians, was easily confused with their life-long enemy, the system of

---

[1] Paper of 29 June 1820: Kaye, *Papers of Metcalfe*, p. 150.
[2] Malcolm, *Political History*, vol. ii, p. 142.

Cornwallis. Yet, on the other hand, they were largely in agreement with certain aspects of the Utilitarian viewpoint. The union of judicial and executive powers in the collector; the simplification of the chaotic jungle of the law to a compact intelligible code which respected Indian custom; the prejudice for a *ryotwar* form of land settlement; and an accurate survey and record of landed rights—in all these reforms they were in agreement with the radical authoritarian strain in Utilitarian thought. But to the spirit of utilitarianism they were as uncompromisingly hostile as Burke. Against the abstract goodness of proposed measures they had no argument; but with the faith of Burke, they countered the new spirit by an appeal to history and experience, and by a counsel of moderation and patience.

Politics to them were experiential in nature, necessarily near-sighted, and essentially limited in their achievement. Hence they were not to be pursued dogmatically along a path of violent change:

The most important of the lessons we can derive from past experience is to be slow and cautious in every procedure which has a tendency to collision with the habits and prejudices of our native subjects. We may be compelled by the character of our government to frame some institutions, different from those we found established, but we should adopt all we can of the latter into our system. . . . our internal government . . . should be administered on a principle of humility not pride. We must divest our minds of all arrogant pretensions arising from the presumed superiority of our own knowledge, and seek the accomplishment of the great ends we have in view by the means which are best suited to the peculiar nature of the objects. . . . That time may gradually effect a change, there is no doubt; but the period is as yet distant when that can be expected; and come when it will, to be safe or beneficial, it must be . . . the work of society itself. All that Government can do is, by maintaining the internal peace of the country, and by adapting its principles to the various feelings, habits, and character of its inhabitants, to give time for the slow and silent operation of the desired improvement, with a constant impression that every attempt to accelerate this end will be attended with the danger of its defeat.[1]

There was no sympathy with the belief in sudden improvement or sudden illumination, which gave to the Utilitarians

[1] Ibid., p. 183.

and Evangelicals the gift of an untroubled assurance. Human nature could never be for them, as with James Mill, 'as plain as the road from Charing Cross to St. Paul's'.[1]

> I have no faith in the modern doctrine of the rapid improvement of the Hindoos, or of any other people. The character of the Hindoos is probably much the same as when Vasco da Gama first visited India, and it is not likely that it will be much better a century hence.

> When I read as I sometimes do, of a measure by which a large province has been suddenly improved, or a race of semi-barbarians civilized almost to quakerism, I throw away the book.[2]

Except for Elphinstone, they had little but contempt for the doctrines of the 'philosophes' and rejected that theory which attributed to government a preponderant influence in the shaping of society.[3] It followed from their notion of the relative ineffectualness of political authority that the function of government was simply one of paternal protection. The passion for legislation which possessed the Utilitarians found no favour with them,[4] for they were convinced that all the great changes in human society came from sources much deeper than the superficial activities of politicians. 'Great and beneficial alterations in society, to be complete, must be produced within the society itself; they cannot be the mere fabrication of its superiors, or of a few who deem themselves enlightened.'[5]

In accordance with their view of politics as an experimental art, they all believed in the need to retain a principle of diversity in Indian government. A centrally imposed uniformity, such as the Utilitarians seemed to contemplate, was anathema to them. Even Elphinstone, who looked with least aversion on the new political lights, rejected the notion of a single 'omni-competent' central government to replace the multiple structure of the three semi-independent Presidencies, a plan which the Utilitarians wished to embody in

---

[1] Cited E. Halévy, *The Growth of Philosophic Radicalism*, p. 451.

[2] Munro to Canning, 30 June 1821: Gleig, *Munro*, vol. ii, p. 57. Letter of Munro, 19 July 1824: ibid., pp. 68–69.

[3] Cf. Munro to his sister, 5 March 1795: *Munro*, vol. i, p. 163. Also Metcalfe, Common Place Book, 5 May 1803: Kaye, *Metcalfe*, vol. i, pp. 109–10.

[4] Cf. Munro's policy as Governor of Madras. Minute of 31 Dec. 1824: Gleig, *Munro*, vol. iii, p. 380: 'For some years past it has been the object of Government to legislate as little as possible.'   [5] Malcolm, *Central India*, vol. ii, p. 281.

the Charter Act of 1833.[1] The dread of a colourless uniformity is, indeed, a facet of the Romantic outlook. Munro
in a half-humorous letter on the political economists and
speculative philosophers bursts into sincere eloquence
against the condition of uniformity to which they would
bring the world:

> to such a state of dull uniform repose, give me a thousand times in
> preference the world as it now stands, with all its beautiful variety of
> knowledge and ignorance—of language—of manners, customs—
> religions and superstitions—of cultivated fields and wide-extended
> deserts—of war and peace.[2]

2. Liberalism and the Policy of Assimilation

So far the administrative history of India before 1818 has
been discussed in terms of the ideas or attitudes governing
the two great rival systems of administration established in
Bengal and Madras. These systems, despite later modification, were to be permanent. Other notions and attitudes were
to arise, but they were accommodated within the framework
of the original structures.

The practical problem of Cornwallis's time had been the
creation of an efficient administrative machinery, which
would provide peace and dispense justice, repair the Company's finances ruined by corruption and misgovernment,
and achieve the ultimate aim of realizing a regular surplus of revenue sufficient to purchase the Company's
annual investment of Indian piece-goods and China tea.
The solution of the problem had entailed sweeping away
the decaying system of indirect rule, initiated by Clive and
continued in another form by Hastings, by which the
Company had attempted to limit its interference and work
largely through the native system of administration. Resort
was now had to the systematic use of English officers in an
English administrative system. The Cornwallis settlement

---

[1] Elphinstone, in his letter to the Select Committee on Indian Affairs in 1832,
stressed the need to retain the legislative independence of the three Presidencies:
Colebrooke, *Elphinstone*, vol. ii, p. 317: 'Our government should still be considered
as in a great measure experimental; and it is an advantage to have three experiments,
and to compare them in their progress with each other.' Munro expressed the same
opinion: Gleig, *Munro*, vol. ii, p. 264.

[2] Munro to his sister, 5 March 1795: ibid., vol. i, pp. 165–6.

of Bengal was a deliberate movement of anglicization, and Munro's work in Madras, although attempting to keep the interference with the existing society to a minimum, carried the same imprint. Both Cornwallis's *zemindari* and Munro's *ryotwari* structures involved the active assumption of the work of government by English officers; both rested on the institution of private property rights in land, secured and maintained by a Western law system. Both might therefore become instruments to inaugurate a fundamental change in the customary modes of land tenure, the heart of Indian society. Yet their spirit was far from revolutionary. Munro had certainly no notion that he was facilitating the commercialization of the land and the break-up of customary society, when he sought to give the Madras peasant a private-property right in his holding. It has been seen how his intention was simply to strengthen the position of the *ryot* and his way of life, by giving him the certainty of a fixed revenue demand and an established tenurial right. With Cornwallis, although the leaning towards change was much more conscious, the temper was still conservative. Cornwallis's intention was to bring order and stability to a society fast dissolving, and not to bring about a social revolution which would effect its complete transformation. His solution was Whig: government reduced to the minimal functions of justice and protection from violence, in a society stabilized by the influence naturally emanating from a great landed aristocracy. His aims were still consistent with the old mercantilist conception of the British position in India, with the notion of reaping a surplus tribute and continuing the monopoly of the East India Company. They were also consistent with the idea of insulating India from the shock of collision with the West by restricting the settlement of Europeans.[1] Whatever his successors may have done with his work, Cornwallis was no apostle of the doctrine of assimilation.

The movement of anglicization in Cornwallis's administrative settlement was thus definite but limited. The move-

---

[1] For Cornwallis's views on the value of the Bengal territories to Britain, and his ideas on the Company's monopoly, see his Minute of 10 Feb. 1790, and his letter to Dundas of 4 April 1790: Forrest, *Cornwallis*, vol. ii, pp. 114, 185 et seq.

ment was, however, to be carried forward in the opening years of the nineteenth century in a much more violent and extreme form. Hitherto it had been confined in its operation to the form and methods of government. With the impetus it was given by the twin force of evangelicalism and free trade, it was now to be consciously directed upon Indian society itself and to become an explicit movement for revolutionary change.

Cornwallis's reforms had undoubtedly owed part of their character to the outlook of his chief advisers, John Shore (later Lord Teignmouth) and Charles Grant, who on retirement both became prominent members of the Clapham Sect and were numbered among the Evangelical Fathers. Cornwallis's distrust and consequent disuse of Indian officials, and his determination to find a solution in an English-officered, English type of administration, certainly reflects the growing contempt in which Indian institutions and methods were held under the influence of this movement of religious revival. To some extent the change in attitude was an inevitable one. The transformation of the English in India from suppliant merchants to a ruling caste, consciously isolated and imbued with a sense of racial superiority, was a natural consequence of their career of conquest. The growth of a considerable European population, in particular of the number of English women, also made for a more regular and settled mode of life, and diminished contact between the races.[1] Yet the change that was everywhere noted as taking shape after Cornwallis came out to Bengal in 1786 was much more than a response to changed political circumstances. The improvement in moral tone was not a merely local phenomenon. It was a change being wrought in the character of the Englishman at his centre; the product of advancing industrialism, of the ascendancy of the new middle classes, and of the emergence of a new ethic for a new society. Originating with Wesley and Whitfield in the form of methodism, the new outlook assumed importance when it began to find adherents among the upper middle classes under the name of the Evangelical revival in the last decades of the eighteenth century. Its influence in English history is

[1] Cf. Percival Spear, *The Nabobs*, chap. viii.

too pervasive to be measured by any conventional yard-stick. Halévy believed it to be the cement which preserved English society from violent dissolution in the Revolutionary era; all historians recognize its importance as the moral agency responsible for Victorian 'respectability', the power which tamed and disciplined the anarchic individualism of the Industrial Revolution. Its connexion with India is par-ticularly intimate, because of Shore and Grant who on their return to England went to live as neighbours to Wil-berforce at Clapham, and, together with Zachary Macaulay, Henry Thornton, and John Venn, formed the Clapham Sect.[1] The influence of this group sprang from its leadership of Evangelical and Methodist opinion on political issues. Wilberforce, as a personal friend of Pitt, and Grant, as a director and for many years chairman of the East India Com-pany, were able to command a powerful minority in the Commons. The two great objects which the Clapham Sect set themselves were the abolition of the Slave Trade and the opening of India to missionary enterprise. The measure of their success in the latter object—'that greatest of all causes, for I really place it before Abolition', as Wilberforce said—has often been recounted.[2] With Grant providing funds, knowledge, and influence, and Charles Simeon at Cam-bridge the spiritual leadership, a small number of Evan-gelical missionaries were sent out to India, the foremost of whom were David Brown, Claudius Buchanan, Henry Martyn, and Thomas Thomason. After years of public controversy, a large measure of freedom was won for missionary enterprise in the Charter Act of 1813, and an Indian Church with a bishop and three archdeacons was established. It is more difficult to estimate the Evangelical influence on the moral tone of European society in India, and probably this was more affected by the wider action of the Evangelical movement on society in England than by any local success. After winning a secure foothold in India, the missionaries directed what political interest they had to

[1] Charles Grant went to live at Clapham in 1794: Henry Morris, *Life of Charles Grant*, p. 168.

[2] Cf. J. W. Kaye, *Christianity in India*, and Morris, *Grant*. Wilberforce's descrip-tion of Indian missions as 'the greatest of all causes': R. and S. Wilberforce, *Life of Wilberforce*, vol. v, p. 126.

securing the legal protection of Christian converts, the suppression of inhuman rites such as 'suttee' and infanticide, and the disconnexion of the British power from the support of temples and Hindu and Muslim religious festivals. Yet if the orbit of its activity had been circumscribed in this manner, the Evangelical movement would have had comparatively little political importance. The fact that it stood for an ultimate transformation of Indian society brought it, however, into alliance with other powerful political currents.

The terms and nature of the alliance were first foreshadowed in the treatise which Charles Grant wrote on his return from India, and which he had privately printed and laid before the Court of Directors in 1797, under the title, *Observations on the State of Society among the Asiatic Subjects of Great Britain, particularly with respect to Morals; and on the Means of Improving it.* This was published as a Parliamentary Paper in 1813 and again in 1832.[1] Naturally it was cast in a moderate and restrained tone, but it gives a fair exhibition of the Evangelical mentality. It would be well to recall the general features of this mentality before dealing with the details of Grant's treatise. The 'notes' of the Evangelical mind were a consuming earnestness and conviction, born of a transfiguring religious experience. The working of this inner experience was the essential gift of the Evangelical faith, the experience of conversion, of being 'born again'. And by the terms it used to describe itself, 'vital religion', 'practical Christianity', it meant an experience actually felt physically and mentally in the anguish and terror of sin and the ecstatic joy of rebirth. Resulting in a complete transformation of the personality, the process of conversion, of 'justification and sanctification', consisted in the soul turning in upon itself, and stripping itself bare of the clothing of habit smothering its awareness. For a man to become alive it was necessary for him to become aware of his thraldom, to know that he did not govern himself, but was a dead thing borne along helplessly by his own appetites and the fashions and opinions of the world. This was the weight of sin which hung upon everyone and could only be thrown off by each man individually coming to terms with his God; it could not

[1] *P.P.*, 1813, vol. x, p. 31 and *P.P.*, 1831–2, vol. viii, Appendix.

be shifted or palliated by other human agency, by the mediation of priest or the performance of outward religious rites. The experience of being saved was one of a sudden illumination coming after the consciousness and repentance of sin, and its fruit was the gift of true self-government, the power of resting on one's own centre and consciously choosing the course of life instead of remaining a slave to outward circumstance and custom. It made the path of duty plain. That path lay, firstly, in the preservation of the soul in its state of grace through prayer and work, and secondly, in the mission to evangelize. Hence the Evangelical gospel, although originating in an intense interior experience, was one of action and mission in the external world. Work, requiring industry, frugality, and perseverance, was an end in its own right, the outward daily discipline of the soul against sloth; but it also afforded the material means for furthering the Kingdom on earth. The communication of the saving knowledge to the millions that dwelt in darkness could only be accomplished by preaching the word among them in a direct assault on their mind. It was not, of course, primarily an intellectual task, for the inward experience could not be reduced to rational terms. All refined worldly learning was a snare for the soul, but certain elementary mental accomplishments were necessary. If salvation was only attainable through the direct encounter of the individual personality with God, it was equally true that knowledge of God was possible only through knowledge of His revealed word. Both Methodists and Evangelicals concentrated, therefore, on securing a minimum standard of education as a prerequisite for conversion, at least sufficient for a person to read and understand the Bible.

The three most important features of the Evangelical mind for the present purpose were its intense individualism and exaltation of individual conscience, its belief that human character could be suddenly and totally transformed by a direct assault on the mind, and finally, its conviction that this required an educative process. These convictions were contained in a cast of mind which was almost Hebraic. To the Evangelicals the hand of God was visible in history, and nowhere more surely than in the miraculous subjugation of

India by a handful of English. Power carried with it an awful responsibility and duty, the evangelization of India's heathen millions. The plight of these millions was desperate, for they were not men with a feeble knowledge of God, but actual worshippers of false gods and graven images. And to the Evangelical their error was not simply false doctrine; it smelt as an unclean thing. The Hindu divinities for Wilberforce were 'absolute monsters of lust, injustice, wickedness and cruelty. In short, their religious system is one grand abomination.'[1]

Grant's treatise was a plea for carrying forward the work of evangelizing India as the great duty and interest of the British power. The major part of his work was devoted to proving the immeasurable degradation into which Indian society was sunk. With a wealth of quotation from Hindu writings and from the observations of European travellers, Grant drew a picture of an India immersed in the most appalling depths of bestial superstition and social corruption, a veritable Sodom and Gomorrah on earth. His indictment is drawn in solemn measured terms:

Upon the whole then, we cannot avoid recognizing in the people of Hindostan, a race of men lamentably degenerate and base; retaining but a feeble sense of moral obligation; yet obstinate in their disregard of what they know to be right, governed by malevolent and licentious passions, strongly exemplifying the effects produced on society by a great and general corruption of manners, and sunk in misery by their vices, in a country peculiarly calculated by its natural advantages, to promote the prosperity of its inhabitants.[2]

In this dread judgement Grant not merely condemned the religions of India but everything which might claim a civilized status for its peoples—their laws, arts, agriculture and handicrafts, and their personal manners and habits. In defining the causes of this degraded state of society Grant argued typically of his century. Character was a product of environment, but of moral rather than physical environment. The great moral force in India was the Hindu form of

---

[1] Speech of William Wilberforce, 22 June 1813: *Hansard*, 1st series, vol. xxvi, p. 164.

[2] Charles Grant, *Observations on the State of Society among the Asiatic Subjects of Great Britain, particularly with respect to Morals and on the Means of Improving it. Written chiefly in Year 1792* (privately printed, 1797), p. 71.

government and law, and above all, the Hindu religion. Their common character was their despotic nature; and here was the source of Indian ills.[1] Despotism destroyed the autonomy of the individual soul and so extinguished the source of virtue, since the man 'who is dependent on the will of another . . . thinks and acts as a degraded being' and 'fear necessarily becomes his grand principle of action'.[2] Admittedly the unrestrained despotism of the Hindu political system had been abolished in the British territories, but the tyranny of the Hindu law and the Hindu religion continued almost unabated. The dominion of the Brahmin class remained unshaken, the 'crafty and imperious priesthood, who feigned a divine revelation and appointment, to invest their own order in perpetuity with the most absolute empire over the civil state of the Hindoos, as well as over their minds'.[3] The root of all evil was this tyranny over the mind, a tyranny which could not be dispelled by a mere reformation in the law. The Hindu law had been and could be further modified, but it was a vital Evangelical doctrine that legislation was powerless to change human character.[4] Everything ultimately rested upon the inward workings of the individual soul. Grant's panacea for India envisaged an Indian counterpart of the European Reformation, capable of liberating the individual conscience from the tyranny of the priest. That tyranny was maintained because of the ignorance of the people and the hold which the vast fabric of superstition exercised over their lives. To free the mind education was the first requirement. To prepare it for the knowledge of Christian truth, it had first to be cleared of error and superstition, and education recommended itself for reasons of prudence. It was the least obtrusive method of evangelizing, the least likely to create any social or political disturbance. It would 'silently undermine . . . the fabric of error', and by restoring to the inhabitants of India the use of their reason would in itself work a great moral revolution.

There is no need to question Grant's sincerity in placing such emphasis on education. Admittedly, it was free from

---

[1] Grant, *Observations*, p. 74.   [2] Ibid., p. 73.   [3] Ibid., p. 83.
[4] Ibid., p. 173. Cf. one of the chief Evangelical authorities, Henry Venn, *The Complete Duty of Man*, 5th edn., 1798, pp. 56–57.

the violent objections raised against direct methods of evangelizing, but it had an intrinsic importance as an integral part of the process of conversion. Grant did not hold that Christianity could be implanted by an attack launched solely at the strongpoints of religious belief. He thought it could only be victorious if the attack were made on a much broader front, so that the Indian character could be subjected to the play of reformative influences from every angle.[1] The whole of the Western mind had to be introduced into India. For the benefits of Christianity were not only religious but also material, and Grant was advancing no less 'than a proposal for the further civilization of a people, who had very early made a considerable progress in improvement, but who, by deliberate and successful plans of fraud and imposition, were rendered first stationary, then retrograde'. The progress of Europe in comfort and wealth was a direct outcome of the liberation of the individual achieved by the Reformation;[2] and Wilberforce echoed Grant, in his speech during the Charter debates of 1813, when he claimed that

Christianity, independently of its effects on a future state of existence, has been acknowledged even by avowed sceptics, to be, beyond all other institutions that ever existed, favourable to the temporal interests and happiness of man: and never was there a country where there is a greater need than in India for the diffusion of its genial influence.[3]

The Evangelical had an almost Hebraic conviction that worldly success and power, although not to be striven for on their own account, attended the faithful pursuit of duty, and were instrumental in forwarding God's purposes in the world.[4] And here was the whole strength of their case. Duty

[1] Wilberforce held the same view. Wilberforce to Lord Wellesley, 6 April 1813: R. and S. Wilberforce, *Wilberforce*, vol. v, p. 111.
[2] Grant, *Observations*, p. 192 n.: 'That grand event introduced new light: and it was diffused among the lower orders, whose instruction became henceforth an object of particular care. The consequences were greater internal order, peace, and stability; thence sprung enlarged industry, adventurous enterprises and all the long succession of prosperity which this country has enjoyed.'
[3] Speech of Wilberforce, 22 June 1813: *Hansard*, First Series, vol. xxvi, p. 8, cited E. H. Howse, *Saints in Politics*, pp. 89–90.
[4] Cf. Wilberforce, *A Practical View of the Prevailing Religious System of Professed Christians*, Griffith, Farran, Okeden & Welsh, London, n.d. [1888?], pp. 113–14, 192 et seq. Also Henry Venn, *Complete Duty of Man*, pp. 277–8.

and self-interest were one. To educate and to evangelize was also to make the earth pour forth her abundance. Released from the chains of immemorial habit, his mind set free from ignorance and superstition, the individual in India would have both the disposition and the knowledge to improve his earthly condition. Grant had reached the crux of his argument. The promotion of civilization and material prosperity in India would immensely further the original and continuing purpose of the British in the East: the great beneficiary would be British commerce.

> In considering the affairs of the world as under the control of the Supreme Disposer, and those distant territories . . . providentially put into our hands . . . is it not necessary to conclude that they were given to us, not merely that we might draw an annual profit from them, but that we might diffuse among their inhabitants, long sunk in darkness, vice and misery, the light and benign influence of the truth, the blessings of well-regulated society, the improvements and comforts of active industry? . . . In every progressive step of this work, we shall also serve the original design with which we visited India, that design still so important to this country—the extension of our commerce.[1]

Hitherto British manufacturers had found only a limited market in India because of the poverty of the people and their unformed taste. Education and Christianity would now remove these obstacles. In this way 'the noblest species of conquest', the spread of true religion and knowledge, would not forfeit its earthly reward; for 'wherever our principles and our language are introduced, our commerce will follow'.

In demonstrating the natural alliance between his views and the interests of British commerce, Grant argued that the key principle of British policy must be 'plainly the principle of assimilation'. At present the British were in every way different from their Indian subjects, in language, manners, customs, sentiments, religion. There must be consequently among the latter a feeling that their interests were opposed. The healing principle which should close the dangerous gulf was that of assimilation. If India were anglicized, a community of interest would be established.[2] In 1813, on the occasion of the renewal of the Company's Charter, the Evangelicals launched a great public campaign

---

[1] Grant, *Observations*, p. 220.   [2] Ibid., p. 204.

to put Grant's ideas into practice. They were victorious in securing an Indian Church establishment, freedom for missionary work, and the appropriation of an annual sum for education. The parliamentary struggle was led by Wilberforce and he drew frankly on Grant's treatise for his arguments. But in the flight of his eloquence, the qualifications which Grant's sense of prudence had imposed were forgotten. Wilberforce voiced the full-blooded doctrine of assimilation:

. . . let us endeavour to strike our roots into the soil by the gradual introduction and establishment of our own principles and opinions; of our laws, institutions, and manners; above all, as the source of every other improvement, of our religion, and consequently of our morals. . . . Are we so little aware of the vast superiority even of European laws and institutions, and far more of British institutions, over those of Asia, as not to be prepared to predict with confidence, that the Indian community which should have exchanged its dark and bloody superstitions for the genial influence of Christian light and truth, would have experienced such an increase of civil order and security, of social pleasures and domestic comforts, as to be desirous of preserving the blessings it should have acquired; and can we doubt that it would be bound even by the ties of gratitude to those who have been the honoured instruments of communicating them?[1]

The Evangelical view stood in complete contrast to the East India Company's traditional attitude. From motives of expediency the Company had always manifested the most scrupulous regard for Indian religions, laws, institutions, and customs. Clive had taught the theory of 'double government', and only with great reluctance had the Company been forced into the open and taken upon itself the direct task of administration. Even after 1772 when it had stood forth 'in the character of Dewan', the Company under Hastings's guidance had been anxious to keep as far as possible to the traditional Indian methods and forms of government. 'We have endeavoured', wrote Hastings of his administrative reforms, 'to adapt our Regulations to the Manners and Understanding of the People, and Exigencies

[1] *Substance of the Speeches of William Wilberforce Esq., on the Clause in the East-India Bill for Promoting the Religious Instruction and Moral Improvement of the Natives of the British Dominions in India, on the 22nd June and the 1st & 12th of July 1813*, 1813, pp. 92–93.

of the Country, adhering, as closely as we are able, to their Ancient Usages and Institutions.'[1] Cornwallis had frankly broken with Hastings's policy in the forms and methods of government, and Teignmouth made a great point of this in defending the Evangelical case against the attacks of Scott Waring and others, who argued that until the mutiny at Vellore the British had always striven to preserve the indigenous system.[2] But Cornwallis's attitude was essentially one of non-interference in Indian society, once the framework of what he considered a sound system of justice and revenue had been established. He had no sympathy with Evangelical hopes for the conversion of the people, considering such hopes utterly visionary.[3] So far as the interests of the Company's subjects were concerned, his aims were enshrined in his Code of Regulations, 'to preserve to them the laws of the Shastre and the Koran in matters to which they have been invariably applied, to protect them in the free exercise of their religion, and to afford security to their persons and property'.[4] Not merely did the Evangelicals now challenge the traditional policy of the Company, they came forward with its direct opposite—the policy of assimilation. And they sought to carry their aims by harnessing their cause to the most powerful political force of their time, the interests of British commerce.

The first generation of the Clapham Sect were, however, unfitted to cement this alliance between the 'civilizing mission' and commerce. They were not cast for the role of revolutionaries, since it was in effect a revolution in the relationship between England and India for which they were calling. In English politics they were decidedly conservative, even numbering themselves among the stern, unbending Tories of the Sidmouth period. With respect to India they had a deep vested interest in the existing order.

[1] Hastings to Court of Directors, 3 Nov. 1772: cited G. W. Forrest, *Selections from the State Papers of the Governors-General of India: Warren Hastings*, vol. ii, Appendix A, p. 277.
[2] *Considerations on the Practicability, Policy, and Obligation of Communicating to the Natives of India the Knowledge of Christianity. By a Late Resident of Bengal,* 1808 [ascribed to Lord Teignmouth in India Office Library Tracts, vol. 96], pp. 23 et seq. For this controversy see Kaye, *Christianity in India.*
[3] David Brown to Charles Simeon, Feb. 1789: Kaye, *Christianity in India,* p. 371.
[4] Preamble to Regulation III, 1793: ibid., pp. 374-5.

They were intimately connected with the Company and publicly defended its commercial monopoly, Grant himself and his sons leading the fight in 1812 for the defence of the Company's privileges. Yet the policy of assimilation and its identification with the interests of British commerce could rest on no other grounds than the closest and freest intercourse with India, and the end of all barriers which opposed the ingress of the West. However staunchly they opposed it, the logical corollary of their policy was free trade, free European settlement, and the complete abolition of the Company as a commercial organ.

The full implications of the principle of 'assimilation' were grasped by the free-trade merchants, who ranged themselves against the Company when the renewal of the Charter was debated in 1813. Their adherence to the principle stemmed from their reading of the trading position. It was certainly true that the economic purpose behind British rule required to be revalued. The Company still continued to look upon it in vaguely mercantilist terms. The Indian trade in itself had ceased to be of first importance after the Company won the command of the revenues of the Bengal territories in 1757. Henceforward the annual 'investment' of Indian piece-goods was considered mainly as a means of transmitting the surplus revenues of Bengal to provide for the dividends of the Company in London; but towards the end of the eighteenth century it had been found more profitable to provide for the Company's dividends by shipping home China tea, purchased out of the proceeds of the Company's opium monopoly. Even Adam Smith, despite his violent attack on the Company, saw nothing wrong with the notion of reaping a tribute from the surplus revenue of the British territories in India;[1] and this mercantilist notion, that political dominion existed for the sake of drawing off a tribute, still lingered into the nineteenth century. In practice, however, Wellesley's conquests had piled up a debt burden which made it impossible to realize. By 1813 the Company had no case for maintaining its monopoly of trade between India and Europe. The sale of Indian piece-goods in Europe had fallen away almost completely; and the British territories no longer afforded a

[1] Adam Smith, *Wealth of Nations*, ed. E. Cannan, 5th edn., 1930, vol. ii, p. 431.

surplus of revenue after the Company's administrative and debt charges had been met. The Company in India had become a purely military and administrative power, and in fact was only able to pay its way with the profits of its opium monopoly, which it used to finance the China tea trade.

The fact that territorial dominion had proved itself to be without profit for the Company and Great Britain was quickly seized upon by the free traders. Not only was the Company's rule without benefit to itself, but it was, they argued, positively ruinous to India. The notion of tribute meant draining the country of wealth and impairing its power to purchase British goods. The Company was uninterested in finding a market for British goods in India, and, in any case, had neither the capital, skill, nor incentive, to develop its vast monopoly trading area, which stretched in the grandiose terms of its Charter 'between the Cape of Good Hope and the Straits of Magellan'. In the eyes of the free merchants the ultimate advantage of political dominion was an indirect one. The proper object of imperial rule was limited, as for government in general, to the efficient provision of law and order. Having established these primary conditions, the question of the profitability of the Indian connexion could be safely allowed to look after itself. For under a free trade India would rise rapidly into prosperity as a market for British manufactures and a source of raw materials. The Company should therefore cease to combine the contrary functions of ruler and trader and renounce all connexion with commerce. Superfluous posts and unnecessary pomp, created by the thirst of the Company's servants for private fortune and of the directors for patronage, should be swept away. The financial burden of the Company's administration should be kept as light as possible, so that the wealth of the people could fructify in their pockets and promote trade. All obstacles hindering the free flow of settlers, capital, and goods should be destroyed.[1] Given these circumstances, the prospects were limitless:

The vast peninsula of India has for centuries been harassed by wars and devastation, rendering property very insecure; but if it becomes open to a free trade, under one mild, liberal, and effective government,

[1] See note A, p. 323.

that could protect the property, laws, lives and liberties of the subjects, what a sudden change we might not anticipate? We should not only see the palaces of the Rajah, and the houses of the Vakeels, Aumils, Shrofs, and Zemindars, furnished and decorated with the produce of English arts and manufactures, but the Ryots, who form so large a part of the Indian population, may, like the British farmers, have a taste for foreign produce, as soon as they can acquire property enough to procure it; and this is only to be acquired to that extent under a free and liberal government, where property is held sacred. Under these circumstances a trade might suddenly grow up beyond the Cape of Good Hope, to take off all the surplus manufactures that Britain can produce.[1]

The Company did not merely deny to India the benefits of free commerce but its whole policy was designed to prevent Indian 'improvement'. Indeed, its chief argument against opening the Indian trade was that the country was incapable of any rapid improvement, its peoples being too rooted in poverty and inveterate habits and tastes ever to have the means or desire to purchase British manufactures on any considerable scale. The Company summoned an impressive array of witnesses before the Parliamentary Committee in proof of this point, including Warren Hastings, Teignmouth, and Munro.[2] The free traders naturally countered by urging that a rapid change in the Indian character was certainly possible, and that, once the establishment of law and order and light taxation had assured the Indian of the enjoyment of the fruits of his labour, he would not be backward in acquiring the requisite means and taste for British manufactures. The argument rested on the belief, common to the whole radical school of thought, that human nature was intrinsically the same in all races. As a later spokesman expressed it: 'We may be assured that in buying and selling, human nature is the same in Cawnpore as in Cheapside.'[3] Such a belief assumed that acquired characteristics were not innate and were readily alterable—an assumption held by the Evangelicals, and providing the

[1] W. Lester, *The Happy Era of One Hundred Millions of the Human Race, or the Merchant, Manufacturer, and Englishman's Recognised Right to an Unlimited Trade with India*, 1813, pp. 39–40.

[2] Evidence of Warren Hastings, 30 March 1813: *P.P.*, 1812–13, vol. vii, pp. 1 ff.; Teignmouth, pp. 9 ff.; Malcolm, pp. 53 ff.; Munro, pp. 121 ff.

[3] Written evidence of Thomas Bracken (a partner in the leading Calcutta house of agency, Alexander & Co.): *P.P.*, 1831–2, vol. x, Appendix, p. 587.

natural basis for the alliance of attitude between the missionary and the merchant. Already by 1813, the free merchants were extending their attack to the whole of the Company's system of government and to its informing principle of leaving Indian customs and institutions undisturbed.[1]

Commercial and missionary opinion were agreed upon the fundamentals of the Indian problem and its solution. Together they generated the colonial policy of nineteenth-century liberalism. This was the policy of assimilation of the anglicizing movement. Because of the close connexion of Grant and Teignmouth with the Company, the alliance of missionary and commercial opinion did not occur in 1813, but by the early eighteen-twenties these groups were rapidly fusing. This was part of a wider process by which Evangelical and non-conformist opinion abandoned its toryism of the Napoleonic War era and went over to the side of reform. It can be best seen in the second generation of the Clapham group. The younger Charles Grant, who in 1813 had delivered one of the finest speeches of his day in defence of the Company, and who continued to defend it in Parliament as late as 1823, passed over to the Whig side, and was the minister for framing the Bill which finally brought the commercial functions of the Company to an end in 1833. His principal assistant on that occasion was the celebrated son of Zachary Macaulay, who to his father's alarm had first imbibed Radical doctrine at Cambridge. In the twenties the British merchants—having won freedom of trade with India in 1813—witnessed with delighted astonishment the cloth and twist of Lancashire displacing even the famed muslin of Dacca in the Indian market.[2] So unexpected a development confirmed their dearest prejudices, and intensified their interest in the measures of government. For the reversal in the balance of trade, brought about by the triumph of imported cottons and the destruction of the Indian export trade in textiles, raised the threat that the potential market

---

[1] David Laurie, *Hints Regarding the East India Monopoly—Respectfully Submitted to the British Legislature*, Glasgow, 1813, pp. 50–51.

[2] Cf. John Prinsep, *Suggestions on Freedom of Commerce and Navigation—More Especially in Reference to the East-India Trade*, 1823, pp. 15–18. None of the free traders had predicted the astonishing rise in the export of British manufactured cottons to India. Technical improvements lowering prices were the main cause.

for British goods would be restricted unless new return products could be found. Measures had to be taken for raising the purchasing power of the Indian population. Thomas Bracken of Alexander & Co. put this quite clearly in his evidence before the Parliamentary Committee of Inquiry in 1832.[1] The actual demands of the merchant community were still largely concerned with their own immediate interests. They had still to acquire the legal right to own land, and to enter the Company's territories without licence. 'The unlimited and unshackled application of British capital and intelligence'[2] was still not fully realized. There were still vexatious customs and internal transit dues to be abolished or reduced. But they instinctively assumed that the path of advance, for themselves and for India, lay in the progressive adoption of English institutions. The great example, constantly before their eyes, was the rise of Calcutta under European control, from a village on a mud-flat to the 'City of Palaces' teeming with a prosperous Indian commercial community. They openly advocated that English law and procedure, with certain modifications, should be gradually extended over the rest of the British territories;[3] and in 1829 the judges of the Supreme Court put forward a scheme which proposed to bring the whole Ganges delta under the Calcutta Supreme Court's jurisdiction as an experimental measure. One of the chief objects of the scheme was to reduce the complexities of Indian land tenures to the simple relations of landlord and tenant, so that Europeans could purchase land in freehold, and individual energy and capital might be applied to Indian agriculture by Indians themselves.[4] The other demand of the mercantile community

[1] Evidence of Thomas Bracken, 14 March 1832: *P.P.*, 1831–2, vol. x, p. 150 (Qu. 1797).
[2] *A View of the Present State and Future Prospects of the Free Trade and Colonization of India*, 2nd edn., 1829, p. 16. The author of the pamphlet was John Crawfurd, who was the representative of the Calcutta mercantile community in the Commons (see p. 62, n. 4). It is ascribed to Crawfurd in the India Office Library Tracts, and in Ross Donelly Mangles, *Brief Vindication of the Hon. East India Company's Government of Bengal from the Attacks of Messrs. Rickards and Crawfurd*, 1830.
[3] Cf. Evidence of Thomas Bracken: *P.P.*, 1831–2, vol. x, Appendix, p. 587. *Bengal Hurkaru*, 11 Sept. 1829 (editorial). Crawfurd, *View of Present State*, p. 85.
[4] Letter from Judges of the Calcutta Supreme Court, 13 Sept. 1830, with enclosures: *P.P.*, 1831, vol. vi, pp. 575 et seq.

was for a revenue system which would impose no more than a light permanent assessment on the soil, instead of the punitive, fluctuating assessments that the Company practised outside the Bengal territories. These were the chief measures which government could be expected to effect. They were what John Crawfurd implied when recommending to the Parliamentary Committee of 1832

that if the Government fulfils its duties, that is, secure an equal and efficient administration of justice, and forbear from imposing burthensome imposts, or throwing needless impediments in the way of private adventure and the free investment of capital, it may very safely and confidently leave everything else to individual skill and competition.[1]

The call for the withdrawal of all governmental interference must not mask the aggressive spirit of the mercantile demands. 'Efficient administration of justice' meant English law, particularly a modern law establishing private-property rights in land, and a system of courts which would ensure that the influence of the law should be fully felt in the remotest hamlet. It meant using law in a revolutionary way, consciously employing it as a weapon to transform Indian society by breaking up the customary, communal tenures. This aggressive spirit filled Crawfurd's powerful pamphlet of 1829. The Indian Government, he asserted, must drop the ridiculous pose of protecting the weaker Indian community from the stronger and more energetic Europeans. Only by the powerful stimulus of competition would India be aroused. The feeble and ignorant must be placed in a state of collision with the strong and intelligent, for this was the only way of sharpening and invigorating their faculties and of raising them in the scale of society.[2] There must be an open assertion of the superior civilization. The Government should stand forward as an English government, instead of masquerading as the feudal subject of the Mughal emperor at Delhi, striking coins with his image, and paying him homage through the British Resident at Delhi. English and not Persian should be used as the language of govern-

---

[1] Written Evidence of John Crawfurd to Queries of Select Committee, in reply to Query 11: 'Can any measures . . . be suggested to advance the interest of Indian Commerce ?': *P.P.*, 1831–2, vol. x, Appendix, p. 588.

[2] Crawfurd, *View of Present State*, p. 101.

ment.[1] Above all, the Government should do everything in its power to spread English education, the great civilizing influence.

The Calcutta mercantile community had its own narrower, more selfish standpoint, but substantially it swelled the great tide of liberalism engulfing the English mind in the eighteen-thirties. Militant in its ardour for expansion, the new outlook renounced all desire for territorial power as an end; impatient of frontiers it wished to secure nothing less than a world empire of trade. As an article in the *Sunday Times* (which the *Bengal Hurkaru* reprinted in 1828) expressed it, it must be 'our policy to abandon altogether a narrow system of colonial aggrandisement which can no longer be pursued with advantage, and to build our greatness on a surer foundation, by stretching our dominion over the wants of the universe'.[2] The most eloquent expression of this English liberalism is to be found in Macaulay. If the new British Empire were to be a dominion not over territory but over the wants of the universe, it followed that it was more important to civilize than subdue.

The mere extent of empire is not necessarily an advantage. To many governments it has been cumbersome; to some it has been fatal. It will be allowed by every statesman of our time that the prosperity of a country is made up of the prosperity of those who compose the community, and that it is the most childish ambition to covet dominion which adds to no man's comfort or security. To the great trading nation, to the great manufacturing nation, no progress which any portion of the human race can make in knowledge, in taste for the conveniences of life, or in the wealth by which those conveniences are produced, can be a matter of indifference. It is scarcely possible to calculate the benefits which we might derive from the diffusion of European civilisation among the vast population of the East. It would be, on the most selfish view of the case, far better for us that the people of India were well-governed and independent of us, than ill-governed and subject to us; that they were ruled by their own kings, but wearing our broadcloth, and working with our cutlery, than that they were performing their salaams to English collectors and English magistrates,

[1] [Gavin Young], *An Inquiry into the Expediency of Applying the Principles of Colonial Policy to the Government of India & of Effecting An Essential Change in its Landed Tenures and Consequently in the Character of its Inhabitants*, 1822, p. 150. Cf. Crawfurd, *View of Present State*, p. 80.

[2] *Bengal Hurkaru*, 21 Oct. 1828 (editorial).

but were too ignorant to value, or too poor to buy, English manufactures. To trade with civilised men is infinitely more profitable than to govern savages. That would indeed be a doting wisdom, which, in order that India might remain a dependency, would make it an useless and costly dependency; which would keep a hundred millions of men from being our customers in order that they might continue to be our slaves.[1]

For Macaulay and many of his contemporaries the political tie with India was by nature brittle and impermanent. His historical judgement taught him that all forms of government were transitory and superficial, and were at the mercy of deeper, irresistible forces which impelled human society. The true wisdom in politics lay in the constant adaptation of institutions to conform with the progress of these forces. To attempt to check them, to oppose an unyielding resistance to their advance, might meet with momentary success, but must ultimately result in a violent explosion as their pent-up pressure broke loose. The governing forces of history were generated by the constant tendency of intelligence and property to increase and diffuse themselves in an ever widening circle; and India could not be insulated from this action. If England were to profit from India she must develop her trade. Wealth and intelligence, at present the monopoly of the English, would then be diffused among the Indians, and political power must ultimately follow this process of diffusion. This was the law of history which Macaulay proclaimed to the Commons in the English Reform Bill crisis of 1831.[2] There was no cause for pessimism in contemplating the future. That the Indian people might one day demand and gain their independence was not a matter for regret. To civilize India was 'on the most selfish view of the case' the proper British policy, for it would create a wealthy and orderly society linked in the closest commercial connexion with England. When this stage had been reached, the political bond would become unimportant and wither away. While the sword won a barren and precarious hegemony, the advancement of a

---

[1] Speech of Macaulay in Charter Debate, 10 July 1833: Macaulay, *Complete Works*, vol. xi, pp. 583–4.
[2] Speech on Reform, 16 Dec. 1831: ibid., pp. 490–5.

society in civilization was a lasting achievement. The permanent and most profitable form of conquest was that over
the mind; and this was the species of conquest which
Macaulay held out to the Commons, at the close of his great
Charter speech of 1833, in a torrent of eloquence which one
of the older members declared would 'console the young
people for never having heard Mr. Burke'.

It may be that the public mind of India may expand under our
system till it has outgrown that system; that by good government we
may educate our subjects into a capacity for better government; that,
having become instructed in European knowledge, they may, in some
future age, demand European institutions. Whether such a day will
ever come I know not. But never will I attempt to avert or retard it.
Whenever it comes, it will be the proudest day in English history. To
have found a great people sunk in the lowest depths of slavery and
superstitition, to have so ruled them as to have made them desirous
and capable of all the privileges of citizens, would indeed be a title to
glory all our own. The sceptre may pass away from us. Unforeseen
accidents may derange our most profound schemes of policy. Victory
may be inconstant to our arms. But there are triumphs which are
followed by no reverse. There is an empire exempt from all natural
causes of decay. Those triumphs are the pacific triumphs of reason
over barbarism; that empire is the imperishable empire of our arts and
our morals, our literature and our laws.[1]

Macaulay had said little that was new; everywhere his
speech rings with ideas which the elder Charles Grant and
Wilberforce had uttered nearly forty years before. And the
instrument which he looked to for gaining this conquest
over the mind of India was no different. The one sphere in
which all Liberal opinion accorded the State a right of
intervention was education.[2] By his entry into the education
controversy of 1835, when he was a member of Council at
Calcutta, Macaulay placed himself at the head of the school
which, in Bentinck's phrase, saw general education as the
panacea for the regeneration of India.[3] Writing to his
father in 1836, Macaulay said that it was his firm belief that,
if the plans for English education were followed up, there
would not be a single idolater among the respectable classes

[1] Speech of 10 July 1833: ibid., pp. 585–6.
[2] Cf. his speech on education, 19 April 1847: ibid., vol. xii, pp. 232 et seq.
[3] Bentinck to Money (Mancy ?), 1 June 1834 (draft): Bentinck MSS.

in Bengal thirty years hence; that this would be effected without any efforts to proselytize; without the smallest interference with religious liberty; merely by the natural operation of knowledge and reflection.[1] In his Education Minute he left no doubt as to the aim of English education. Never was the doctrine of assimilation so baldly and crudely stated. Explaining his support for the 'diffusion' theory, which envisaged applying the Bell and Lancaster technique of instruction to the mass of the Indian population, Macaulay said the first object must be to raise up an English-educated middle class 'who may be interpreters between us and the millions whom we govern—a class of persons Indian in colour and blood, but English in tastes, in opinions, in morals, and in intellect'.[2] Macaulay was backed by the great bulk of the Calcutta mercantile community in his fight for English education. But its most ardent advocate was Macaulay's young brother-in-law, Charles Trevelyan, in whose person the fusion of the Evangelical and Radical outlook was most completely realized.[3] In his pamphlet on the *Education of India* Trevelyan expounded in its fullest development that Liberal policy towards India, which Macaulay had outlined in his own speech of July 1833, and which was implicit in his reading of history. It is worth citing at length because it contains the kernel of the outlook of the Age of Reform, its passionate conviction that the ideals of altruism and the strongest claims of self-interest coincided. Substantially it represents the permanent Liberal attitude to India, which survived intact to the end of British rule, which, despite hesitations, was ready with an answer for Indian nationalism, and which has finally triumphed in our own time.

The existing connection between two such distant countries as England and India, cannot, in the nature of things, be permanent: no effort of policy can prevent the natives from ultimately regaining their independence. But there are two ways of arriving at this point. One

---

[1] Macaulay to his father, Zachary Macaulay, 12 Oct. 1836: G. O. Trevelyan, *Life and Letters of Lord Macaulay*, 1908 edn., pp. 329–30.

[2] Macaulay, Minute on Education, 2 Feb. 1835. One of the few reasonably accessible books which reproduces this minute in its entirety is G. O. Trevelyan, *The Competition Wallah*, 1864, pp. 410 et seq. Also *Selections from Educational Records*, Part I, 1781–1839, ed. H. Sharp, pp. 107 et seq.

[3] See note B, p. 323.

of these is through the medium of revolution; the other, through that of reform. In one, the forward movement is sudden and violent; in the other, it is gradual and peaceable. One must end in the complete alienation of mind and separation of interests between ourselves and the natives; the other in a permanent alliance, founded on mutual benefit and good-will. The only means at our disposal for preventing the one and securing the other class of results is, to set the natives on a process of European improvement, to which they are already sufficiently inclined. They will then cease to desire and aim at independence on the old Indian footing. . . . The political education of a nation is a work of time; and while it is in progress, we shall be as safe as it will be possible for us to be. The natives will not rise against us, we shall stoop to raise them; there will be no reaction, because there will be no pressure; the national activity will be fully and harmlessly employed in acquiring and diffusing European knowledge, and in naturalising European institutions. The educated classes, knowing that the elevation of their country on these principles can only be worked out under our protection, will naturally cling to us. . . . The change will thus be peaceably and gradually effected; there will be no struggle, no mutual exasperation; the natives will have independence, after first learning how to make good use of it; and we shall exchange profitable subjects for still more profitable allies. The present administrative connection benefits families, but a strict commercial union between the first manufacturing and the first producing country in the world, would be a solid foundation of strength and prosperity to our whole nation. If this course be adopted, there will, properly speaking, be no separation. A precarious and temporary relation will almost imperceptibly pass into another far more durable and beneficial. Trained by us to happiness and independence, and endowed with our learning and political institutions, India will remain the proudest monument of British benevolence; and we shall long continue to reap, in the affectionate attachment of the people, and in a great commercial intercourse with their splendid country, the fruit of that liberal and enlightened policy which suggested to us this line of conduct.[1]

3. *The Utilitarians and India*

Against the setting of the two great tendencies animating British policy, it would naturally be expected that utilitarianism stood in the vanguard of the tendency towards assimilation, and that it would form the spearhead of the movement for reform generated by the alliance of merchant,

[1] C. E. Trevelyan, *The Education of the People of India*, pp. 192–5.

manufacturer, and missionary. The Utilitarians were intimately connected with Indian affairs, for in 1819 James Mill,
to be followed shortly by his son, was admitted into the
executive government of the Company. Admittedly this
connexion was not free from embarrassment. As the unqualified champion of reform, the *Westminster Review* had
to maintain an awkward silence with regard to the East India
Company; a point which Hazlitt was quick to seize upon.[1]
Yet on larger grounds Bentham and James Mill might well
feel that this embarrassment was of little consequence, compared with the immense practical opportunities which the
appointment afforded. Given the post of an assistant examiner
in 1819, and in 1830 succeeding to the chief executive
office, that of Examiner, James Mill was at the very centre
of power and in a position to carry into practice the principle of utility as he had expounded it in his *History of British
India*. Writing to Dumont in his early period, when he was
assistant examiner in charge of revenue affairs, Mill proudly
pointed to the kingdom that had been delivered into his
hands:

> The time of attendance is from 10 till 4, six hours; and the business,
> though laborious enough, is to me highly interesting. It is the very
> essence of the internal government of 60 millions of people with whom
> I have to deal; and as you know that the government of India is
> carried on by correspondence; and that I am the only man whose
> business it is, or who has the time to make himself master of the facts
> scattered in a most voluminous correspondence, on which a just deci-
> sion must rest, you will conceive to what an extent the real decision on
> matters belonging to my department rests with the man who is in my
> situation.[2]

John Stuart Mill in his *Autobiography* also laid emphasis on
this aspect of his father's career:

> In this office [of assistant examiner], and in that of Examiner,
> which he subsequently attained, the influence which his talents, his
> reputation, and his decision of character gave him, with superiors who
> really desired the good government of India, enabled him to a great
> extent to throw into his drafts of despatches, and to carry through the

---

[1] Hazlitt, 'The New School of Reform': *The Plain Speaker* (Everyman edn.), p. 183.
[2] James Mill to Dumont: *The Works of David Ricardo*, ed. R. Sraffa, vol. viii,
'Letters 1819–21', p. 40 n.

ordeal of the Court of Directors and Board of Control, without having their force much weakened, his real opinions on Indian subjects. In his History he had set forth, for the first time, many of the true principles of Indian administration: and his despatches, following his History, did more than had ever been done before to promote the improvement of India, and teach Indian officials to understand their business. If a selection of them were published, they would, I am convinced, place his character as a practical statesman fully on a level with his eminence as a speculative writer.[1]

John Stuart himself entered the Company's service in 1823, the year of the foundation of the *Westminster Review*, and was, in his own words, 'in a few years practically the chief conductor of the correspondence with India in one of the leading departments, that of the Native States'. Although he was to remain in high administrative office in the Company until its abolition in 1858, eventually succeeding to the examinership, he had neither his father's opportunities nor his bent for the practical realization of the Utilitarian theories. Some of the early despatches on education, which he drafted, preached the word of utility, but for the main part of his career his duties were confined to handling the political relations with the Indian states.[2] In any case the scale of opportunity after his father's death was very much reduced by events within India; for the great administrative foundations in law, revenue, and the form of government had been settled in Bentinck's time, and the decade of wars after 1839 was no atmosphere for measures of internal reform. The reorganization of the India House after the loss of the Company's commercial functions in 1834 also greatly weakened the influence of the Examiner and his assistants. Before 1834 the entire burden of supervising the preparation of despatches to India was placed on the Committee of Correspondence, consisting of only nine of the twenty-four directors of the Company. In these circumstances the draft despatches prepared in the Examiner's office were usually accepted without demur, and a forceful man like James Mill was able, as his son says, to assert his views. After 1834 all the twenty-four directors were employed on the administrative

---

[1] J. S. Mill, *Autobiography*, ed. H. J. Laski (World's Classics, repr. 1949), pp. 22–23.   [2] See note C, p. 323.

side, and the result was that they paid 'infinitely more attention to the administration of India than they used to do, when they were encumbered with a great trade'.[1] They showed a much greater readiness to alter draft dispatches; and on J. S. Mill's own admission there was

less disposition to lay down general principles than there was formerly, perhaps in consequence of the greater interest now taken by individual members of the Court in the proceedings, and the greater application of their minds to them than formerly; for that very reason there is a greater number of objections, and it is more difficult to frame any statement of principles that shall command a majority.[2]

Yet perhaps the real secret why J. S. Mill left relatively so small a mark on Indian policy was that he was unfitted by temperament or belief to take over the leadership of the doctrinaire programme laid down by his father. Undoubtedly, his authority as a political economist did much to gain general acceptance for his father's doctrine of the Indian land revenue and for upholding peasant proprietorship. But one has the impression that he lacked the clear objectives, the range of opportunity, and the enthusiasm for Indian affairs, which his father had possessed. He makes little mention of India in his *Autobiography*, and his most recent and most thorough biographer completely omits any account of his work at the India House.[3]

The other assistant examiner, appointed at the same time as James Mill in 1819, was Edward Strachey, who was placed in charge of judicial matters. Strachey was described by Carlyle as 'a genially abrupt man; Utilitarian and Democrat by creed'.[4] He was a friend and correspondent of Mountstuart Elphinstone, and they discussed the applicability of Bentham's theory of law to Indian circumstances, when Elphinstone was the Governor of Bombay. Strachey paid a visit to Bentham and secured Elphinstone a present of the master's works.[5]

[1] Evidence of J. C. Melville, Secretary to the Company, 6 May 1852: *P.P.*, 1852–3, vol. xxx, p. 30. For the system before 1834, cf. C. H. Philips, *East India Company 1784–1834*, chap. i.

[2] Evidence of J. S. Mill, 21–22 June 1852: *P.P.*, 1852–3, vol. xxx, pp. 315–16, 333.   [3] M. St. John Packe, *Life of John Stuart Mill*.

[4] Thomas Carlyle, *Reminiscences*, 1887 edn., vol. ii, p. 124. Edward Strachey was father of Sir John Strachey and grandfather of Lytton Strachey.

[5] Colebrooke, *Elphinstone*, vol. ii, p. 115.

Bentham had always been eager to take a hand in framing the law system of India. In 1793 he had made an offer of his services, as a sort of Indian Solon, to Dundas, at this time President of the Board of Control; and Bentham's papers show that he toyed with the notion of constructing an Indian constitutional code. The important essay *On the Influence of Time and Place in Matters of Legislation* was composed with the object of considering what modifications were required in order to transplant his system of law codes to Bengal.[1] When the Mills entered the India House his earlier interest revived, and with the appointment of a reforming Governor-General in 1827, on intimate terms with Grote and his circle, Bentham's influence seemed complete. Before leaving for India in December 1827, Bentinck was given a farewell dinner at Grote's house, where he was feasted on 'the pure milk of the Benthamite word'. His professions in reply gave every satisfaction. 'I am going to British India, but I shall not be Governor-General. It is you that will be Governor-General', James Mill reported him as saying.[2] When on arrival in India Bentinck asked the public for suggestions of reforming measures, Bentham was overjoyed. It appeared to him 'as if the golden age of British India were lying before me'.[3] The head of the old philosopher was full of schemes. He instructed 'our friend James Young' (as Mill spoke of the Radical head of the Calcutta house of agency, Alexander & Co.) to expound the full details of the Benthamic principles to the new Governor-General; and Young had soon acquired an influence over the Supreme Government, with access to confidential papers, that Malcolm

---

[1] Bentham to Dundas, 20 May 1793: Bentham, *Works*, vol. x, p. 292. Fragment entitled 'Exordium cod. Ind.': Bentham MSS., folder clxix, f. 97. 'On the Influence of Time and Place in Matters of Legislation', *Works*, vol. i, pp. 171 et seq.

[2] Bentham to Col. Young, 28 Dec. 1827: *Works*, vol. x, pp. 576–8. It is not absolutely clear from Bentham's account of the dinner to whom the statement was addressed, but it would appear to be James Mill. Certainly Halévy was wrong in saying that Bentinck 'went to receive Bentham's philosophic blessing' before leaving for India, and that it was on this occasion that the statement was made (Halévy, *History of the English People 1830–41*, 1926 edn., p. 233). Bentham in fact never met Bentinck (*Works*, vol. x, p. 590). Other historians have reproduced Halévy's error; cf. K. N. Bell and W. P. Morrell, *Select Documents on British Colonial Policy*, p. xxx; J. S. Furnivall, *Colonial Policy and Practice*, p. 29.

[3] Draft letter, Bentham to Bentinck, 18 Nov. 1829: Bentham MSS., Box X, ff. 179–82.

thought improper.[1] Ram Mohan Roy, the bright morning
star of the new India, had long been catechized. In the
House of Commons 'in the service of British India' was
Daniel O'Connell, 'the best of legislators'.[2] Apart from these
specific instances of influence in high places, Bentham's
ideas were being disseminated amongst the young Indian
civilians at the East India Company's College at Haileybury.
William Empson, the Edinburgh Reviewer, who in 1824
succeeded Sir James Mackintosh as Professor 'of general
polity and laws', used Bentham's writings in his course.[3]
Sir George Campbell, who was at Haileybury in the eighteen-
forties, described Empson's teaching as 'not the law of
English lawyers but good first principles. He was a good
deal of a Benthamite, and I came away from Haileybury
with a very sound belief in the greatest happiness of the
greatest number.'[4]

It would be natural to expect the Utilitarians interested in
India to ally themselves with the general current of reform,
as it has already been described. And for the most part they
did. Free trade with cheap and efficient government, designed to affect the rapid modernization of India, were ideals
shared by all reformers. Yet the specific influence of utilitarianism, especially that exerted by James Mill and Bentham, was surprisingly distinct and isolated from the broad
body of Liberal opinion. This was not due to the much
closer definition and precision of their actual practical ideas,
but to an alienation in sentiment such as narrowed them into
a sect in England, drawing upon them Hazlitt's sting and
making them a butt for Dickens's caricature in *Hard Times*.[5]
James Mill was naturally suspect to the free traders, from

---

[1] James Mill to Brougham: A. Bain, *James Mill*, p. 391; Bentham, *Works*, vol. x,
pp. 590–1, vol. xi, p. 2. Malcolm to Bentinck, 4 Oct. 1829: Bentinck MSS.
[2] Draft letter, Bentham to Bentinck, 9/10 April 1829: Bentham MSS., Box X,
f. 178.
[3] Evidence of W. Empson, 2 July 1832: *P.P.*, 1831–2, vol. xii, p. 129, Qu.
1076 et seq. On Empson, cf. *D.N.B.*, vol. vi, p. 783. Mackintosh, while not a
disciple of Bentham, was on friendly terms with him and was among the chosen
few invited to Bentham's dinner-parties: *Works*, vol. x, p. 533. Mackintosh's conception of law was obviously affected by Bentham's theories; cf. his report as Re-
corder of Bombay on a draft Code of Police Regulations, cited W. H. Morley,
Analytical Digest of Reported Cases, vol. ii, p. 516.
[4] Sir George Campbell, *Memoirs of My Indian Career*, vol. i, p. 10.
[5] Hazlitt, 'The New School of Reform': Essay XVII in *The Plain Speaker*.

the time when he took service in the enemy's camp in Leadenhall Street. But even when he appeared as their champion in his great work on India, when he arraigned the Company before the bar of history and condemned it under the laws of utility, his standpoint was quite distinct and separate.

James Mill's *History of British India* was principally an attempt to make a philosophic analysis of Indian society and assess its place in the 'scale of civilization'.[1] Undoubtedly, one of his main aims was to dispel what he considered the silly sentimental admiration of oriental despotism which had marked the earlier thinkers of the Enlightenment. Even such a 'keen-eyed and sceptical judge' as Voltaire had succumbed,[2] and the conservative tendencies of the Enlightenment had been mischievously strengthened. Mill's indictment of so-called Hindu and Muslim civilization is a *tour de force*, more formidable in its relentless piling of evidence than even Grant's treatise. In India there was 'a hideous state of society', much inferior in acquirements to Europe even in its darkest feudal age.[3] So far from any diffidence on account of his entire lack of personal experience of India, Mill prided himself that the severity of his judgement was all the more justified by its very disinterestedness. His astonishing arraignment of the entire populations of India and China shows the fantastic authority which he was prepared to grant to the philosophic intelligence.

Even in manners, and in the leading parts of the moral character, the lines of resemblance [between the Indians and Chinese] are strong. Both nations are to nearly an equal degree tainted with the vices of insincerity; dissembling, treacherous, mendacious, to an excess which surpasses even the usual measure of uncultivated society. Both are disposed to excessive exaggeration with regard to every thing relating to themselves. Both are cowardly and unfeeling. Both are in the highest degree conceited of themselves, and full of affected contempt for others. Both are, in the physical sense, disgustingly unclean in their persons and their houses.[4]

Mill was not only in agreement with Grant and the Evangelicals

[1] James Mill, *History of British India*, 2nd edn., 1820, vol. ii, p. 135. Cf. Duncan Forbes, 'James Mill and India', *Cambridge Journal*, vol. v (1951–2).
[2] Mill, *History*, vol. ii, p. 137.
[3] Ibid., pp. 146 et seq., p. 186.
[4] Ibid., p. 195.

over the condition of Indian society, but his diagnosis of the causes of its ills ran in a similar direction. At the root of this primitive and barbaric state of society was despotism—a vast political and religious tyranny.

We have already seen, in reviewing the Hindu form of government, that despotism, in one of its simplest and least artificial shapes, was established in Hindustan, and confirmed by laws of Divine authority. We have seen likewise, that by a division of the people into castes, and the prejudices which the detestable views of the Brahmens raised to separate them, a degrading and pernicious system of subordination was established among the Hindus, and that the vices of such a system were there carried to a more destructive height than among any other people. And we have seen that by a system of priestcraft, built upon the most enormous and tormenting superstition that ever harassed and degraded any portion of mankind, their minds were enchained more intolerably than their bodies; in short that, despotism and priestcraft taken together, the Hindus, in mind and body, were the most enslaved portion of the human race.[1]

Certain broad similarities have often been detected in the thinking of Utilitarians and Evangelicals.[2] Both had turned against the tolerance and respect for Indian civilization characteristic of the ages of Clive and Warren Hastings. Both agreed in many general aims. Evangelicalism and utilitarianism were movements of individualism, both seeking to liberate the individual from the slavery of custom and from the tyranny of noble and priest. Their end was to make the individual in every society a free, autonomous agent, leading a life of conscious deliberation and choice. Although there was, of course, a profound gulf between their actual practising ideas, the assumptions of the Evangelical theology and the Utilitarian philosophy were remarkably similar. For both, man was a creature of sensation, of pleasure and pain. His failure to attain his end of happiness was the result of ignorance or miscalculation. Because of these he tended to prefer present pleasure to a more remote but lasting happiness. Knowledge would show men their true state and enable them to calculate aright. But until men were fully

[1] Mill, *History*, vol. ii, pp. 166–7.
[2] Cf. G. M. Young, *Victorian England—Portrait of an Age*, pp. 11–12. Also Halévy, *History of the English People in 1815*, 1924 edn., pp. 509–11.

educated, and until they had sufficiently disciplined themselves to forgo immediate pleasure for the sake of lasting
happiness (the Evangelicals would say until men are 'born
anew'), a 'severe schoolmaster' was necessary in the form of
law. For the Evangelicals this meant the Divine or Mosaic
Law, whose first use was to punish ignorance and to 'slay the
sinner'.[1] For the Utilitarians it meant that the human legislator must assist men to avoid harmful acts by artificially
weighting such acts with the pains of punishment. The
Utilitarians admitted that there were other 'sanctions' in-
fluencing conduct. Public opinion and education were important in affecting men's views and conduct in pursuit of
happiness. But these were as nothing in the scale when compared with the might of law. The primary influence determining human character was the legislator and his commands,
that is, the form of government and the laws. The Utilitarians, completing the work of their intellectual ancestors,
abolished God and substituted human for Divine Justice.
But for the Evangelicals the Law-Giver and the Law were
predetermined. Their business was limited to admonition
and persuasion, to make men conscious of Him and His
dreadful commands; and they had no faith in the power
of mere human laws to shape conduct and transform
character. In its largest sense their solution was that of
education.

This is the crux of the difference which sets the Utilitarians apart from Evangelical and Liberal opinion in its
analysis and proposed solution of the Indian problem. It is
the immense and indefinite influence which the Utilitarians
allowed to the power of law and government. Mill gave the
most finished expression to his general theory in his *Encyclopaedia Britannica* article on 'Education'.[2] Education,
understood in its largest sense of the various external influences forming the individual mind, was of course all-
important. But in its ordinary meaning of schooling, of
technical education, it was the most subordinate branch. The

---

[1] Cf. John Wesley, 'Sermon XXIX—The Original Nature, Property, and Use of
the Law', *Forty-Four Sermons*, 1944 edn., p. 391.
[2] James Mill, article on Education, reproduced in *James and John Stuart Mill on
Education*, ed. F. A. Cavenagh, 1931.

influence of the home (domestic education), the influence of public opinion (social education), were of much greater importance. But 'the keystone of the arch' was the form of government and laws, that is political education, upon which the strength of the whole depended. Political education determined directly the moral forces acting upon the individual. It also determined those more indirect forces arising out of the physical condition of the people, for the progress of wealth and the standard of living were equally dependent upon the form of government. Without an adequate amount of food and leisure in the great body of the people, all education, according to Mill, was impotent. The vices and defects of the mass of mankind arose not from a lack of schooling but from poverty. He applied this theory to the Indian problem. 'The form of government is one', wrote Mill in his *History*, 'the nature of the laws for the administration of justice is the other, of the two circumstances by which the condition of the people in all countries is chiefly determined.' There was one corollary. 'Of these two primary causes no result to a greater degree ensures the happiness or misery of the people than the mode of providing for the pecuniary wants of the government.'[1] It will be necessary to examine Mill's theory of human nature rather more closely, but it is already evident that, with the gesture of one demonstrating a geometrical theorem, he had simplified the Indian question to three issues—the form of government, the nature of the laws, and the mode of taxation. Reform these, argued Mill, and the whole of Indian society would undergo a vast transformation, setting it on a rapid advance up the scale of civilization. All other measures were secondary and comparatively unimportant. Explicitly he rejected the notion, so firmly held by Evangelical and Liberal opinion, that the schoolmaster could provide India's panacea. In the *Fifth Report* of 1812 the Bengal district judges had put forward the proposal of reform through education. Mill dismissed the idea in striking fashion in his *History*. Something 'far beyond the power of mere schooling' was required. A fundamental change had first to take place in the state of government and law, 'the primary sources of good and evil',

[1] Mill, *History*, vol. i, p. 247.

before any change could take place in the stream they sent forth:

> It has been alledged above, that most of the Indian judges point to education as the only power from the operation of which a favourable change can be expected in the moral character of the people; on this subject however, if Sir Henry Strachey be excepted, their views are superficial. The most efficient part of education is that which is derived from the tone and temper of society; and the tone and temper of society depend altogether upon the laws and the government. Again: ignorance is the natural concomitant of poverty; a people wretchedly poor are always ignorant; but poverty is the effect of bad laws, and bad government; and is never a characteristic of any people who are governed well. It is necessary, therefore, before education can operate to any great result, that the poverty of the people should be redressed; that their laws and government should operate beneficently.[1]

This difference over the efficacy of education was crucial. It has been usual to associate the Mills with the movement for English education which Macaulay carried to victory by his Education Minute of 1835. A recent writer has gone so far as to assert that: 'The Minute on Education is James Mill's philosophy expressed in Macaulayese.'[2] This is to give a wholly erroneous impression. It is true that Macaulay shared with Mill a profound contempt for oriental culture, but his minute owes more to Charles Grant's treatise in every way. James Mill was no Anglicist. He was convinced that the vernacular languages were far better vehicles of instruction. The passion for English education was patently for him the outcome of a narrow patriotic prejudice, while in contrast the only truly scientific criterion for judging the content and medium of instruction was that of utility. This was the whole burden of the education dispatch of 1824 which has been generally attributed to him.[3] But what is of far greater importance is his striking scepticism about the effectiveness in India of any type of formal education, whether in English or the vernacular. In his evidence before the Select Committee in 1832 he made no attempt to conceal

---

[1] Ibid., vol. v, pp. 541–3.
[2] Duncan Forbes, 'James Mill and India', *Cambridge Journal*, vol. v (1951–2), p. 23.   [3] See note D, p. 324.

his pessimism. The progress of education so as to produce any very perceptible effect would, he thought, be exceedingly slow, and any very general diffusion of the English language among the natives of India was to be despaired of.[1] This chill, sceptical attitude to the dearest of Liberal hopes is the measure of Mill's isolation.

The divergence between James Mill and the main stream of English Liberal opinion requires emphasis. It has been common to neglect this divergence, and to assume that utilitarianism was a more strictly logical and programmatic form of Liberal belief. While in the broadest sense this may well be true, it fails to take into account the increasing isolation in which the Utilitarians found themselves in the eighteen-thirties. Their doctrines, when pressed into rigorous and systematic form, drove them into positions which questioned the comfortable assumption of progress held by Liberal opinion. Ricardo had revealed the fundamental disharmony in the workings of a free economy, and drew attention to the permanent cleavage of interest between the landlord and every other class in the community. And Malthus's law of population, upon which Ricardo first formulated the principles of the Iron Law of Wages, threw serious doubts on the belief in a society given over to the free play of individual instinct. This new, coldly scientific and recondite political economy, of which James Mill was the expounder, possessed none of the warmth of common life or the readability of Adam Smith. And while it might provide an oracular authority for arguments against the Corn Laws and in favour of free trade, it seemed to take perverse delight in destroying those confident prejudices upon which the new middle-class optimism was founded. Their impatient expansive spirit, which believed that Britain's future hung upon the extension of her foreign trade and the winning of a world-wide market, was sharply corrected by Ricardo and Mill. Foreign trade was simply an exchange and not a creation of wealth; what mattered was the rate of capital

[1] Evidence of James Mill, 21 Feb. 1832: *P.P.*, 1831–2, vol. ix, p. 55. For the difference between the Mills's and the Macaulay view on Indian education, cf. K. A. Ballhatchet, 'The Home Government and Bentinck's Educational Policy', *Cambridge Historical Journal*, vol. x (1951), p. 224.

growth and not the extent of the market. Admittedly, trade brought about an international division of labour and so increased the mass and variety of commodities, but it was not the life-blood of the nation as the manufacturing and commercial classes chose to argue.[1] Mill would never join with those clamorous partisans who, as we have seen, held out prospects of visionary wealth, if once India were open to free trade. He would never agree that a surplus of capital or goods was the cause of the periodic slumps in the new industrial economy, or that new markets were a vital necessity as an outlet for the surplus. Such common claims that 'India might afford a field for the employment of a greater portion of the unemployed capital of the country' were to him nonsensical.[2] By definition there could never be a general glut of capital or commodities. In this way Mill stood aloof, agreeing that free trade was correct as a principle, but refusing to be carried along by the tide of popular prejudice which regarded it as the key to happiness. It is small wonder that by the thirties this form of political economy, whose arguments were always abstract and bloodless, should have fallen from favour, and that later economists broke away from its leading strings to preach a more optimistic and comfortable doctrine. And it is significant that the new generation should be known as the Manchester School. The sectarianism of Bentham's and Mill's younger followers had already, before the Whig victory of 1832, alienated ordinary Liberal opinion. Hazlitt, the Radical, declared them to be 'a kind of Ishmaelite, whose hand is against others'. In 1829 Macaulay declared this alienation in the strongest of terms.

We wish to see a broad and clear line drawn between the judicious friends of practical reform and a sect which, having derived all its influence from the countenance which they have imprudently bestowed upon it, hates them with the deadly hatred of ingratitude. There is not, and we firmly believe that there never was, in this country a party so

---

[1] Cf. James Mill, *Commerce Defended*, 1808, p. 106. Cf. K. E. Knorr, *British Colonial Theories 1570–1850*, chap. viii.

[2] Cf. an article in the *Scotsman*, 23 May 1829, reproduced in the *Bengal Hurkaru* of 17 Sept. 1829. The claim was also made in the Commons by Whitmore, who acted with John Crawfurd as a parliamentary spokesman of the Calcutta mercantile community; cf. Commons debate of 14 May 1829, reported in the *Bengal Hurkaru* of 8 Sept. 1829.

unpopular. They have already made the science of political economy—
a science of vast importance to the welfare of nations—an object of
disgust to the majority of the community. The question of parliamentary reform will share the same fate if an association be formed in
the public mind between Reform and Utilitarianism.[1]

This was written before the authoritarian implications of
Bentham's constitutional theories had become apparent in the
centralized bureaucracy which his disciples, Chadwick and
Southwood Smith, were to fashion from the Poor Law Commission and the Local Government Board.

The Mills were naturally suspect with regard to India
because of their employment in the Company; and to their
influence was attributed the marked silence of the *Westminster Review* and the Radical *Morning Chronicle* with regard
to this stronghold of outworn privilege. The Radical news-
paper of Calcutta, the *Bengal Hurkaru*, bitterly lamented
James Mill's defection:

He is a man of the highest order of intellect, and would doubtless
have done much for this country, and among other things would have
finished his long promised supplementary volumes of his history [of
British India], but for one slight impediment, which does honor to the
sagacity of at least one party to the bargain. He has now a retainer from
the other side. Honor, gratitude, and complacent self-love have won
him, and kept him on the non-popular side of one great public question
—that between the Company and England.[2]

The Mills were accused of betraying their principles, and
'judging of Indian questions by rules and standards the very
opposite of those they employ to decide all other questions
whatever. Demagogues at home, they are despots abroad.'
It has been seen, however, that James Mill differed from the
English mercantile community before he entered the Company's service, that he disliked their selfish prejudices, and
believed himself to possess a scientific solution of India's ills
peculiarly his own. In his *History* he had belittled the hopes
centred on education, and had attacked two of the dearest
convictions of the English merchants—their faith in the
virtues of English law and English courts, and their faith in

[1] Macaulay, *Edinburgh Review*, June 1829. Article on 'Westminster Reviewer's
Defence of Mill', *Miscellaneous Writings and Speeches of Lord Macaulay*, 1889 edn.,
pp. 203-4.   [2] See note E, p. 324.

the virtues of Cornwallis's land revenue system. The Supreme Courts, established in the Presidency towns and presided over by judges appointed directly by the Crown, were regarded by the English inhabitants as the shield and defence of their rights and liberties against the despotic government of the Company. But as depositaries of English law, they were also regarded as representative of a higher order of civilization, which should gradually be allowed to expand from out of its narrow confines and spread over the face of British India. In 1829 the judges of the Supreme Court at Calcutta, Sir Charles Grey and Sir Edward Ryan, seriously ventured to propose the extension of an English form of property law to a part of Bengal, as a preliminary measure. Similarly, while cherishing few illusions as to the character of the majority of the Bengal *zemindars*, the principles of Cornwallis's settlement of the land revenue appeared to the mercantile community to be absolutely correct. These principles were the permanent and known limitation of the State demand, and the conferring of a freely alienable private property right; and they carried with them the complementary notions of the restriction of executive power and the subordination of all landed rights to the sole authority of the courts of law. It was hoped that with the progress of society the ownership of the great landed estates of Bengal would pass out of the hands of the old *zemindar* type into those of a modern Indian *entrepreneur* class. Munro's alternative of trying to create from the actual cultivators a property-owning yeomanry stood condemned, because his system meant arming the executive with preponderant power, preventing the accumulation of capital and the rise of a capitalist class, and so blocking the only line of development capable of producing a progressive agricultural revolution.

Mill's irreverence for English law, and his disrespect for the Supreme Courts as a check on the executive power,[1] were forgivable, so long as he stood forth as the champion of a better and more efficient law system; but his advocacy of Munro's *ryotwar* system set him permanently at odds with

[1] Mill, *History*, vol. iv, pp. 267 et seq. Cf. also James Mill's Evidence, 21 Feb. 1832: *P.P.*, 1831–2, vol. ix, p. 50.

the Calcutta merchants.[1] The suggestion he put forward in
his *History* that the State should absorb the whole rental of the
soil as revenue was too daring to be understood or considered.[2]
In 1828 the *Bengal Hurkaru* was congratulating its readers—
quite mistakenly as it proved—that 'the *Cornwallis* system
is beginning to emerge from the eclipse into which it has
for the last twenty years been thrown by the interposition of
the *Munro* system; and that we may hope to see disastrous
twilight succeeded by a light shining brighter and brighter
unto the perfect day'.[3] The *ryotwar* system, with its fluctuating assessments collected annually from the individual cultivator, appeared to give the executive despotic power and
to make impossible the establishment of effective private-
property rights. Crawfurd, who had been appointed as a
spokesman in England for the Calcutta merchants, denounced it with fierce indignation:

> . . . it is not to a land-tax in the abstract that I object, but to an
> Asiatic land-tax—to a tax which aims at the entire absorption by the
> State of all that it can seize of the rent of a country, nearly the whole
> industry of which is rural,—to a tax, therefore, which makes it im-
> possible that capital should accumulate, and a people advance in
> prosperity,—to a tax which, in its very essence, must be unequal and
> uncertain,—to a tax which is proved by long experience subjects the
> contributor, beyond any other, to the violence, venality and corrup-
> tions of a host of tax-gatherers,—and finally to a tax which, with all
> these characteristics, there is no escaping from, because it presents the
> object taxed—exposed, naked, palpable, and defenceless to arbitrary
> power and fiscal rapacity.[4]

There were other disquieting tendencies in the Utilitarian programme. Bentham's name commanded immense
respect in the field of jurisprudence, and many of his arguments were excellent ammunition in the Radical assault on
the anomalies of existing laws and institutions. But his
belief in the single judge, his depreciation of juries, his

---

[1] Mill, *History*, vol. v, p. 416.   [2] Ibid., vol. i, pp. 277–8.
[3] *Bengal Hurkaru*, 21 Feb. 1828 (editorial).
[4] John Crawfurd, *An Appeal from the Inhabitants of British India to the Justice
of the People of England. A Popular Inquiry into the Operation of the System of Taxation in British India* (1839), pp. 34–35. Crawfurd was the paid Parliamentary Agent
of the Calcutta merchants; cf. Crawfurd's Evidence, *P.P.*, 1830, vol. v, p. 285; vol. vi,
p. 342.

eulogy of the summary mode of procedure, were all sus-
piciously un-English, and made his ideas difficult of entire
acceptance even to those who counted themselves as advanced Radicals. The *Bengal Hurkaru*, which steadily
supported Bentham and hailed his idea of a rational and
codified law system, could not conceal its misgivings on his
notions of procedure. It saw how close they came in their
authoritarian cast to the hated system of Munro, who had
frankly set out to perpetuate Indian tradition and oppose
English innovation.

The framing of a penal code for all persons in India, the Judges
think, would take but a few months, under the care of a Judge of the
Nizamut Adawlut and an intelligent English lawyer; but as the Judges
say the 'arrangement of a system of Courts for carrying the code into
execution is another matter'. It is indeed; there is the problem to solve,
and the true mean to hit between the technical and what the philosophers have been pleased to phrase the natural mode of procedure:
between the ARCADIAN plan of governing and judging, in which your
Governor and Judge sit under a tree; your simple plan which finds
favour in the eyes of Bentham and Mill and (for extremes meet)
of Sir Thomas Munro, in which the Judge examines the plaintiff,
defendant, and the witnesses—hears, decides, and executes judgement
summarily, and on the spot; a plan which supposes Judges always to be
what they are very ready to suppose themselves to be, all-sufficient in
point of capacity, honesty and labour, and to require no aid, no watch-
ing, and plaintiffs and defendants quite competent to conduct their
own affairs in the best possible manner; between these and similar
plans, and the technical plan, with its array of intermediaries,
Advocates, Attornies, and Officers of Court, lies the mean. . . .[1]

Instances of this difference with Liberal opinion can be
readily multiplied. The Utilitarian contempt for the Whig
reverence of the separation of powers, its lack of suspicion
of executive power *per se*, its conception of the legislature as
entirely sovereign with the judiciary and executive as mere
executants of its will, such ideas offended deep-seated
prejudices. James Mill's notion of a Government of India,
supreme over all courts and persons, including the Supreme
Courts, and entrusted with an absolute and binding authority

---

[1] *Bengal Hurkaru*, 1 June 1832 (editorial). For many complimentary references to
Bentham and suggestions for the applications of his ideas to India, cf. *Bengal
Hurkaru*, 8, 9, 15 April, and 23 June 1828.

equivalent to that of the British Parliament; his advocacy of a single legislative council composed entirely of a few experts and in no way representative of English inhabitants as in a colonial legislature; his insistence that Englishmen in the interior should be subject to the same law and courts as Indians; all these positions advanced in his evidence of 1832 before the Parliamentary Committee were hardly calculated to endear him to the narrower type of Englishman in Calcutta. And he was equally estranged from 'the large-hearted English liberalism' which wished to see educated Indians increasingly associated in the work of government. This sentiment, to be expressed by later generations in the maxim that good government was no substitute for self-government, awakened no response in the elder Mill, although it was to be among the important qualifications with which his son was to dilute the Utilitarian doctrine. Happiness and not liberty was the end of government, and happiness was promoted solely by the protection of the individual in his person and property. In his evidence before the Commons Committee of 1831, James Mill confessed that he did not share in the widely entertained opinion that the natives of India should be more largely employed in the business of government. The great concern of the people of India, Mill argued, was that the business of government should be well and cheaply performed, but that it was of little or no consequence who were the people who performed it. He rejected the suggestion put to him that the employment of Indians in the higher branches of the administration would tend to elevate the character of the people as a whole. To elevate the character of any people, the important thing was to protect them. 'Elevation is the natural state of a man who has nothing to fear; and the best riches are the effects of a man's own industry; effects which never fail when the protection is good.'[1] In the great explanatory despatch which accompanied the new Charter Act of 1833, and of which Mill has always by tradition been considered the author, this view was set forth. Its cold Utilitarian logic struck through the woolly sentiment of the new dispensation which purported to abolish all disqualifications of race or creed for Government

---

[1] Evidence of James Mill, 4 Aug. 1831: *P.P.*, 1831, vol. v, p. 396.

employment. Macaulay, the Liberal, had declared that to the last day of his life he would be proud of having assisted in framing the Bill which contained 'that noble clause, which enacts that no native of our Indian empire shall, by reason of his colour, his descent, or his religion, be incapable of holding office'. In words very similar to those which James Mill had used in his evidence before the Commons Committee, the Public Despatch of 1834 toned down the implications of this clause and poured cold water on its warm-hearted, liberal sentiments:

> . . . we must guard against the supposition that it is chiefly by holding out means and opportunities of official distinction that we expect our Government to benefit the millions subjected to their authority. We have repeatedly expressed to you a very different sentiment. Facilities of official advancement can little affect the bulk of the people under any Government, and perhaps least under a good Government. It is not by holding out incentives to official ambition, but by repressing crime, by securing and guarding property, by creating confidence, by ensuring to industry the fruit of its labour, by protecting men in the undisturbed enjoyment of their rights, and in the unfettered exercise of their faculties, that Governments best minister to the public wealth and happiness.[1]

All that mattered for James Mill was that the machine of government should be efficiently designed and conducted. Unsympathetic to Indians being admitted to government service, he strenuously resisted any suggestion for establishing representative institutions for India, such as had been urged by some Liberal enthusiasts like Sir Alexander Johnston and Robert Rickards.[2] It was wholly out of the question, he replied to the committee.[3] For Mill the only control that

---

[1] Public Despatch to India, 10 Dec. 1834, para. 109; cited C. Ilbert, *The Government of India*, p. 530. James Mill's authorship was declared to be an office tradition by J. W. Kaye, *The Administration of the East India Company*, p. 137 n.

[2] Johnston had been Chief Justice of Ceylon in 1805. He favoured legislative councils for India which would have included elected Indian representatives; cf. his evidence, 5 July 1832: *P.P.*, 1831–2, vol. xii, p. 139, Qu. 1130. In 1806 he had submitted a most radical scheme of constitutional reform to Charles James Fox: ibid., p. 147. Robert Rickards was one of the Company's most persistent opponents, and his pamphlets attracted considerable attention. For his scheme of a native council, cf. his evidence of 14 May 1830; *P.P.*, 1830, vol. vi, pp. 274, 284, 286.

[3] Evidence of James Mill, 21 Feb. 1832: *P.P.*, 1831–2, vol. ix, p. 49, Qu. 364; cf. *Edinburgh Review*, vol. xvi (April 1810), p. 155: 'A simple form of arbitrary government, tempered by European honour and European intelligence, is the only

could properly be exerted over the administration was that
of Parliament and the Home Authorities.

If Mill's study of the Indian problem lacked the condensa-
tion of a finished philosophical exposition, it nevertheless
aimed at the same simplicity of analysis as his *Essay on
Government*. He admitted that his *History* was 'a motley kind
of production, having been written at such distant times,
and with so many interruptions', but he hoped it would
'make no bad introduction to the study of civil society in
general', and that it would lay open 'the principles and laws
of the social order in almost all its more remarkable states,
from the most crude to the most perfect with which we are
yet acquainted'.[1] Above all he strove to deduce the Indian
problem and its solution from a single principle, to break
through the loose arguments and suggestions of ordinary
opinion and to reason with the rigorous logic of his 'abstract
or geometrical method'. His solution was designed to look
simple, to rest upon a 'grand discovery of modern times' as
with the problem of government as a whole. He had rejected
the solution of education in its conventional sense. The
winning of the active co-operation of the Indian peoples was
unnecessary; the task of persuading them by education and
rewarding them by gradual admission to office and power
was laborious, and would fail to achieve any large effect.
The solution lay simply in a reconstruction of the machine
of government.

For the source of India's ills was no different from that of
the rest of mankind's: quite simply it was bad government.
In his *Essay on Government*, Mill had set out a chain of
deductive reasoning from 'the principles of human nature'
which was intended to be a summary exposition of the whole
Utilitarian doctrine. Man, as a sensum seeking pleasure and
shunning pain, strove for wealth as a chief means to his end.
Given no interference with the law of attraction and repulsion,

form which is now fit for Hindustan.' Article attributed to Mill: A. Bain, *James Mill*,
p. 109.
   [1] James Mill to Ricardo, 6 Oct. 1816, 19 Oct. 1817: *Works of David Ricardo*, ed.
Sraffa, vol. vii, pp. 75, 195–6.

each man would automatically avoid the pain of labour by seeking forcible possession of his neighbour's wealth; but this tendency was self-defeating, because the condition of insecurity which it generated destroyed the very motive to labour on which the existence of wealth depended. Government originated in order to provide security for the motive to labour and accumulation; it existed to supply that 'basis of expectation' which was property. Law created property by defining rights and securing them under the threat of punishment. Since, therefore, law always operated at the expense of liberty and by the infliction of pain, it was important that it should be precisely adjusted so that the pain inflicted was outweighed by the pain prevented.

It was to the lack of an efficient system of law, founded on the science of jurisprudence, that Bentham in his early years explained the source of misgovernment and poverty. Given such a system which perfectly reconciled liberty and security and laid on individual action no further restraint than was beneficial, Bentham believed that wealth, and therefore happiness, would be—in his own language—'maximized'. Logical and practical considerations ultimately drove him on to see that this lack was caused, not by ignorance, but sinister design. What security was there that the man or group of men to whom the supreme legislative power was confided would prefer 'the greatest happiness of the greatest number' to their own immediate happiness? If in the absence of restraint men seek to avoid the pain of labour and possess themselves of their neighbours' goods, what was to prevent a government of one or a few men from preying upon the community and framing the law in their own sinister interests? Bentham's experience of trying to get his schemes accepted confirmed this reasoning; so that by the time Mill formulated the Utilitarian theory in the *Essay on Government*, he could state as an axiom that the fewer the persons holding sovereign power the worse a government became. Despotism was the low-water mark in the scale of political evil. Only as far as the governing few could be brought under the control of the governed many, could there be security for laws which aimed at maximizing wealth and happiness. Mill found the solution in what he termed 'the grand discovery of modern times', the device of representative democracy.

Now only half of this chain of reasoning applied to India. It has already been observed that, while ascribing all India's ills to the lack of good government, Mill had ruled out its chief security, representative democracy. That check could not be applied by the people of India themselves; it had to be supplied by the submission of the Indian Government to the control of the British Parliament. Mill seemed untroubled at this prospect and obviously believed India was a case where autocracy need not lead to tyranny. Bentham in his earlier years had rested his hopes on enlightened despotism, and they may still be detected in the grandiose boast he made at the end of his life when he pictured himself as the uncrowned philosopher-king of India's millions: 'Mill will be the living executive—I shall be the dead legislative of British India.'[1]

Mill had traced the retrograde and debased state of Indian society to the despotism of native government. This despotism caused the depredation of the many by the few, and led to an entire absence of security for individual rights, and the sapping of the motive to labour.[2] The resultant poverty, according to Mill, brought in its train all the moral vices and defects which afflicted the Indian character. Poverty bred crime, cruelty, licentiousness, apathy, listlessness, servility, superstition, and an entire loss of independence and self-reliance.[3] The remedy was simple and obvious:

What then upon the whole of this induction is the general result? That, in a state of extreme poverty, the motives which usually restrain from transgression; respect for the laws, dread of the laws, desire of the esteem and affection, dread of the contempt and abhorrence of mankind, sympathy with the pains and pleasures of our fellow creatures, lose their influence upon the human mind, while many of the appetites which prompt to wickedness acquire additional strength. If, therefore, the government of India would lessen the tendency to crime, which is manifested among its subjects to so extraordinary a degree, it must lessen the poverty which prevails among them to so extraordinary a degree. . . .

[1] Bentham, *Works*, vol. x, p. 490.
[2] Mill, *History*, vol. i, p. 412.
[3] Ibid., vol. v, pp. 535-7.

The mode of increasing the riches of the body of the people is a discovery no less easy than sure. Take little from them in the way of taxes; prevent them from injuring one another; and make no absurd laws, to restrain them in the harmless disposal of their property and labour. Light taxes and good laws; nothing more is wanting for national and individual prosperity all over the globe.[1]

Mill's remedy is designedly simple, a 'discovery' deduced from the science of human nature and capable of solving not merely one isolated problem but of setting off a chain of results embracing the whole. The simplicity is of course deceptive. Mill was proposing a revolution of Indian society carried through solely by the weapon of law. The purpose of the revolution was the same as the end of all government; it was to release individual energy by protecting its efforts, freeing it from the despotism of custom and communal ownership, and from the tyranny of priest and noble. Set at liberty in this way and given free scope for capital and labour, Indian society would be stirred out of its inveterate stagnation and set moving along the path of improvement. The individualist, competitive society, which Mill regarded as the acme of an advanced civilization, would be inaugurated. For India, the definition and protection of individual rights meant principally the definition and protection of rights in the land. Mill was too good a Benthamite to suggest a frontal assault on Indian customs and prejudices; but clearly the marking off of individual property rights in the soil would act as a solvent of the traditional joint-ownership and communal control, which he considered to be the marks of a primitive state of society.[2] He recognized that in India the judiciary had not merely to protect established rights but had first to seek out and define those rights. It was his great complaint against Cornwallis's permanent *zemindar* settlement of Bengal that, apart from creating a vast inequality of

[1] Ibid., vol. v, pp. 537–8.
[2] Ibid., vol. i, pp. 210 et seq. While asserting the universal applicability of his principles of law, Bentham admitted that the details would require modification to suit local conditions. It was important in his eyes that the law should as far as possible harness popular prejudices to its service so as to strengthen its influence. In his essay *Of the Influence of Time and Place in Matters of Legislation* he expressly considered some of the modifications which would be required in an ideal code for it to be established in Bengal: Bentham, *Works*, vol. i, pp. 171 et seq.

property harmful to economic and social progress, Cornwallis had merely defined the rights of the *zemindars* and left all beneath them in confusion. This great preliminary work of definition was being accomplished, as Mill knew, in the recording of landholdings which characterized any *ryotwar* type of settlement, and which was given its most developed form in the 'record of rights' forming part of the settlement procedure of the North-Western Provinces after 1822. In this way a 'Domesday' survey would be made, the Government by an authoritative act recording all rights and interests in the soil, and giving a fixed, written, and legal form to what had hitherto been vague, unwritten, customary, and shifting. The result would be a register of land titles adequate for all ordinary purposes, the peasant being put in possession without effort on his part of a clear individual property title, which he could freely sell, mortgage, or bequeath. A further advantage, in Mill's eyes, of the *ryotwar* system of settlement was that the State demand was fixed on the actual peasant landholder, whereas in Bengal the *zemindar* exacted the revenue arbitrarily from all beneath him.

Rights so defined needed to be secured by an adequate judicial system. In his *History* Mill had pointed out the appropriateness of Bentham's *Draught of a New Plan for the Organization of the Judicial Establishment in France* for Indian conditions.[1] The scheme sketched in Bentham's paper followed logically from his ideas on the function of government and law. The security of individual person and property depended upon the certainty of their protection. The law must therefore be efficient and swift, clear and easily intelligible, simple and readily available. If its action were automatic, if every infraction of right were met with peremptory punishment, crimes and litigation would soon cease, and human conduct would be permanently canalized into beneficial or harmless courses. To realize this ideal it was necessary that all law should be scientifically designed, and embodied in a written form in codes. This 'pannomium', as Bentham termed his set

[1] Mill, *History*, vol. v, p. 515 n. Bentham, 'Draught of a New Plan for the Organization of the Judicial Establishment in France' (1790), *Works*, vol. iv, pp. 305 et seq. This gives the most succinct account of Bentham's ideas on judicial organization: cf. also Halévy, *Philosophic Radicalism*, Part III, chap. ii, 'The Organization of Justice and of the State'.

of codes, would in brief compass contain the whole of law, and with the aid of the printing press, the will of the legislator expressed in simple rational language could be known directly to every man of ordinary intelligence. The monopoly of the legal profession, which Bentham regarded as the origin of the expense and delay of English justice, would be broken; every man would be his own lawyer, just as the more extreme Evangelicals hoped that, armed with the Bible, every man would be his own priest. To administer this scientific body of law, Bentham planned a judicial system in which the main feature was to be a myriad of local courts. Once the law had been framed in a rational manner and the old obscurities, inconsistencies, and technicalities afflicting it had been removed, Bentham considered that its actual administration would not be a difficult affair. He therefore proposed to give these local 'parish' and 'district' courts jurisdiction over every sort of case. In this way justice would be brought to every man's door, Bentham's ideal being that no inhabitant should be farther from a court than a day's return journey on foot. Much of the inconvenience and expense of the law would in this manner be avoided. Cheapness, speed, and simplicity, demanded that the form of procedure should exhibit the same qualities. Bentham proposed a summary, non-technical method in which the suitor would orally state his plea and personally confront the defendant. For reasons of speed, economy, and simplicity, there would be only one judge, and only one appeal from his decision to a single metropolitan court of appeal. The process of appeal would consist simply in a view of the recorded proceedings of the original court. This could be transmitted by post, without incurring the inconvenience and expense of personal attendance by parties and witnesses. Bentham and Mill believed that this scheme was the only solution to the pressing problem of providing an adequate judicial system for India. They were particularly insistent on the virtues of the local 'omnicompetent' courts, and seemed to consider that these could work, in conjunction with a regular survey, to produce the register of landed rights which they deemed indispensable.[1]

---

[1] See p. 147. Cf. Bentham to Bentinck, 20 Nov. 1829 (draft): Bentham MSS., Box X, f. 184. Also James Mill's evidence, *P.P.*, 1831, vol. v, pp. 302–3.

Bentham published no full work on the ideal administrative structure of a state; and only a small part of his *Constitutional Code* appeared before his death. Mill had not dealt with the question in his *History*. But the guiding principles are clear. Bentham's political philosophy was in origin authoritarian, a product of the century of enlightened despotism; and when it later took sides with democracy it could not root out its parentage. Its conception of the nature and exercise of political power sprang from Hobbes. Government was an artifact, a creation and expression of will. Sovereignty was single and indivisible; its instrument was law speaking the language of command. Rights had no meaning except as they were a creation of law; liberty was but the absence of restraint, and found place only where the law was silent. Bentham's problem was to make Leviathan the slave of the demos, but the nature of Leviathan remained unchanged. It was that of a great machine, and as with a machine its virtue lay in speed, efficiency, economy, regularity, and uniformity. There was admittedly danger of its power being abused; yet this danger was to be averted, not by reducing its speed and efficiency, but by ensuring effective control over the hands to whom its operation was entrusted. The normal functions of government were executive, that is, essentially authoritative in character. To attempt to control government in the interests of the community by dividing its powers, and setting them as a mutual check against one another, was to frustrate its purposes. This was the error of the Whig theory and of its leading exponent, Montesquieu.[1] Once the commands of the legislator had been identified with the popular will, through the device of representative democracy, the executive and judiciary should be nothing but creatures to carry them into effect. To permit a power of interpretation to the judiciary, or to allow it to challenge the commands of the legislator, was clearly to set up another will in defiance of the popular will. To prevent the executive abusing its power, by deliberately allowing a constant friction to occur between judiciary and executive, was to make the machine of government unnecessarily complicated and inefficient, as well as to prevent the prompt

[1] See note F, p. 324.

execution of the sovereign legislative will. Bentham's constitutional scheme merely proposed to transform into concrete practical arrangements the cloudy metaphysical notion of the General Will expounded by the French revolutionaries. Although he was impressed with the federalism of the United States, it was more natural for him to think in terms of a central controlling mind; and both he and his immediate disciples looked to the example of the French centralized bureaucracy. If the transformation of India was to be achieved by law, it appeared essential to Bentham and Mill that a sovereign legislative body should be established, and that the government of India should be transformed from an anomalous congeries of semi-independent authorities into a uniform and centralized state. This meant ending the independent power of legislation enjoyed by Madras and Bombay, and vesting all legislative authority in a central law-making organ. From this legislative organ would issue that body of codes which was to work India's regeneration.

There remained, however, the question of the organization of the judicial and executive arms. Here Bentham again had a number of firm principles. Whig theory had maintained that to prevent administrators and judges abusing their authority, it was important to make the exercise of power impersonal and collective, through the agency of boards, committees, or benches of judges. For Bentham the Whig notion suffered from the same defects as their vaunted principle of the separation of the powers. A board, or a bench of judges, was a screen. It was not merely wasteful, many hands performing what could be done by one, but it could not be made accountable. The individual was neither stimulated to exert himself by the prospect of individual distinction, nor deterred from indolence or the abuse of power by the threat of individual punishment. Hence arose Bentham's 'single-seatedness' principle, which he supported with such slogans as: 'Official aptitude maximized, expense minimized', 'Minimize confidence, maximize responsibility'. To make the most economical use of an official, to exact from him his full energy and sense of responsibility, and to guard against the abuse of power, Bentham argued that he must be employed singly and not jointly, so that he could be held personally responsible for his actions. His accountability was to be reinforced in a number of ways; firstly, by making his official actions as public as possible; and secondly, by subjecting him to official inspection.[1] The first method laid him open to the fullest public criticism, especially through the press; the second made him officially accountable, by compelling him to keep detailed records and accounts and to submit frequent reports of his acts to a higher official.

These were Bentham's principles of publicity and inspectability. The principle of inspectability involved an important distinction. It was a distinction by which Bentham in some measure sought to reintroduce the Whig separation of the powers, stripped of its traditional defects. This was his distinction between controlling and executive functions. It was merely stating in another form the necessity for a disciplined administrative hierarchy. If inspectability were to be achieved, then the work of inspection and control had to be kept entirely separate from that of actual execution. If the controlling authority also engaged in executive functions, there would in practice be no check. Similarly, if an appeal judge entirely re-heard a case, again taking evidence of facts, he would not be conducting a proper appeal, which was to ensure that the law was correctly applied to certain facts, but would be repeating the original trial. There would be no check on the conduct of the first judge. The work of inspection could in fact be usually performed through the examination of written reports, although personal inspection carried through without warning was a useful adjunct. Bentham's ideal state was therefore envisaged as a hierarchy of individual officials, related to one another in a military form of subordination, with a perfectly clear chain of command and distribution of responsibility. The area of a state was to be divided into a number of districts, sub-districts, and smaller divisions, each area having an individual head. Complementary to the geographical distribution of the work of government was the logical distribution. Each head of an area, from the chief of state to the local headman, would be aided by departmental subordinates. In this way unity of design was to be harmonized with the advantages of division of labour.

[1] See note G, p. 325.

Bentham's constitutional ideas were imperfectly publicized in his lifetime, the main bulk of the *Constitutional Code* not appearing until Bowring's collected edition of his works in 1843. But the execrations which met his disciples, Chadwick and Southwood Smith, when attempting to apply his ideas to the problems of poor law, public health, and local government, are an indication of how foreign his scheme of a great administrative bureaucracy appeared to contemporary England. The objection did not, however, occur in the case of India. The British could govern India only through a bureaucracy. By the eighteen-twenties there was a pressing need to make that bureaucracy more economical and more efficient, and Bentham's principles had an obvious attraction. The need could be met only by reducing the status of the semi-independent presidencies of Madras and Bombay to subordinate units of one strong central government, and so imposing unity and uniformity. Furthermore, for efficient control within these units it was necessary to establish a firm chain of command and subordination. Cornwallis's system had proved wasteful and inefficient. Pursuing Whig notions, he had established a host of collective bodies to supervise the land revenue and justice, in the form of the Provincial Revenue Boards and the Provincial Courts of Appeal; yet their control over the district judge and over the collector had proved ineffective. Bentham's principles of 'individual agency', of personal accountability, of a systematic bureaucratic hierarchy, had an obvious relevance.

There remained the final, but in some ways, the most vital point at which the Utilitarian theory touched the Indian question. This was the land revenue. It was the heart of the British administrative system, and the one subject which brought British rule into intimate contact with the lives of the Indian peasantry. Symptomatic of its decisive part in forming the whole administrative structure is the official title of Collector, by which the head of the district is still known throughout most of the Indian provinces. The persistent conflict of ideas between the Cornwallis and Munro traditions began and continued to be fought as a battle of land-revenue systems. All the great issues, the union or separation of judiciary and executive, the law to be administered and the rights to be protected, hinged upon it. More than half of the revenue of the State was derived from the taxation of land; and the fact that the State demand absorbed almost the whole surplus produce of the soil, after allowing for the bare subsistence costs of the cultivator, made it the determining influence in shaping the structure of Indian society. Except in the cities, every class above the immediate cultivators lived upon allowances or alienations of land revenue. Consequently, the British as sovereigns held in their hands the most powerful agency affecting the composition of Indian society. The first question with which they were confronted was the form of revenue collection, whether payment should be effected through intermediaries, such as the Bengal *zemindars*, or directly from the individual peasant. James Mill, in company with the school of Munro, favoured the latter solution. His antipathy towards landed aristocracy was not alone responsible for his attitude. It will be remembered that his scheme for the regeneration of India depended upon a close definition and protection of individual rights, and both he and Bentham had laid emphasis on the importance of a survey and recording of landholdings as the basis of an effective judicial system. This could only be secured in a system such as the *ryotwar* where the State entered into direct administrative relations with the mass of the people.

Undoubtedly one of Mill's chief influences was to show how Munro's essentially conservative system could be transformed into an instrument for the radical transformation of Indian society, through the means it afforded of defining and securing individual rights. But it was not this aspect which excited him most deeply. Where he felt he had a unique contribution to make was in showing the applicability of the new truths of political economy to the other problem of the land revenue: the principles which were to govern its assessment. It has been seen how in Mill's analysis the question of taxation was given the highest importance; it was for him the third great influence moulding human society and character, the other two being the form of government and the administration of justice. Now, the central principle of the new scientific political economy, and the great advance it claimed over the work of Adam Smith, was the discovery of the law of rent. When correctly defined rent was an element which did not enter into costs of production, and did not affect prices or wages. As such it was held by Ricardo and James Mill to be a particularly suitable source of taxation, because a tax on rent in no way retarded economic progress. In England rent property was in private hands, and the practical and political difficulties in the way of meeting the financial needs of the State out of rent were insuperable. The practical influence of political economy in England was, in consequence, largely confined to acting as a useful tool of the commercial and industrial classes in their campaign to reduce the economic intervention of the State to a minimum. In India there was the same work to be done; the Company's commercial functions and the internal and external tariff barriers had still to be destroyed. But the fact that the land revenue absorbed almost all that could be defined as rent left the State in the position of universal landlord, and gave it a decisive role in the Indian economy. Against every instinct of the ordinary English mind, and against the professed intentions of both the Munro and Cornwallis systems, James Mill preached that the British power should not withdraw from this position, but substantially maintain it. Mill claimed that the State could exact the full economic rent of the soil as land revenue, and that so long as the limits of rent were not exceeded no harm would result to India's economic progress. In fact, there would be the positive benefit that eventually the whole of the public needs could be met from the land revenue, and all tariffs on trade or vexatious taxes like the salt monopoly could be entirely abolished.

To determine the rent of land in India was, as Mill readily admitted before the Parliamentary Committee of 1831, a formidable problem in actual practice. It could only be done by a minute inquiry into the yield of different soils, the costs of production, and the history of agricultural prices. It presupposed a highly trained and efficient administration, possessing a familiar knowledge of the people and their agricultural system, such as had hardly begun to exist when Mill wrote his *History*. When, therefore, in his effort to make the solution of the Indian problem appear simple, Mill referred merely to 'light taxes and good laws' as the panacea, he was deliberately minimizing the magnitude of the task. These easy words masked a great reform programme—the establishment of a strong central government possessed of exclusive legislative authority for the whole of British India, the embodiment of all law in a set of scientific codes, an entire reorganization and expansion of the judicial system, a complete overhaul and reshaping of the administrative service, the survey and registration of all landholdings, and a scientific assessment of the land revenue based on detailed statistics of agricultural production. Even in its final and unfinished shape, this programme was to occupy the British administration for more than a half-century after the publication of Mill's *History* in 1818.

Mill was aware that it could not be directly executed from the India House in London. He acknowledged to the Parliamentary Committee that the orders of the Home Authorities had usually to be cast in the form of a statement of principles or of a retrospective survey of past events. It was true that the refashioning of the superior structure of Indian government could be carried out in England by Act of Parliament, and it will be seen how strong was Mill's influence on the main provisions of the Charter Act of 1833. But the inferior administration could be dealt with only in India, and in particular a workable land revenue administration could only be developed through local experience. These were not, however, the most serious limitations on the Utilitarian influence, for it was soon able to count on influential converts amongst the Company's officials in India. The limitation consisted rather in the transposition of utilitarianism to the Indian setting. As in England its intellectual cast meant that in a pure form it could never be more than the creed of a minority. To obtain any success it had not merely to provide practical ideas for the solution of practical issues, but it had to link itself with some larger tendency. In India the great administrative traditions had already been established, and it remained to be seen whether the authoritarian paternalism of Munro, or the impersonal libertarianism of Cornwallis's system, would prove the best suited to the changing purpose of British rule. Superficially, there could be no doubt that the movement towards modernization, as embodied in the pressure of liberalism, must eventually favour the system of the rule of law and pursue the tradition of Cornwallis. That it did not do so entirely was due to the success of utilitarianism in showing how the originally conservative system of Munro might be transformed into a most powerful instrument for change.

The authoritarian character of Mill's proposals has already been noticed. To carry them into effect involved a general issue of principle which, not only in India but also in England, perplexed and divided the Utilitarian ranks, and laid bare the difference between their authoritarian and their *laissez-faire* assumptions. This was no less than the extent to which the executive arm of the State should be strengthened and expanded. The controversy which gathered round the 'Bashaws of Somerset House' and Chadwick's assistant commissioners had its counterpart in India. The Bengal school, which had the support of the whole European mercantile community, was instinctively hostile to strengthening the collector's authority, or in any way weakening the separation of the judicial and executive powers which Cornwallis had believed so vital. Utilitarians like Alexander Ross believed that a Benthamite judicial system could, on its own, form a revolutionary agency for breaking up the indigenous society, with its communal and customary basis; and that by their definition and protection of individual property rights, the courts of law could inaugurate the individualist competitive society of the modern world. The Bengal School were powerful in the counsels of the Governor-General in the eighteen-twenties and thirties, but their ability to influence the British territories beyond the confines of Bengal, Bihar, and Orissa, was diminishing. This was because of the very different administrative problems created in the North-Western Provinces and Bombay Deccan by the admitted undesirability and impracticability of a permanent settlement on the lines of the great *zemindar* system of Bengal. The protracted nature of the settlement operations in these territories, and the fact that the Government saw no alternative but to settle with peasant proprietors, led to the creation of an extensive administrative organization combining revenue, police, and magisterial powers. The inspiration of this revenue and administrative system came from Munro; but its achievements attracted men of reforming energies, versed in the new political economy and the simple authoritarian logic of the Utilitarian mind. This disciplined hierarchy of individual officials—a quasi-military administrative army, freed of the pedantic red-tape mentality of the old Bengal bureaucrat—had all those qualities of energy, speed, efficiency, and decisiveness, dear to the reformer's heart.

The Utilitarian influence in India thus divided, one stream looking to the energizing of the Cornwallis system and to the rule of law applied aggressively by an efficient judiciary: the other seeking its fortune in the North-Western Provinces and later in the Punjab among the heirs of Munro, the Tory Evangelicals; or applying its scientific bent to the engine of social and economic transformation which Wingate and Goldsmid were constructing in the form of the Bombay survey and settlement. This division was not to be permanent. Long after the Utilitarians had ceased to be a distinctive party, and only the rigorous logic of their mentality was remembered, Indian administration was finally made uniform under a system which harmonized a strong executive with the rule of law. In the sixties and seventies of the nineteenth century there eventually emerged a structure which substantially realized James Mill's ideals of Indian government.

II

POLITICAL ECONOMY AND
THE LAND REVENUE

1. *The Doctrine of Rent and the Land Tax*

THE core of the Utilitarian philosophy, its professed scientific foundation, was the new political economy developed by Ricardo. At the heart of Indian administration lay the land revenue system. The one was to react upon the other with results of the deepest importance for Indian society. In this field James Mill was the master. Himself an expert on political economy, he was from 1819 until 1830 immediately responsible for drafting the Revenue despatches to India. The lustre of Bentham's name has to a large extent distracted attention from Mill's work and led to the belief that the Utilitarians were principally law reformers. Such a view fails to acknowledge the comprehensiveness of their philosophy of government; and from a practical standpoint the Utilitarian hopes of inaugurating a competitive society, based on individual rights in the soil, depended as much upon the revenue assessment, and the registration of landholdings which accompanied it, as upon the superstructure of judicial codes and establishments.

By inheriting a position in which the main revenue of the State consisted of a large portion of the produce of the soil, the British found themselves confronted with problems touching the fundamental principles of political society. How far were they to go on relying on the land as the chief fiscal source; and, more important, on what principles were they to regulate the assessment and collection of the land revenue? The systems of Cornwallis and Munro offered contrasting solutions, but they proceeded on certain common assumptions. There was no question of continuing existing Indian practice unaltered. Greatly decayed by years of anarchy, its uncertainty and irregularity afforded scope for the grossest corruption and oppression, with a resulting decline in cultivation and serious damage to the revenue resources of the State. It was generally agreed that certainty and regularity could be restored only by some formal definition of the State demand which drew a clear line of distinction between public and private rights. Hitherto rights over land had had no more than a precarious existence, taking their origin in the unwritten customary law of the agricultural communities, but suffering constant modification from the efforts of arbitrary rulers to determine the State share of the produce and the agency of collection at their own discretion. Even at its best, tradition provided no model to follow, for it gave rights no secure definition and certainly supplied no safeguard against the malpractices of the Company's revenue officials. The British mind found incomprehensible a society based on unwritten custom and on government by personal discretion; and it knew of only one sure method of marking off public from private rights—the introduction of a system of legality, under which rights were defined by a body of formal law equally binding upon the State as upon its subjects. Such a system required the revenue demand to be fixed, and the remaining produce of the soil recognized as private property in the full legal sense. Absolute precision and security for private property were obtainable if the fiscal demand of the State were to be guaranteed against all future enhancement, and if the tax were to be levied as a definite monetary sum on the land and not as a fixed share of the produce. The weight of the tax also affected property rights. Apart from its influence on the incentive to improvement and on the prospective revenue resources of the State, a tax which absorbed so much of the produce as to leave no more than the bare expenses of cultivation would deprive land of all saleable value. Private property would consequently have no effective existence, and the State would remain as the universal landlord of the soil. Only by limiting the land tax so as to leave a private rent could saleable property rights be established. Such was the chain of reasoning which occurred instinctively to the generation of Englishmen for whom Arthur Young had spoken, when he declared that the magic of property turned sand into gold.

These ideas lay behind Cornwallis's Permanent Settlement of Bengal in 1793. Unable to reduce the existing demand, Cornwallis declared it unalterable and left the great *zemindars*, whom he recognized as proprietors, to obtain a private rent from opening up the vast tracts of cultivable waste within their domains. By this action he also recognized the necessity and desirability of meeting the future financial needs of the State from other sources, and principally from taxes on internal commerce.

Munro was moved by much the same considerations in the Madras Presidency. He did not differ from Cornwallis over the institution of private-property rights in land, but only over the hands in which they were to be lodged. He maintained that his assessment was equally permanent, but he was opposed to a formal declaration of its unalterability in order to leave the State a taxable reserve for a time of great emergency.[1] Similarly, he did not see why the State should renounce its revenue rights over waste land, as Cornwallis had done when he recognized the extensive waste tracts of Bengal to form part of the *zemindars'* estates. Yet his decision, to retain the unassessed waste and to vest the right of property in the *ryot* or peasant, meant that there could not be the same withdrawal of the State from its position as landlord or the same absence of executive interference with private rights. In Bengal, the collector (at least in theory) had simply to take receipt, from a relatively small number of persons, of a sum fixed permanently at the level at which it happened to stand in 1793; and the State freed itself from all concern with the work of detailed assessment and collection. But in settling with the *ryot* Munro committed the administration to the vast undertaking of assessing and collecting the demand for each cultivated field. Furthermore, since no margin of waste land was left to the *ryot* as proprietor, the State had to determine a principle of assessment which would assure to him a private rent and a saleable value for his property. All this meant a much more inquisitorial investigation into the private concerns of the people, and placed the decision as to what constituted public

---

[1] Cf. Minute on the State of the Country and the Condition of the People, 31 Dec. 1824: Gleig, *Munro*, vol. iii, pp. 319 et seq.

and private rights in the hands of an army of executive officials.

Munro took for his principle of assessment the traditional criterion of good Indian rulers that the State share of the produce should not exceed one-third. He believed it could be shown empirically that, when the demand was kept within this limit, private saleable property rights in land emerged. It was, in fact, because this limit had so rarely been observed in the past that the general absence of such rights in India was to be explained. In his settlement of the Ceded Districts of Madras, from 1800 to 1807, he sought to frame for each field a cash sum representing an estimated one-third of the gross produce; but in practice he modified the assessment by reckoning the sum an area could fairly pay, in the light of its past revenue history and present condition, and then distributing this sum in detail by altering the original figure for each field proportionately.[1] Despite his assertion that this field assessment was equally as permanent as that of Cornwallis, the practice of the *ryotwar* system denied the claim. The Madras *ryot* lived too near the margin of subsistence to commit himself in perpetuity to the revenue demand on his holding. Accordingly, he was given the right to make annual engagements and to vary the number of fields he cultivated from year to year. But even the sum fixed on each field could not be maintained unaltered. Not merely did allowance have to be made for crop failures, but the demand proved generally too high to be met except in years of bumper harvest. The *ryotwar* system thus exhibited in its actual working all the features of an annual assessment and of a fluctuating, uncertain demand. Nevertheless, this was an outcome not anticipated by Munro, who claimed to be pursuing the same ideals as Cornwallis—the institution of private property rights, and the commutation of the State share of the produce to an unalterable money tax.

A third, intermediary type of settlement had been formed

[1] Cf. B. H. Baden-Powell, *Land Systems of British India*, vol. iii, pp. 37 et seq. For the *ryotwar* system cf. *Fifth Report*, 1812; A. J. Arbuthnot, *Sir Thomas Munro: Selections from his Minutes* . . . (especially for Munro's Report as Principal Collector of the Ceded Districts, 15 Aug. 1807, vol. ii, p. 93); A. D. Campbell's paper on the Madras system and Minute of Madras Board of Revenue, 5 Jan. 1818: *P.P.*, 1831-2, vol. xi, Appendix, pp. 9-48, 411-36.

in northern India, in the Ceded and Conquered Provinces, which Wellesley had acquired between 1801 and 1803. There the early settlements had been made neither with great hereditary revenue farmers like the Bengal *zemindars* nor with the humble cultivators as in Madras, but generally with the co-sharing village brotherhoods. These groups usually cultivated holdings of their own, and also shared among themselves the payments which inferior cultivators made to them as overlords for the right of occupying the remaining village lands. In quite a large number of instances, however, the settlements had been made with single individuals—either temporary revenue-farmers, or more established local magnates termed *taluqdars*—who contracted for the revenue payment for a whole group of villages. The early settlements were temporary, lasting generally from three to five years. The government demand was based on an estimate of what the *taluqdars* or the village brotherhoods derived ultimately from the immediate cultivators, together with the profits on their personal holdings on a similar basis. The only sources of information were the notoriously imperfect traditional revenue records, kept by the local revenue officials (the *qanungo* and *patwari*), and their estimates of the revenue assets of each village. The British officials sought vainly to get behind these to discover the true extent of the area under cultivation and the true rate of payment made by the immediate cultivators. The question of proprietary right fell into great confusion, but the presumption inherited from Bengal was that the person engaging for the revenue acquired the proprietary right. That right, made freely alienable by the British and subject to public auction in default of revenue payment, was held to consist of the traditional commission of 10 per cent. on the revenue collected. The situation was comparable to that of Bengal, except that in place of the great *zemindars* a different class of intermediaries was given the right to engage for the revenue and enjoy the proprietary right. In the absence of any class equivalent to the Bengal *zemindars*, and with the prior claims of the village brotherhoods too strong to be ignored, the Supreme Government in Calcutta accepted the different proprietary position; but it sought in accordance with Bengal tradition to render proprietary rights secure by the conclusion of a permanent settlement. In 1807 (Regulation X) it proclaimed such a settlement, subject to the approval of the Home Authorities. Its action was disallowed. Munro had successfully sowed the seeds of doubt about the virtue of the whole Cornwallis tradition. The Home Authorities resolved that no permanent settlement could be considered, until the vexed question of proprietary right had been properly investigated, the security of the immediate cultivator provided for, and the revenue resources of the country more fully developed by the cultivation of a larger proportion of waste land. On the other hand, the ideal of an ultimate permanent settlement was not contradicted or renounced.

It will be noted that the institution of private saleable property rights, through the permanent limitation of the State demand and the relinquishment of a private rent to the proprietor, was a motive common to all types of revenue settlement. Their differences merely concerned the class of person to be given the proprietary right, and the timing and method of framing of a permanent money tax. Munro's system captured the support of the rising lights of Indian administration, especially Metcalfe, Malcolm, and Elphinstone; and the celebrated *Fifth Report* of 1812 of the Commons Select Committee secured Munro's prestige with the authorities in London. But Cornwallis's errors in application could not for long defeat the power of his principles. To the support of the latter there now rallied the rising forces of the English mercantile community, increasingly convinced that the expansion of the Indian market rested on the rapid introduction of the capitalist mode of production into Indian agriculture. For them, whatever his intentions, Munro's *ryotwar* system exhibited all the faults of traditional oriental practice—property rights left at the mercy of a host of corrupt petty officials, levying annually an uncertain fluctuating demand, and the benefits of any limitation of the demand squandered among a myriad of improvident cultivators. Instead of encouraging the emergence of a régime of substantial farmers using wage labour, Munro's system perpetuated the *petite culture* of a backward peasant agriculture. On the other hand, whatever his faults of detail,

Cornwallis had proceeded on the right lines, seeking to establish substantial units of property, cutting the State completely free from the oriental position of universal landlord, and limiting State interference in the land to the receipt of an unalterable tax.

Set out in these terms it would naturally be supposed that the Utilitarians would support the forces of 'progress'. Instead James Mill fiercely assailed the Cornwallis settlement.[1] Much of his wrath was no doubt kindled by what he considered to be an attempt to create in Bengal a replica of the hated English aristocracy, and much could be explained by his desire to see property in the hands of the greatest number.[2] But his hostility to the Cornwallis system went much farther, and struck at the root of those assumptions on which not only the Cornwallis but every other revenue settlement was based. It was not a question as to the class which should be recognized as proprietors, nor the timing and method of framing a permanent tax. What Mill denied was the assumption that the sole method of establishing private rights in land was by permanently limiting the State's fiscal rights and so creating private rent property. He came forward with the daring proposal that the State should remain as the landlord and that each peasant should hold directly from the State as its tenant. To advocate an agricultural system based on relatively small peasant holdings was in itself sufficiently startling for a man of Mill's political leanings; but to advocate State ownership or nationalization of the soil was to strike at the whole Liberal tradition for which the institution of private property was the tap-root of progress and individual liberty.

James Mill believed that the new Utilitarian science of political economy contained a novel truth, of the utmost significance for India, stemming from the law of rent. The East India Company had been quick to appreciate the importance of the new science, and its college at Haileybury had been the first institution to establish a chair in the subject. It was as a result of preparing a course of lectures for the young civilians that Malthus, the first holder of the chair from 1805 to his death in 1834, 'discovered' the law of rent

---

[1] James Mill, *History of British India*, vol. v, chaps. v, vi.
[2] See p. 147.

in 1815.[1] Refined by the later criticism of Ricardo and Say, the law claimed to show that rent was a special portion of wealth, distinct from profits or wages, and determined in an exact scientific manner. It originated from the propensity of population to outgrow food resources and the consequent necessity of resorting to increasingly poorer soils as society progressed in population and wealth. Rent constituted the differential advantage enjoyed by all soils of a higher quality than the last taken into cultivation. On the last quality of land, at the margin of cultivation, the capital employed merely replaced itself and yielded the ordinary prevailing rate of profit. But all other soils yielded a surplus or rent beyond this. The element of rent could, therefore, be exactly determined by subtracting from the total or gross produce the cost of wages and the ordinary rate of profit on the capital employed. An alternative term for rent was the net produce. In the competitive economies of advanced countries, where land was under private ownership, the landlord had been able to get his land cultivated by a capitalist tenant-farmer working for the ordinary rate of profit and to separate off the element of rent as his own property. Malthus regarded this surplus as a special bounty of Providence, making possible the existence of a leisured class, civil freedom, and all the arts of civilized life. But Ricardo, the friend of James Mill and the high priest of the Utilitarian economic doctrine, interpreted it in a much more sinister manner. He demonstrated rent to be a monopoly value which arose because land as an instrument of production was limited in quantity and variable in quality, and because, unlike air, it could be appropriated as private property. In his account the landlord performed no economic service and lived as a parasite on the community. In answer to Malthus's contention that 'the interest of the landlord is strictly and necessarily connected with that of the State', Ricardo replied that 'the interest of the landlord is always opposed to every other class in the community'.[2]

[1] T. R. Malthus, *The Nature and Progress of Rent*, London, 1815. The Preface states that 'the Tract contains the substance of some Notes on Rent which . . . I have collected in the course of my professional duties at the East India College'. Cf. *D.N.B.*, vol. xii, p. 887.

[2] T. R. Malthus, *Principles of Political Economy*, 1st edn., 1820, p. 217. Ricardo,

In that striking vein of pessimism which marked his doctrine Ricardo held out the gloomiest prospect for an advanced society. The conditions of its early state would no longer prevail. Then its population was small, fertile land abundant, and rent practically non-existent. Consequently the rate of profit was high, capital accumulation was rapid, and the constant scarcity of labour prevented wages from falling to their natural subsistence level. But with the growth of population and wealth, a stage was reached when less fertile land had to be taken into cultivation. The same quantity of labour and capital now returned a smaller amount of produce. The rate of profit was therefore reduced, and the surplus profits enjoyed by capital on the superior soils were appropriated by the landlord as rent. At the same time it was increasingly difficult for food production to keep pace with the natural rate of population growth, and so wages tended to fall to their natural subsistence level. Ricardo prophesied that ultimately a 'stationary state' would be reached. The rate of profit would fall so low that capital accumulation would cease; and, with the elimination of profits, the entire produce of the country would go as rent to the landlord except for the barest subsistence wage of labour.[1]

This bitter truth, that the course of economic progress benefited only the landlord at the expense of every other class in the community, governed the Utilitarian doctrine of taxation. The unearned increment constituting rent seemed, on grounds of justice alone, a peculiarly suitable subject for taxation; but a tax on rent was recommended also by compelling economic arguments. Every other tax was open to the objection that it tended to check production, either directly or indirectly. On the other hand, rent could be wholly absorbed by taxation without in the smallest degree interfering with profits, wages, or the prices of necessities. For rent neither affected the rate of profit nor the price of corn, since these were determined by the costs of production on the least fertile land in cultivation which yielded no rent.

Essay on the Influence of a Low Price of Corn on the Profits of Stock, London, 1815, p. 20. Cf. J. H. Hollander in Ricardo, *Notes on Malthus' 'Principles of Political Economy'*, ed. J. H. Hollander & T. E. Gregory, 1928, pp. xxiii–iv, xlviii.
[1] Ricardo, *Principles of Political Economy*, 1821 edn., chaps. v, vi.

The Radical bearings of such a doctrine of taxation were rendered harmless when the Utilitarians came to apply it to English conditions. Ricardo drew back from advocating a special class taxation on landlords; and James Mill, who was much more eager for the State to intervene and rectify the unjust distribution of wealth resulting from the constant tendency of the rent element to increase, recognized the force of Ricardo's objection. At best he cautiously suggested an idea, later taken up by his son, that the future unearned increment of rent should be liable to a special levy.[1]

India was, however, an altogether different question, for there private rent property had never been permitted to emerge. Even before he entered the service of the East India Company, James Mill had seen the importance of the rent theory for India and had touched upon its implications in his *History*.[2] From 1819, as assistant examiner responsible for drafting the Revenue despatches, he was able to propagate his ideas in an authoritative manner. Doubtless because of his official position he did not publish his views, and our knowledge of them is derived from the evidence he gave to the Select Committees on Indian affairs from 1830 to 1832. It has been seen that Mill took up the startling position that the British power in India should not renounce but maintain the traditional right of an oriental sovereign to the ownership of the soil. Like Malthus, Mill equated the right to levy the land revenue with a landlord right to appropriate the entire rent of the soil in its exact scientific sense.[3] In his *Elements of Political Economy*, published in 1820, he had developed the idea of the peculiar suitability of rent as a subject of taxation, and his enthusiasm led him almost to overlook Ricardo's teaching that rent, so far from being a creation of wealth, added nothing to the resources of a country and did not enable it to maintain fleets and armies.[4] To the Commons Select Committee of 1831, clearly surprised

[1] James Mill, *Elements of Political Economy*, 1821, pp. 200–1. Halévy, *Philosophic Radicalism*, pp. 360–2. J. S. Mill, *Principles of Political Economy*, Book V, chap. ii, s. 4. L. Stephen, *The English Utilitarians*, vol. iii, pp. 232–3.

[2] Mill, *History*, vol. i, pp. 324–7.

[3] Malthus, *Principles of Political Economy*, p. 155.

[4] Ricardo, *Principles*, pp. 485–6. Also cf. pp. 164–5.

that such a view should come from the executive head of the India House, Mill laboured his argument:

Nine-tenths probably of the revenue of the Government of India is derived from the rent of land, never appropriated to individuals, and always considered to be the property of government; and to me that appears to be one of the most fortunate circumstances that can occur in any country because in consequence of this the wants of the state are supplied really and truly without taxation. As far as this source goes the people of the country remain untaxed. The wants of government are supplied without any drain either upon the produce of any man's labour, or the produce of any man's capital.[1]

His practical conclusions were that no permanent settlement should be granted. By denying itself the future increment of rent (even if the assessment represented the full economic rent at the time), the State would ultimately have to resort to taxes which fell upon capital or profits and so checked production. In any event, since 'the sources of production are the source of taxation', taxes on commerce must fall ultimately on the land as being almost the sole source of wealth in India; only, unlike a tax on rent, they would fall in an injurious form.[2] If, however, it was the true principle for the State to exact the full economic rent, it was equally important that the assessment should not exceed it. Otherwise the assessment would trench upon profits, hinder capital accumulation, and retard the progress of the country. This meant that any form of revenue collection employing middlemen, such as the Bengal *zemindars*, or the *taluqdars* and village brotherhoods of the Ceded and Conquered Provinces, could only be paid for out of the rent fund, a fund which in Mill's view was the rightful property of the State. Yet unless the State defined the assessment for each peasant cultivator there was no security that a rapacious middleman would not exact more than the true rent and do untold harm to the country. A detailed *ryotwar* settlement was therefore essential whatever the form of collecting agency ultimately adopted. But what point was served in leaving the function of collection to middlemen? It entailed giving up a much

---

[1] Evidence of James Mill, 2 Aug. 1831: *P.P.*, 1831, vol. v, p. 292, Qu. 3134. Cf. James Mill, *Elements of Political Economy*, p. 199.

[2] *P.P.*, 1831, vol. v, p. 359, Qu. 3839.

greater share of the public rent fund, and all experience showed that 'the persons who own rent, and live upon rent, consume it all'.[1] It was idle to expect that rent owners would accumulate capital and invest it in agricultural improvements; only the immediate cultivator would do this.

With inexorable logic Mill declared himself in favour of an outright *ryotwar* system in which the State carried out the entire work of assessment and collection from each peasant cultivator.[2] But he differed from Munro's model over the two principles which Munro shared in common with Cornwallis. Mill objected to any permanent limitation of the assessment, and to any relinquishment of rent designed to give the peasant a private rent property. For the peasant would act no differently from a middleman; given the whole or a portion of the future increment of rent he would lease out his land and live parasitically as a rent-receiver.[3] Mill's plan for India was for the State to be the sole landlord, with the immediate cultivators as its tenants. The State would grant leases for twenty or thirty years to provide sufficient incentive and security for the investment of capital; but it was its right and duty to revise its assessment on the renewal of the leases so as to appropriate the unearned rental increment. The peasant would have as substantial and secure a title as that of the tenant farmer in England, the only difference being that his landlord would be the State.

The law of rent provided, therefore, both a coherent policy for the demarcation of public and private rights in the land, and a clear criterion of assessment. Munro's system offended in this last respect. He had professed to adopt the traditional Indian principle of taking a fixed proportion of the gross produce as the basis of the government demand. Here Mill broke decisively with native tradition. He was prepared to accept the oriental role of the State as landlord of the soil, because this happened to coincide with his views on taxation. But he had nothing of the reverence of the paternalists for the time-hallowed practice of Indian

---

[1] *P.P.*, 1831, vol. v, p. 372, Qu. 3974. For the argument of this paragraph, cf. James Mill's paper, 'Observations on the Land Revenue of India', 15 Aug. 1832: *P.P.*, 1831-2, vol. xi, Appendix No. 7.

[2] *P.P.*, 1831, vol. v, p. 292, Qu. 3135.   [3] Ibid., p. 372, Qu. 3974-6.

tradition. To accept the criterion of assessment of 'the rude governments which preceded ours' was to adopt the ignorant error that lay behind the poverty and backwardness of the East. Political economy and not Indian tradition was to be the tutor of policy, for it demonstrated that the principle of taking a fixed share of the gross produce, if strictly enforced, must prevent all but the superior soils from being cultivated. This was because the poorer soils yielded little or no rent, and any tax taking indiscriminately a fixed proportion of the crop, without regard to the fertility of the soil, could only be met out of profits. Such a tax would discourage the employment of capital on the poorer land and raise the cost of production. In chain reaction, it would lead to a general rise in price of agricultural products, in the money (but not real) wages of labour, and in the level of rents. The final result would be to lower the general rate of profit and so of capital accumulation.[1] The proper principle was that the assessment should fall only upon the element of rent, or, in other words, upon the surplus or *net produce* which remained after defraying from the gross produce the wages of labour and the normal profits of capital.

It will be simpler to trace the influence of the law of rent on the theory and method of assessment, before embarking on the wider questions of property right which formed the other part of Mill's programme. In his evidence before the Parliamentary Committee of 1831 he declared that for many years instructions had been sent from London in keeping with his view that the assessment should be strictly confined within the limits of the net produce or rent. He admitted the serious practical difficulties in ascertaining rent —experiments in India were clearly revealing these by 1831 —and recognized that the only safeguard was to make the assessment so moderate that it ran no danger of over-stepping the prescribed limits. In effect this meant that Mill was prepared to allow a small portion of rent to remain with the cultivator. He had also to admit that his principle had made little headway as yet with the majority of settlement officers,

[1] Evidence of James Mill, 2 Aug. 1831: ibid., p. 296, Qu. 3162. Ricardo, *Principles*, pp. 174–5.

who had 'no very clear ideas about rent, nor very distinct notion of what it consists'. But he could truthfully state that 'the most explicit instructions have been given to consider that all that the government is entitled to take, or can take with safety to its own interests, is the surplus of the produce of the soil, after a full remuneration to the cultivator for his labour and stock'.[1] As a practical instance where this principle had been employed he pointed to the survey and settlement of the Bombay Deccan under R. K. Pringle.[2]

The doctrine of rent had, however, made an earlier and more influential convert. In 1819, the year in which James Mill entered the India House, Holt Mackenzie penned his 'masterly and exhaustive' Memorandum on the land revenue problems of the Ceded and Conquered Provinces in northern India. As Secretary to the Supreme Government in the Territorial Department at Calcutta, he was the leading revenue expert from 1817 until his retirement in 1831. While Pringle's work in the Bombay Deccan was to prove isolated and short-lived, Mackenzie's Memorandum became the seed-plot of the revenue systems adopted throughout northern and central India. Despite his fame as an administrator little evidence has survived of his personal life and character. He had the reputation of being 'of retired and studious habits, and gifted with a keen and comprehensive intellect'.[3] Malcolm suspected him as a typical Calcutta bureaucrat lacking in practical experience and local knowledge. Writing to Lord William Bentinck, the Governor-General, in 1828, Malcolm deplored that

on the early development of superior abilities, he was employed to reform, to plan, to scheme. His talent in writing, and the ingenuity of his mind, combined with his general knowledge, obtained great currency to his opinions, but he displays a spirit of speculation which gives me alarm. There is in his papers too great a reliance on the principles of Political Economy, and general conclusions from assumed fact, and so little attention to the actual state of our possessions in India.[4]

---

[1] P.P., 1831, vol. v, p. 364, Qu. 3884. Also cf. p. 296, Qu. 3162; pp. 334–5, Qu. 3555–6.   [2] Ibid., p. 364, Qu. 3882.

[3] J. Thornton, 'The Settlement of the North-Western Provinces', reprinted from Calcutta Review, No. 24 (Dec. 1849): P.P., 1852–3, vol. lxxv, p. 463.

[4] Malcolm, 'Secret and Confidential Memorandum for Lord William Bentinck', 24 Jan. 1828: Bentinck MSS. For Holt Mackenzie see Biographical Notes, p. 331.

Certainly Mackenzie had the type of mind which was sensitive to the reforming current of utilitarianism. It was on his initiative that the General Committee of Public Instruction was set up in 1823, with the object of 'diffusing useful knowledge', and in his minutes the term utility is to be found used in its technical Benthamite sense.[1] Having studied to good purpose under Malthus at Haileybury, he was quick to see the bearings of the Utilitarian teachings on political economy. He cited Bentham as an authority when arguing for the abolition of the legal rate of interest, and, above all, within four years of its promulgation by Malthus, he fully grasped the law of rent and saw its significance for India.

In his Memorandum of July 1819 he equated the land revenue rights of the State with the right to enjoy the full economic rent, and at the same time issued a warning against trespassing beyond this limit and trenching 'on the necessary profits of stock and wages of labour'.[2] The Government Resolution of 1 August 1822, which set the seal of official approval on Mackenzie's views and which was almost certainly drafted by him, spoke in similar terms. As with James Mill the effect of the rent theory was to set up a highly authoritarian conception of the rights of the State. In particular, it refuted the suggestion that the State demand was limited by custom and tradition, or that these could provide a correct standard of assessment. The State was free to determine its demand, guided solely by its own discretion; and, in any case, a general principle like that of the Emperor Akbar, stipulating the State share of the produce to be one-third, stood convicted of harmfulness by the laws of political economy.[3] Munro's adherence to traditional theoretical principles was swept aside, and the Resolution of Government spoke in terms of ascertaining the rent or net produce in a manner similar to that suggested later by James Mill: 'The object being to ascertain and record . . . the fiscal

---

[1] *Personal Records*, vol. xvii, f. 729. Bentinck cautioned him against the wisdom of using Bentham as an authority to advocate ending the legal limitation on the rate of interest. Mackenzie to Bentinck, 24 Oct. 1829: Bentinck MSS.

[2] Mackenzie, Memorandum, 1 July 1819, para. 369 n.: *Selections from the Revenue Records of the North-West Provinces 1818–1822*, Allahabad, 1866.

[3] Resolution of Supreme Government, 1 Aug. 1822, para. 127: *P.P.*, 1831-2, vol. xi, Appendix, pp. 210 et seq.

capabilities of the different *mehals* [estates], their extent and produce, the value of that produce and the cost of production. . . .'[1] But if the law of rent was envisaged as supplying the correct theoretic criterion of assessment, Mackenzie was extremely cautious about its application. His immediate practical concern was to establish safeguards against the two evils which had hitherto afflicted the revenue administration of the Ceded and Conquered Provinces: over-assessment and unintentional interference with existing landed rights.

Convinced in his own mind that the total assessment on the Provinces had reached its safe limit, he was fearful of the effects of the Home Authorities' demand for more detailed statistics to prove the adequacy of the existing assessment; for they were still being pressed by the Indian Government to declare a permanent settlement. Any detailed investigation of the revenue resources of the country proceeding on the method of matching theoretical rights against actual revenue collections was bound in his view to give an exaggerated figure. It was, in fact, impossible to discover any general principle governing the State demand in local practice, and to proceed universally by applying a uniform customary principle, like that of a fixed proportion of the gross produce, would be not merely objectionable on the argument from political economy, but would wantonly set aside the multiplicity of local practice which constituted the existing system of private rights. This infinite variety, between village and village and caste and caste, made impossible even the application of the net produce criterion, for 'even the bare calculation of profit and loss will vary greatly from other causes than the mere nature of the soil'.[2] So far from imposing a uniform equality the first object was to maintain the existing distribution of private rights and interests, whatever subsequent arrangements might be made to dispose of the new form of property which would emerge if the demand were limited for a long period of years. There was no alternative but to set out on a laborious and detailed inquiry into the circumstances governing the existing assessment on each field. Only when all information on crop, soil, stock, agricultural

---

[1] Resolution of Government, Aug. 1822, para. 20: *Revenue Selections 1818–1822*, pp. 5–6.   [2] Ibid., para. 100.

caste, and past history, had been carefully gathered, would there be grounds for arriving at an equitable assessment in each separate case. In these detailed inquiries the principal aim would be to discover the aggregate of payments made by the immediate cultivators to the revenue engagers. The cultivated area would need to be accurately measured, and, where payment was made in kind by means of a division of the crop, the gross produce would have to be ascertained and an estimate made of the value of the share of produce allotted to the State in local village practice. Where payment was made in money the accuracy of the village accountant's records would need to be tested. These estimates of revenue resources required to be treated with the greatest caution, and evidence of past collections and other general considerations were to be given most weight. In all this the net produce criterion was envisaged as able to supply no more than an independent check on the demand.

At least these seem to have been Mackenzie's general intentions in framing the new settlement system, which was formally adopted under Regulation VII, 1822. No clear directions appear to have been given to the settlement officers. The Board of Revenue of the Western Provinces (as the Ceded and Conquered Provinces were now termed) merely forwarded to them copies of the Regulation, and of the long discursive Resolution of Government of 1 August 1822, together with a specimen tabular form for recording the settlement data.[1] In such circumstances it was not to be wondered at that when in 1826 Mackenzie came to review the first settlements made under Regulation VII, 1822, all of them had ignored the net produce criterion, their groundwork being no more than various estimates of the actual payments made by the immediate cultivators. Nevertheless, Regulation VII, 1822 has always been held to have aimed at an assessment embodying the net produce criterion.[2]

---

[1] Board of Revenue, Western Provinces, Proceedings, 24 Oct. 1822.

[2] Baden-Powell, *Land Systems of British India*, vol. ii, p. 25. Also cf. C. Grant, Offg. Accountant N.W.P., 25 March 1842; Indian Revenue Consultations, 20 May 1842, No. 11, Appendix C: '... Instead of attempting to ascertain the productive powers of each field from a minute inquiry into the costs of seed, cultivating etc., when compared with the produce, as was erroneously thought practicable to the framers of Regulation VII of 1822 ....'

The aim appears to have been more strongly pursued after Mackenzie's Memorandum of 1826. In suggesting amendments to the statistical record compiled by settlement officers he proposed that inquiries should be carried out into the yields and the costs of production on the lands of a specimen cultivator.[1] But the voluminous statistics which the settlement officers were required to gather do not appear to have been useful to them in arriving at a workable assessment, and each officer continued to seek out, in his own way, what was customarily payable by the immediate cultivators. William Fraser, the local commissioner of the Delhi Territory, apparently made the strongest efforts to introduce an assessment founded on the theory of rent, but, on reviewing 1,012 completed settlements, he had to admit complete failure:

They seem to be made on different grounds, some by rates on produce, some on estimates of gross produce, taking a half or third as the right of Government; others on a classification of soils and rates applied, some on the year's produce, a great number on bargain, i.e. how much the people will give and not go away; not one that I have seen on a thorough based estimate of cost, produce, and profit as the groundwork, and advertence to local free-will rent as the rule.[2]

Mackenzie himself, in his written evidence before the Select Committee of 1832, certainly declared that the net produce criterion had been an important principle; the object of the exhaustive inquiries being to ascertain 'the extent and productiveness of the land, including in the term all circumstances, natural or artificial, that affect its power of yielding rent, or a surplus beyond what is required for the wages of labour and the replacement and use of stock'. 'The foundation of the proposed assessment had been an estimate of the proceeds and expenses of husbandry',[3] but as he readily admitted, in practice it had proved impossible to achieve this object because the variety of local customs and prejudices prevented agricultural prices and existing rent payments

[1] Mackenzie, Memorandum, 19 Oct. 1826, paras. 658, 664: *P.P.*, 1831-2, vol. xi, Appendix, pp. 243 et seq.
[2] Cited by Bentinck, Minute, 20 Jan. 1832, para. 54: *Selections from the Revenue Records of the North-West Provinces, Vol. ii, 1822-33*, Allahabad, 1872, p. 369.
[3] Written evidence of Holt Mackenzie: *P.P.*, 1831-2, vol. xi, pp. 298, 301.

from following the economic laws of supply and demand. He continued, however, to advocate the use of the net produce criterion as a test to ensure that the assessment did not wholly absorb the rent; and thought it necessary 'to form for each village, and in some cases for each class of cultivators, an estimate of the gross and net produce of farms, grounded on a statement of the average of gross produce which may be expected from each field one year with another'.[1]

The restraint and caution which marked the employment of the net produce criterion in the settlement of the Western Provinces was entirely absent from the settlement of the Bombay Deccan. On the submission of the Bombay Government's plans in 1825, the Home Authorities had condemned the proposal of taking one-third of the gross produce as the basis of assessment.[2] With the Revenue despatches being filled increasingly with short disquisitions on the principles of political economy, it was understandable that the Bombay Government should appoint an able young officer versed in the new science to be the Superintendent of the Revenue Survey and Assessment of the Deccan. Robert Keith Pringle, whom Mill pointed out to the Select Committee of 1831 as a practical exponent of the rent doctrine, had been one of Malthus's best pupils at Haileybury and had distinguished himself by winning the medal in political economy. In September 1828 he drew up an elaborate report describing the principles which he was employing in his operations. Having demonstrated the truth that an assessment proportioned to the gross produce checked production by impeding the cultivation of poorer soils, he struck out boldly for the net produce criterion.[3] His method involved the calculation of the average gross produce per *biga* ($\frac{2}{3}$ acre)

---

[1] Mackenzie, ibid., p. 302.

[2] Revenue Letter from Bombay, 15 June 1825, para. 72. Memorandum of Rules proposed for a Revenue Survey and Assessment of the Deccan, 29 Dec. 1824, No. 4, Head Assessors, para. 3: *Selections of Papers at the East India House*, vol. iii, pp. 880–1. Revenue Despatch to Bombay, 14 Nov. 1827, para. 28.

[3] R. K. Pringle, Report on the Survey and Assessment of the Deccan, 6 Sept. 1828; Revenue Letters from Bombay, vol. viii, ff. 169–251. For Pringle's early career: E. Dodwell and J. C. Miles, *List of Hon. East India Company's Bombay Civil Servants*, 1839, and *East India Register and Directory for 1821*, 1st edn., p. xl.

for nine separate soil qualities, turning this into a money value, and finally deducting the cost of production and interest on the stock employed, so as to arrive at the net produce. He went into almost ridiculous detail, claiming that 'no circumstance however minute is omitted which may appear to contribute to the accuracy of the result'. The total demand on a district was fixed on general considerations of its past revenue history and present condition, but everywhere the demand was distributed as a fixed proportion of the estimated net produce, and as far as possible this was made to approximate to 55 per cent. throughout the area under settlement. In this way the old Mahratta apportionment of the revenue among villages and among different fields was almost entirely disregarded.

It is interesting, in view of the notoriety of Pringle's settlement for severe over-assessment, that he himself considered it to represent a deliberate act of self-sacrifice on the part of the Government.[1] Like Mackenzie he emphasized that the whole of the net produce could be absorbed as revenue without impairing the resources of the country in any way. By limiting itself to taking just over half the estimated net produce, the State was giving up a large part of its rightful dues in order to leave a rent property in private hands. In this respect Pringle followed Malthus and the general liberal instinct for establishing private-property rights. But on the whole James Mill could rest well content, and the Home Authorities gave Pringle's work their blessing. While delivering a warning against the excessive relinquishment of the revenue rights of the State, they treated the Bombay Government to a short lesson on the principles of political economy in order to demonstrate the general correctness of Pringle's plan. It is more than likely that the despatch was the work of Mill.

In estimating what amount of assessment the land, which is of all degrees of fertility, can bear, he [Pringle] is right in considering that

---

[1] The Civil Finance Committee, of which Holt Mackenzie was the leading member, condemned Pringle's settlement for this reason, although even Pringle himself recognized that his original rates were excessive by at least 33 per cent.: *P.P.*, 1831-2, vol. viii, p. 187; R. K. Pringle, Final Report on the Survey and Assessment of the Deccan, 18 July 1831, para. 73, Bengal Revenue Consultations, 27 Dec. 1832, No. 102.

the charge of cultivation, including the outlay of the cultivator, re-muneration for his labour and the customary profit on his stock, ought all to be deducted in the first instance, and the surplus, namely what remains of this produce after this deduction is made, is the fund from which the revenue of the State is to be drawn. This surplus, which Mr. Pringle calls net produce, is that which remains to the owner of the soil after the cultivator is reimbursed and remunerated; and in Europe is called rent. At Bombay, wherever Government has not disposed of this fund, by transferring it to other parties . . . it belongs in whole to the Government. . . . A light assessment would leave part of this rent to the cultivator, and such an assessment we desire wherever practicable; but at the same time it is to be considered the unappropriated rent, [and] is the great fund from which the wants of the State have to be supplied.[1]

Although aware of the practical difficulties surrounding the use of the net produce criterion, James Mill and Holt Mackenzie continued to urge its value as an independent and scientific test of assessment, when they gave evidence before the Select Committees of 1831 and 1832. Mill especially pointed to the work of Pringle 'as a particular instance where care has been taken to ascertain the capabilities of the soil, the cost of production, and the surplus that may remain after remuneration to the cultivator'.[2] Despite this influential support from Mill, now the executive head of the India House, and from Holt Mackenzie, a newly appointed Com-missioner of the Board of Control, the net produce method was destined to suffer an eclipse.

The decision to abandon it was taken by the Indian authorities after the settlement operations, both in the Western Provinces and in the Bombay Deccan, had shown clear signs of failing. In July 1830 Bentinck, the Governor-General, set on foot an official inquiry into the causes of the negligible progress made in the settlement of the Western

[1] Bombay Despatches, 15 June 1831, para. 42. The original draft of the last sentence read: '. . . it is to be considered the unappropriated rent of the land, is the property of the Government, and is the great fund from which the wants of the State have to be supplied.' The deletion of the phrase, 'is the property of the Government' was made at the Board of Control and initialed '18 June 1831'. Is it fanciful to suggest that the original draft was Mill's, and that the Board of Control found his assertion of State proprietorship too outspoken and too radical?

[2] Cited Bentinck, Minute, 26 Sept. 1832, para. 49: *Revenue Selections 1822–33*, p. 403.

Provinces under Regulation VII, 1822. In the same year Pringle's operations were curtailed, initially on grounds of expense; but they were never resumed because of increasing doubts concerning the principles on which Pringle had proceeded. Much of the failure was due no doubt to the attempt to carry through a most complicated and detailed form of settlement with the aid of an administrative staff entirely inadequate in numbers, training, and discipline. Bentinck's remedial measures consequently embraced the reform of the whole administrative structure in the Bengal territories. Carried into effect between 1829 and 1831, they provided for the establishment of the divisional commissioner, the strengthening of the collector by vesting him with police and magisterial authority, the expansion of the European and Indian district staff, and the welding of all these authorities into a firm, disciplined chain of command. At the same time the procedure of settlement itself was subjected to an entire revision, with the aim of making it much less cumbrous and slow, and stripping it of all detailed inquiries which were not immediately essential for settlement purposes. Experience had shown that all attempts at founding an assessment on a theoretical criterion had led to no workable result, whether the criterion was the traditional Indian one of taking a fixed proportion of the gross produce, or was the net produce criterion itself. The elaborate and lengthy calculations of gross produce and conversion into money values, which both methods required, were now looked upon as unnecessary. Revenue officers had grown confident that a sound pragmatic judgement was the best aid in determining what a given area could safely be made to pay. Summarizing their views, Bentinck could fairly state it as 'the general opinion that the minute researches which have been hitherto made can lead to no practically useful results'. Although he valued James Mill's approbation highly (as he acknowledged to Mrs. Grote), he felt bound to expose the fallacy of Mill's confidence in the net produce criterion and pointed to Pringle's failure as decisive proof.[1]

---

[1] Bentinck, Minute, 20 Jan. 1832, para. 58: *Revenue Selections 1822–23*, p. 371. Minute, 20 Sept. 1832, para. 49: ibid., p. 403. Bentinck to Mrs. Grote: Bain,

Having toured the Western Provinces, Bentinck brought the protracted consideration of the revenue problem to a final conclusion at a conference of revenue officials held at Allahabad in January 1833. As a result Regulation IX, 1833 was passed, and gave its name to the new system of revenue settlement. There was no sharp break with the past; rather was the old procedure abbreviated and simplified. The main change was that, instead of dealing separately with individual villages, these were now formed into homogeneous groups and the assessment was determined for each group as a whole. The assessment was fixed in the light of payments over the previous twenty years, the relative growth or contraction of the cultivated area, and the general state of prosperity which the villages exhibited. No hard and fast method of assessment was prescribed. A total sum for an area arrived at in this way could be tested for suitability by seeing how it fell as a rate per acre (the 'revenue rate'). There was no pretence at any great precision in these calculations. 'In fact the older system was one of a sort of enlightened guess, or estimate, which was arrived at on general considerations, and was afterwards justified to the controlling authorities by various calculations.'[1]

In the Bombay Deccan Pringle's assessment was entirely set aside in 1835, and there was a much more decisive break in method. Just as much greater reliance had been placed in Bombay on an assessment arrived at deductively from the pure theory of rent, so the reaction in favour of an entirely empirical method was the more striking. In laying the foundations of the new Bombay system after 1835 H. E. Goldsmid and (the later Sir) George Wingate made their new empirical method as precise and rigorous as possible. Their survey and classification of the soil was a much more exact and scientific affair than the rough survey methods used after 1833 in the (North) Western Provinces. It took the form of a proper cadastral survey carried down to the individual field, with each field being minutely classified for

James Mill, p. 367: 'I read his [Mill's] evidence, with great pleasure, and much more profitable instruction, I suspect than the E[ast] I[ndia] Committee. You mention his approbation of my administration. None could gratify me more, because he is one of the very few men who can form a correct judgement.'

[1] Baden-Powell, *Land Systems of British India*, vol. ii, p. 43.

soil quality. The assessment was arrived at in much the same manner as in the North-Western Provinces, villages being formed into homogeneous groups and a sum fixed for a whole area in the light of its past history and general condition. But again, the method used was a careful and skilful use of statistics in place of the rough empiricism of the north. The statistical material was assembled in the form of a graph which showed the interrelation of the amount of assessment, the actual sum collected, and the acreage under cultivation, over a period of ten to twenty years. By tracing the relative movements of these three elements, Wingate believed that the diagram would demonstrate scientifically what precise pitch of assessment was required for securing the highest amount of revenue to the State without giving rise to a contraction of cultivation or the growth of balances in arrears.[1]

It might be supposed that such entirely empirical methods had deprived the law of rent of all practical importance. This was far from true. In the North-Western Provinces the law of rent remained the governing theory, despite the fact that all attempt to calculate the economic rent deductively in the form of the net produce was given up, the amount of assessment being decided finally on 'the judgement and sound discretion' of the settlement officer. James Thomason's authoritative *Directions for Settlement Officers* (1844) show the apparently contradictory situation in which the theory of the net produce was retained but the practice rejected. The *Directions* said it was 'desirable that the Government should not demand more than two-thirds of what may be expected to be the net produce. (By net produce is meant the surplus which the Estate may yield, after deducting the expenses of cultivation, including the profits of stock and wages of labour. . .).' At the same time the assessment could not be determined 'with certainty by any fixed arithmetical process, or by the prescription of any rule, that a certain portion of the gross or net produce of land shall be assigned to the Government and to the proprietors. . . . Not only would the actual

---

[1] On the revised Bombay system, cf. Joint Report, 2 Aug. 1847, Joint Report, 17 Oct. 1840; Report by Captain G. Wingate . . . on the Survey and Assessment of the Bunkapoor Talook, 29 Sept. 1846: *P.P.*, 1852-3, vol. lxxv, pp. 296, 361, 383.

ascertainment of the net produce of an estate be a fallacious basis, but it is in itself most difficult to accomplish, and the attempt to effect it is likely to produce many serious evils.'[1] The net produce criterion had been abandoned because of the difficulties in its practical use and not because of a revolt from the principles of political economy. Another method was now attempted in order to give them effect.

Baden-Powell, the standard authority on the Indian land revenue, gives a somewhat misleading impression in his general description of the methods employed in the early settlements under Regulation IX, 1833.[2] One would imagine from his account that they were rough and ready in the extreme, and that the various forms of calculation were used merely to support a figure of assessment arrived at almost entirely on the general judgement of the settlement officer. Certainly there was a great variety of methods employed, and in some cases these might be greatly lacking in precision, but it would be misleading to ignore the genuinely scientific element which R. M. Bird, the leading figure in the new settlement system, was trying to introduce. Baden-Powell places this attempt at scientific precision at a later period, after 1850, although in fact it was at work from the beginning. Essentially it was the adoption of an empirical in place of the former deductive method for ascertaining economic rent. Instead of trying to calculate rent in the form of the net produce (which involved an estimation of the average gross produce of different soils and the subtraction of nominal values for profits and wages), the attempt was now made to seek out actual free-will cash-rents and calculate the general rental value of an area from them. As early as 1832-4 R. M. Bird was suggesting the use of specimen rent-rates; and even when competition cash rents were not in existence, some officers, like Thornton in Muzaffarnagar, laboriously constructed specimen rent rates by converting existing payments in kind into money rates per acre.[3] Once the settlement

[1] 'Directions for Settlement Officers', paras. 50, 52: *P.P.*, 1852-3, vol. lxxv, pp. 18-19.　　　[2] Baden-Powell, *Land Systems*, vol. ii, pp. 42 et seq.
[3] Extract copy of letter of R. M. Bird in H. M. Elliot's notebook 'Revenue Extracts', ff. 151-9: 676 MS. Eur D.310, India Office Library. Bird's letter is undated but from its context would appear to belong to the period 1832-4. For Thornton's settlement of Muzaffarnagar, cf. *P.P.*, 1852-3, vol. lxxv, p. 194. Other

officer had obtained an estimated rental value for the tract under settlement, by the use of two or three specimen rent rates for the different qualities of soil, he brought the theoretical principle of assessment into action. Committed to leaving a portion of rent in private hands, as will be described later, Bentinck had decreed that the State should limit itself to two-thirds of the rental value.[1] Employing this criterion the settlement officer was left in possession of a figure which usually had an important influence in helping him to frame his ultimate demand. Certainly the history of assessment practice in the North-Western Provinces after 1833 was that of a sustained attempt to bring the demand closer and closer to its theoretical and scientific standard. By 1855 agriculture had become sufficiently commercialized for an alteration of method to be formally authorized. Under the Saharanpur rules of that year 'the aggregate-to-detail' procedure was abandoned. No longer was a lump sum levied on a whole group of villages, but each village was separately assessed on the basis of its prevailing rent rates. Finally after 1878, when the settlement system had been perfected and the village records brought to a high degree of accuracy, it became possible to aggregate the rentals of individual fields as recorded in the village rent roll, and to make the total the basis of the government demand. The stricter method of assessing introduced in 1855 made necessary a lowering of the theoretical standard to one-half of the rental assets, and after 1878 the assessment was brought into very close correspondence with this standard on the basis of actual competition rents.[2]

In Bombay it was not possible to follow this system. Because of the absence of an intermediary proprietary class between the Government and the cultivators, no rent or quasi-rent payments were in existence. Free-will tenant payments had appeared rapidly in the North-Western Provinces. Each village community (or the acknowledged proprietor or proprietary group) had been recognized as the

---

settlement reports are printed in *Reports on the Revenue Settlement of the N.W. Provinces under Regulation IX, 1833*, 2 vols., Benares, 1862-3.
[1] Bentinck, Minute, 26 Sept. 1832, para. 11: *Revenue Selections 1822–33*, p. 389.
[2] Cf. Baden-Powell, *Land Systems*, vol. ii, pp. 49 et seq.

lawful owner of the surrounding waste, and, with the growth of population and trade under the *pax Britannica*, the proprietors let out the waste tracts to tenant cultivators for cash rents. In the Bombay Deccan, however, the Government had followed the *ryotwar* tradition and had asserted the proprietary right of the State to all waste land. The expansion of cultivation consequently took the form of peasants 'renting' fresh land from the State, and the assessment was actually termed 'the Government rent'. Under these circumstances the payments of cultivators were not adjusted as a free-will bargain between cultivator and private landlord, but were fixed authoritatively by the Government as its assessment. There was therefore no opportunity for employing a theoretical standard of assessment, such as a fixed proportion of actual rent assets. Yet it would be quite false to conclude that the authors of the Bombay system had flouted the doctrines of Mill and renounced the teaching of the rent theory. They believed, in fact, that they were carrying them into effect in more perfect form despite the fact that practical difficulties prevented them from using a theoretical standard. In the Joint Report of 1840, drawn up in reply to the adverse criticism of the authorities in the North-Western Provinces, Wingate and Goldsmid accepted the theoretical correctness of the rent theory without question:

From the difficulty of ascertaining the true rent of different descriptions of land we have not assumed any theoretical proportion of this for the standard of our assessment; but we fully coincide in the justice of the principle of limiting the Government demand to a portion of the true rent, and believe 50 to 60 per cent thereof, as laid down by the Board [of Revenue, North-Western Provinces] would form a liberal assessment.[1]

If such a principle were capable of being carried into practice, they declared, it would open a new era in the history of the agricultural classes, and they boldly laid claim to its accomplishment. Purely on the empirical evidence of 'the unexampled rapidity with which cultivation has everywhere

---

[1] Joint Report by H. E. Goldsmid and G. Wingate, 17 Oct. 1840, para. 17: *P.P.*, 1852–3, vol. lxxv, p. 364.

extended', they argued that their assessment had left a liberal portion of rent with the cultivator.

All the revenue systems agreed on the truth of the rent doctrine; their differences arose over the method by which it should be put into effect. The Home Authorities were reluctant to see the abandonment of the net produce criterion in the North-Western Provinces, and while bowing before the united voice of local experience they expressed the opinion that the attempt to calculate costs of production, and so obtain an absolute test of the pitch of assessment, had been too hastily given up.[1] But the abandonment by the new Bombay system of any theoretical standard of assessment whatever was a matter for more serious concern, because it became difficult to defend the system against the charge of being one of arbitrary exaction. The outspoken doubts of Manchester magnates, who were troubled at the production costs of Indian raw cotton, could only be silenced by the demonstration that the Indian land revenue was not a crushing burden on agriculture but was simply a modest portion of the net produce or rent. When Madras came to revise its revenue system in 1855, the Home Authorities made their influence felt. The Madras Government had proposed adhering to Munro's principle of assessment, although lowering the standard to one-fourth of the gross produce.[2] Naturally, their proposal was rejected on the ground that it offended against the received doctrine of taxation drawn from the law of rent. The instruction from London was that 'the assessment should be proportioned to the net and not the gross produce'.[3] It was admitted that the experience of the North-Western Provinces had shown that this criterion was 'imperfectly attainable in practice'. But the choice was between the Bombay system with no theoretical standard and the net produce criterion; for the *ryotwar* system precluded the possibility of founding the assessment on the rental payments

[1] Revenue Despatch to Bengal, 12 April 1837, para. 16.
[2] Extract Minutes of Consultation, 14 Aug. 1855, No. 951, para. 19, and Madras Revenue Letter, 11 Oct. 1855 (No. 44 of 1855), para. 5: 'Papers relating to General Revenue Survey of the Madras Presidency', pp. 8, 75–76, in *Selections from the Records of the Madras Government*, O.S. liii, Madras, 1858.
[3] Revenue Despatch to Madras, 17 Dec. 1856 (No. 17 of 1856), para. 18: ibid., p. 186.

made by the immediate cultivators to an intermediary proprietary class as in the North-Western Provinces. Despite the
opposition of Sir Charles Trevelyan to the net produce
criterion—he had apparently had experience of it under
William Fraser in the Delhi Territory in the late eighteen-
twenties—Sir Charles Wood, as Secretary of State in 1864,
eventually decreed that the Madras assessment should be
based on the standard of one-half of the net produce.[1] In this
way the net produce method returned after an eclipse of
thirty years. It necessitated calculations of average produce,
prices, and expenses for different qualities of soil, just as
James Mill and Holt Mackenzie had wanted to see introduced. It was too much to expect, however, that an assessment founded on a deductive method drawn from abstract
theory could stand up unmodified to the hard facts of everyday experience. The assessment proved excessive except on
the better soils, and it was found necessary to adjust the total
assessment on a tract of country on general considerations
and to alter the revenue rates accordingly. The final result
was something similar to Pringle's system. While general
considerations played the final part in determining the
quantum of assessment, the sum was distributed in relative
proportion to the net produce of the soil.[2]

The rent doctrine had triumphed, in large measure, in the
forming of the assessment theory and method of the land
revenue systems of India, which together constituted the
great administrative achievement of British rule. The system
elaborated in the North-West Provinces was later extended
in a modified form to the Punjab and the Central Provinces
after their annexation in the middle of the century. One-
half of the rental assets remained the standard of assessment
right down to the nineteen-twenties, although from Curzon's
time it was exacted with steadily diminishing stringency. In
Madras and Burma, where the *ryotwar* settlement prevailed,

---

[1] Sir Charles Trevelyan, Minute, 20 Nov. 1859: 'Papers Relating to General
Revenue Survey', vol. ii, p. 351, in *Selections from the Records of the Madras
Government*, O.S. lxxiv, Madras, 1863. (Trevelyan was Governor of Madras
from 1859 to 1860.) Revenue Despatch to Madras, 24 Feb. 1864, paras. 11, 15, cited
R. C. Dutt, *The Economic History of India in the Victorian Age*, 7th edn., 1950, p. 310.

[2] *Moral and Material Progress Report for 1882–83*: P.P., 1884–5, vol. lx,
p. 115.

the standard was one-half of the net produce. Only Bombay was left without any theoretical standard at all.

2. *The Effect of the Rent Doctrine on Indian Land Tenures*

The method of assessment had been merely one part of James Mill's design. Perhaps of greater importance was the influence of the rent doctrine in determining the weight of the land revenue demand and in shaping the type of private-property right established by British rule. It will be recalled that Mill, in standing out for the extreme logic of his theory, had wanted the State to absorb the whole of the true rent as revenue and to prohibit the growth of a private rent property. Not only did he wish to prevent the emergence of a land-owning aristocracy or gentry, but he rejected the idea of peasant proprietorship in the ordinary sense, because he foresaw that, once in possession of a portion of rent, the peasant would just as readily let out his land and become an idle rent-receiver.[1] The only concession he was prepared to make was that any assessment pitched short of the full economic rent (to allow for the practical difficulties of ascertaining the precise limit of rent) should go to benefit the immediate cultivator.

Mill's doctrine was, of course, too extreme to find acceptance, but it exercised a powerful influence. Holt Mackenzie had drawn much the same theoretical conclusions, identifying the land revenue right of the State with the economic rent and arguing that no harm would result from its entire absorption by the State.[2] He considered, however, that the traditional employment of a middleman agency in the revenue collections of northern India, and the British recognition of the right to engage for the revenue as a property right, had alienated one-tenth of the rent fund as private property, this being the customary commission enjoyed by a middleman on his collections. Beyond this concession Mackenzie asserted a highly authoritarian view of State rights. There had been in his view far too little consideration of the question as to where the line of demarcation between public

[1] See p. 92, n. 3.
[2] Mackenzie, Memorandum, 1 July 1819, para. 369 n.: *Revenue Selections 1818–22.*

and private property should properly be drawn. The right to the office and perquisites of revenue management had been fatally confused with the right to the soil itself; and the confusion had been worst confounded by making such a right freely alienable and saleable. Cornwallis's conversion of the hereditary revenue collectors of Bengal, the *zemindars*, into landed proprietors was the most glaring example of the error, but Munro had also been guilty in this respect. He had passed to the other extreme and given the right to engage for the revenue, and with it the property right in the soil, to the immediate cultivator. The result had been a profound and unjust derangement of existing rights, and in the case of Cornwallis a wanton and ill-considered sacrifice of the revenue rights of the State. The first swept into limbo the rights of all classes other than that vested with the revenue engagement. The second gave to such a favoured class the entire benefit of the limitation of the State demand irrespective of justice or expediency. These errors could have been avoided if there had been a proper study of existing rights, and if the two types of right—the right to collect the revenue and the right to the soil—had been kept mentally distinct.

It would have been noticed that the true private-property right, that of regulating the occupation and cultivation of the soil, belonged to the primary tenure of Indian agrarian society, the co-sharing village community. Doubtless this tenure had been enfeebled over most of India by the misrule of the eighteenth century, and only in the (North) Western Provinces had it proved too strong to be ignored. Altogether distinct from this tenurial right was that of collecting the revenue dues of the State. This was essentially a public right, and could only be converted into private property by a distinct grant of the State or by prescriptive hereditary usage. In any case, the right extended to no more than that of collecting a sum fixed by the State—its proper theoretic limits were the economic rent—and of enjoying a traditional commission of one-tenth on the revenue collected. Now in the great majority of instances, Mackenzie argued, the *taluqdars* and revenue farmers of northern India had no shred of title to hereditary rights of collection. They had gained their position through force or fraud in the disturbed conditions prevailing before and immediately after British annexation. The State had a perfect right to resume their offices and confer them upon any class it wished. If the office had become to some extent hereditary, the holder could be compensated for its loss. In the comparatively rare instances where a *raja* or other individual could show ancient hereditary claims, then he might be continued in his office, but his perquisites would be strictly limited to the proper commission by defining the revenue he was to collect from the villages in his dependency. Although Mackenzie is always looked upon as the man who wanted to avoid preconceptions and to make a careful 'Domesday' survey of every grade of existing right and interest in the land, it will be noticed that his interpretation of the rights of the aristocratic classes fitted in well with Utilitarian prejudice. For him right and expediency went happily hand in hand. He believed that, from a purely impartial reading of the evidence, the original private-property right in the soil belonged to the village community; that the State was entitled to set aside the existing agency of collection and confer it upon whom it wished; and that right and expediency argued equally in favour of conferring the agency of collection and the formal proprietary title on the village community. The man who stated his aim to be that of avoiding 'those sudden revolutions which our operations appear to have so strong a tendency to produce, even where no change has been distinctly contemplated', and of making 'our general system of administration fitted to the frame of society' was in fact quietly advocating an agrarian revolution destined to destroy the aristocratic classes of northern India. Of the expediency of this policy he was in no doubt. Sharing Mill's fervent belief in the parasitic nature of rent-receivers, he argued that the continued agency of the aristocratic classes in the revenue collection would be bought too dearly; for the State could realize far more if it collected itself directly from the village communities, and the portion of public rent relinquished to the aristocracy as remuneration would only be wasted on non-productive consumption. It was a most dangerous illusion to think that they could be transformed into an improving capitalist class ploughing back their gains into agriculture. In almost the same words that Mill used twelve years later before the Commons Select Committee, Mackenzie expressed his conviction that the cultivator was the sole hope of Indian agriculture.[1]

What was the nature of the property right which Mackenzie proposed to vest in the village community or brotherhood? In keeping with the Utilitarian distrust of private rent property, he envisaged a right that was strictly limited. It was to amount to no more than the allowance of a tenth on the *existing collection*, which the revenue manager traditionally enjoyed; and the village brotherhood were to be prevented from collecting in excess of this allowance by the framing of a *ryebundee* or register of cultivators' payments in each village. The rates so recorded would be protected against enhancement for the duration of the settlement. But what of the additional increment that would accrue if the government demand were limited for a lengthy period instead of being varied every few years? Mackenzie was deeply concerned at the prospect of an increasing amount from the rent fund being alienated into private hands without any serious considerations as to its use. He used the language of the Utilitarian:

But holding 9/10ths of the clear rent of the country as a fund to be administered for the public good, the Government may, I think, justly be regarded as under a very solemn obligation to consider more fully than has hitherto been usual, how it can dispose of *that fund* so as to produce the greatest sum of happiness.[2]

He saw no point in distributing the increased portion of private rent among the whole mass of the co-sharing communities, since the amount each individual received would be so small. It was much better, he considered, to separate off this additional amount and turn it into a quasi-hereditary property for the remuneration of a leading village officer.[3]

Apart from this last suggestion, Mackenzie's proposals were generally accepted and became the basis of the settlement

---

[1] Holt Mackenzie, Memorandum, 1 July 1819, para. 636. Also cf. paras. 473, 634, 745–7: *Revenue Selections 1818–1822*.

[2] Mackenzie, Memorandum, 19 Oct. 1826, para. 426: *Revenue Selections 1822–1833*, p. 148.

[3] Ibid., paras. 509–11.

system under both Regulation VII, 1822 and Regulation IX, 1833. It was provided under the first regulation that the proprietor should be accorded an income of not less than 10 per cent. of the assessment, but where an increase was made on the existing assessment the allowance should be raised to 20 per cent. Now the paramount need to maintain the existing level of revenue demand was undoubtedly the most cogent argument for keeping the proprietary allowance within such narrow limits; the regulation itself stipulated that no decrease in the existing assessments would be sanctioned 'unless on the clearest grounds of necessity'. But political economy provided a powerful theoretic justification, with its equation of the immediate cultivators' payments with rent, and its demonstration that these could be wholly absorbed as revenue, apart from a small proprietary allowance for the risks and costs of collection. The inadequacy of even 20 per cent. was soon recognized. By Regulation IX, 1833, it was raised to 30 to 35 per cent. Despite all their high-minded pleas for moderation of assessment, the Home Authorities condemned this new increase as excessive, and one cannot doubt that the source of their inconsistency was the spell which the rent doctrine had woven over their minds.[1] The responsibility of the rent theory for the over-assessment practised generally in the period before the Mutiny is such an important question that it will need to be examined at a later stage.

Mackenzie's other proposals regarding the right to the revenue engagement and to the proprietary title were also incorporated into the settlement system of the North-Western Provinces. Wherever possible the right was vested in the village community and all superior tenures were extinguished. Again, there were other influences besides the Utilitarian making in this direction. From the earliest settlements there had been no practical alternative over wide areas, and, despite the havoc wrought by the practice of public sale for revenue default, the village type of settlement remained the

---

[1] Revenue Despatch to Bengal, 15 Feb. 1833, No. 2, paras. 34–36. The wording of the despatch suggests James Mill's authorship; cf. para. 15 on *ryot* rights with the wording of Mill's 'Observations on the Land Revenue of India, 15 August 1832', *P.P.*, 1831–2, vol. xi, Appendix, p. 48, and a letter to his son, James, in Bain, *James Mill*, pp. 397–8.

prevailing one. The Munro tradition also exerted a strong anti-aristocratic bias. But the systematic way in which the aristocratic classes were set aside after 1822 owed a great deal to the rent theory, with its doctrine of the parasitic nature of rent-receivers and of the right of the State to dispose of the rent fund at its own discretion. When the settlement system came up for review in Bentinck's time, the Governor-General expressed his agreement with James Mill that the original right to the soil belonged to the *ryot* or peasant, and that the tenures of the great *zemindars* and *taluqdars* were artificial creations of the State. Bentinck confirmed Mackenzie's principle that the proprietary right should generally be vested in the village communities.[1] Under the eye of Robert Bird, who looked upon the inchoate aristocracy of revenue assignees and farmers as nothing more than 'a host of un-productives', the supersession of the *taluqdar* class was pressed forward with great severity.[2] Where they could not be ousted without flagrant injustice, they were kept in office, but a sub-settlement was made with the subordinate village communities which rigidly limited the *taluqdari* allowance to 18 per cent. on the assessment, and only 10 per cent. of this was allowed as hereditary property. John Stuart Mill was a true son of his father in favouring peasant proprietorship, and in the *Principles of Political Economy* (1848) gave his blessing to the developments in the North-Western Provinces. Quoting his father's denunciation of the Bengal Permanent Settlement at length, he branded the rent owners in Bengal as 'useless drones on the soil', and expressed his satisfaction that in other parts of India, including the North-Western Provinces, 'the blunder has been avoided of endow-ing a useless body of great landlords with gifts from the public revenue.'[3] The rigour with which the aristocratic classes were excluded from the revenue settlement appalled T. C. Robertson, a lieutenant-governor recruited from Bengal. He found Bird's system 'a fearful experiment', cal-

---

[1] Bentinck, Minute, 26 Sept. 1832, paras. 18–20, 42: *Revenue Selections 1822–33*.

[2] R. M. Bird, Minute, 25 Sept. 1832, para. 12: *Revenue Selections 1822–33*, p. 423. Cf. *P.P.*, 1852–3, vol. lxxv, pp. 46–49, 160, 242, 252, 255, 263, 265, 270, 288–93, 474–5.

[3] J. S. Mill, *Principles of Political Economy*, ed. W. J. Ashley, pp. 325–8.

culated so as to 'flatten the whole surface of society as eventually to leave little of distinguishable eminence between the ruling power and the cultivators of the soil'.[1] The social revolution which the settlement system helped to bring about partially explains the reason for the Mutiny taking on something of the character of a general uprising in this region.

The other cardinal point in James Mill's teaching was that the State should not permanently alienate the public rent fund by granting a freehold property title and declaring the assessment unalterable. His view had been backed with increasing conviction by Holt Mackenzie.[2] The Indian Government had never, however, abandoned the idea of a permanent settlement, and it will be remembered that the principle commanded support not only from the Cornwallis tradition of Bengal but also from the paternalist school. It was in fact to Munro's authority that Bentinck appealed when he suggested in 1835 that the assessment should be declared permanent on the cultivated area of surveyed 'estates'; and it was from Metcalfe, a disciple of Munro's, that the original proposal came.[3] The only serious opposition in the Supreme Council came from Alexander Ross, who as a Judge of the *Sadr* Court had proclaimed himself 'a disciple of the Benthamite school of jurisprudence', and who—as the Calcutta Radical, James Young, told Bentinck—had 'while recently at home, had the benefit of adding to his previous acquirements *all* that [James] Mill and his School could teach'.[4] Like Mill, Ross held that 'the rent of land being the most unobjectionable of all sources of public revenue', it would be wrong to exclude the State from benefiting in the natural growth of the rent fund. The permanent limitation of the assessment in Bengal had made necessary the imposition of injurious taxes, like the salt and opium monopolies, and the town and transit duties, which were levied on internal commerce. Their effect was to prevent the extension

---

1 T. C. Robertson, Minute, 15 April 1842, paras. 29–30: *P.P.*, 1852–3, vol. lxxv, p. 125.

2 Written evidence of Holt Mackenzie: *P.P.*, 1831–2, vol. xi, p. 308.

3 Revenue Letter from Bengal, 20 July 1835, para. 2. Bentinck, Minute, 19 March 1835: Board's Collections, vol. 1559, Register No. 63873, f. 18.

4 A. Ross, Minute, 26 March 1835: ibid., f. 21. Evidence of Ross, *P.P.*, 1831, vol. vi, p. 508. James Young to Bentinck, n.d. [1828]: Bentinck MSS.

of manufactures and trade, and, by confining the labour of the people to the single employment of growing food, the country had been kept in a state of extreme poverty. London gave Ross its unqualified support, and summarily rejected any suggestion for vesting the Indian Government with a discretionary power to declare the assessment permanent in individual cases. Instead they agreed to sanction leases for periods not exceeding thirty years, as James Mill had recommended to the Commons Committee of 1831.[1] That Mill was the *éminence grise* of the Home Government's revenue policy was detected even in the remote Straits Settlements, where the vociferous demands of the European mercantile community for land on freehold title were again met by the uncompromising refusal of London. W. R. Young, a special commissioner sent out from Bengal, considered the local demands reasonable but was compelled to abide by the rule laid down; a rule which, he said, 'appeared to be founded upon the theory of taxation originating with the late Mr. Mill. . .'.[2]

The direction to grant leases or settlements for periods of thirty years was extended to Bombay and Madras, but Mill's principle did not triumph without a final struggle. The English mercantile community had never accepted the principle without demur; and in 1861, in the aftermath of the Mutiny, when paternalism was for the moment in the ascendant under John Lawrence, the proposal for a permanent settlement or a permanent redemption of the land revenue was again formally put forward by the Government of India and accepted in principle by the Secretary of State, Sir Charles Wood.[3] Many voices were raised in protest,

---

[1] Revenue Despatch to Bengal, 12 April 1837, para. 3. Evidence of James Mill, 19 Aug. 1831: *P.P.*, 1831, vol. v, p. 367, Qu. 3911.

[2] W. R. Young, Commissioner to the Eastern Settlements, to H. T. Prinsep, Secretary to Government of India, General Dept., 27 Sept. 1838, para. 69: *Correspondence Relating to the Land Revenue System of the Straits Settlements 1837–1844*, Singapore, 1883.

[3] Cf. R. C. Dutt, *Economic History of India in the Victorian Age*, chap. iv. Cf. Letter from Sec., Bombay Chamber of Commerce, to Bombay Government, 21 Jan. 1841: *P.P.*, 1847–8, vol. ix, p. 513: 'Nothing short of the absolute and perpetual property in the land (subject of course to a fixed rate of taxation) will give that confidence which is necessary to cause capital, time, health and labour, to be fully expended upon it.'

uttering the traditional arguments of the rent theory—that the land revenue, being a portion of economic rent, was the ideal mode of taxation, and that to sacrifice the right of the State to enjoy the unearned increment of rent, which accrued naturally from the increase of population and wealth, was wanton folly. Sir George Wingate, Ross Donelly Mangles (sometime chairman of the East India Company), and the rising collector of Moradabad, the future Sir John Strachey, all turned to the authority of the writings and teaching of the two Mills.[1] Events proved to be on their side. Faced by the inflation of the eighteen-sixties and the steady depreciation of silver as its currency medium, the Indian Government found its financial situation seriously endangered. Renounced by the Indian Government in 1871, the idea of a permanent settlement was finally laid to rest by the Secretary of State in 1882.[2]

Although the radical policy was adopted of setting aside the aristocracy, rejecting a permanent settlement, and basing the method of assessment squarely on the rent theory, it should not be supposed that the settlement system of the North-Western Provinces entirely realized James Mill's ideal. For the system as it stood contained certain conservative features which the radical-minded were not prepared to see made permanent. Mackenzie, Bird, and Thomason had been influenced sufficiently by the paternalist creed for them to refrain from the vigorous enforcement of individual proprietary title and individual revenue responsibility. Fearful of the social effects of a sudden dissolution of the co-sharing village communities, they upheld the custom of joint proprietorship or of joint revenue management (where the village lands were held in severalty). In order to give added support to the forces holding the members of the village communities together, and to keep the stranger out of the village, the Government allowed the communities a right of pre-emption where the interest of any member had to be sold up for default of revenue or mortgage payments.

---

[1] See note H, p. 325.
[2] Letter of Governor-General in Council, 20 May 1871, para. 16; printed in A. Colvin, *Memorandum of the Revision of Land Revenue Settlements of the N.W. Provinces*, Calcutta, 1872, p. 72.

Naturally these customs hampered the transferability of land, imposed considerable restrictions on individual enterprise, and generally stood in the way of progress towards a free economy. The law had, however, always provided a remedy for overcoming such restrictions by permitting any co-sharer to apply for a separation of his own individual interest, so that the practice of joint ownership and responsibility for the revenue rested largely on the force of custom and the personal influence of the district officers. These supports grew steadily weaker as cash crops and a more commercialized form of agriculture were introduced. Land acquired a mort-gageable value, and the peasant's desire to be free from communal ownership or control was consequently sharpened. The movement towards individual properties was assisted by the 'record of rights', which provided for the detailed registration of individual interests, and gave precise legal definition to what had hitherto been a matter of unwritten custom. Finally, the very simple procedure adopted for the transfer of title gave a fearful facility to the peasant to sell or alienate his land. By the eighteen-forties paternalism as a creed was wearing thin in the North-Western Provinces; Thomason, appointed Lieutenant-Governor in 1843, found that his own Board of Revenue was in Radical hands, and actively encouraging the partition of joint estates and the ending of joint responsibility for the revenue.[1] Within a year of his death, in 1853, the transfer of land to the owner-ship of the money-lending classes had gone so far that an official inquiry was made into the growing volume of sales in execution of decrees for debt. Despite the lamentations of the paternalists and even a suggestion from one of them to prohibit the alienation for debt of land held by hereditary cultivators, it was the young and radical John Strachey who voiced prevailing opinion. Whatever sentimental regret might be caused by the break-up of the old village communi-ties and the transfer of ownership to the money-lending classes, these things were part of the unalterable march of progress. No government interference could preserve the

[1] Thomason, Minute on Joint Responsibility in Undivided Estates, 30 Dec. 1848: *Selections from the Records of Government N.W. Provinces. Mr. Thomason's Despatches*, vol. i (Calcutta, 1856), p. 462. See Biographical Notes, p. 333.

vitality of a system which natural causes were breaking up, because the village communities were necessarily 'doomed to decay with the establishment of good government and the progress of civilization'.[1]

The other cardinal feature of the paternalist system was the preservation of the status of the subordinate cultivators through a village rent roll which recorded and secured their existing payments for the duration of the settlement. Before the Mutiny this feature remained intact, but it could not permanently withstand the pressure of radical forces. When, after 1855, the attempt was made to bring the assessment into the closest conformity with the new standard of one-half of the rental assets, there was a corresponding movement to bring the customary rates of hereditary cultivators more into line with the competition cash rents paid by tenants-at-will. Once again the old paternalism was defeated. Metcalfe and his school in the twenties and thirties had looked to a permanent limitation of subordinate cultivators' payments as the proper counterpart of a permanent limitation of the assessment on the village proprietors. Now, the Utilitarians had rejected this corollary with their rejection of the idea of a permanent settlement.[2] One wing, represented by Alexander Ross and in closer sympathy with the European mercantile community, had gone so far as to suggest that all governmental interference between proprietor and subordinate cultivator was wrong. In the words of their spokesman, Gavin Young, the European community saw the one hope of progress 'in reducing the present complexity of tenures to the simple relation of landlord and tenant', and considered that attempts to establish fixed rent rates for subordinate cultivators were both futile and injurious.[3] Ross supported them in their plea for free competition and for the unrestricted right of a proprietor to contract freely with his cultivators. He drew his argument from the doctrine of the wage fund, asserting that the mass of the cultivating classes

---

[1] J. Strachey, Collector of Moradabad, 16 July 1855: *Selections from the Records of Government N.W. Provinces*, vol. iv (Agra, 1854), p. 212.

[2] See pp. 92, 110. Also cf. Revenue Despatch to Bengal, 9 May 1821, para. 60.

[3] [Gavin Young], *A Further Inquiry into the Expediency of Applying the Principles of Colonial Policy to the Government of India and of Effecting an Essential Change in its Landed Tenures, &c.*, London, 1828, p. 96.

must necessarily pass into the position of agricultural labourers, and that the portion of the produce falling to them as wages was inexorably limited by the laws of political economy. If the State interfered with the operation of these laws and arbitrarily fixed the payments of subordinate cultivators, it would be giving them a right 'which would be superior to, and incompatible with, the right of property in the soil which has been recognized to be vested in the zemindars'.[1] This view had been defeated in the early eighteen-thirties, and even the more moderate standpoint of Bentinck and Holt Mackenzie had been overridden. R. M. Bird, with the support of the Home Authorities, established the right of almost every grade of subordinate cultivator to have his payments fixed for the duration of the settlement.[2] Despite, however, the strong wording of the Revenue Despatch of 15 February 1833, which James Mill probably drafted, there was no question of Mill going to the lengths of the paternalists who stood for the permanent fixing of subordinate rent payments. The movement which took place after 1855 to allow such payments to rise to a true economic level did not contradict his viewpoint. Before 1859 a proprietor could only secure an increase of rent by resorting to the expensive and hazardous procedure of a regular suit in the civil courts. But with Act X of 1859 jurisdiction over rent cases was given to the revenue officers, who were bound to award an increase if it could be shown that there had been a general rise in prices or that the existing rent was substantially below the average for land held by tenants of similar status. Finally, in the Land Revenue Act of 1873, settlement officers were empowered to raise tenant rents on the periodical revision of settlements, whilst proprietors still remained entitled to sue for further increases of occu-

[1] A. Ross, Minute, 6 March 1827, paras. 13, 14: *P.P.*, 1831–2, vol. xi, Appendix, pp. 125–6. Also Minute, 5 Nov. 1829, paras. 29 et seq.: *P.P.*, 1831–2, vol. xii, Appendix, p. 462.
[2] For Bird's views, cf. Minute, 25 Sept. 1832: *Revenue Selections 1822–1833*, p. 419. For Bentinck's views, cf. Minute, 26 Sept. 1832: ibid., p. 385. For Mackenzie's views, cf. undated paper 'Mr. Mackenzie's Remarks on Mr. Bird's Memorandum respecting Settlements': Bentinck MSS. For regulation of question, cf. 'Directions for Settlement Officers', paras. 130, 135, passim; also cf. E. Thornton, 'The Settlement of the North-Western Provinces of India': *P.P.*, 1852–3, vol. lxxv, pp. 32–33, 473–4.

pancy rents at ten-year intervals.[1] In all this Mill's point was maintained: the State continued to define and fix the demand down to the lowliest cultivator, but at the same time rejected the notion of a permanent limitation of cultivators' payments. The retention and enforcement by the State of the power to fix rents was another instance in which the Utilitarian influence, assisted by the paternalist tradition, succeeded in restricting the attributes of landed property rights and in defeating the claims of ordinary liberalism for an entirely *laisser-faire* economy. The authoritarian role exercised by the Indian Government was hailed by John Stuart Mill as a model to be followed in dealing with the Irish agrarian problem; and it was Liberals with Indian experience, like the younger Mill and Sir George Campbell, who first taught their party that the State might justly lay hands on the sacred institution of private landed property.[2]

It was in the Bombay Presidency that the revenue system came nearest to James Mill's ideal. Admittedly it abandoned the deductive method inherent in the use of the net-produce criterion, which Pringle had employed and Mill had blessed; but it will be recalled that the systematic empiricism of Wingate and Goldsmid claimed to embody in a more faithful manner the teachings of the rent doctrine. In all other respects the Bombay system was bluntly radical and amply fulfilled James Mill's requirements. The State settled directly with the individual cultivator, and fixed its demand on the individual field. All intermediaries were excluded. The State made no renunciation of its position as universal landlord, and the joint proprietary right of the State and the cultivator was explicitly affirmed. The cultivator was recognized as possessing a permanent, freely-alienable property right, indefeasible except for failure to pay the government demand. As if to emphasize the ultimate landlord right of the State, the official term given to the demand was 'the Government

---

[1] Sir Auckland Colvin, *Memorandum on the Revision of Land Revenue Settlements in the North-Western Provinces 1860–72*, Calcutta, 1872, pp. 110–12. Baden-Powell, *Land Systems*, vol. i, chap. iv; vol. ii, chap. ii, sect. v.

[2] J. S. Mill, *Principles of Political Economy*, pp. 332 passim. Sir George Campbell applied his Indian experience in his pamphlet, *The Irish Land* (1869), which had considerable influence in prompting Gladstone's Irish Land Acts of 1870 and 1881: *D.N.B.*, vol. xxii, p. 384.

rent', and the term 'occupancy tenant' was used rather than 'proprietor'.[1]

The apportionment of the demand was made on a strictly egalitarian basis. This was in direct contrast to Pringle, who had set out to make his assessment bear a uniform proportion to the net produce in the full knowledge that he was reversing the egalitarian trend of later Mahratta revenue practice. His aim, he declared, had been to place all lands exactly in the same relative position which they would have held if no assessment had existed at all; 'that is, to enable them to yield a rent to the owner, progressively increasing in amount from the worst to the best soils according to their quality'.[2] Pringle's critics could truthfully claim that this was in fact to remunerate the cultivator, 'not in proportion to his labour, but in proportion to the value of the field on which he laboured'.[3] It was to consecrate the fundamental injustice of private rent property, that it arose not from individual energy and capital, but from a legal monopoly of the richer soils. Wingate's principle, in contrast, held that if private rent property were to be created the State must intervene to repair Nature's injustice. 'Where the labour, the stock and the outlay required are equal, so ought also to be the profit'.[4] But this implied a highly authoritarian approach. It argued 'as though Government were the universal landlord and the cultivators its servants, and if that were the case it would undoubtedly be unjust to leave one man a greater proportionate share of the fruits of his labour than another'. On the other hand, if the assessment were regarded as a land tax on existing private property, the plan of taking 'a certain share of the net produce' was the only fair one.[5] Wingate deliberately rejected the principle followed in the North-Western Provinces and

---

[1] Baden-Powell, *Land Systems*, vol. iii, pp. 269 et seq.

[2] R. K. Pringle, Report, 6 Sept. 1828, para. 39: Revenue Letters from Bombay, vol. 8, f. 167.

[3] Lieut. A. Nash to S. Mansfield reporting on the survey and assessment of the Indapur Taluka, n.d. [1838], para. 8: *Selections from Records of Bombay Government*, N.S., vol. cli (Bombay, 1877), p. 88. Also cf. G. Wingate, Supt. Revenue Survey to R. Mills, Principal Collector, Poona, 4 Aug. 1838: ibid., Appendix ii, p. 102.   [4] Ibid., para. 8, p. 105.

[5] T. Williamson, Revenue Commissioner, Poona, to Bombay Government, 12 Oct. 1838, para. 14: *Selections . . . of Bombay Govt.*, N.S., vol. cli, Appendix iv, p. 125.

later in Madras. Although not going so far as James Mill in wanting to suppress the emergence of private rent property entirely, he was determined that the portion of the public rent fund relinquished into private hands should be distributed as far as possible in the form of a general and uniform increase in the profit rate of agricultural capital.[1] His test in this respect had to be an entirely empirical one, since he distinctly renounced all attempt to discover rent from a calculation of gross produce and costs of production. A correct distribution of the assessment was empirically demonstrated when cultivators paid no attention to differences of soil quality on applying to take up waste land.[2]

The egalitarian and radical quality of the system was also evident in the treatment of the native tenures. In the North-Western Provinces strong efforts were made to 'fit the administration to the frame of society'; and for the first twenty- and thirty-year settlements under Regulation IX, 1833, joint responsibility for the revenue, recognition of the superior status of the village brotherhood, acceptance of privileged grades of cultivators, and allowances for caste and special circumstances, were all permitted to modify the uniformity and equality of the assessment. This tenderness to ensure that the assessment did not bear too harshly against the existing form of society and its traditional inequalities of payment was entirely absent at Bombay. Although Wingate and Goldsmid freely admitted that the practice of joint management and responsibility had been 'universal in the Deccan' up to the time of British rule, they condemned the principle as being 'unjust in itself' and 'in opposition to nature'. It constituted a drag on individual exertion, and if allowed would once again throw the mass of cultivators into the power of the village officers and the more influential members of the community. In contrast the effect of their own system had been to confine every man's liabilities to his own concerns.[3] In the North-Western Provinces the dominant co-

---

[1] James Mill did not object to the cultivator being allowed a portion of rent so long as it was not large enough to allow him to cease cultivating and live as a rent receiver. Cf. evidence of James Mill, *P.P.*, 1831, vol. v, p. 372, Qu. 3974–6; p. 398, Qu. 4225.

[2] H. E. Goldsmid and G. Wingate, Joint Report, 17 Oct. 1840, para. 14: *P.P.*, 1852–3, vol. lxxv, p. 363.   [3] Ibid., para. 38.

sharing groups, the joint *zemindars* and *pattidars*, had been recognized as proprietors of the whole of the village lands, with a right to levy payment from the inferior cultivators. In the Deccan the punitive revenue assessments of the Mahrattas had greatly weakened the corresponding groups, the *mirasdars*, making them anxious to relinquish responsibility for land not in their own immediate cultivation. Wingate and Goldsmid now enforced a rigorous equality. So far from trying to restore the position of the *mirasdars*, they sought as far as possible to eliminate the *mirasi* tenure and to reduce all cultivators to an equality of status. The *mirasdars* lost all right to regulate the occupation of the village lands, and the only distinguishing mark left to them was the right of bequeathing their property according to the Hindu law of inheritance. The ordinary occupancy tenant was compelled to devise his occupancy right according to the law of primogeniture, the object being to avoid the excessive subdivision of holdings inherent in the Hindu law of joint division among heirs.[1] The *mirasdars* were allowed no special consideration in fixing the assessment, and the old customary deference to caste and position, which in the North-Western Provinces made for great inequalities in the payments of similar fields or even villages, was summarily swept aside. Such action was justified by the laws of political economy, for to permit differential assessment rates on such grounds would create 'different rates of profit on capital employed in agriculture' and so 'would interfere with its natural and most advantageous distribution'. Capital would be attracted away from cultivated lands to the lowly-assessed waste of villages where the inhabitants happened to be poor agriculturists; and 'by enabling the latter to meet the Government demand without the application of the same degree of capital and skill required in the case of the better cultivated villages, it would foster in the former a slovenly and unremunerative mode of husbandry'.[2] By maintaining joint proprietorship and joint revenue management, and by giving the village

---

[1] J. Thornton, Memorandum, 11 July 1850, paras. 4–9: *P.P.*, 1852–3, vol. lxxv, p. 439. Survey Rules: ibid., pp. 313 et seq.
[2] H. E. Goldsmid, Capt. G. Wingate, and Capt. D. Davidson, Joint Report, 2 Aug. 1847, para. 67: *P.P.*, 1852–3, vol. lxxv, pp. 308–9.

communities the right of pre-emption, the North-Western Provinces' administration had hoped to guard against too rapid social change brought on by the free play of economic forces. Wingate would have none of this. The best safeguard against control of the land by a poverty-stricken peasantry and the excessive subdivision of land was

to afford the greatest possible facilities for its conveyance from one party to another, so that when a cultivator becomes impoverished, and by his inability to cultivate his land properly, deprives the community of the wealth it is capable of producing, the land may get into the hands of some one better able to turn it to advantage. The customs and native revenue systems of India are adverse to such transfers, and it is therefore all the more necessary to adopt measures for giving them effect.[1]

While in the North-Western Provinces the state had interfered hesitantly and gradually with the prevailing forms of Indian society, in Bombay it acted boldly and drastically. An assessment levied authoritatively on each field and payable directly to the Government; the whole complex of native tenures reduced to one simple form of individual occupancy right devolving under the Western law of primogeniture; the assessment regulated to ensure a uniform rate of profit on farming capital instead of leaving a private rent to accrue according to the varying fertility of the soil; these formed a system closest to the Utilitarian ideal. The *ryotwar* system of Munro, intensely conservative in aim, had been transformed into an aggressive instrument of social change.

There remained one serious charge that could be brought against the Bombay system. It could be plausibly maintained that the system inhibited the growth of a capitalist mode of production by setting up a mass of petty peasant proprietors, without capital or position, who were not able to commit themselves beyond an annual engagement, despite the fact that the assessment was guaranteed against enhancement for thirty years. The classical economists, as represented by McCulloch, had always held the view that smallholders were the mark of a primitive type of agriculture, and taught that progress inexorably demanded a capitalist organization em-

---

[1] G. Wingate to E. H. Townsend, Revenue Commissioner, Southern Division, 23 Dec. 1848, para. 13: *P.P.*, 1852–3, vol. lxxv, p. 348.

ploying wage labour as in manufacturing industry. Wingate was ready with an answer to this charge. Firstly, the system of annual engagements or leases permitted the immediate expansion or contraction of cultivation in direct response to the variations in the country's stock of capital. The peasant had all the advantages of a long lease in that his rent was secured against increase for thirty years, while the country enjoyed all the advantages of mobility of capital.[1] Secondly, Wingate held that there were few grounds under any circumstances for anticipating the establishment of a class of wealthy agriculturalists cultivating large farms. And this was not to be regretted; 'for the problem, as to the best distribution of national wealth, has been by no means so satisfactorily solved as to enable us, in my opinion, to pronounce decidedly in favour of one or the other of these systems.'[2] It will be recalled that James Mill had also pronounced in favour of the *ryotwar* settlement, arguing that only the immediate cultivator in India would accumulate capital. James Mill's aberration from what may be regarded as the conventional line of Liberal thought was made into a general issue by his son. In the *Principles of Political Economy* (1848) John Stuart Mill devoted a large section to applauding the merits of peasant proprietorship.[3] Wingate was in fact one of J. S. Mill's most unquestioning disciples. When he came to refute the proposal for a permanent redemption of the land revenue in 1862, he quoted extensively from the *Political Economy*, and gave the most perfect expression to the Utilitarian doctrines on the Indian land revenue.

Rent, in the estimation of modern economists, results from land varying in fertility and advantages of situation, which makes it to be of more value in one place than another. On the more valuable land a greater amount of produce can be raised from the same outlay than on the less valuable land, but as the latter must suffice to remunerate the occupier, the excess of produce yielded by all kinds of land above that of the worst in cultivation constitutes a rent which can have no influence in enhancing the cost of cultivation, as this is determined by the cost of cultivating the least favourably situated land which yields no rent. Rent

---

[1] Joint Report, 2 Aug. 1847, paras. 6–9: *P.P.*, 1852–3, vol. lxxv, pp. 296–7.
[2] Wingate to Townsend, 23 Dec. 1848, para. 8: ibid., p. 347.
[3] A good summary of the whole question is given in Stephen, *The English Utilitarians*, vol. iii, pp. 184–94.

may, therefore, be received entirely by a landlord, or be shared between him and other parties in many different ways, without affecting the cost of agricultural production. . . . The land assessment of India . . . as in the surveyed districts of the Bombay Presidency, is merely a share of the natural rent that the land must yield when in cultivation and has therefore no prejudicial influence upon production. And herein consists its distinction from taxation in any form. The latter raises the price of the commodity taxed, and so interferes with its consumption. Taxes upon imports are usually paid by the consumers, and check trade. Taxes upon exports are usually paid by the producers, and also check trade. Taxes upon income, necessaries, or personal expenditure, all tend to diminish consumption and check trade. But a public revenue derived from rent neither enhances prices nor diminishes consumption. The whole result is, that the rent is shared between the Government and the ostensible landlord but the rent itself is neither greater nor less than it would have been had this division not existed, so that the productive power of the country remains unaffected. And as the amount of rent constantly increases with the progress of society, without any effort on the part of the landholder, it may justly be looked upon as the natural inheritance of the public, and forms beyond all question a most legitimate fund for contributing to the expenses of Government.'[1]

This doctrine, drawn directly from the teaching of the two Mills, was adopted as the official theory of the Indian land revenue. It supplied the principles of assessment, and justified the withholding of a permanent settlement and the denial of freehold rights in land. Although its practical conclusion, that the main tax burden should be laid on the land and commerce be left free, was undoubtedly congenial to the European business interests, these remained wedded to the principles of Cornwallis, and continued to look with distrust on the *ryotwar* and village form of settlement with their authoritarian and un-English character. The East India Company was always sensitive to the persistent criticism of the Manchester textile magnates that the mode of assessment impeded cotton cultivation. Traditional Indian assessment methods had always regulated the demand according to the type of crop under cultivation, and paternalists like Metcalfe saw nothing wrong with the practice of making land under

---

[1] Sir George Wingate, Memorandum regarding Proposals by the Government for the Sale of Waste Lands and the Redemption of the Revenue, 2 May 1862, paras. 6–7: *Selections . . . of Bombay Government*, N.S., vol. cli, pp. 154–5.

the more valuable crops pay at a higher rate. In the (North) Western Provinces the traditional methods tended to be incorporated in the settlements made under Regulation VII, 1822, and were noted by the Home Authorities to persist as late as 1832.[1] In this question London issued peremptory instructions; for it was one in which powerful commercial interests and the rent theory were in agreement. The practice of making land under the more valuable crops, like cotton, tobacco, and sugar, pay a heavier assessment was open to the same objection as a tax levied according to the gross produce. Unlike a tax on rent it raised the cost of production of the produce, enhanced its price, and so placed 'an obstruction in the way of exportation; while the prevention of that enhancement will encourage it and give an impulse to trade'.[2] The only consideration was to be the general productiveness of the soil and not the particular crop being grown. Bentinck accepted this teaching in his Revenue Minute of 2 January 1832, and only Metcalfe questioned the break from native practice.[3] As a corollary of the net-produce principle it was enunciated alongside it, and when the Home Authorities in 1837 issued prohibitory orders against 'this objectionable mode of assessment', they listed nineteen despatches sent since 1822 laying down the correct criterion. These were among the despatches to which James Mill referred in his evidence before the Parliamentary Committee of 1831, when he said that the 'most explicit instructions' had been sent concerning the net-produce principle.[4] The Indian Government under Lord Auckland now promised strict compliance.[5]

The British mercantile community were, however, slow to bow before the teachings of political economy, and continued to believe that cotton cultivation in India was being

---

[1] Revenue Despatch to Bengal, 12 April 1837, para. 33.

[2] Revenue Despatch to Bengal, 15 Feb. 1833, No. 2, para. 42.

[3] Metcalfe, Minute, 29 June 1832: Bengal Revenue Consultations, 27 Dec. 1832, No. 66. Governor-General to Sudder Board of Revenue on Deputation, 7 April 1831, paras. 114–19: *P.P.*, 1831–2, vol. xi, Appendix, pp. 312–13. Also Bentinck, Minute, 2 Jan. 1832, para. 25: Bengal Revenue Consultations, 27 Dec. 1832, No. 48. Written evidence of James Mill; *P.P.*, 1831–2, vol. xi, p. 278.

[4] Revenue Despatch to Bengal, 12 April 1837, para. 35. Evidence of James Mill: *P.P.*, 1831–2, vol. v, p. 364, Qu. 3882–4.

[5] Revenue Letter from Bengal, 12 April 1838.

retarded by the heavy assessment on the soil. In England they voiced their opinions through the British-India Society, which was formed in 1839, with George Thompson as travelling secretary and John Crawfurd as a prominent sponsor. Thompson stumped the country, fiercely denouncing the Indian Government for its land revenue system which, he claimed, was destroying India's resources and causing famine and depopulation. Crawfurd supported him in an impressive pamphlet entitled *An Appeal from the Inhabitants of British India to the Justice of the People of England*.[1] In July 1839 the society held a public meeting in London at which Brougham was persuaded to take the chair. This attack on the Indian authorities, then under a Whig Governor-General, Auckland, was thought serious enough to justify a reply from the *Edinburgh Review*. The number of January 1840 already contained Macaulay's great essay on Clive; but the matter was considered sufficiently important to include another article on the subject of India—a subject which even Macaulay had readily confessed was 'not only insipid but positively distasteful' to the majority of English readers.[2] Ten years earlier, before the Whig accession to power, the *Review* had allowed Crawfurd to publish an unsparing denunciation of the Indian authorities in its pages, almost at the same time as it had published Macaulay's attack on James Mill and the Utilitarians.[3] Now the roles were reversed, and it was Mill's authority to which it made appeal in order to rebut Crawfurd's charges. The *Review* rehearsed the arguments Mill had put forward at the Parliamentary Committee of 1831, showing the advantages of deriving the State revenue from land rent and proving how this left a country's economy unaffected.[4] The identification of the Indian land revenue with rent in the technical sense was supported by quotation from Malthus;

---

[1] Quoted on p. 62.

[2] *Edinburgh Review*, vol. lxx (1839–40), p. 391. Article on 'The Revenue System of British India'.

[3] *Edinburgh Review*, vol. xlvii (1828), p. 134. Article on 'Indian Taxation of Englishmen', attributed to Crawfurd by W. A. Copinger, *Bibliographiana No. 2 On the Authorship of the First Hundred Numbers of the Edinburgh Review* (privately printed at the Priory Press, Manchester, 1895), p. 41.

[4] The passage from Mill quoted by the *Edinburgh Review* is given above, p. 91.

and to show that this was not 'merely a theoretical opinion of certain writers' but 'a doctrine thoroughly understood, and practically acted upon, by the British Government' in India, the *Review* quoted Holt Mackenzie and Bentinck's Minute of 26 September 1832. That the difficult and unattractive topic of the Indian land revenue should have entered the stately pages of the leading organ of English opinion, and that it should be expounded exactly in accordance with Mill's views, was a triumph for his influence on India. It only remained to quote Ricardo to drive home the truth that rent did not influence the price of produce in any manner, and so dismiss as fantastic the British-India Society's charge that the Indian land revenue had driven up the import price of Indian cotton, sugar, silk and tobacco. 'The truths on which we have insisted are so elementary', declared the *Review*, 'that we feel ashamed to lay them down with such particularity.' It was necessary to do so because of the widespread misunderstanding which was misleading philanthropists over the Indian problem. The real evils in India were admittedly poverty, moral degradation, spiritual tyranny, and above all ignorance. But the true cure for these—and here the *Review* broke away from Mill to repeat the orthodox Liberal opinion—was education.

When the Commons Committee on the Growth of Cotton in India sat in 1848, with Bright as Chairman, it was evident that Mill's cause was won and his opponents silenced. The committee, of which George Thompson was a prominent member, were unable to counter the classical theory. The great names of the Indian revenue administration rose up to support it; Ross Donelly Mangles, who had served with Bird in the North-Western Provinces, George Wingate of Bombay, and John Sullivan, the former president of the Madras Board of Revenue. All maintained, Mangles actually quoting James Mill, that so long as the land revenue was kept within the limits of rent in the technical sense, it could not possibly affect the costs of cotton production.[1] Even Crawfurd, who had hitherto been so bitter in his criticism

[1] Evidence of Ross D. Mangles: *P.P.*, 1847–8. vol. ix, pp. 282, 386, Qu. 3383, 3652. Letter of G. Wingate: ibid., p. 333. Evidence of J. Sullivan: ibid., p. 397, Qu. 4532.

of the Indian revenue system, recanted his earlier views and gave his assent to Mill's theory.[1] All the committee could suggest was that European control over the subordinate revenue officials was so difficult that the proper limits of the assessment were often in practice exceeded. It could not even maintain the opinion, common in mercantile circles, that the assessment differentiated unfavourably against land cultivated with cotton; F. W. Prideaux, the assistant examiner in charge of the Revenue branch, placing before the committee the despatch of 1837 that has already been noticed.[2]

Not only, however, did the Ricardian theory of rent serve to prevent a perpetual limitation of the assessment, but it also encouraged an attitude which saw no harm in taking an exceedingly high proportion of the land rental as revenue. This may be illustrated by the views of such a man as Sir Edward Ryan, a typical Liberal of the eighteen-thirties and a close friend of Macaulay, but certainly no doctrinaire Utilitarian. In a letter to Bentinck in 1832 he wrote:

I think the view (and here the Political economists differ from each other) which Mill long ago took in his treatise and which he takes again in his evidence before the house, is the true one, that revenue derived from the *rent* of land does not effect [*sic*] the industry of the Country and that of all sources of revenue it is best adapted to supply the exigencies of the state. I need not say that the truth of the proposition rests entirely upon the correctness of the theory of rent long ago promulgated by West and Malthus—namely that *rent* is the surplus of the produce of land after replacing the capital expended on its cultivation with the ordinary profits of stock—so that if the whole rent of land were taken by the state it would not diminish in any way the profits of the Cultivator. It is obvious of course that under a permanent settlement with an increase of population, the rent of land must rise, —this increase the Zemindar now possesses in Bengal instead of the Government, the result of which is that the Revenue derived from land is only 13,500,000 while the gross revenue . . . is 22,000,000. The difference between the two sums is raised as I believe by a tax on the productive industry of the country in the shape of customs, transit duties, etc. which but for a permanent settlement might eventually have been abandoned. . . . If the whole of the Revenue cannot be derived from rent, it would still be desirable for the Govt. to

1 Evidence of John Crawfurd: *P.P.*, 1847–8, vol. ix, p. 358, Qu. 4132.
2 Ibid., pp. 45–46, Qu. 611. See p. 129, n. 4.

appropriate as large a portion of the rent in the unsettled Provinces as they can with a just consideration of the rights of *all*.[1]

The excessiveness of the demand was later recognized, but that it was not obvious in the pre-Mutiny era to some of the most intelligent and gifted revenue officers that were ever to serve the British administration, must, in some part at least, be laid at the door of the Utilitarian political economy. The constant view held by the Home Authorities under James Mill's influence was that expressed in the Revenue Despatch to Madras of 12 December 1821. In the belief that they were inculcating a principle of moderation, the Home Authorities argued that, since minute accuracy could not be obtained in calculating the assessment, 'we shall avoid all material evil, if the surplus produce (i.e. the whole rent of the land) is, in all cases, made the utmost extent of our demand'. With this view they had opposed the reduction of the assessment standard in the North-Western Provinces to two-thirds of the rental assets, as sanctioned by Bentinck.[2] Yet the Saharanpur Rules of 1855 recognized that even Bentinck's standard was still excessive: 'two-thirds, or 66 per cent., is a larger proportion of the *real* average assets than can ordinarily be paid by proprietors, or communities, in a long course of years.'[3] The standard was accordingly reduced to half the rental assets, and this standard was authorized as the general rule throughout India by Sir Charles Wood in 1864. The Administration Report of the North-Western Provinces for 1882–3 was much more emphatic about the pre-Mutiny assessments:

It is now generally admitted that the proportion of the rental left to the proprietors by the old assessments in the N.W. Provinces was much less than was absolutely necessary to provide for the support of themselves and their families, bad debts, expenses of management, and vicissitudes of season. . . . It is only since the late revision that they have been left a sufficient margin to enable them to live at all and count with certainty on being able to meet their liabilities to the State.[4]

[1] Sir Edward Ryan to Bentinck, 5 July 1832: Bentinck MSS.
[2] Bentinck, Minute, 20 Jan. 1832, para. 57: *Revenue Selections 1822–33*, p. 370. Revenue Despatch to Bengal, 12 April 1837, No. 2, paras. 34–36.
[3] Cited R. C. Dutt, *The Economic History of India in the Victorian Age*, p. 48.
[4] *North-Western Provinces and Oudh Administration Report 1882–83*, p. 46.

In Bombay, also, the theory of rent must be held responsible for blinding the authorities to the high pitch of the government demand. Pringle had maintained the total at the level exacted by the Mahrattas in the anarchic years at the end of their rule. He recommended that the total should be reduced by one-third, but he himself argued the innocuousness of exacting the full rent, and his own assessments, he claimed, represented only 55 per cent. of the net produce or rent.[1] In the desperate attempt before the Mutiny to balance the Indian finances, it was little wonder that his recommendation was disregarded.

The results of Pringle's settlement were depicted in the darkest colours by the Bombay Administrative Report of 1872. Pringle's settlement

had the result of aggravating the evil it had been designed to remove. From the outset it was found impossible to collect anything approaching the full revenue. . . . Every year brought its additions to the accumulated arrears of revenue and the necessity for remission and modification of rates. . . . Every effort, lawful and unlawful, was made to get the utmost out of the wretched peasantry. . . . Numbers abandoned their homes and fled into the neighbouring states. Large tracts were thrown out of cultivation; and in some districts no more than a third of the cultivable area remained in occupation.[2]

These views were reiterated by the Deccan Riots Inquiry Commission of 1878, using the evidence of the authors of the new settlement system, Wingate and Nash.[3] Pringle has probably suffered unduly at their hands, over-assessment being a common feature of all early British revenue settlements. These were based on the demand found prevailing under native governments, the great difference being that they were now levied in cash and not in kind. This feature, together with the precipitous fall in grain prices which it probably caused, resulted in the first assessment-rates being grossly excessive in all regions of India. Munro's settlements failed on these grounds. It is fair to say, however, that the prevailing theory of rent prevented the authorities from

---

[1] See p. 100.
[2] *Bombay Administration Report 1872–73*, pp. 41–42: cited R. D. Choksey, *Economic History of the Bombay Deccan and Karnatak 1818–68*, Poona, 1945, p. 92 n.
[3] *P.P.*, 1878, vol. lviii, p. 236.

realizing the excessiveness of the land revenue demand until bitter experience had forced the truth upon them.

Even then the sharp lessons of practical experience did little to threaten the supremacy of the rent theory. The progressive reduction in the proportion of net produce, or rental assets, to be taken as revenue was merely regarded as a necessary measure for the more effective institution of private property rights. Some doubts were raised as to the validity of the law of rent in Indian conditions, but these were generally brushed aside. The most striking example of this tendency was to be found in J. S. Mill. In his authoritative *Principles of Political Economy* Mill substantially accepted Richard Jones's argument that the Indian *ryot* was a type of cottier-tenant similar in many ways to the Irish peasant. He was neither a wage labourer nor a capitalist farmer, but a peasant raising his subsistence from the soil by his own labour and stock. His rent in consequence did not follow the ordinary workings of economic law. In classical political economy the rent of a capitalist farmer was determined by the competition of capital, the size of the population, and the varying fertility of the soil. The competition of capital decided the prevailing rate of profit; and the size of the population determined the demand for agricultural produce and so the amount of capital to be employed in agriculture. Because of the tendency of all capital to earn a uniform rate of profit, anything that was earned above the prevailing rate of profit, by virtue of the varying fertility of the soil, was rent. Rent could be measured from either the extensive or intensive margin, where capital returned only the ordinary rate of profit; that is, from the worst quality of soil in cultivation or from the last dose of capital on any quality of soil. Mill expressly acknowledged that cottier-rent was not determined in this way. Instead it was decided directly by the proportion between population and land, rather than between population and capital. The regulating factor was not the competition of capitals but the competition of tenants for land. 'The effect, therefore, of this tenure is to bring the principle of population to act directly on the land, and not, as in England, on capital.'[1] In other words, a capitalist farmer would only pay as rent that

[1] J. S. Mill, *Principles of Political Economy*, p. 319.

surplus which the land yielded above the prevailing rate of profit; whereas the cottier, forced to cultivate land as the only means of livelihood, would pay as rent almost all the produce except the bare amount necessary for subsistence, if the competition for land were sufficiently severe. Mill agreed with Jones that, because of the traditional monopoly of land-ownership by the sovereign in India, payments for land had never been regulated by competition but by the mere will of the ruler, although modified to some extent by custom. The British Government had lowered the rapacious demand it had found in existence; but in the greater part of British India, where it engaged directly with the peasant, it had continued to determine its 'rent' at its own discretion rather than put up the land to competition. The *ryot* tenure under British rule was therefore a modified and improved type of cottier tenancy.[1] But whether the *ryot* payments were determined by competition, or custom, or the will of the ruler, Mill had admitted that they were in no sense economic rents in the meaning of the classical economy. It was remarkable that, despite this admission, Mill should still continue to assert elsewhere the doctrines of his father concerning India. In his anonymously published *Memorandum of the Improvements in the Administration of India during the Last Thirty Years* (1858) he was still maintaining that the land revenue formed a portion of rent in the classical sense, and that therefore the people of India could be said to be so far untaxed:

Nearly two-thirds of the revenue of India consists of the rent of land. So far as this resource extends in any country, the public necessities of the country may be said to be provided for, at no expense to the people at large. Where the original right of the State to the land of the country has been reserved, and its natural, but no more than natural, rent made available to meet the public expenditure, the people may be said to be so far untaxed: because the Government only takes from them as a tax, what they would otherwise have paid as a rent to a private landlord. This proposition undoubtedly requires modification in the case of a ryot or peasant cultivating his own land; but even in his case, if the Government demand does not exceed the amount which the land could pay as rent if let to a solvent tenant (that is, the price of its

---

[1] J. S. Mill, *Political Economy*, pp. 324–8.

peculiar advantages of fertility or situation), the Government only reserves to itself, instead of conceding to the cultivator, the profit of a kind of natural monopoly, leaving to him the same reward of his labour and capital which is obtained by the remainder of the industrious population. Any amount whatever of revenue, therefore, derived from the rent of land, cannot be regarded, generally speaking, as a burthen on the tax-paying community.[1]

Relying on J. S. Mill's authority, leading revenue experts like Wingate constantly repeated these assertions. They were employed, it will be remembered, against the proposal of a permanent settlement and in favour of preserving the right of the State to the 'unearned increment' of the land. They were similarly used to deny the claim that the price of Indian raw cotton was affected by the weight of the revenue demand, although J. S. Mill had acknowledged that a cottier-type rent could enter as an element in price.[2] The matter is the more remarkable in the case of Wingate since he was one of the authors of the Bombay revenue system which explicitly refused to use any theoretical standard to determine the assessment. Yet Wingate continued to assert, without a shred of actual evidence, that the assessment was a share of rent in its classical sense. The passage from J. S. Mill's *Memorandum*, together with supporting quotations from Henry Fawcett, was reproduced by Sir John Strachey in his book *India*; and this remained a semi-official handbook for more than twenty years after its publication in 1888.[3]

The law of rent was never in fact to be dethroned as the general explanation of the Indian land revenue. The standard of assessment remained at one-half of the rental assets in the United Provinces, the Punjab, and Central Provinces, and at one-half of the net produce in the *ryotwar* areas of Madras, until the nineteen-twenties. Moreover, the official assumption continued to be that the rental assets (viz. rents actually or hypothetically paid) could be identified with economic rent in the strict sense. Sir Edward Maclagan, in the 1909 edition of the *Imperial Gazetteer of India*, still

---

[1] [J. S. Mill], *Memorandum of the Improvements in the Administration of India during the Last Thirty Years* (1858), pp. 20–21. For Mill's authorship, cf. MacMinn, &c. (ed.), *Bibliography of the Published Writings of J. S. Mill*.

[2] J. S. Mill, *Political Economy*, p. 481.

[3] Sir John Strachey, *India*, pp. 75–77. The book went into its 4th edition in 1911.

continued to defend the land revenue on this ground; although he was aware of the caution of contemporary economists over taxation of rent, admitted that custom rather than competition was still a cardinal feature of India, and knew of Indian economists who argued that the State exacted a rack-rent.[1] The maintenance of the rent theory until so late a date can be explained on practical grounds. It suffered a temporary eclipse in the eighteen-sixties, when the disruption caused by the Mutiny and subsequent famine in the North-Western Provinces enabled the protagonists of the agricultural community—whether favouring the landed aristocracy or the peasantry—to raise again the question of a permanent assessment. But the eclipse was only temporary. The price rise of the eighteen-sixties and the later fall in the sterling value of the rupee changed the Government of India's mind towards relinquishing future enhancements of land revenue. For a time it continued to uphold a policy of moderation on reassessment, but when the famines and the agrarian unrest of the seventies were past there was a further hardening in its attitude. Faced by the fresh financial difficulties caused by the Second Afghan War, and fortified by the opinion of the 1880 Famine Commission that the land revenue had no connexion with the famines of the seventies, the Government decreed that its right to exact a half-share of the rental assets or net produce should be stringently enforced. Under the influence of men like Sir Edward Buck and Sir Denzil Ibbetson, an attempt was made after 1886 to shorten the periods of settlement so that the revenue demand could be raised more quickly, and it was only the opposition of the India Office which defeated this attempt.[2] The school of revenue officials represented by Buck and Ibbetson took the view that agrarian poverty and indebtedness were not caused by the high pitch of the revenue demand. In fact a low-pitched demand, they thought, encouraged improvidence and careless farming and so directly contributed to indebtedness and lack of resistance to famine. A reduction

---

[1] *Imperial Gazetteer of India. The Indian Empire*, vol. iv, 1909 edn., chap. vii, p. 234.
[2] Minute of Sir J. O. Miller: Government of India, Department of Revenue and Agriculture, File No. 90 of 1909, p. 21.

of the assessment would merely result in extending the chain of parasitic rent-receivers who intervened between the State and the cultivator. This attitude, it has been said, can be explained on practical grounds: the financial position of the Government, the absence of major famine between 1880 and 1896, and the desire to benefit the revenues from the rise in land values due to irrigation and railway developments. But there were also deeper convictions involved. J. S. Mill's support of the Land Tenure Reform Association, in its campaign in England to promote his scheme for taxing the 'unearned increment' of land, did much to prolong the life of the rent theory. Furthermore, Buck and Ibbetson were characteristic of a school of British officials which continued to press, until the end of the nineteenth century, for a policy of cold administrative efficiency and the uncompromising application of the truths of political economy, rejecting on principle all appeals founded on sentiment or popular preju-dice.[1] It was they who upheld most faithfully the ideas of James Mill and the early Benthamites, and it was fitting that the rent theory should find among them its last con-vinced adherents.

[1] See pp. 281 *et seq.*

III

LAW AND GOVERNMENT

1. *The Reform of the Administration*

THE form of taxation was but one of the three component elements which in James Mill's analysis determined the degree of progress achieved by any given political society. The two other elements were the form of law and the form of government. In India these latter two were so intimately connected that they cannot be discussed apart.

Bentham's ambition to be the law-giver of India, the nature of his ideas, and the growth of their influence over the Indian administration, have already been touched upon.[1] His doctrines naturally first asserted themselves as a criticism of the existing order. That order had been founded by Cornwallis, and had survived with little modification in the vast area of northern India subject to the Bengal Presidency. In Madras, however, it had been altered in important directions by Munro. Setting out with the aim of substituting the rule of law for the rule of personal discretion, Cornwallis had sought to embody the commands of government in formal legislative acts, and entrust their administration to an independent judiciary. Such a system, he hoped, would constitute a secure foundation for private property and personal rights and would also establish a sure defence against the abuse of executive power. He had remodelled the administration accordingly. Stripping the head of the district executive, the collector, of all judicial and police powers, he appointed for each district a European judge who combined the office of civil judge with that of criminal magistrate. To assist in the disposal of the smaller civil cases various grades of 'native commissioner' were recruited from among Indians. Over the district judges were placed Provincial Courts of Appeal, which heard original suits of large amount as well as civil appeals from the decisions of the district judges. At the

[1] See pp. 50, 60–75.

same time the provincial courts performed the function of courts of circuit, trying the more serious criminal cases and hearing appeals from the decisions of the district judge in his capacity as criminal magistrate. The armed retainers of the great *zemindars* were disbanded and an entirely governmental police force was set up, grouped into subdistricts or *thanas* under the general supervision of the district judge. Standing at the apex of the whole judicial system was the chief civil and criminal court, the *Sadr Diwani and Nizamat Adalat* at Calcutta.[1] Filled with admiration for such a system founded on the 'principles of the British constitution', Wellesley ordered its introduction into Madras before he left India in 1805. But here it was to encounter the hostility of Munro and the paternalist school. Munro's charges against it were directed against its wholly artificial and foreign character. He saw it as a system which set aside the immemorial institutions of the people, excluded them from all share in the settlement of their own disputes, and substituted an incomprehensible technical form of law in every way unsuited to their needs. Above all, it destroyed the simple intelligibility of the Indian political tradition in which the *hakim* or ruler invariably bore the sword of justice in his own person. By taking from the collector all judicial and police powers, the one visible representative of government was left powerless to punish crime and redress wrong; and by confiding the sole administration of justice to distant courts presided over by foreigners and employing a highly technical procedure, the peasant was in effect deprived of justice.

Munro's remedies were to restore the jurisdiction of the village *panchayets*, or customary tribunals, composed of village elders; to invest the village headman with limited powers in petty civil and criminal cases; to appoint new grades of Indian 'native judges' with greatly extended jurisdiction; and to limit the right of appeal from the lower courts. These measures he succeeded in carrying into effect, between 1814 and 1816, as part of his general aim to restore the everyday

---

[1] It will be remembered that the Company's *Sadr* Courts in the three Presidency towns were altogether distinct from the Supreme Courts set up by the Crown. The Supreme Courts had jurisdiction only within the limits of the Presidency towns, except for cases involving Europeans.

THE JUDICIAL AND ADMINISTRATIVE STRUCTURE OF THE BENGAL PRESIDENCY

(1) *On Bentinck's arrival in* 1828

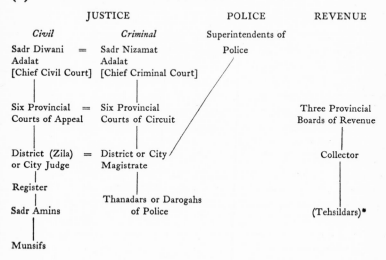

(2) *After Regulation I of* 1829

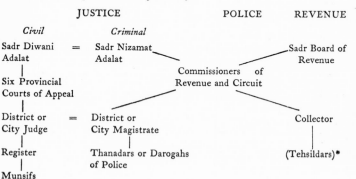

= denotes that offices are united.

* denotes in Upper Provinces only.

(3) *After the Reforms of* 1831

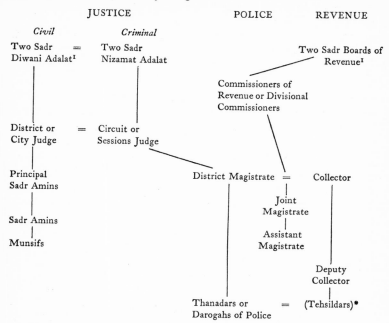

JUSTICE   POLICE   REVENUE

Civil   *Criminal*

Two Sadr = Two Sadr   Two Sadr Boards of
Diwani Adalat[1]   Nizamat Adalat   Revenue[1]

Commissioners of
Revenue or Divisional
Commissioners

District or = Circuit or
City Judge   Sessions Judge

Principal   District Magistrate = Collector
Sadr Amins

Joint
Magistrate

Sadr Amins

Assistant
Magistrate

Munsifs

Deputy
Collector

Thanadars or = (Tehsildars)*
Darogahs of Police

(*Note: The Provincial Courts of Appeal were not finally abolished until* 1833)

Diagram illustrating the changes in the administrative and judicial system in the
Bengal Presidency, 1829–31

administration of civil justice into the hands of the people.
Finally, Munro ended the rigid separation of powers by
which the judiciary was exalted at the expense of the executive. At the district level the executive arm was now given
paramount influence and authority, by vesting in the collector summary powers to decide boundary and rent disputes, and by transferring to him the office of magistrate and
the function of local chief of police.[2] All local governmental
powers were thus united in a single hand. The importance

---

[1] One for Western, one for Lower Provinces.

[2] For Munro's reforms, see *Selections of Papers from the Records at the East-India
House relating to the Revenue, Police, and Civil and Criminal Justice under the
Company's Government in India*, vol. ii (1820), pp. 236 et seq. The essential points
are outlined in Munro's letter to the Madras Government, 24 Dec. 1814; ibid.
p. 292, and cited Gleig, *Munro*, vol. i, pp. 417–23. Also Madras Regulations, iv–
xii, 1816.

of the collector's office was additionally heightened by the fact that the Madras district was of far greater size than its Bengal counterpart, and was large enough to be split into subdivisions (*talukas*) under sub-collectors.[1] Ranged into a clear chain of command proceeding from the collector, the personal semi-military organization of the Madras district stood in contrast to the divided and impersonal administrative system of Bengal. The Madras collector was answerable directly to the Board of Revenue at the seat of government, while in Bengal three Provincial Boards of Revenue interposed, exercising an impersonal control by correspondence rather than relying on personal inspection and direct command. Otherwise the administrative and judicial structure above the district was similar in both Presidencies.

The ultimate logic of paternalism was, however, for a unitary form of government which allowed of no separation of powers. It was Metcalfe, when Resident of the Delhi Territory from 1811 to 1819, who gave this a practical shape, and who later, as Vice-President of Bentinck's Council, brought the gospel of paternalism to bear upon the administrative reorganization of the Bengal territories. Untrammelled by the Bengal Regulations, whose writ did not run in the Delhi Territory, Metcalfe was free to preserve the Mughal tradition of discretionary government, and with the aid of two or three European assistants to combine in his own person the functions of governor, chief judge, revenue collector, and commander-in-chief. Like Munro, he sought to avoid disturbance of the institutions of the people, and tried as far as possible to let them settle their own disputes through their *panchayets* and headmen.[2] Indeed, by leaving the existing revenue system more or less intact and by refraining from setting up courts of justice outside the city of Delhi, Metcalfe adhered to a much more primitive and patriarchal form of rule than was ever employed at Madras.

[1] After 1803 the Madras Presidency contained about 140,000 sq. miles of territory, and the number of districts has varied from 20 to 27. In 1892 Hunter gave the average size of the district in Madras as 5,646 sq. miles, Bengal 3,224, and the North-Western Provinces and Oudh as 2,194 sq. miles (W. W. Hunter, *The Indian Empire*, p. 516).

[2] For a description of Metcalfe's 'Delhi System', see Percival Spear, *Twilight of the Mughuls*, chap. v.

With the attempt to preserve or revive indigenous institutions the Utilitarians could have little sympathy. Steeped in the conviction of their incurable rottenness, James Mill was loath to see the British power have recourse to archaic Indian practices. His mind leant naturally towards Cornwallis's ideals of substituting the rule of law for that of personal discretion, reducing all law to a written statutory form and confiding its entire administration to a modern system of pure and efficient courts. These would strike at the root of India's troubles, which Mill had ascribed to the threefold evils of unbridled discretionary power, the lack of any certain definition of individual rights, and the prevalence of a largely unwritten body of indigenous law devoid of any clear rule of action. Despite this apparent identity of aim James Mill showed no tender regard for Cornwallis's labours. In his *History*, which ended at 1805, he had not to consider the merits of Munro's contrasting methods. He devoted himself entirely to a sustained attack on Cornwallis. In his judicial reforms he acknowledged that Cornwallis had been prompted by the best of intentions. The idea of containing all law in the Bengal Code of Regulations and of setting up a modern system of courts to administer it deserved the fullest praise. But Cornwallis had suffered from the fatal national prejudice of esteeming the unreformed system of British justice to be the acme of perfection. In transposing it almost unmodified to the Bengal territories he had succeeded merely in wreaking havoc. Without remedying the defects of the uncertain customary laws of India he had laid on the country the additional affliction of the vices of the English system. Indeed, the one merit possessed by Indian judicial practice had been discarded by substituting for its summary and non-technical process 'a mode of procedure loaded with minute formalities, rendered unintelligible, tedious and expensive by technical devices'.[1] So far from defining and protecting existing rights, Cornwallis had thrown all into confusion by vesting an almost absolute property right in the great *zemindars* and leaving all sub-

---

[1] James Mill, *History*, vol. v, p. 425. Cf. Bentham's similar condemnation of transplanting English judicial procedure to Bengal: 'Essay on the Influence of Time and Place in Matters of Legislation', *Works*, vol. i, pp. 187–8.

ordinate interests undefined. The mass of litigation which had ensued from the Permanent Settlement was left to be dealt with by a judicial organization wholly inadequate in scope and arrangement. The length and cost of the judicial process had grown so huge as to be tantamount to a virtual denial of justice and 'a destructive anarchy'. Similarly, in trying to reduce the Hindu and Muslim law into a written form, Cornwallis had proceeded on entirely erroneous lines. Sir William Jones, to whom he had entrusted the task, had been content to assemble a heterogeneous mass of texts, commentaries, and opinions; 'a disorderly compilation of loose, vague, stupid or unintelligible quotations and maxims: selected arbitrarily from books of law, books of devotion, and books of poetry; attended with a commentary which only adds to the mass of absurdity and darkness; a farrago by which nothing is defined, nothing established'.[1] The task was essentially one for the philosophic jurist, who would proceed to adapt the ideal universal law codes, envisaged by Bentham, for the special prejudices and customs of the people of Bengal. An equal chaos prevailed in the penal law, which in its existing form ran counter to all the Benthamite criteria. 'Clearness, certainty, promptitude, cheapness, with penalties nicely adapted to the circumstances of each species of delinquency; . . . in all these, without one exception, the penal law set up by the English in India is defective to a degree that never was surpassed. . .'.[2]

Mill's panacea was threefold: 'an accurate code, an adequate judicial establishment, and a rational code of procedure' would effect 'a complete deliverance'.[3] Now the master code of substantive civil or penal law, which Bentham hoped would require 'little more than manual labour' to adapt to the special circumstances of Bengal, never appeared. Mill could therefore recommend only a written digest of existing law at this stage.[4] But Bentham had devoted himself to an exhaustive study of judicial procedure and organization. The mine of papers which he produced on judicial procedure was dipped into by James Mill and Dumont as editors, and

---

[1] Mill's *History*, vol. v, p. 513.   [2] Ibid., pp. 474–5.   [3] Ibid., p. 521.
[4] Ibid., pp. 432–3. Cf. Mill's evidence, 29 June 1832: *P.P.*, 1831–2, vol. xii, p. 126, Qu. 1060.

finally published by the younger Mill in five volumes under the title of *The Rationale of Judicial Evidence*.[1] For the organization of the judiciary Mill had a much readier source in Bentham's *Draught of a new Plan for the Organization of the Judicial Establishment in France* (1790), and he referred to it as his authority when making his proposals for law reform in the *History*.[2] His immediate plans were for a huge increase in the number of local courts, the adoption of a summary non-technical procedure, and the registration of existing land rights. In a letter to Ram Mohan Roy written about 1828, Bentham described Mill's aims:

For these many years the grand object of his [Mill's] ambition has been to provide for British India, in the room of the abominable existing system, a good system of judicial procedure, with a judicial establishment adequate to the administration of it; and for the composition of it his reliance has all along been, and continues to be, on me. What I have written on these subjects wants little of being complete; so little that were I to die tomorrow, there are those who would be able to put it in order and carry it through the press. What he aims at above all things is—the giving stability and security to landed property in the hands of the greatest number throughout British India—and for this purpose, to ascertain by judicial inquiry, the state of the *customs* of the people in that respect. For this purpose a great *increase* in the number of judicatories, together with the *oral examination* of all parties concerned, a *recordation* of the result will be absolutely necessary; the mode of proceeding as simple as possible, unexpensive and prompt, forming in those respects as complete a contrast as possible with the abominable system of the great Calcutta Judicatory; natives of unmixed blood and half-caste, both of whom could serve on moderate salaries, being on my system, as much employed as possible.[3]

Now the main outlines of this programme—for a straightforward comprehensive digest of law, for a registration of tenurial rights, and for a system of local courts using a simple

---

[1] *An Introductory View of the Rationale of Evidence for the Use of Non-Lawyers as well as Lawyers*, ed. James Mill, n.d. [1810?]. E. Dumont, *Traité des preuves judiciaires; Ouvrage extrait des MSS. de M. Jérémie Bentham . . . par Et. Dumont*, 2 vols., Paris, 1823. *Rationale of Judicial Evidence*, ed. J. S. Mill, 5 vols., London, 1827. Bentham had high hopes of his work on judicial procedure being used in India; cf. Bentham to Ram Mohan Roy, *Works*, vol. x, pp. 590–1: 'But from the influence possessed by Mr. Mill, and the intense anxiety he has been manifesting for some years past for the completion of it, my hopes have in relation to your country been rather sanguine.' [2] Mill, *History*, vol. v, p. 515 n.
[3] Bentham to Ram Mohan Roy, n.d. (*c.* 1827–8): *Works*, vol. x, p. 590.

oral procedure—had widespread support outside the Utilitarian fold. They had long been urged by the school of paternal conservatism led by Munro. Despite their ultimate divergence of spirit and aim, the Utilitarian and paternalist tended to be thrown together in common opposition to Cornwallis's revenue and judicial plan. Metcalfe's 'Delhi system', with its entire absence of a formal administrative organization, and its reliance on the personal capacity of British officers to work informally through existing local institutions, was a passing idyll. Even Metcalfe, for all his angry explosions against the Bengal régime, knew in his heart that his patriarchal rule of Delhi could not be a permanent and universal model. Some more formal administrative arrangements were required, without sacrificing too much of the simpler forms of justice and government characteristic of Indian tradition. The Utilitarians appeared to offer a partial solution; for Bentham's administrative scheme for a modern state exhibited a number of principles cherished by the paternalists. Bentham condemned the Whig addiction to complexity, and its apparatus of check and balance, which in India had led Cornwallis to establish collective boards and to set up the judiciary over against the executive. Instead he taught the virtues of simplicity, with power devolved downwards to assignable individuals through a disciplined chain of command.

Mountstuart Elphinstone's governorship of the Bombay Presidency from 1819 to 1827 supplies an illustration of the way in which paternalism could harmonize with the advanced ideas of Bentham. For the administrative organization of the huge territories annexed to Bombay in 1818 Elphinstone relied almost entirely on Munro's example, adopting the *ryotwar* system of land settlement and the corresponding administrative structure which united the office of magistrate and collector. He favoured the careful gradation of authority in the hands of single officers,[1] and in his appointment of a Superintendent of the Deccan he was advancing towards the later system of divisional commissioners controlling the district officers. Anxious to avoid the

[1] Cf. Elphinstone, 'Report on the Territories conquered from the Peshwa', cited G. W. Forrest, *Official Writings of Mountstuart Elphinstone*, p. 322.

mistakes made by Cornwallis in Bengal, particularly the obliteration of indigenous laws and institutions, Elphinstone sought a means of reconciling the Indian and European forms of government. As the most intellectual and politically advanced of the paternalist group, he was naturally attracted to the solution offered by Bentham: a rationally designed and simple code of laws which would supply a complete instrument of administration and at the same time preserve the customary rights and laws of the people in a written and consistent form. Edward Strachey, his friend at the India House who held the post of assistant examiner responsible for judicial matters, secured for him a present of Bentham's works from the master himself.[1] Elphinstone was 'much struck with the good sense' of Bentham's 'rules for transplanting a system of laws, and some of his maxims regarding the introduction of a foreign government'. 'I have long since changed my irreverent notions of Bentham for great respect and admiration', he confessed.[2] Elphinstone was unable to achieve his ambition of reducing the local Hindu law, both written and customary, into a comprehensive and consistent code; and he had to content himself with a digest of the British Regulation law, whose only difference from the Cornwallis Code was that it included a complete body of criminal law. The Bombay Code of 1827, consisting of twenty-seven consolidatory regulations, certainly has no claim to its title under Bentham's definition of a code; and Macaulay found it valueless in his own work of codification in the eighteen-thirites. But however little it satisfies the Benthamite criteria, its inception was clearly the product of Bentham's influence.[3] James Mill had been 'a sincere trumpeter of Panopticon', Bentham's model penitentiary;

---

[1] Elphinstone to Strachey, 3 Sept. 1820: Colebrooke, *Elphinstone*, vol. ii, p. 115.
[2] Elphinstone to W. Erskine (who was later on the committee which framed the Bombay Code of 1827), 4 Aug. and 1 Nov. 1818; ibid., pp. 45, 51.
[3] Cf. Letter from the Indian Law Commissioners, 2 May 1837, para. 9: printed C. D. Dharker, *Lord Macaulay's Minutes*, p. 262. The minor differences with the law under the Cornwallis Code were all reforms advocated by Bentham. Cf. evidence of Hon. M. S. Elphinstone before Committee of House of Lords, 25 March 1830: *P.P.*, 1830, vol. vi, pp. 154–5: 'There are some minor differences between it [the Bombay Code] and the Bengal code. An admonition is made use of, instead of an oath, in examining witnesses; there is no limit to the interest of money; and there is no imprisonment for debt after a person gives up his property.'

and the prisons constructed at Poona and Ratnagiri, together with the introduction of an improved system of prison discipline, were symbolic of the new current of ideas which the Utilitarians were directing upon Indian administration.[1]

The cause of reform had to await the arrival of Bentinck in 1828 before it was allowed its head. Reform was not, however, prompted solely by the happy conjunction of a reforming Governor-General with the new school of ideas. It was dictated by hard facts. Bentinck was sent out to set the Company's house in order before the issue of the renewal of its Charter came before Parliament; and his immediate tasks were to improve the efficiency of the civil service and to wipe out the annual deficit of $2\frac{1}{2}$ crores of rupees.

Minor modifications in Cornwallis's judicial system were found to be necessary at an early date; and from 1814 the Home Authorities were pressing upon the Bengal Government the need to consider measures similar to those carried out by Munro in the Madras legislation of 1816.[2] It was not, however, until the Mahratta and Burmese wars had been concluded that the question was taken up in earnest. In the interregnum before Bentinck's arrival, the Bengal Government under the direction of two civil servants, Butterworth Bayley and J. H. Harrington, proceeded to consider the proposals first made from London in 1814. In a huge despatch of 1827, running into nearly 300 folio pages, they accepted the need to multiply the number of courts on a vast scale, and for this purpose to overthrow entirely Cornwallis's virtual prohibition of an extensive use of Indians as subordinate judges.[3] They also claimed that a great deal had been done to overcome the length and delays of the judicial process. But they would not contemplate any radical alteration of the Cornwallis structure. They rejected the revival of *panchayets* and the restoration of police powers to

---

[1] See note I, p. 325.

[2] Judicial Despatches to Bengal, 9 Nov. 1814, 8 Dec. 1824.

[3] Judicial Letter from Bengal, 22 Feb. 1827: printed *P.P.*, 1831–2, vol. xii, pp. 235 et seq. By 1821 various amendments had already raised the powers of Indian subordinate judges in Bengal, known as *amins* and *sadr amins*, well above the limits fixed by Cornwallis. Cornwallis had restricted them to hearing suits to the value of 50 rupees. By 1821 this limit had been raised to 300 rupees and in special circumstances to 500 rupees. Cf. W. H. Morley, *The Administration of Justice in British India*, pp. 62–65.

village headmen as a retrograde step, and in particular (although prepared to allow the collector a summary jurisdiction in disputed rent cases) stood firm against any serious infringement of the separation of judicial and executive powers, which formed the keystone of Cornwallis's work. A permanent system for the district ought to envisage, they argued, three separate and distinct officials: the district judge, the magistrate, and the collector.

Bentinck on his arrival in 1828 rapidly came to the conclusion that a much bolder approach was required. He first turned his attention to the functioning of the executive. The failure to make any appreciable headway with the revenue settlement of the Western Provinces under Regulation VII, 1822, was proof to his mind of the existence of a state of affairs bordering on administrative breakdown. Despite the work of the Provincial Boards of Revenue, which conducted a great mass of correspondence with the Supreme Government and the collectors of districts, there was clearly no effective control over the district revenue administration, and no co-ordinating authority to watch over the operation of the judicial and revenue system as a whole. Holt Mackenzie was ready with a scheme for reform.[1] Its essential feature was the abolition of the Provincial Boards, and the setting up of a new form of control over the local executive authorities in the shape of local commissioners, each in charge of a division comprising a number of districts. It was vital to his scheme that the new method of control should be individual and personal. Collective deliberative boards trying to supervise the collectors almost entirely by correspondence had shown themselves powerless to detect or prevent the grossest mismanagement. The executive officials must be placed directly under the eye of a superior controlling officer to whom they would be personally and individually accountable and who in turn would himself be held responsible for their actions. This meant that the territorial division under the new commissioner's command should be no larger than the area he could control by personal inspection. Instead of largely relying on written reports put up by the collectors, as the

---

[1] Holt Mackenzie, Report, n.d.: Enclosure No. 2 in Revenue Letter from Bengal, 10 Dec. 1828, printed in *P.P.*, 1831–2, vol. xii, pp. 385–9.

Provincial Boards had done, the commissioner would go on tour through his division and check the revenue work by personally examining the papers of a certain number of villages in each *pargana* or revenue sub-district. He was, however, to confine himself solely to the work of inspection and checking, and not to undertake any kind of executive duties: 'if we would really establish an efficient system of control, the controlling and executive authorities must be kept distinct'. These ideas went back, of course, to Munro; but they also adhered closely to Bentham's administrative notions—his advocacy of the individual officer as against the collective board, his principle of 'inspectability' and of reducing 'the field of service' to the limits in which personal control could be effectively exercised.

The scheme was widened to deal with part of the judicial problem. The Home Authorities had reproved the complacent view of the Bengal Government, expressed in the Judicial Letter of 1827, that little radical alteration was needed to the Cornwallis system; they had pointed to the figure of 123,651 suits in arrears at the end of 1824 as testimony of the critical position.[1] On the production of Mackenzie's plan for the reform of the executive, Butterworth Bayley now suggested (in 1828) that the judicial position would be eased if the judges of the Provincial Courts of Appeal were relieved by transferring their functions as criminal judges to the new commissioners. He also proposed entrusting the commissioners with the functions of the superintendents of police, whose offices could then be abolished with a beneficial saving to the treasury.[2] He salved his conscience over infringing 'the principles of 1793' by arguing that this union of administrative and judicial functions was taking place in the controlling and not the executive authorities.

[1] Judicial Despatch to Bengal, 23 July 1828, para. 3: *P.P.*, 1831–2, vol. xii, p. 195.

[2] W. B. Bayley, Minute, n.d.: ibid., pp. 404–5. Leaving the police under the wing of the district judge and magistrate, with no further specialized or superior control, proved unsuccessful. Between 1808 and 1810 superintendents of police were appointed, one for Calcutta, Decca, Patna, and Murshidabad, the other for Benares and Bareilly. In 1816 their duties were enlarged and the whole police system confided to their supervision; cf. W. H. Morley, *Administration of Justice in British India*, pp. 76–77.

These proposals of Mackenzie and Bayley gave Metcalfe, as the senior member of the Governor-General's Council, opportunity to voice his strongly-held views. Readily concurring in the substitution of the new commissioners of revenue and circuit for the Provincial Boards, his one regret was that the reform was not to be more complete. He deplored 'the continued separation of the office of judge, magistrate, and collector, the limitation of the judicial powers of the commissioners to criminal trials, and all other parts of the old and new system which tend to produce division in the administration of our rule'.[1] Instead he stood out for a complete union of powers. The best form of government, in the interests of the people, was that which was 'most simple and most free from artificial institutions'; and, in the interests of preserving British dominion, was that which was 'most conducive to a union of powers, and most free from the elements of collision and counteraction'. Such a form of government was also the most economical. The structure he envisaged was military in form. One European officer was to be placed in charge of each district and was to exercise 'all the local powers of judicature, police and revenue in all its branches, having under him native officers entirely subject to his orders'. Districts were to be grouped into divisions on a similar pattern, with each division under a commissioner 'who should exercise the highest powers in all branches of the administration'. In turn the commissioners would be responsible to a board of control at the Presidency. The final supervising authority would be the Supreme Government, 'which should exercise authority in all branches of the administration, including the revising, correcting and altering of judicial decisions, wherever it might deem its interference necessary from good and sufficient cause'. The scheme derived from Metcalfe's experience in the Delhi Territory, and was infused with the emotional attitude of paternalism: 'Every functionary, from the highest to the lowest, ought to strive to make the administration of our Government beneficial and paternal; much, or rather most, would depend on superintendents of districts; and the happiness of the people would be greatly influenced by the degree of benevolence

[1] Metcalfe, Minute, n.d.: *P.P.*, 1831–2, vol. xii, pp. 407–8.

and affection felt by those officers towards them.' Here is to be found the cult of the district officer, the kindly autocrat dwelling among the people, which forms the heart of Metcalfe's outlook and supplies the key to paternalism. From it stemmed the belief that British rule in India could only be rightly carried out by men vested with full undivided powers, acting from personal observation and experience, and linked into a military chain of command.

There was no question, of course, of Metcalfe's ideal of administration being carried into practice. In practical terms he merely lent support to Mackenzie's proposals. The result was that Bentinck sanctioned Mackenzie's scheme for divisional commissioners, himself justifying it on the analogy of Munro's system of collectors and sub-collectors in Madras.[1] By Regulation I, 1829, the Bengal Presidency was partitioned into twenty divisions, each under a commissioner of Revenue and Circuit, and with each division comprising three or four districts. The commissioners replaced the Provincial Boards of Revenue, took over the function of the superintendents of police, and also became judges of circuit and session in place of the Provincial Courts of Appeal. With the abolition of the three Provincial Boards of Revenue, a chief or *Sadr* Board of Revenue was re-established at Calcutta as the controlling authority set over the divisional commissioners.

The measures of 1829 did not complete the chapter of reforms and were to be modified by the subsequent measures of 1831. But it would be well to pause to consider the significance of the establishment of the commissioner system. Admittedly it had no title to novelty. It was the ordinary form of administration for newly acquired territories and derived from the simple forms of military government. The Ceded Provinces of Oudh had been ruled in this fashion from 1801 to 1803. Metcalfe had managed to retain the principle in his government of the Delhi Territory, and in Cuttack, and wherever the Bengal Regulations were not at first extended, it was usual to keep governmental powers united in the hands of commissioners. Yet these had always been regarded as temporary expedients, necessary because of the unsettled

---

[1] Bentinck, Minute, n.d.: *P.P.*, 1831–2, vol. xii, p. 385.

condition of newly annexed country. The commissioner principle was now to be entrenched at the heart of the orthodox form of administration founded by Cornwallis. Admittedly, the commissioners in the Bengal Presidency did not absorb the role of the judiciary and their permanent judicial powers were confined to land revenue questions; but the establishment for each division of the country of a permanent chief, himself part of an ordered administrative hierarchy, was to be of lasting importance. For it was the method which alleviated the weakness inherent in the rule of law when applied to subject territories, and restored to the executive arm a preponderant authority and prestige. The commissioner system formed a principal feature of the administration of the North-Western Provinces under Bird and Thomason, and from there passed on to the Punjab, under the Lawrence brothers, in the perfected form envisaged by Metcalfe. It was introduced into Burma and was later adopted throughout the whole field of British colonial administration. The credit for its establishment must be largely ascribed to the paternalist tradition; but Holt Mackenzie, its final author, spoke for it with all the arguments of Bentham, and it may justly be regarded as one of the signal examples where paternalism blended with the authoritarian wing of Benthamite thought.[1]

The overhaul of the revenue and executive administration cleared the path for a major reform of the judiciary. In November 1829 Butterworth Bayley followed up the ideas put forward in the Judicial Letter of 1827, of which he had been one of the authors.[2] He produced a scheme for dealing with the choking of the courts by arrears of business, proposing a sweeping increase in the number of local courts, and appointing Indian subordinate judges with wider powers for this purpose. By giving the European district judge power to refer all cases below the value of 5,000 rupees to his Indian subordinates, his functions for all practical purposes would be confined to those of an appeal judge. The six Provincial

---

[1] For the Benthamite tone of Mackenzie's language, cf. Mackenzie, Memorandum, Enclosure 'Paper A' in Revenue Letter from Bengal, 10 Dec. 1828 (Board's Copies, vol. 16, ff. 347–8).

[2] W. B. Bayley, Minute, 5 Nov. 1829: *P.P.*, 1831–2, vol. xii, pp. 449–54.

Courts of Appeal would in turn become superfluous and could be abolished; but, in view of the additional burden which would be thrown on the *Sadr* Court at Calcutta, Bayley suggested the establishment of a separate Chief or *Sadr* Court for the Western Provinces at Allahabad. Bayley's scheme agreed with the broad outlines of Bentham's solution—the multiplication of local courts by means of the extensive employment of Indian subordinate judges, and the reduction in the number of stages of appeal.[1] But Bayley's inspiration was not Benthamite. His was rather a practical attempt to expand the judicial establishment at the minimum cost, and to satisfy the Liberal desire of his day for modifying Cornwallis's harsh exclusion of Indians from positions of trust and responsibility. In this respect Bayley's proposals did no more than bring the Bengal Presidency into line with Madras and Bombay.

Bayley reaffirmed his adherence to Cornwallis's ideal of the supremacy of the rule of law, and of its practical corollary, the separation of the judicial and revenue functions. But the majority of the judges of the Calcutta *Sadr* Court saw in his proposal to abolish the Provincial Courts of Appeal, and to vest summary jurisdiction over rent cases in the collector, an impious infringement of the structure and spirit of Cornwallis's hallowed system. It was left to one of their number, Alexander Ross, the avowed 'disciple of the Bentham school of jurisprudence', to proffer the true Benthamite solution. Founding his argument apparently on Bentham's *Draught of a New Plan for the Organization of the Judicial Establishment in France*, he criticized Bayley's scheme as a half-measure which ignored important questions of principle.[2] Bayley had continued the old error of arranging the system of courts according to the monetary value at stake in lawsuits, and had disregarded the important distinction between original and appellate jurisdiction by leaving these functions united in the hands of the district judge. His proposal to set up a separate chief court for the Western Provinces endangered

---

[1] Cf. Bentham to Ram Mohan Roy, cited p. 147. Also 'Draught of a New Plan for the Organization of the Judicial Establishment in France', *Works*, vol. iv, p. 328. 'Constitutional Code', *Works*, vol. ix, p. 469.

[2] A. Ross, Minute, n.d.: *P.P.*, 1831–2, vol. xii, pp. 458–70.

the uniformity of judicial interpretation. On principle it was preferable to have only one high court; and the problem created by the extra volume of work thrown upon the existing *Sadr* Court, because of the abolition of the Provincial Courts of Appeal, might easily be met by increasing the number of *sadr* judges.

Instead of elaborating the arguments on these points Ross passed into a sketch of the ideal revenue and judicial administration as he conceived it. The contrast with Metcalfe's scheme is so marked as to symbolize a rival political philosophy. Metcalfe had contended for an administration almost military in form, and on the plea of unity, simplicity, and the need for the intervention of the protecting arm of the State in native society, one stream of Utilitarian opinion was ready to accept some such authoritarian framework. With this view Ross broke sharply; and in his insistence on the supremacy of the rule of law he was doubtless in the more orthodox Utilitarian tradition. The crucial question was the union or separation of revenue and judicial powers; and to Ross's mind there could be no doubt that, not only must they be separated, but the revenue must be made firmly subordinate to the judicial. However much he might oppose the Cornwallis structure and the dead weight of administrative traditionalism it had come to represent, he was in fact contending for its vital creed. And inasmuch as the main current of Utilitarian opinion swung away from the bureaucratic authoritarianism of Bentham and inclined towards liberalism, Ross was the more orthodox in demanding not the destruction, but the remodelling and refurbishing of the structure built by Cornwallis.

His actual proposals for the internal government of the Bengal territories are striking parallels of Bentham's ideas. Like Bentham, Ross proposed a division of the country into equal administrative areas. His unit was to be a 'district' with some 100,000 inhabitants, and these 'districts' were to be grouped in tens to form *zillahs*. In every district there was to be a court of primary jurisdiction, the *munsif*'s court; in every *zila* a superior court of primary jurisdiction, the *sadr amin*'s court; and supervising and hearing appeals from these primary courts a *zila* court of appeal. The courts of primary jurisdiction were to be 'omnicompetent', 'empowered to receive and try, in the first instance, suits of all descriptions and for any amounts'. Plaintiffs had the option of initiating their suits in the *munsif*'s court close at hand, or in the *sadr amin*'s court, which was more distant but had the advantage of a judge with superior qualifications; and defendants were generally to have a similar option to choose the court where they were to appear. This, in Bentham's terminology, would provide for 'intercommunity of jurisdiction'.[1] The *zila* court of appeal, presided over by a European judge, was also to be omnicompetent in its appellate jurisdiction, and its decisions were to be final; its proceedings being only subject to revision by the *Sadr* Court at the Presidency. The Indian subordinate judges—the *munsifs* and *sadr amins* —would be liberally paid to raise them above all corrupt temptation. There would be no fees on the institution of suits, costs being paid by the losing party; and every person would have the option of pleading in person or by means of a professional pleader. Criminal justice was to be administered on the same basis as the organization of civil justice. The existing *thanadar* principle was to be followed, native police officers exercising petty criminal jurisdiction. In each *zila* there was to be a separate magistrate, appeal from whom would lie to the judge of the *zila* court of appeal. Alongside this judicial system was to be a much-attenuated revenue arm. In the Lower or permanently-settled Provinces there was to be a collector for every two *zilas*, and in the Western Provinces two collectors for every *zila*. They were to be divested of all judicial powers and functions, and even of the work of forming revenue settlements, which was to be confided to special settlement commissioners. Ross believed that a procedure which dispensed with all minutiae and granted long leases would rapidly complete the work of settlement. The collector would in fact be reduced to the status his name implied, a mere collector of revenue; and as such he had no need to be controlled by commissioners of revenue or provincial boards. He was to be paid a salary of 1,000 rupees, which would be no more than that of the native *sadr amin*, only two-thirds of that of the *zila* magis-

[1] See note J, p. 325.

trate, and a mere third of that paid to the judge of the *zila* court of appeal. Nothing could be more symbolic of the new dispensation.

The judicial part of Ross's scheme clearly follows Bentham's plan. Bentham's three grades of court—the parish or canton court, and the district court, both exercising only original jurisdiction; and above them a provincial court of appeal—closely resemble Ross's arrangement.[1] They were likewise to be omnicompetent, without institution fees or stamp duties, and provided with 'intercommunity of jurisdiction'. Certainly Bentham's attempt to achieve only a single stage of appeal and a general uniformity in the interpretation of the law caused him considerable hesitation over an intermediate appellate court, such as his proposed provincial court of appeal;[2] and Ross's scheme would have left the Bengal Presidency with fifty-two such courts of final appellate jurisdiction, subject merely to a revision of proceedings by the *Sadr* Court. The exact details are not so important, however, as the manner in which Ross used the Benthamite teaching. Bentham had imagined his judiciary as the close partner of a strong executive, but Ross rejected this conception. To him the great instrument of social change was not to be executive power but solely the rule of law itself. Made swift, certain and efficient, the law could of itself, by its ordinary operation through the courts of judicature, inaugurate the individualist competitive society of the West, in place of the age-old corporate and customary society of India. The whole paternalist view is denied and the administrative structure springing from it. The commissioner and his lieutenant, the district officer, are to be swept away. Given security for the fruits of each man's industry, which a proper system of law would provide, society would best develop of itself, unhampered and unoppressed by the hand of government.

It was left to Holt Mackenzie to trace the permanent solution.[3] He was in broad agreement with Ross over the organization of the judiciary and accepted the main

[1] Cf. Bentham, 'Judicial Establishment', *Works,* vol. iv, p. 323.
[2] See note K, p. 326.
[3] Holt Mackenzie, Minute, 1 Oct. 1830: *P.P.,* 1831–2, vol. viii, pp. 135–60.

Benthamite principles. Like Ross he wanted an absolute divorce of original jurisdiction from the controlling function of appeal, and agreed that the European district judge ought to be relieved entirely from hearing original suits and his work confined simply and solely to hearing appeals. This would enable him to exercise effective control over the Indian subordinate judges, to whom the entire field of original jurisdiction would be made over. Similarly, he accepted with Ross the Benthamite doctrine which condemned the classification of cases and courts according to the monetary sum in dispute; and likewise objected to the existence of two forms of procedure, the regular and the summary.

But where Mackenzie differed profoundly from Ross was in his conception of the role and power of the executive. Ross would have reduced the function of the executive arm to the bare task of tax-collecting, and would have left the European district judge as the symbol of government within the district. In contrast, Metcalfe wanted to perpetuate the principles of his Delhi system and make the executive the sole custodian of authority, with the administration of justice confided to its hands. Mackenzie looked to a solution which gave neither branch a predominant position, but which harmonized the action of each and prevented a destructive conflict between them. In this he reverted to the spirit in which Bentham had envisaged the relations of the judiciary and executive in his *Constitutional Code*. To him, as for Bentham, the most important requirement was that the machine of government as a whole should function with a close unity of purpose and action. Cornwallis's rigid separation of the judicial and revenue arms, leaving no authority short of the Supreme Government itself to co-ordinate their operations and watch over the system as a whole, was a glaring mistake.

In a word to disjoin the several parts of government in a country which is not self-governed, is like placing the different members of the body in charge of different physicians, severally acting with their respective limbs according to individual theory without treatment of other parts, and each holding in his hand the power of destroying life, but helpless to save from the blunders of his brethren. It is to animate the lifeless frame with a plurality of souls.

To confide to the judicial authorities the control of the police, properly a function of the executive government, had been an error 'against all sound principle'; but to leave the judiciary entirely uncontrolled was even more misguided. 'The judicial is the chief branch of the executive administration. Though in free countries it may belong to the people, in a despotism it must belong to the ruler or his delegates; and to put judges arbitrarily over the people, whom the people cannot control, and leave them uncontrolled, is to abandon the most sacred duty of supreme power.' No one could be more bitter as to the effects of the Bengal Regulations when left to the free operation of the courts, without any form of control by the Government. The disastrous effects on the village communities, the mainstay of the social order, had been particularly marked in the Western Provinces. But for all his plea 'for the completest possible unity of purpose throughout all departments' he did not suggest the union of judicial and revenue powers as a permanent system. While vital for the moment in areas where the settlement operations would take many years to complete, it was at best a temporary expedient. Eventually property rights would have to be founded on the careful judgements of proper judicial tribunals, and the revenue officers relieved of their judicial powers.

His proposals to meet the immediate situation embraced a unitary form of administration for the Western Provinces. In each district there was to be a European collector-magistrate in personal command of the subordinate revenue and police officials. Likewise there was to be a European district judge, who would try criminal cases committed for trial by the collector-magistrate and hear civil appeals from the Indian subordinate judges, over whom he would exercise a close 'superintendence, direction, and control'. Above the districts there were to be 'circle' or divisional commissioners, and, in turn above them, three *sadr* or chief commissioners, who would not only supervise the revenue and police work of the divisional commissioners, but would also act as *sadr* or chief judges controlling the district judges and hearing appeals from their decisions. In Bengal and the permanently-settled districts, however, the more permanent form of organization would be introduced, with the offices of *sadr* commissioner and *sadr* judge kept quite separate; but otherwise, both the judiciary and executive were to be constructed on the principle of a hierarchy of individual officers instead of collective bodies. The decisions of the *sadr* judges were to be carefully scrutinized by the Government; and to make this scrutiny and control effective and to give a unity of design to the whole machine, provincial lieutenant-governors should be established for Bengal and the Western Provinces with power to stay court decisions and refer them to the Supreme Government.[1] In this way Mackenzie envisaged a powerful executive arm set alongside the judiciary, but both designed rather as co-ordinate arms of government than as comprising a system of mutual check and counterbalance.

Mackenzie nowhere refers to Bentham's authority—it will be recalled that Bentinck had cautioned him against doing so when Mackenzie had proposed abolishing the usury laws—but it is Bentham's principles which he constantly advocated. In particular, the plea for 'individual' as against 'collective agency' went to the root of Bentham's doctrine. The issue was taken up by the Calcutta Civil Finance Committee, which Bentinck had set up to co-ordinate the financial economies of the three Presidencies and of which Mackenzie was the presiding spirit. The committee, on which the representatives of Madras and Bombay, Hill and Bax, were keen champions of the Munro tradition of personal government, fastened upon the suggestion of the Home Authorities that administrative boards were uneconomical and inefficient. The suggestion had probably come originally from James Mill; certainly the Revenue Despatch to Bengal of 18 February 1829, which the committee quoted, bears all the familiar inciseness of Mill's style:

It is a common but trite observation that responsibility is lessened by being divided, and there is, we believe, no doubt that more business can be done by the same number of persons acting separately than in conjunction. If the business of your Revenue Boards is now divided and a distinct portion allotted to each member; then the utility of such division is already practically admitted, and the Board may be deemed

---

1 Mackenzie, Minute, 10 Oct. 1830, paras. 36–41; also Minute, 20 July 1830, para. 21: *P.P.*, 1833, vol. xxv, p. 202.

to exist principally for the purpose of receiving collectively praise or blame for measures, the merit or demerit of which belongs to one of its members. . . .[1]

A further aspect of Cornwallis's constitutional principle of check and balance, the system of boards had been designed in part to prevent the abuse of executive power. Promptitude of executive action had been looked upon as more a defect than a virtue, and it was thought that the danger of hasty and possibly corrupt decisions would be guarded against by making the controlling authorities collective and delibera- tive bodies, bound to record all their proceedings in writing.[2] Mackenzie's Civil Finance Committee struck at these assumptions with the same arguments as Bentham. Not only did collective bodies perform far less work jointly than their members could get through individually, but they suffered equally from the defect that no 'clear and direct responsibility' was exacted from each member. Having already admitted the virtues of the principle of 'individual agency', by re- placing the Provincial Revenue Boards with commissioners of revenue, the Government ought to apply the principle consistently 'by substituting universally single commis- sioners for collective Boards, acting under the immediate control of Government in the superintendence of the officers employed in the administration of the country'.[3]

The greater part of Bayley's and Mackenzie's scheme was accepted by Bentinck and passed into legislation in 1831. The chief measure was the transfer of the criminal jurisdic- tion of the commissioners of revenue to the district judges (Regulation VII, 1831) who in turn relinquished the office of magistrate to the collector. A separate *Sadr* Court was set up for the Western Provinces (despite Ross's protest), and with the extensive new powers given to Indian sub-

[1] Letter from Calcutta Civil Finance Committee, 13 Dec. 1830, para. 2: *P.P.*, 1831–2, vol. viii, Appendix, p. 232. Cf. Holt Mackenzie's unfavourable opinion of boards, Minute, 1 Oct. 1830, para. 43: ibid., p. 149.

[2] Cf. Burke for the Whig view of the advantages of collective boards. Speech on Mr. Fox's East India Bill, 1 Dec. 1783: *Works*, 8th edn., Boston, 1884, vol. ii, p. 502.

[3] Letter of Civil Finance Committee, 13 Dec. 1830, para. 13. Mackenzie's influence over the committee is illustrated by the fact that this phrase is taken unchanged from his Minute, 1 Oct. 1830, para. 42.

ordinate judges, paved the way for the abolition of the Provincial Courts of Appeal. Mackenzie was not so successful, however, in carrying the 'single-seatedness' principle into the superior controlling authorities. Although agreeing to the proposal for *sadr* commissioners for the Western Provinces, each with a specific area under his supervision, Bentinck decided that they should sit as a Board of Revenue when issues of general policy were under consideration. He also refused to unite the superior revenue and judicial authorities of the Western Provinces, setting up instead the separate *Sadr* Court. Mackenzie's proposal to give the Government power to stay the execution of the *Sadr* Court's orders he indignantly rejected; but as a compromise agreed that for the Western Provinces one of the *sadr* commissioners of revenue should sit as a member of the Court when cases touching land revenue policy were heard.[1] The establishment in 1834 of a separate government for the (North) Western Provinces to some extent, however, met Mackenzie's views on the need for a superior co-ordinating authority for the revenue and judicial system as a whole.

The reforms of 1831 completed those of two years earlier. Throughout the Bengal territories the executive was welded into a single chain of command. Admittedly the judiciary was kept distinct, but at the local level the authority of the collector was powerfully reinforced. Exercising the office and dignity of magistrate, with command of police functions and with summary jurisdiction in rent cases, the collector was now more properly termed the district officer. The double institution of the divisional commissioner and district officer permanently modified the Cornwallis structure and supplied the orthodox model for future British colonial administration. The divisional commissioner readily accorded with Bentham's constitutional ideas, but the union of the collector and magistrate commanded no such definite theoretical support. The Utilitarians displayed no consistent attitude. James Mill's opinion is unknown, apart from his common

---

[1] Letter from Secretary to Governor-General, 26 Jan. 1831: *P.P.*, 1831–2, vol. xii, pp. 490–5. Bentinck, Minute, 24 Jan. 1831; *P.P.*, 1831–2, vol. viii, Appendix, pp. 239–40. Letter from Secretary to Governor-General, 15 June 1831, para. 6: Board's Collections, vol. 1353, No. 53665, f. 10.

rejection with Bentham of the division of powers as a constitutional principle. Bentham was certainly not averse to an
officer uniting all executive and judicial functions at the local
level, as the powers of 'Local Headmen' in his *Constitutional
Code* indicate.[1] But it was not a question that could be
readily argued from general principle. Even Holt Mackenzie
admitted the union of judicial and executive functions as a
temporary measure. Its strongest support came from the
Munro tradition, and Bentinck, who had governed Madras
in Munro's time, looked to him as mentor. He urged upon
the Home Authorities, as the best means for improving the
efficiency of the civil service, that they should

confirm and persevere in the system long since recommended by them
to the Madras Government, upon the authority of Sir Thomas
Munro, of uniting the appointments of collector and magistrate, of
destroying the independence of each other of every officer employed in
the same district, of making the collector's a great office, consisting
of deputy collectors and joint magistrates and assistants, subordinate to
one head, and acting upon the same system.[2]

The question of uniting the offices of collector and magistrate proved the issue upon which reforming opinion divided.
While men like Macaulay and Ross, who had been deeply
affected by Bentham's teachings on jurisprudence, stood out
for the supremacy of the rule of law, and the re-energising of
Cornwallis's principles through an efficient system of courts
and procedure, reforming officials of the 'unsettled' provinces, who had been drawn to the authoritarian element in
the Utilitarian doctrines, accepted the administrative tradition of Munro's school. The reforms of 1829 and 1831 were
a victory for the latter, but the long struggle was by no means
concluded. Owing to changes in the Court of Directors the
India House no longer looked with favour upon the Munro
tradition. Although, as late as 1824, the Court was still
pressing upon the Bengal territories to consider the adoption
of Munro's judicial scheme enacted for Madras in 1816, by
1831 it was barely prevented from disallowing Bentinck's
new plan for commissioners of revenue and circuit. Only

---

[1] Cf. James Mill, cited Halévy, *Philosophic Radicalism*, p. 420; Bentham,
'Constitutional Code', *Works*, ix, pp. 612 et seq.

[2] Bentinck, Minute, 10 Nov. 1831, para. 28: *P.P.*, 1831–2, vol. ix, p. 749.

the action of the Board of Control, in overriding the formal dissent of the Court, stopped the definite prohibition of any union of revenue and judicial powers, except as a strictly temporary measure.[1]

On this general issue Ross had to accept at least temporary defeat, and his visionary scheme of administration was in any case as far from practical realities as the contrasting plan of Metcalfe. But his Benthamite criticism of Bayley's proposals for a reformed judiciary was not wasted.[2] In condemning the principle whereby the class of judge to try a suit was determined by the monetary value of the matter at issue, Ross was assailing a practice which all the eloquence and authority of Macaulay as Law Member was to prove powerless to remove. Similarly, his objections to stamp duties on plaints and legal documents and to fees levied on the institution of suits were equally unavailing. Where he did obtain fair success was in managing to sweep away many of the restrictions with which Bayley had proposed to hedge the 'omnicompetence' of Indian subordinate judges, particularly of the lowest grade—the *munsifs*— whom Bayley had tried to limit to suits for personal but not real property. More important was the question of procedure in appeals. Bayley had provided for appeals to be heard by the next superior Indian subordinate judge, allowing a right of special or second appeal to the district judge. Ross attacked this as an infringement of the important Benthamite rule that original and appellate jurisdiction should always be exercised by completely separate judges. Making the decision of a *munsif* appealable to a *sadr amin*, or that of a *sadr amin* to the new rank of Indian judge proposed by Bayley, of principal *sadr amin*, was to make their courts tribunals both of first instance and appeal. Instead appellate jurisdiction should be reserved exclusively for the European district judges, while at the same time they should be freed entirely

---

[1] The Board of Control struck out a paragraph in the Draft Judicial Despatch No. 582 (eventually Judicial Despatch to Bengal, 26 Feb. 1831) and the Court formally recorded their dissent: Appendix Court Minutes, vol. 5, ff. 60–65. Also Judicial Despatch to Bengal, 11 Sept. 1833, paras. 7 et seq.

[2] A. Ross, Minute on Draft Regulation for extending powers of Munsiffs, &c., 31 Jan. 1831: Board's Collections, vol. 1353, No. 53664, ff. 191–216. Also Minute, n.d.: *P.P.*, 1831–2, vol. xii, pp. 458–70.

from hearing original suits in order to devote themselves to a close supervision of the subordinate judges. The final arrangement (embodied in Regulation V, 1831) provided for an extension of the powers of subordinate judges as Bayley had proposed—for *munsifs* power to try suits up to 300 rupees, for *sadr amins* up to 1,000 rupees, and for the newly created principal *sadr amins* up to 5,000 rupees. Appeals from the decisions of all grades of subordinate judge were to lie, as Ross had proposed, direct to the district judge (although a second or special appeal to the *Sadr* Court was allowed from decisions of the principal *sadr amin*). It was a strictly limited success, for no absolute distinction between appellate and original jurisdiction was established. The district judge was still empowered to try any case in first instance if he chose, and he was obliged to do so in the rare suits above 5,000 rupees in value. Ross scored a number of other small points for his master's doctrines, such as the remuneration of *munsifs* by salaries instead of by institution fees on suits or stamp duties, and the removal of many legal formalities encumbering the institution of a suit. Although Ross's objection to establishing a separate *Sadr* Court for the Western Provinces was passed over, his proposal for introducing Bentham's 'single-seatedness' principle into the high court bore fruit. By Regulation IX, 1831, it was declared, subject to certain provisions, 'competent to a single judge of the Court to hold a sitting of the Court on all matters within the cognizance of the Sudder Dewanny Adawlut, and to pass orders or judgement in conformity to the Regulations'.

The chapter of Bengal reforms had its counterpart in the other Presidencies. Both at Madras and Bombay there was a widespread extension in the employment and powers of Indian subordinate judges.[1] Malcolm, as governor of Bombay from 1827 to 1830, showed himself an ardent adherent of the principle of 'individual agency'. The administrative system was assimilated to that of Madras by the appointment of principal and sub-collectors, the number of collectorates having been reduced in number and their size increased. Above them was placed a revenue commissioner and assis-

---

[1] Cf. *Cambridge History of India*, vol. vi, p. 67. Morley, *Administration of Justice in British India*, pp. 86, 108.

tant, while the Southern Mahratta Country was kept under a separate commissioner exercising both revenue and judicial powers. Although Holt Mackenzie did not consider that the system of principal and sub-collectors drew sufficient distinction between executive and controlling functions and wanted the Bengal model of commissioners adopted, the direction of reform was the same. Likewise Malcolm launched an attack on the various boards within the government, and succeeded in abolishing the Military Board.[1]

2. *The Reform of the Superior Government*

So far as it lay in Bentinck's power the subordinate administration had been reformed, and his work undoubtedly led to a marked increase of efficiency. Yet the superior government was still untouched. The powers of the Governor-General in Council and the structure of the subordinate Presidencies had been laid down by Parliament and could only be altered at Westminster. The problem was, however, fully considered in India, and the proposals of the Indian authorities had considerable influence on the new system of government established by the Charter Act of 1833.

The anomalies of the unreformed order were demonstrated in the matter of the Indian high courts. The jurisdiction of the Supreme Courts established by Parliament at the three Presidency towns had never been clearly defined, and the situation had given rise to serious conflicts with the Company's courts, and even with the local governments. A violent and undignified contest between Malcolm and the Chief Justice of Bombay in 1829 made reform imperative. Suggestions were made by the Bengal Government and the judges of the Supreme Court at Calcutta for dovetailing the jurisdiction of the King's and Company's courts, but the most important issue raised was that of legislative powers. It was not merely the existence of two ill-defined jurisdictions, but the fact that two different bodies of law were administered in them, which gave rise to the greatest anomalies. The

[1] Malcolm, Minute, 10 Nov. 1830, para. 114: *P.P.*, 1831–2, vol. xii, p. 517. Letter of Civil Finance Committee, 20 Sept. 1830, para. 4: *P.P.*, 1831–2, vol. viii, p. 183. Malcolm to Bentinck, 2 Dec. 1830: Malcolm, *The Government of India*, Appendix, pp. 178 et seq.

Supreme Court at Calcutta administered generally the Common and Statute Law of England prevailing in 1726 (with any subsequent modifications effected by statutes relating to India), together with such Regulations of the Governor-General in Council as had been registered in the Court. This situation was repeated at the other Presidencies with the difference that each administered its own Regulations. In cases where Hindus or Muslims were defendants they were admittedly entitled to the benefit of their personal law; but the general situation was one of great confusion. The Bengal Government in a letter to the judges suggested that the evil was twofold—the lack of a single legislative authority and the lack of a single law system.[1] The twin problem posed by this correspondence became the central issue in the Charter discussions on the form of the Indian Government. It resulted in the two leading ideas of the Act of 1833; the need for a single omnicompetent legislative and executive authority, realized in the creation of the Government of India and its Legislative Council, and the need for a uniform and codified law system, realized much later and in more fragmentary form in the Indian codes.

These two ideas were put forward semi-officially to Ellenborough at the head of the Board of Control,[2] and were later elaborated in the proceedings of the Calcutta Civil Finance Committee. Its presiding genius, Holt Mackenzie, approached the question of the form of the superior government by taking for his governing principle the distinction between executive and controlling functions.[3] This distinction, it will be recalled, had been constantly employed in the discussion over the Bengal judicial and administrative reforms, both on the establishment of the commissioners of

---

[1] Cf. 'Observations . . . as to the Formation of a Code of Laws', Enclosure in Letter to Government from the Judges of the Supreme Court, 13 Sept. 1830: *P.P.*, 1831, vol. vi, Appendix, p. 579. Letter of Bengal Government, 14 July 1829: ibid., pp. 469–71. Macaulay's description of the confusion of laws is more picturesque. Macaulay, Speech on Charter Act, 10 July 1833: *Complete Works*, vol. xi, p. 579.

[2] In a letter to Bentinck of 19 May 1829 (Bentinck MSS.), Ellenborough, as President of the Board of Control, had asked for suggestions for the future frame of government. He himself was in sympathy with a semi-military form of rule on the lines envisaged by Metcalfe.

[3] Holt Mackenzie, Minute, 20 July 1830: *P.P.*, 1833, vol. xxv, p. 195.

Revenue and Circuit, and on the extension of 'native agency'. The principle had the sanction of Bentham. He had used individual responsibility and inspectability to weld his administrative chain and form the means of exercising control over the executive, in opposition to the Whig method of attenuating executive power and subjecting it to independent checks.[1] The distinction between the functions of execution and control is at the root of Bentham's division of original and appellate jurisdiction; it is the key to his theory of the true use of the jury, and it makes its appearance wherever an office of executive authority is established in his *Constitutional Code*.

Employing this principle Mackenzie stressed the need for a Supreme Government in India, relieved of all executive and local duties, and having as its task 'to superintend, control, and direct the proceedings of the subordinate Governments'. His idea was that the Governor-General and his Council should be entirely freed from the local administration of the Bengal Presidency and invested with a new and more complete authority. The subordinate Presidencies, which for so long had conducted their internal administration more or less independently of the Governor-General, and corresponded directly with the Home Authorities, were accordingly to have their powers closely shorn. Instead of their existing semi-sovereign state, each with a Governor and Council and with powers of legislation, they would simply be territories under lieutenant-governors, without independent legislative, financial, or diplomatic powers.

The function of the subordinate governments being mainly executive in character, the existing councils at each Presidency would be replaced by secretaries of state, each with departmental responsibilities. The subordinate governments were in all things to act 'under the vigorous control of the Governor-General'; their hallmark was to be 'energy and despatch'.

The Governor-General in Council was to be clothed in a new authority; in him was to centre all civil and military power. Relieved of local responsibilities, he would be free to proceed to any part of the country in order to control the

[1] See note L, p. 326.

work of the subordinate governments.[1] As the sole legislative authority he would be assisted by a legislative council, which would draft and enact laws for the whole of British India. There was, however, a difficulty. In one aspect the Governor-General was the head of the whole executive; but viewed in his relation to the subordinate governments and in his character as legislator, his functions were not executive, but deliberative and controlling. How were the functions of deliberation and execution to be distinguished at this level? *Quis custodiet custodem?* It was easy enough to discard the Councils at the subordinate Presidencies; and Mackenzie's first instinct was to do likewise with the Governor-General's Council and replace it with merely a consultative body of departmental heads. But he relented, and his reasoning is significant. There were two problems in his mind. Firstly, there was the need to exercise some form of control over the Governor-General while maintaining his individual responsibility and leaving his executive efficiency unimpaired. Secondly, there was the difficulty of combining executive and legislative functions in a single person or body. Now these problems were also present in Bentham's thought, as part of the wider question of reconciling law as the command of the sovereign and law as the collective expression of the will of the community. The one required a military organization of individual executive authorities; the other required collective deliberation and control. Mackenzie found the solution to the first question in existing practice. The Governor-General would act through his Council, but would retain full power to override it or to act without it. The Council would serve as a restraining influence in the case of an impetuous or inexperienced Governor-General; and in matters of a legislative nature—that is as regarded 'changes of law and system'—it would introduce a 'well-informed caution, a certain sluggishness'. The principle was exactly that of Bentham. In addition to the single-seated judge Bentham had made

---

[1] Bentinck had proposed transferring the seat of the Government to Agra, but the Home Authorities declared such a step illegal. In consequence he abandoned his tour of the Western Provinces after setting out in 1829. In his later tours he had to leave his Council at Calcutta.

provision for a 'quasi-jury' in appeal cases. This was to be a small group of jurors who would form a means of exerting the influence of public opinion over the judge's actions. The 'quasi-jury' would deliver its opinion, but this was not to be binding on the judge.[1] This principle Bentham had also applied to the question of government. He had expressly approved the constitution of the Indian governments, whereby a governor was assisted by the advice of a council and subjected to the influence of its opinion, but was left with full power and responsibility for all decisions.[2]

The second problem, that of providing for the legislative function in India, was to be solved, Mackenzie proposed, by instituting a separate legislative council. In his evidence before the Select Committee of 1832 he expanded this view.[3] It was his conviction that 'the legislative authority should be kept quite distinct from the executive'. The existing practice whereby the same persons exercised both functions was to be regretted, 'for though it be impossible to carry on the executive government of a country if shared by a multitude of persons, yet laws should not ordinarily be enacted without the concurrence of many councillors'. Bentham had solved the problem by providing for a 'multi-seated' legislative and a 'single-seated' executive, the latter kept strictly subordinate to the former. The legislature, although unicameral, was to be governed by certain rules to prevent precipitate legislation. But this separation of legislative and executive functions was not possible in India, and Mackenzie rejected any notion that the extraordinary authority of the Governor-General to legislate in an emergency should be shared with a small council. He maintained that 'the responsibility for the safety of India must always rest on the Governor-General alone, and that the power should be absolute so long as we govern India on the present system'. Ordinarily, however, he was unfavourably impressed with the lack of deliberation with which laws were passed. He suggested a large legislative council, to include representatives of the subordinate govern-

[1] For the quasi-jury see 'Principles of Judicial Procedure', *Works*, vol. ii, pp. 141 et seq. Also 'Constitutional Code', *Works*, vol. ix, pp. 554 et seq.
[2] See note M, p. 326.
[3] Evidence of Holt Mackenzie, 6 March 1832; *P.P.*, 1831-2, vol. ix, pp. 91 et seq.

ments, the judges of the Supreme Court, and nominated Indian members. The dual problem of controlling without impairing the authority of the Governor-General, and of drawing the necessary distinction between executive and legislative functions, was solved on broadly Utilitarian lines. A unified administrative system was to be established with an all-powerful head, the eighteenth-century despot in altered guise; and a degree of control was to be introduced by subjecting the measures of the Governor-General to the deliberation of an executive and a legislative council. Yet there is a lack of rigour and symmetry about Mackenzie's ideas that suggests a qualified assent to the full Benthamite gospel, and his opinions on a codified law system seem to support this view. It was in fact James Mill who was to crystallize these ideas before they took permanent shape in the Charter Act of 1833.

Metcalfe and Hill (the representative of Madras on the Civil Finance Committee) were in agreement with the spirit of these proposals, but it would be false not to see that the outlook of men of the Munro tradition was essentially conservative, while that of Mackenzie was at least potentially more aggressive.[1] The difference lay in the degree of centralization and uniformity envisaged by each. In the strict Utilitarian theory, as Bentham outlined it in his *Constitutional Code*, government proceeded downwards through a chain of command. There was, therefore, a strong tendency to enhance the power of the central authority and to reduce the subordinate agents to mere executants of its will. Mackenzie represented this tendency. On the other hand, Munro, Metcalfe, Malcolm, and Elphinstone favoured the delegation of wide discretionary powers to local agents. This was the basis of Malcolm's plan for a lieutenant-governorship of central India; and it was because he considered that his powers were insufficient that Metcalfe resigned as Lieutenant-Governor of the North-Western Provinces in 1838. They had supported the idea of a single law system and of a code; but again they meant something very different from the Utilitarians. The notion of a compre-

---

[1] Metcalfe, Minute, 18 Oct. 1830: *P.P.*, 1833, vol. xxv, pp. 224 et seq. Hill, Minute, 16 June 1830: ibid., pp. 189 et seq.

hensive body of laws, collected for ready reference into a few volumes, and made easily intelligible in its language and arrangement, was of course of early origin. Cornwallis cherished the idea and attempted to realize it in his Regulations of 1793, which were known as the Cornwallis Code. He also encouraged Sir William Jones to compile a digest of indigenous law. Sir Alexander Johnston, in a letter to Fox in 1806, pursued the notion of a codified body of law for the whole of British India.[1] Munro's school partook of this liberal current of ideas, but their conception of a code was essentially that of a defensive instrument designed to preserve Indian rights and customs against the aggression of European laws and institutions. Hence they favoured local variety and detested uniformity. Elphinstone, who had studied Bentham, who had been responsible for the Bombay Code of 1827, and who could be claimed as the most liberal of his group, took his stand in 1832 over the question of a uniform system. It was far better, he argued, in a country so diverse and little known as India, to have the benefit of three different experiments in administration and law which the existing system of provincial autonomy allowed, than to attempt to force the whole country prematurely into one uniform mould.[2]

Perhaps because he felt that the proposal to relieve the Governor-General from local responsibilities might lessen his effective power, Bentinck would not support the plan to create two new governments for the Bengal Presidency and to sever the local connexion of the Supreme Government with Bengal.[3] Certainly he considered that greater control over the subordinate governments of Madras and Bombay was necessary, and he was in favour of a single army and a single legislative council for the whole of India. But he does not convey the impression of a mind devoted to centralized rule. He did not think it 'desirable that a minute interference with the administration of the subordinate Governments should take place; the interference should be rather of check,

---

[1] *P.P.*, 1831–2, vol. xii, pp. 138 et seq.

[2] Letter of Evidence to Select Committee of 1832: cited Colebrooke, *Elphinstone*, vol. ii, p. 317. Cf. Malcolm, *Political History*, vol. ii, p. 13; Gleig, *Munro*, vol. ii, p. 264.

[3] Bentinck, Minute, 14 Sept. 1831: *P.P.*, 1833, vol. xxv, p. 237.

of a preventive and restraining, than of an active and meddling character. . . . Its business would be to preserve the system as already approved from innovation.' He may have dallied with the scheme of Metcalfe and Holt Mackenzie for lieutenant-governors, without the old councils, and forming part of a hierarchy of individual authorities. But his later views were more cautious and less addicted to change. His refusal to abolish the system of board management in the revenue and other departments was matched by a similar opposition to the abolition of the Councils at the subordinate Presidencies.[1]

The ideas that issued from India during these discussions were those upon which the new political forms of the Charter Act of 1833 were founded.[2] But they came dressed in qualifications, even from Holt Mackenzie, the most radical of Indian authorities. It was left for the reformers seated at the centre of power in England to take up these ideas and champion them in their original untrammelled conception.

In his evidence before the Select Committee of 1832, James Mill had given the Utilitarian blessing to Mackenzie's plan for a Supreme Government divested of all local administrative responsibility, the sole channel of communication with the Home Authorities, and the sole legislative organ. He agreed that the authority of the Supreme Government over the provincial governments should be absolute and unquestioned, and that the latter should be headed merely by lieutenant-governors without councils.[3]

The suggestions for a legislative council and a law commission, which had originated during the discussions of 1829–30 with the judges of the Calcutta Supreme Court, had come, however, in a more questionable shape.[4] All

---

[1] Cf. Bentinck to H. St. G. Tucker (Chairman of the Court of Directors), 11 Aug. 1834: Bentinck MSS.: 'It is quite unintelligible to me, how in a *settled regular* Government, the pure monarchical principle, the institution of so many Anglo-Indian Rajahs can be deemed preferable to a collective and deliberative Council.'

[2] Cf. Charles Grant to Bentinck, 25 Dec. 1833: Bentinck MSS.: 'The papers written by the members of the Civil Finance Committee, and the Judges of the Supreme Court and the members of your Council, and your own Minutes, have furnished invaluable materials of which we have availed ourselves. . . .'

[3] See evidence of James Mill, 21 Feb. 1832: *P.P.*, 1831–2, vol. ix, pp. 42 et seq.

[4] Cf. Sir Edward Ryan (judge of the Calcutta Supreme Court) to Bentinck,

Indian authorities had envisaged the legislative council as necessarily large and varied in composition. It was generally proposed that it should include the members of the Governor-General's Council, the judges of the Supreme and *Sadr* Courts at Calcutta, some official representatives from the other Presidencies, and possibly a number of unofficial native gentlemen. Holt Mackenzie had favoured such a plan in the belief that a legislative body should be made as broad and as popular in composition as possible. James Mill brought to these ideas the rigorous precision and authoritarian cast of his mind and political principles.[1] Firstly, in keeping with Bentham's constitutional theory, he condemned the notion of the judiciary having any share in the making of laws, as had been intended in the proposal to admit the judges to the legislative council. The judiciary must be kept as a strictly separate and subordinate arm. Further, he rejected all idea of popular representation through a large and varied body. The fashioning of the legislative organ is conceived by him on the most absolute lines. The legislative council was to be omnipotent, subject merely to the control of the Home Authorities. So far from being a large body, in order to secure the widest representation of opinion, it 'should consist of so small a number of persons as offer a reasonable prospect of their having all the requisite knowledge among them'. The argument against numbers was the argument against boards, that they lessened responsibility, or, as Mill termed it, that they diminished 'adequate motives for fidelity; by fidelity meaning not only honesty, but diligence also in the execution of the trust'. Public opinion would indeed exercise greater influence over the members if they were few rather than many. Beyond this consideration lies the older conception of the legislator. His pedigree is that of the eighteenth-century *philosophe*, and it reaches back to Solon. Legislation is a science, a task for the ablest philosophic mind, a subject for dispassionate study

13 Jan. 1831: Bentinck MSS. For Ryan's proposals for a codified law system, see 'Some Observations Suggested by the Governor-General in Council as to the Formation of a Code of Laws for the British Territories in the East Indies', signed by Sir C. Grey and Sir E. Ryan; Enclosure No. 2 in Letter from judges of Supreme Court, 13 Sept. 1830: *P.P.*, 1831, vol. vi, Appendix, p. 579.

[1] Evidence of James Mill, 21 Feb. 1832: *P.P.*, 1831–2, vol. ix, p. 45, Qu. 345.

and expert knowledge, and not the sport of political passion or of popular and ignorant prejudice.[1] Bentham found himself more at home with the enlightened despots than turbulent political assemblies, for is not the legislator in some sense necessarily single and despotic?

Undoubtedly Mill took his ideas of the legislative process from Bentham. In the *Codification Proposal* of 1822 Bentham had himself sought to combine his authoritarian and democratic views; and his solution for drafting a complete law system was similar to that devised in the *Constitutional Code* for regulating the entire relations of the government and the governed. Control was not to be purchased at the expense of efficiency. Indeed control was always enhanced by vesting power in a single and known individual rather than an impersonal collective tribunal. For this reason, and in the interests of the consistency and symmetry of a codified law system, 'the greatest happiness of the greatest number requires—that every draught . . . be from beginning to end, if possible, the work of a single hand. *Hands not more than one.*'[2] Bentham had pursued this idea in his arrangements for a fully democratic legislative assembly in his *Constitutional Code*. Here he had to reconcile the right of the individual member to initiate legislation with the need to make all legislation conform to its scientific criteria. This Bentham achieved by providing for a legislation minister through whom all legislative measures had to pass. It was his task not only to attend to the intrinsic qualities of their drafting, but also to ensure that they could be accommodated harmoniously into the existing body of codes.[3] Later John Stuart Mill, probably impressed with the work of the Indian Law Commission and Legislative Council, was to advocate the establishment of a Legislative Commission to remedy the defects of laws enacted by a numerous assembly.[4]

The elder Mill was, therefore, in the best Benthamite tradition when he argued for a small, expert body rather than a numerous legislative assembly for India. Since the political

---

[1] See note N, p. 327.   [2] *Works*, vol. iv, p. 554.
[3] 'Constitutional Code', *Works*, vol. ix, pp. 430–3.
[4] J. S. Mill, 'Representative Government', *Utilitarianism, Liberty, and Representative Government* (Everyman edn.), pp. 235–9.

and moral condition of India put popular representation out of the question, the problem was to form a body as small as was consistent with requisite knowledge. He proposed a commission of four members—one to have special knowledge of English law, to prevent collision with parliamentary enactments; one to be an official of the Company with long experience of India; one an educated Indian with special knowledge of the customs and feelings of the people; and finally, a master-mind, 'a person thoroughly versed in the philosophy of man and of government'.[1] The conception was obvious. A disciple of Bentham's jurisprudence was to frame a code for India, helped where necessary by the local and detailed knowledge of an English lawyer, an English Company official, and a native gentleman. Again the inspiration was that of Bentham. The law-giver like Solon was to be a foreigner, versed in the universal principles of legislation, and free from local prejudice and interest.[2] Local knowledge was of minor importance. The science of legislation had its universal immutable laws as valid as those of the physical sciences; and it was knowledge of these great philosophic principles that was the prerequisite qualification of the legislator. To adjust these principles to suit a particular country was a secondary and relatively simple task.

The great outlines, which require to be drawn, will be found to be the same for every *territory*, for every *race*, and for every *time*: only in this or that *territory*, only for this or that *race*, only for this or that *time*, as distinguished from this or that other, will the *filling* up of those lines be found to require to be, on this or that point, more or less different.

The task of the legislation committee was therefore merely to assist the law-giver with its local knowledge to fill up 'the great outlines' which he alone was permitted to draw.[3] Mill was insistent that his proposed body should form part of the Government itself. It was not to be a subordinate commission or board, but was to be added to the Governor-General's executive council, so forming a supreme council for the purposes of legislation. He admitted that his scheme was

---

1 Evidence of James Mill, 21 Feb. 1832: *P.P.*, 1831–2, vol. ix, p. 46, Qu. 346.
2 Bentham, 'Codification Proposal', *Works*, vol. iv, pp. 560 et seq.
3 Ibid., p. 562.

hastily conceived, and it was not in practice adopted. Never-theless, the two component ideas bore fruit; firstly, a com-mission to frame a body of codified law for the whole of British India, headed by a man of distinguished intellectual ability; and secondly, the recommendation of adding to the executive council expert opinion on the science of legislation, when laws were considered or discussed. These ideas materialized in the Law Commission under Macaulay, and in the Legislative Council of India, which was formed by joining a fourth or law member to the ordinary Executive Council of the Governor-General. Both these bodies were kept small as Mill had advocated. The authoritarian argu-ment for a small expert body to draw up an Indian Code, rather than a large miscellaneous assembly, was accepted by the framers of the Charter Act, and Macaulay advanced Bentham's and Mill's view in his famous Commons speech of 10 July 1833:

The work of digesting a vast and artificial system of jurisprudence is far more easily performed, by few minds than by many, by a Napo-leon than by a Chamber of Deputies and a Chamber of Peers, by a government like that of Prussia or Denmark than by a government like that of England. A quiet knot of two or three veteran jurists is an infinitely better machinery for such a purpose than a large popular assembly, divided, as such assemblies almost always are, into adverse factions.[1]

The Charter negotiations were largely concerned with the financial settlement consequent on the decision to abolish the Company's monopoly of the China tea trade, and to end its commercial functions. The Directors were too little con-cerned or too resigned to contest the political arrangements of the proposed Act very strongly. But they did have some success in modifying its provisions concerning the internal government of India. The proposals of the Whig Govern-ment were forwarded to the Court sixteen days before the Bill was due to have its second reading on 10 July 1833.[2] Officially its author was Charles Grant, the President of the

---

[1] Macaulay, *Complete Works*, vol. xi, p. 582.
[2] 'Summary of provisions of proposed Bill enclosed with a Letter from Rt. Hon. Charles Grant, 24 June 1833': *P.P.*, 1833, vol. xxv, pp. 142 et seq. An account of the negotiations is given in Philips, *East India Company*, pp. 285–98.

Board of Control; but undoubtedly his assistants at the Board had a more powerful influence in its modelling. Over these James Mill's teaching exercised great influence. Macaulay was the foremost among them; and it is not difficult to trace the influence of Holt Mackenzie, who was also by now a member of the Board. Hyde Villiers was another of the Board's officials who had come under the Benthamite spell.[1] The framing of the measure was undertaken at a time of great political excitement, and bitter party feeling marked the relations of the Ministry with the Court of Directors. The Court was unwise enough to adopt an obstructionist attitude, and held back important information.[2] There was every reason, therefore, for the Ministry to agree with the more radical plans for reform, which would throw complete power for the local government of India into the hands of the Governor-General, their own nominee.

The plan which Grant submitted to the Directors was in effect a compromise between Bentinck's and Mackenzie's. It was proposed to form a separate presidency out of the Western Provinces of Bengal, to be known as the Presidency of Agra; but the Governor-General was to continue to act as Governor of Lower Bengal. His general authority was to be made more complete: 'the whole Civil and Military Government of India' was to be vested in him. The Supreme Government was to be the sole legislative authority, and this authority it was to exercise over 'all persons, British or Native, Foreigners or others, and all Courts of Justice. The Governor-General will thus be empowered to issue laws binding, to a certain extent, on the Supreme Courts, especially as to jurisdiction.'[3] The Supreme Government was also to have 'a more defined and efficient control' over

---

[1] See note O, p. 327.

[2] Cf. Philips, op. cit., p. 287. Also cf. Ryan to Bentinck, 29 April 1832: Bentinck MSS. (referring to the reluctance of the Directors to produce the relevant papers): 'It was with the fear that this course might be adopted that I ventured to give Whitmore the means of calling for the papers relating to a legislative Council, a code of laws and system of Courts, and after a struggle and great delay I am happy to say that these papers are now before the Committee.' (Whitmore was the M.P. who made the original motion for an inquiry into the Company's affairs in 1829; cf. H. H. Wilson, *History of British India*, vol. iii, p. 333.)

[3] Summary of Provisions of Proposed Bill: *P.P.*, 1833, vol. xxv, p. 143.

the subordinate governments; 'and for this purpose it shall have a precedent and preventive, in place of a subsequent and corrective control'. The governors of the subordinate Presidencies were no longer to have councils. There was to be a Law Commission appointed by the Governor-General in Council, to inquire into 'the nature, administration, etc. of the existing laws, into the courts of justice, modes of judicature, and police throughout British India. The Commission to submit alterations and propositions tending to establish a legislation, approximating to as much uniformity as may be consistent with the differences of castes, manners, usages and feelings of the people in different parts of the country.' Europeans were to have greater facility of access to the interior, and were to be allowed to hold land on leasehold tenure. They were with certain temporary exceptions to be 'subject to the same laws and the same jurisdiction with the natives' and in particular, 'subject to the same criminal laws and criminal courts'. The Council of the Governor-General was to be enlarged to five members, the intention being obviously to have a representative from each of the Presidencies of Bengal, Madras, Bombay, and Agra; the fifth member would be a person not in the Company's service, and his post was to be that of law member to aid the Council in its new legislative capacity. Already the Radical programme for transforming British India from a loose confederacy of diverse governments and law systems into a strong, unified, and centralized state had been modified in Grant's scheme. A central government, with its capital in the heart of Hindustan and entirely free from local administrative responsibilities, was perhaps too visionary at this stage. Grant's proposal meant that the new Government of India would still have Calcutta as its capital, and that it would still be burdened with local administration, although this would be confined to Lower Bengal alone. The subordinate governments would still retain their privilege of direct communication with the Home Authorities. Despite these modifications the scheme of government outlined in the 'Summary of Provisions' reflected the influence of the principles of uniformity and centralization. The Court of Directors singled them out for attack. Firstly, they doubted 'whether the

British Empire in India, embracing a vast population of multiform castes and usages, has yet reached the point at which it may be possible for its foreign rulers to accomplish that desideratum of uniformity of law, which has not yet been found attainable in our long-settled and highly civilized country'.[1] And secondly, they held that the Governor-General under the proposed arrangements would 'have a sway almost absolute', which would have the effect of making the other Presidencies subordinate to him rather than to the Home Authorities. They considered that 'the vast powers' which Grant's plan gave to the Governor-General would make it 'scarcely possible always to select a person fit to be entrusted with authority of such magnitude'. They had no conception of the new philosophy of government: 'Division of labour, the best means we submit for securing efficiency, is the present system. Consolidation of labour, to a degree quite incompatible with efficiency, would we think, be the effect of the change contemplated.' Most power, they felt, must always rest with the subordinate local governments, 'and that power will be liable to abuse unless checked by the association with the Governors of persons of character and eminence in the service'. In consequence of these views the Directors opposed the abolition of the councils at the subordinate Presidencies; they were even hostile to the erection of a new Presidency of Agra, and in fact they condemned every new departure from the existing system of Indian government. It was the irony of history that James Mill as Chief Examiner was compelled to draft and transmit these views of the Directors when they were so completely opposed to his own.

There was a respectable body of opinion that was ready to support some of the Court's contentions. Malcolm and Elphinstone had spoken against excessive uniformity and centralization; and Bentinck had upheld the system of councils for the subordinate Presidencies. In the course of its passage through Parliament modifications had to be introduced into the Bill. The original phrasing declaring that 'the whole civil and military government of all the said territories

---

[1] Letter from chairman and deputy chairman to Rt. Hon. Charles Grant, 2 July 1833: *P.P.*, 1833, vol. xxv, p. 169.

and revenues in India shall be . . . vested in a governor-general and counsellors' was softened down to the older phraseology of the previous Acts, that 'the superintendence, direction and control' should be thus vested. The constitution of the subordinate governments, that is of a Governor with a Council, was to remain unchanged, although the Company was empowered to reduce the number of councillors or to suspend the councils entirely, if it saw fit.[1] Outwardly at least, Bentham's principle of centralization was unfulfilled. But the sacrifice was one of form rather than substance. In order to end the conflict of laws and jurisdiction, and to make British subjects amenable to the Company's courts outside the Presidency towns (before permitting them unrestricted access to the interior), Parliament agreed to the proposal that the Governor-General in Council should have power

to make laws and regulations for all persons, whether British or Native, foreigners or others, and for all Courts of Justice, whether established by Her Majesty's Charters [i.e. the Supreme Courts] or otherwise, and the jurisdiction thereof and for all places and things within . . . the whole . . . of the said territories and for all servants of the said Company.[2]

Their legislative acts were to have the force of parliamentary statutes. The Supreme Council was to have three ordinary members, besides the Governor-General and the Commander-in-Chief (who might be appointed as an extraordinary member). There was to be a fourth or law member to provide expert legislative opinion when the Council sat in its capacity as the Legislative Council; and the Governor-General was directed to appoint a commission of four, to inquire into the system of Indian laws and propose their amendment. In practice, therefore, the Utilitarian ambitions had been fulfilled. There was to be only one legislative authority in India, supreme over all courts and all persons; and this made the failure to strip the subordinate governments of their semblance of independence comparatively unimportant.

[1] See note P, p. 327.
[2] 3 & 4 Wm. IV, c. 85, s. 43.

3. *Macaulay as Law Member*

Further progress in judicial reform, after Bentinck's measures between 1829 and 1831, waited upon the arrival of the new law member and the setting-up of the Law Commission. But suggestions of detail were made by the Home Authorities which show the influence of James Mill's opinions. In his evidence before the Select Committee of 1832 Mill had rehearsed the chief tenets of Bentham's doctrine of jurisprudence.[1] Besides the question of an adequate number of local tribunals and the need to record customary property rights and interests, Mill's emphasis was laid upon efficient judicial procedure. In his view one of the most defective parts of the Indian system had been that of appeal. Original and appellate jurisdiction had erroneously been joined, and courts whose primary function was that of appeal were absorbed in trying cases in first instance. Bentham had insisted that the distinction between appellate and original jurisdiction corresponded to the distinction between the controlling and executive function. If the distinction was confused, then the requisite check and control was lost.[2] But Mill was more concerned in his evidence with efficiency. The notion of appeal had been incorrectly viewed, he contended. Courts trying cases in appeal had considered themselves competent to take new evidence, which meant that they were in effect conducting a fresh trial, and merely doing the work of the original tribunal over again. Hence cases determined in this way were not really allowed the right of appeal. Mill's objections to the taking of fresh evidence he described as quite radical. For like his fellow Benthamites he believed that there were discoveries to be made in the science of law and government as efficacious and as revolutionary as those made by the mechanical inventions in industry. The great problems of society could each be solved by a simple principle; the problem of crime by the Panopticon; the problem of government by representative democracy, and the problem of universal education by the monitor system

---

[1] Evidence of James Mill, 29 June 1832: *P.P.*, 1831–2, vol. xii, pp. 119 et seq.

[2] Bentham, 'Judicial Establishment', *Works*, vol. iv, p. 352; and 'Principles of Judicial Procedure', *Works*, vol. ii, p. 165.

of Lancaster.[1] In the field of law the problem was, on the one hand, to secure prompt, accessible, and cheap justice with the minimum of inconvenience to witnesses and parties; and on the other, to establish an efficient control for preventing maladministration and abuse. The principle that solves the dilemma is the Benthamite conception of appeal. If appeal is limited to a consideration of the evidence and judgement of the original trial, then there is no need to hear the parties, the witnesses, or even their counsel again. The controlling and regulative function which appeal performed could be effected without the delay and inconvenience usually associated with it. All that was required was to consider the original proceedings, and these could be transmitted by post. If fresh evidence arose or there was reason to believe that the original evidence was incomplete, then a re-trial by a court of first instance should be ordered. This notion of appeal, as merely the consideration of a written record transmitted by post, meant that the distance of the appeal court from the domicile of the parties was immaterial. Hence the Benthamite ideal is achieved—a myriad of omnicompetent local tribunals controlled by a single court of appeal at the metropolis.[2] Now Mill emphasized the importance and advantage of centralizing appellate jurisdiction in one tribunal even more than Bentham. Not only would this mean that appeals would have the benefit of the best tribunal, but also that a single appellate court would ensure a greater uniformity of decision. He went so far as to propose that appeals from native judges should no longer be heard by the district judge but should go directly to the *Sadr Adalat* at Calcutta. And on the principle of uniformity he condemned, like Ross, the erection of a separate *Sadr* Court for the Western Provinces of Bengal.

The other defect of the Indian judicial system was in procedure. Admittedly the full technicalities of English pleading had never been introduced into India. But there was

---

[1] Cf. Bentham, 'Panopticon', *Works*, vol. iv, p. 39: 'Morals reformed—health preserved—industry invigorated—instruction diffused—public burthens lightened —Economy seated, as it were, upon a rock—the gordian knot of the Poor Laws not cut, but untied—all by a simple idea in Architecture.' Cf. James Mill, *On Government*, ed. E. Barker, p. 34; Leslie Stephen, *The English Utilitarians*, vol. ii, p. 19.

[2] Cf. Bentham, 'Judicial Establishment', *Works*, vol. iv, pp. 348–50.

considerable room for improvement, Mill considered, in defining at the outset the points at issue in a suit. This would obviate the necessity of attendance by witnesses who were summoned on the mere possibility of their being called to give evidence. Such a definition of the real issues could not properly be attained by written pleadings. In this matter there had been a retrogression from the traditional native practice of 'parties appearing personally before the judge and stating their own case'; for 'few things would be more efficient for the purposes of justice than oral pleading', which if properly managed would be an instrument of inestimable value. Mill also disapproved of the monetary classification of suits. This was

the principle of one sort of court for sums of small amount, another sort of court for sums of higher, the best tribunals for the highest sums, the worst tribunals for the lowest; declaring in fact, that more care is due to prevent wrongs done to the rich than wrongs done to the poor. The opinion which has obtained but too generally appears to me most erroneous, that suits for small sums are suits of the least importance. I think, in point of importance, the reverse is the right order.[1]

In all this he was, of course, simply following the principles of Bentham—Bentham's idea of appeal, of oral pleadings and confrontation of parties, of omnicompetent tribunals, and of courts organized geographically instead of on the metaphysical or pecuniary principle.[2] Bentham had condemned the distribution of jurisdiction according to the type of cause (the metaphysical principle), or according to the value of the sum in dispute (the pecuniary principle), as leading inevitably to complication, fraud, expense, and delay. His solution was for local courts, sufficient in number to be within easy reach of every person, and competent to hear every type of cause for any amount. Similarly, Mill's advocacy of courts under single rather than under a number of judges was merely the 'single-seatedness' principle of Bentham. Mill believed, again like Ross, that this measure would

---

[1] James Mill's evidence, 29 June 1832: *P.P.*, 1831–2, vol. xii, p. 123, Qu. 1046.

[2] Cf. Bentham, 'Judicial Establishment', *Works*, vol. iv, pp. 338–53, on appeal; pp. 328–38, on 'the modes of parcelling out jurisdiction'. For the question of oral pleadings and the confrontation of parties, cf. 'Rationale of Judicial Evidence', *Works*, vol. vi, pp. 138–9; 'Principles of Judicial Procedure', *Works*, vol. ii, pp. 74 et seq.

release a considerable number of judges and make possible an immediate increase in the number of courts.

His opinions represent the nature and direction of further judicial reform. In January 1832 a Judicial Despatch was urging the adoption of Ross's proposal for the introduction of the 'single-seatedness' principle in the *Sadr* Court at Calcutta.[1] In December 1833 the Benthamite teaching on appeal was being expounded, and emphasis was laid on its importance because under the Regulation of 1831 original jurisdiction had almost wholly been vested in Indian judges.[2] This meant that appeal became essentially a controlling and inspective function, and it was therefore particularly important that it should be kept quite distinct from original jurisdiction. In September 1835 the Home Authorities were advocating a return to the oral examination of parties to a suit, on the grounds that 'a recurrence to the ancient oriental practice which still prevails in several parts of our Indian Empire might produce a salutary effect in the decision of suits'.[3]

In October 1835 there was a remarkable Judicial Despatch which may well have come from James Mill's hand.[4] Against the general trend of opinion usually expressed by the Court, the despatch suggested judicial inspectors to supervise the subordinate courts. A stationary chief court at Calcutta could not effect the close superintendence that was necessary; for 'a real acquaintance with what is going on in the country is only to be obtained by persons on the spot'. It was proposed, therefore, that the commissioners of revenue, who had recently been relieved of their duties as judges of circuit, should assume this new function and be invested 'with the powers of control, enquiry and general supervision over the whole judicial and magisterial administration in their respective Districts'. Here was the union of powers recommended in its most radical form. The commissioners were to

---

[1] Judicial Despatch to Bengal, 11 Jan. 1832, paras. 5 et seq.: *P.P.*, 1831–2, vol. xii, p. 209.

[2] See note Q, p. 328.

[3] Judicial Despatch to Bengal, 8 Sept. (No. 3) 1835, paras. 3–4.

[4] Judicial Despatch to Bengal (Lower Provinces), 7 Oct. (No. 5) 1835. Mill had in the same month published an article on law reform in the *London Review*: cf. Bain, *James Mill*, p. 395.

hear complaints against all judicial functionaries, and they were to be 'held personally responsible for any neglect or abuse which shall not have been inquired into and corrected'. Is not this, we may ask, Bentham's principle of inspectability which he had applied to the judiciary in the *Constitutional Code*?[1] And the great apparatus of statistical control, which the despatch recommended, would seem to confirm the Benthamite inspiration. The commissioners were to submit half-yearly reports which would embrace 'the operation of the Civil, Criminal and Police systems, the condition and morals of the people, and should convey any suggestions they may desire to offer, with a view to promote in any way the public welfare'.[2] These reports were in no way to supersede 'the means of superintendence and control over all judicial officers which consists in their rendering with perfect accuracy regular and complete returns of the duty performed by them'. The function of the *Sadr* Court was emphasized as not that of mere judicial decision of appeals, 'but also a Board of Superintendence over the other tribunals'. Like Bentham's Appellate Judicatory it was to exercise an inspective as well as its ordinary function. Finally, it was important that as an appeal court it should not be carried beyond its proper limits. Bentham's doctrine of appeal was once more enunciated.[3] The larger organization recommended by the despatch was not in fact realized. James Mill died in 1836 and from 1837 the judicial despatches were for some years firmly anti-Benthamite in tone. But in itself this despatch of October 1835 is a monument to Bentham's influence at the India House so long as Mill remained at its head.

Similarly in India, in the period before Macaulay's arrival, the Utilitarian influence was pushing the judicial

---

[1] 'Constitutional Code', *Works*, vol. ix, pp. 598–9.

[2] Cf. Bentham, 'Rationale of Reward', *Works*, vol. ii, p. 232. Cf. Mill, *History*, vol. v, pp. 430–1: [Speaking of Cornwallis's judicial reforms] 'To require periodical reports from the judges, for the purpose of making known the evils which remained without a remedy, is a measure deserving no common tribute of applause. Were a similar operation carried out over the whole field of government, and made sufficiently faithful and searching, the melioration of governments, and with it the happiness of the human race, would proceed with an accelerated pace.' The passion for statistics reached its height in England during the eighteen-thirties; cf. G. M. Young, *Victorian England*, pp. 32–33.

[3] Judicial Despatch to Bengal, 7 Oct. 1835, para. 15.

reforms of 1831 to what appeared their logical conclusion. The Supreme Government felt that any alterations could be most usefully effected as part of the larger work of consolidating and digesting the various enactments governing the judicial organization of Bengal. A Company's judge, Frederick Millett, was appointed in 1833 for this task; and it was particularly suggested to him that the restrictions on the powers of Indian judges should be abolished, the monetary limits governing the original jurisdiction of principal *sadr* amins removed, and the latter given power to hear original suits for any amount.[1] To quicken the procedure, it was suggested that the rule by which all suits tried by Indian subordinate judges had first to be referred to them by the district judge, should be done away with, and that instead they should receive suits directly. Similarly, it was proposed that the requirement for the district judge to confirm the orders of Indian subordinate judges should be dispensed with, and the limitations (prescribed in Regulation V of 1831) excluding British or American subjects from the civil jurisdiction of Indian judges should likewise be removed. These alterations were clearly in answer to the demands of reformers, such as Ross, who were striving after the Benthamite ideal of 'omnicompetence' for the Indian courts.

The more ambitious ideal of an entirely codified law was also being actively discussed. It had been officially adopted by the Supreme Government as a solution to the problem of competing law systems.[2] It was being pressed by the reforming group at Calcutta, Ross and Ryan and Young.[3] Bentinck

---

[1] Judicial Letter from India, 18 April 1835.

[2] Cf. Letter of Government to the judges of the Calcutta Supreme Court, 9 Oct. 1830, para. 18: *P.P.*, 1831, vol. vi, Appendix V, p. 147: 'We likewise entirely assent to your suggestion, that as soon as possible, one code of law should be established for all persons and all places within the same [territories of British India], reserving of course the special laws and usages which depend upon the religious creed of the different classes of our subjects. . . .'

[3] Sir Edward Ryan, a judge of the Calcutta Supreme Court, was toasted at a dinner as 'the sergeant-major of the march of intellect'; Bentinck to Grant, 18 Dec. 1832: Bentinck MSS. He was reprinting publications of the Society for the Diffusion of Useful Knowledge, and was asked to form with Bentinck a 'Corresponding Committee of the Society' at Calcutta; Ryan to Bentinck, 29 Jan. 1832: Bentinck MSS. Ryan had been instrumental in bringing the question of a code before Grant, the President of the Board of Control; see p. 180, n. 2. Cf. also Ryan to Bentinck,

asked Ross for a report on the question, preparatory to bringing it before the Supreme Government.[1] All these measures were avowedly interim, and waited upon the Law Commission and Legislative Council, established by the new Act, to carry them into action. Nevertheless, they show that the ground where Macaulay had to labour was far from unprepared, and that there was a body of official opinion actively thinking along the lines he was to pursue.

Macaulay's arrival as law member to the new Legislative Council of India appeared to herald a golden age of reform that would entirely eclipse Bentinck's previous achievement. Why were these expectations unfulfilled, and the tangible results comparatively so meagre? One may ascribe it to the lack of time, the uncertainty from a change of masters, and to the re-emergence of pressing diplomatic and military problems. Macaulay was in India from June 1834 until the beginning of January 1838, a period of no more than three and a half years. The first Governor-General under whom he served, Bentinck, left India in March 1835; Metcalfe succeeded temporarily, but the post was not permanently occupied again until Auckland's arrival in March 1836. And from the end of 1836 the attention of the Governor-General was increasingly distracted from domestic affairs by the problem of the North-West Frontier and the gathering of the Afghan storm-cloud. These conditions were hardly favourable for devising comprehensive measures of law reform and carrying them swiftly into effect. But it is possible to detect a more deep-rooted cause than adverse circumstance. In India there was also something of the hesitancy and slackening of the central impulse which affected the Whigs in England on the morrow of their great political triumph of 1832. The main position won, the cause of reform broke down into a number of separate and smaller issues, and slowly the larger conception was lost. In the discussions before the Charter Act, law had been looked upon as part

25 Aug. 1830: Bentinck MSS. Cf. Col. Young to Bentham, 30 Sept. 1828: Bentham, *Works*, vol. xi, p. 9.

[1] Cf. Ross to Bentinck, 5 April 1834: Bentinck MSS. Bentinck, Minute, 11 July 1834: Board's Collections, vol. 1555, No. 63507, f. 21. Ross, Minute on Codification, 30 Dec. 1833; ibid., ff. 23 et seq.

of the larger problem of government. From the time of Bayley's original proposal of 1828 the whole question of the nature and constitution of British political authority in India had been ventilated. With Macaulay, despite the range of his mind, there was a marked absence of that reference to first principles which characterized Metcalfe, Holt Mackenzie, and Ross. For Macaulay government rested on certain unquestioned assumptions rather than on a theory that had to be elaborated and defended.[1] His minutes are *tours de force*, but they remain essentially practical documents. They are the work of a lawyer advocating his cause with brilliance but with a strictly legal relevance. It is as though the laws of evidence excluded him from the discussion of larger principles and purposes.

Macaulay had at one time employed his talents in a frontal assault on James Mill and the Utilitarian philosophy of politics; but even in those articles of 1829 for the *Edinburgh Review* he acknowledged his respect for Bentham's contribution to jurisprudence.[2] He had taken an important part in the framing of the Charter Act of 1833, and in his speech, as well as in the terms of the Act, the ideal of a codified law system for India figured largely. Probably on that account James Mill had magnanimously canvassed his appointment as law member.[3] Macaulay's mind is indeed symptomatic of the assimilation of the Utilitarian science to the Whig outlook. He rejected the Utilitarian ideal of a general renovation of society by means of an abstract universal theory, from

---

[1] Cf. Macaulay, speech on Parliamentary Reform, 2 Mar. 1831: *Complete Works*, vol. xi, p. 409: 'I rest my opinion on no general theory of government. I distrust all general theories of government.' Cf. Macaulay's defence to the charge of the *Westminster Review* that he assailed the Utilitarian theory of government without being able to produce one of his own; Macaulay, 'Westminster Reviewer's Defence of Mill' and 'Utilitarian Theory of Government' in *Edinburgh Review*, June and Oct. 1829.

[2] Macaulay, 'Westminster Reviewer's Defence of Mill', *Miscellaneous Writings and Speeches of Lord Macaulay*, pp. 184–5: 'However sharply he [Bentham] may speak of us, we can never cease to revere in him the father of Jurisprudence. He has a full right to all the privileges of a great inventor; and in our courts of criticism, those privileges will never be pleaded in vain.' Cf. the eulogy on Bentham in his Essay on Mirabeau (*Edinburgh Review*, July 1832): *Miscellaneous Writings and Speeches*, pp. 267–9.

[3] Cf. Trevelyan, *Life and Letters of Lord Macaulay*, p. 244. Macaulay frequently saw Mill at his house at this time; Bain, *James Mill*, p. 370.

which the minutest practical detail was deduced. Instead he adhered to expediency and pragmatism, which he dignified with the authority of Bacon's inductive method. Reform had place only when time and circumstance proved it necessary. The prejudice was in favour of the existing historical society, and the burden of proof on the innovator.[1] Instead of meaning the entire transformation of society, reform was simply the remedying of certain specific defects in the machinery of government as and when they occurred. Certainly they required the services of the expert, but he was to be confined to his particular task and skill.[2] Macaulay accepted Bentham's jurisprudence but not the general political theory that attached to it.[3] Law reform meant for him the urgent necessity to make the law rational and efficient, and he was relatively unconcerned with the more speculative object of fashioning it into an instrument by which society could be reordered and transformed. There was, too, a difference of political creed. Bentham's philosophy gave to government a function and importance to which Macaulay's Whig instincts were opposed. Macaulay might accept remarkable extensions to the role of the State, if special circumstances proved these necessary, but as a principle he inherited the Whig suspicion of political power. The great improving agency of history, the progress of moral and intellectual knowledge, was a product of voluntary action and free enterprise, and its hereditary enemy was political power. There could be no sympathy for the planned, centralized, bureaucratic state, which Bentham had envisaged in all its minutiae in the *Constitutional Code*. The end of government could still be described for Macaulay in terms of the Whig revolution formula, 'the protection of

[1] Cf. speech on second reading of the Charter Bill, 10 July 1833: *Complete Works*, vol. xi, p. 568.

[2] Macaulay had a great veneration for the expert, cf. Minute, 17 April 1835; Indian Judicial Proceedings, 11 May 1835, No. 12: Board's Collections, vol. 1555, No. 63502, f. 109: 'The principle of the division of labour holds good in this and in most other cases. A militia is no match for a regular army, the amateur artist is hardly ever equal to a professional artist.'

[3] Cf. speech on the exclusion of judges from the House of Commons, 1 June 1853: *Complete Works*, vol. xii, p. 305: 'Of Mr. Bentham's moral and political speculations, I entertain, I must own, a very mean opinion: but I hold him in high esteem as a jurist.'

persons and property', or more simply as 'the administration of justice'. Certainly he had no sympathy for that authoritarian element which had lent its support to the strengthening of the executive and the closer union of powers in India. With his arrival the movement of reform in Bengal ceased to threaten the overthrow of the Cornwallis structure. The tide which had reached full flood with the establishment of the commissioner system and the union of magistrate and collector, was turned aside by Macaulay to cleanse and widen the old channels rather than carve out new. The system of Cornwallis, the incarnation of the Whig philosophy, was left secure; and the aim now was not to destroy it, but to render it efficient.

Macaulay was appointed to the post of fourth or legislative member of the newly constituted Government of India, and it was only later that he voluntarily took over the direction of the Law Commission. His immediate tasks were outlined at length in the Public Despatch of 10 December 1834, written on good tradition by James Mill himself.[1] The despatch distinguished between the immediate and prospective changes contemplated by the new Charter Act. The ultimate prospect was that 'a general system of justice and police, and a code of laws common (as far as may be) to the whole people of India, and having its varieties classified and systematized, shall be established throughout the country'. Preparations for such a system and code were to be begun at once, and for this purpose the Law Commission had been appointed. Yet such a task would obviously require a number of years, and it was expedient and necessary in the meantime to carry out certain immediate reforms. The new legislative powers of the Supreme Government had been conferred by Parliament to provide for this situation and to enable experimental measures to be conducted, prior to the introduction of a general system. But the immediate consideration for arming the Supreme Government with new legislative power was the lifting of all restrictions on the free admission of Europeans into the interior, and the con-

---

[1] Printed *in extenso*, C. Ilbert, *The Government of India*, pp. 492 et seq. For authorship: Kaye, *Administration of the East India Company*, p. 137 n.; also Ilbert, p. 92.

sequent necessity of making them subject to the authority
and jurisdiction of the Company's Government and its
courts, instead of merely to the Supreme Courts and the
laws these administered. It was, therefore, expressly enjoined that British-born subjects, except in capital cases,
should be subject 'in all other criminal respects and in all civil
respects whatever to the ordinary tribunals of the country'.
The powers and jurisdiction of the Supreme Courts were to
be regulated to prevent the past evils of conflicting laws and
authorities; and the Charter Act provided the Government
of India with the necessary legislative power for this purpose.

There were therefore 'good reasons for collecting and
uniting all the functions of legislation in one central and
metropolitan Government'; and the immediate task for the
new Legislative Council was to establish this power on a
proper basis, by settling at the outset the mode of promulgation and the procedure for considering and passing legislation. To avoid precipitate or thoughtless laws, it was
instructed to provide by positive rules that every legislative
proposal should travel through a defined succession of
stages before adoption, allowing ample time for discussion
at each stage and adequate intervals between stages for
reflection and inquiry.[1] The mode of authentication was to
be laid down by enactment, and provision made for cheap
vernacular copies of the laws to be obtainable. These were
all good Benthamite principles. Bentham had declared the
necessity of proper authentication and the widest publicity
in order to make the law certain and known.[2] He had also
laid emphasis upon a carefully regulated procedure for the
passage of legislation. The Whig method of avoiding precipitate legislation was the device of a second chamber, but
Bentham had rejected this as a needless complication which
could be used to frustrate the will of the greatest number.
He was, however, alive to the need for proper deliberation
and discussion. 'Everything which renders reflection and
order necessary in the proceedings of a free people', he
wrote, 'is the assured safeguard of their rights.'[3] In his *Essay*

---

[1] Public Despatch to India, 10 Dec. 1834, para. 16.
[2] Bentham, 'Judicial Establishment', *Works*, vol. iv, pp. 311–12.
[3] Bentham, 'Essay on Political Tactics', *Works*, vol. ii, p. 354 n.

on Political Tactics he had emphasized the need for definite rules to govern the passage of ordinary legislation.

James Mill's despatch went on to stress the importance of the fourth councillor or law member. He was not simply to be a substitute for the function of registration previously performed by the Supreme Court; indeed his dissent or even absence during the enactment of a law was not of vital importance and would not in any way invalidate it. His task was rather the great intellectual work of preparing the laws. The despatch described him in terms of Bentham's legislator seated at the centre of power.

> His will naturally be the principal share, not only in giving shape and connexion to the several laws as they pass, but also in the mighty labour in collecting all that local information, and calling into view all those general considerations which belong to each occasion, and of thus enabling the council to embody the abstract and essential principles of good government in regulations adapted to the peculiar habits, character, and institutions of the vast and infinitely diversified people under their sway.

Suggestions regarding legislative measures were to be invited from the subordinate governments, from outside bodies, and from the public at large, but the law itself was to be 'really your own, the offspring of your own minds, after obtaining an adequate knowledge of the case'.[1] Thus a measure of publicity was to be achieved, whilst reserving the whole power of initiation to the Supreme Council. From the content and tenor of these instructions there is every reason to believe that James Mill was attempting to strengthen the Benthamite inspiration of the Charter Act after its attenuation by criticism in Parliament. The despatch was at pains to emphasize the importance of the new powers conferred by clause 39;[2] for the wording of this had been softened in face of the charge of over-centralization levelled at the Bill.

---

[1] Public Despatch to India, 10 Dec. 1834, para. 33. Mill apparently feared that the subordinate governments might retain the substance of legislative power. 'We say this, knowing as we do how easily the power of delegating a duty degenerates into the habit of neglecting it, and dreading lest at some period, under the form of offering projects of laws, presidencies should be left to legislate for themselves, with as little aid from the wisdom of the Supreme Government as when the power of legislating was ostensibly in their own hands.'

[2] 3 & 4 Wm. IV, c. 85, s. 39: 'The superintendence, direction and control of the

The powers here conveyed, when the words are interpreted in all their latitude, include the whole powers of government. And it is of infinite importance that you should well consider and understand the extent of the responsibility imposed upon you. The whole civil and military government of India is in your hands, and for what is good or evil in the administration of it, the honour or dishonour will redound upon you.

Although Macaulay arrived in India in the hot weather of 1834, there was little he could do in his official capacity in framing and drafting laws until the newly established Government of India was stabilized and instructions from home were to hand. The arrangements for the new Government of Agra, and the famous education controversy, in which Macaulay secured the ascendancy of English language and literature as the medium of higher education, took up the period until Bentinck's departure in March 1835. By that time the instructions from the Home Authorities—the great despatch which has just been discussed—had arrived and were ready to be acted upon. In the course of the education controversy, however, Macaulay had aroused the hostility of Thoby Prinsep, at that time a Secretary to Government, and now with Bentinck's departure a fully fledged member of Council.[1] Prinsep appeared determined to oppose every measure put forward by Macaulay, on the assumption that it was part of a design to subvert the whole Cornwallis system. It was not the first time in India that the motto 'Reform to preserve'[2] should thus be mistaken for a revolutionary creed; but at the outset it indicates the narrowness of the area of conflict in Macaulay's era of reform. The prejudice rather than the details of Prinsep's opposition is significant. Macaulay carried all before him in that tide of authoritative argument and eloquence before which the greatest parlia-

whole civil and military government of all the said territories and revenues in India shall be vested in the said Governor-General in Council.' Public Despatch to India, 10 Dec. 1834, para. 78.

[1] Cf. D.N.B., vol. xvi, p. 392. Prinsep's autobiographical memoir; I. H. Sharp and J. A. Richey, Selections from the Educational Records, vol. i, pp. 132 et seq. Also Auckland to Hobhouse, 9 April 1837: Add. MS. 37690: 'he [Prinsep] and Macaulay butted at each other like wild bulls, blind to everything but to their own joust of brains and the contest was not advantageous to either.'

[2] Cf. 'Review of Hallam's Constitutional History', Sept. 1828: Lord Macaulay's Essays, 1903 edn., p. 98.

mentarians sometimes quailed. His first measures were to provide for the authentication of laws, and the framing of rules for the legislative process, as James Mill's despatch had enjoined. Act X of 1835 provided that the printing of a law in the *Official Gazette* was to be sufficient evidence of its authenticity, and Macaulay's Standing Orders for the Legislative Council were likewise accepted. Macaulay summarized the objects of the latter with his fine economy and clarity of statement:

We ought to provide securities against precipitate legislation. We ought to ensure a fair hearing to the minority, however small. We ought to reserve to ourselves the power in great emergencies of legislating with the utmost promptitude, and yet to put this power under such checks as may render it very difficult for ourselves or our successors to abuse it. We ought to give the public an opportunity of expressing its opinions concerning our laws before they are finally passed.[1]

He concluded that an interval of six weeks between the publication and passing of an Act would normally be sufficient; although in the case of emergency legislation or unimportant amendments the Council would be able to suspend its standing orders after recording its reasons. Every member could demand that the rest of the Council should individually record its views on any law, and certain other delays were to be allowable to ensure that minority opinion was permitted a fair hearing.[2] Prinsep's objections, his attempt to reduce the powers of the Legislative Council by a condition that all laws should first be considered by the Executive Council in the department to which they belonged, were of no avail. Macaulay not only vindicated the parity of the Legislative Council with its form as the Executive Council, but also the right of the fourth member to be present at the discussion of a law in all its stages.[3]

A question of principle had, however, arisen, which revealed the deeper sources of division. On 13 April 1835, during the discussion of a measure proposed by the new Government of Agra, Prinsep took occasion to object to the

---

[1] Macaulay, Minute, 28 May 1835: C. D. Dharker, *Lord Macaulay's Legislative Minutes*, p. 150.

[2] Standing Orders of the Council of India, adopted on 6 July 1835: ibid., pp. 302–3. [3] Macaulay, Minute, 13 June 1835: ibid., pp. 153–8.

new form in which Macaulay was casting the laws.[1] The old method of prefixing a title and preamble had been discarded, and the terse concision of the new laws—some of them consisted of barely three lines of print—was well calculated to alarm conservative prejudices. Prinsep tried to argue the matter as a legal one, maintaining that the Council was bound in this respect by Regulation XLI of 1793 and a parliamentary enactment of 1797 (37 Geo. II, c. 142); and more generally he rested his case on the conservative grounds that a title and preamble were sanctioned by established practice and followed the venerable model of the British Parliament. That the new legislative authority of the Governor-General should be questioned appeared to Macaulay a point of importance. To signify the distinctiveness of this authority from that wielded in the past, Macaulay had given the laws of the new Government the name of Acts rather than continue the old nomenclature of Regulations. The latter were 'mere by-laws' whereas the new enactments were of the same effect as Acts of Parliament and extended over all courts, persons, and places in the Indian Empire. That a legislative body could be permanently fettered by its previous enactments was, of course, anathema to any mind read in Bentham's doctrines.[2] In this instance Macaulay was supported by Ross, Ryan (the Chief Justice), and eventually by the Home Authorities, that old Acts of Parliament or past Regulations did not bind the Government to a prescribed form of legislation.[3]

Yet a difficulty had arisen which was inherited from Bentham. The criterion of a law in Bentham's teaching was that it should be short, simple, and above all the expression of command. On this ground Macaulay had pared away the title and preamble. At the same time, to induce obedience, to render his motives intelligible, and to impart instruction, Bentham had emphasized that the legislator should always

[1] H. T. Prinsep, Minute, 13 April 1835: India Legislative Proceedings, 27 July 1835, No. 1 (Board's Collections, vol. 1555, No. 63505).

[2] Macaulay, Minute, 11 May 1835: Dharker, op. cit., p. 145. Cf. Bentham, 'Book of Fallacies', *Works*, vol. ii, pp. 402–7.

[3] Macaulay, Minute, 31 May 1835: Ind. Leg. Proc., 27 July 1835, No. 6 (Board's Collections, vol. 1555, No. 63505, f. 39). Ryan had become Chief Justice in 1833.

give reasons for his acts. The problem was to combine the enactive with the expositive, the law with its rationale, while keeping each distinct. Bentham had been certain as to the principle of keeping them distinct, but had not been dogmatic about the method.

To assign the reasons for a law is a separate operation, which ought never to be confounded with the law itself. If it be desirable to instruct the people, it may be done in a preamble, or in a commentary which accompanies the law; but an imperative law ought only to contain the simple expression of the will of the legislator. Intended to serve as a rule of conduct, it cannot be too simple, too clear, too free from dispute.[1]

Macaulay was wholly in agreement with Bentham's principles of conciseness and simplicity. His writing has all the enthusiastic conviction of a proselyte.

... I would resist the very beginning of an evil which has tainted the legislation of every great society. I am firmly convinced that the style of laws is of scarcely less importance than their substance. When we are laying down the rules according to which millions are, at their peril, to shape their actions, we are surely bound to put those rules into such a form that it shall not require any painful effort of attention or any extraordinary quickness of intellect to comprehend them. Why it has been so much the fashion in various parts of the world to darken by gibberish, by tautology, by circumlocution, that meaning which ought to be as transparent as words can make it, is a question which I will not discuss here. It is certain that in many countries not one in a thousand of those who are bound under the most severe penalties to obey the laws can read a page of any law without being altogether bewildered by the unnecessary intricacy and exuberance of the language.[2]

Macaulay was similarly convinced of the need for legislators to give public reasons for their acts; but he felt that this was a matter of acute difficulty. A legislative body might be unanimous as to the passing of a measure, while each member held different and opposite reasons for its desirability.[3] A preamble was therefore usually a tissue of vague generalities

[1] Bentham, 'Essay on Political Tactics', 1791, *Works*, vol. ii, p. 356. See the whole of this essay; also 'On the Promulgation of Laws', *Works*, vol. i, pp. 159–63.

[2] Macaulay, Minute, 11 May 1835: Dharker, op. cit., p. 148. Cf. Bentham, 'Nomography', *Works*, vol. iii, pp. 231 et seq.

[3] Macaulay, Minute, 11 May 1835: Dharker, op. cit., p. 148: 'I fully agree with Mr. Ross and with that eminent writer whom he has quoted [i.e. Bentham] and from whose opinions on a question of jurisprudence it is rarely safe to dissent, in thinking it most desirable that the Government should, in some manner or other, give to the

to embrace a multitude of different reasons; or it was merely
a bare statement: 'Whereas it is expedient. . . .'[1] The only
solution that Macaulay could suggest was the publication of
the minutes of members of Council on questions of legislation, a course which he admitted would expose the dissen-
sions of the Council to the public eye and might even
aggravate their differences.

In dispensing with the preamble, although not perhaps
with the title, Macaulay was generally following Bentham.[2]
As the master's opinions had grown more democratic, however, he had laid increasing stress on the importance of the
'rationale'. In the belief that the giving of reasons was a form
of publicity and was the best popular check against the abuse
of legislative power, Bentham favoured making the rationale
an integral though clearly defined portion of the laws.[3] A
preamble he thought a clumsy instrument, not merely
because of the vague and prolix generalities of which it
usually consisted, but because he believed that every enactive
clause of law should be immediately accompanied by the
ratiocinative.[4] His later views were largely concerned with
codes of law, and for these he had devised an elaborate
method for interweaving the rationale with the text.

public the reasons for its legislative measures.' Bentham had recognized the difficulty
of securing agreed reasons for laws; cf. *Works*, vol. ii, pp. 356–7.

[1] Macaulay, Minute, 11 May 1835: Dharker, op. cit., p. 147. Cf. Bentham,
'Papers on Codification', *Works*, vol. iv, p. 480: ' "Whereas it is expedient"—only
upon British legislators could such a phrase pass itself off in the character of a
reason, or for anything better than a mark of dotage.'

[2] As a general rule Bentham thought the most effective method of indicating the
contents of a statute was by enumerating the sections and prefacing it with a table
of contents; cf. 'Nomography', *Works*, vol. iii, pp. 265–7. He also employed
chapter and section titles in his 'Constitutional Code' and other works. In the
drafting of deeds he favoured the use of titles as an aid to the layman; cf. 'Humphrey's
Real Property Code', *Works*, vol. v, p. 394: cited Dharker, op. cit., p. 28 n.

[3] This is one aspect of the central problem in Bentham's constitutional theory:
how to combine the speed, certainty, and efficiency of despotism with democratic
control. The giving of reasons in legislation he regarded as providing democratic
control. Cf. 'Papers on Codification', 1817, *Works*, vol. iv, p. 526.

[4] Bentham, 'Nomography', *Works*, vol. iii, p. 249 n.: cited Dharker, op. cit.,
p. 27: 'Of all instruments of long-windedness, the most unmerciful is that which is
called a Preamble. It is a sort of excrescence growing out of the head of a section.
If it be apart, it never forms any more than a part of a section, or even so much as a
grammatical sentence. When the preamble is concluded, the principal part of the
sentence is not yet begun.' Macaulay noted with approval Bacon's advice to omit
preambles; 'Essay on Bacon', *Lord Macaulay's Essays*, pp. 401–2.

This method was now recommended by Ross for Indian enactments; and he referred explicitly to Bentham's *Codification Proposal* as his authority.[1] He defended Macaulay's omission of titles, failing a complete code of laws in which the subject-matter would be scientifically classified, and likewise his omission of the preamble. But he wanted the principles and reasons incorporated in contiguous Notes, to be published as an integral part of every law, and disagreed with Macaulay that it was impossible to find agreed reasons. With this interchange of views the matter was referred to the Court of Directors.[2] Meanwhile the Acts of the Government of India were published without title, preamble, or a statement of reasons. When the views of the Home Authorities were received they proved far from favourable. James Mill had died in 1836 and the cause of reform at the India House languished. The despatch of 1 March 1837 disapproved of Macaulay's innovations; and after Macaulay's departure from India the old practice of employing title and preamble was revived.[3] The style of the laws passed between 1834 and 1837, far more than this somewhat minor question, is perhaps the best testimony to Bentham's influence. Their brevity and simplicity show that Macaulay was more apt in applying the Benthamite principles than Bentham himself. He succeeded in giving these principles a practical embodiment such as was never attained in English parliamentary legislation.

A host of miscellaneous questions arose in day-to-day business that were occasions for expressing the Benthamite view. The Chief Magistrate of Calcutta, D. M. Macfarlan, proposed to introduce the principle of the single judge into the magistracy of Calcutta in place of the existing rules by which offences under the by-laws were heard by two magistrates. In support of the principle he quoted Bentham at

---

[1] Bentham, 'Codification Proposal', *Works*, vol. iv, p. 543: 'The greatest happiness of the greatest number requires, that, of this Rationale, the several parts be placed in the most immediate contact with the several arrangements to which they respectively apply. Rationale, interwoven not detached.' A. Ross, Minute, 1 May 1835: Ind. Leg. Proc. 27 July 1835, No. 2 (Board's Collections, vol. 1555, No. 63505, f. 19).

[2] Judicial Letter from India, 24 Aug. (No. 2) 1835, para. 108.

[3] Legislative Despatch to India, 1 Mar. (No. 4) 1837, paras. 22–25. The last of the series of Acts regularly without title or preamble was Act XX of 1839.

length. There was opposition from a section of the European inhabitants led by T. E. M. Turton, a barrister of the Calcutta Supreme Court, who was prominent in the attack on Macaulay in the 'Black Act' controversy. In a later complaint they argued that 'the vesting of such power in one individual had a nearer relation to the spirit which prevails in governing India under Muslim rather than under British rule'.[1] But Macaulay was no man to heed such petitioners; and the measure was carried into law as Act IV of 1835.[2] The same principle of 'single-seatedness' was reiterated in the matter of a draft regulation from the Bombay Government concerning the reconstitution of the Bombay Court of Requests. Macaulay took the opportunity to preach an object-lesson in Bentham's doctrines. Not only was the single judge advocated, but the proposed limitations on the Court's powers of jurisdiction and execution, the distinction made between real and personal property, and the whole pecuniary classification of suits, were roundly assailed.[3] To the system of fees on suits Macaulay said he objected altogether. The expenses of the judicial establishment ought to be borne by the State, although if the State could reimburse itself by fining the party in the wrong, so much the better. But to take fees from a plaintiff before his cause had been tried was simply to punish him for asking for justice, a detestable practice which he hoped would be speedily ended.[4] The prolixity and tautology of the draft act were alone sufficient in Macaulay's view for refusing to pass it. It was sent back to the Bombay Government for reconsideration, with the ready concurrence of Ross and Ryan.

[1] D. M. Macfarlan to C. Macsween, Secretary to Government, 1 June 1834: Bengal Judicial Consultations (Crim. L.P.) 15 Sept. 1834, No. 21 (Board's Collections, vol. 1555, No. 63492, f. 53). Macfarlan's quotations are taken from Bentham, 'Judicial Establishment' in *Works*, vol. iv, pp. 325–6. For the petition against the Bill; Ind. Leg. Proc. 30 May 1836, No. 15: cited Dharker, op. cit., p. 78.

[2] Judicial Letter from India, 24 Aug. (No. 2) 1835, paras. 22–25. Act IV of 1835 is a good example of the conciseness and simplicity of Macaulay's drafting. The whole of the Act is contained in one sentence: 'Be it enacted, that from the 14th day of March, 1835, all powers in Criminal Cases which, by virtue of any law now in force, may be exercised by two Justices of the Peace for the Town of Calcutta, shall be exercised by one such Justice.'   [3] See note R, p. 328.

[4] Macaulay, Minute, 17 April 1835, para. 12. On the question of fees cf. Bentham, 'Rationale of Judicial Evidence', *Works*, vol. vii, pp. 327–8.

It was during these early months of his residence in Calcutta that Macaulay, doubtless animated by his swift successes as law member, was led to declare his larger objectives. By June 1835 Millet had completed his work of consolidating the laws relating to the judicial system of the Bengal Presidency, and of drafting certain amendments.[1] Macaulay sensed the danger that consolidation might be substituted for codification,[2] and that a comparatively limited measure of reform, capable of immediate enactment, might be seized upon by conservatives to forestall a radical scheme of renovation. He proposed therefore that Millett's work, which comprised in effect 'the whole or almost the whole of what Mr. Bentham would call the civil law adjective of the presidency of Fort William and Agra', should be considered by the Council as part of the general question of a careful revision of the whole judicial system. The matter should then be referred with the Council's recommendations to the Law Commission. He was full of sanguine expectation. The Law Commission, he hoped, would be able 'in a few months . . . to frame a complete Code of Civil Procedure for the whole Indian Empire', or at least for Bengal and Agra.[3] The time had therefore come for a statement of his general views on the reform of the judicial organization and its procedure. There was little direct reference to Bentham, but there can be no question that the great source of his inspiration was Bentham's *Draught of a New Plan for the Organization of the Judicial Establishment in France*, which Macaulay later in his life declared to be among the most valuable of Bentham's writings.[4] The similarity of his views with those expressed by James Mill before the Select Committee in June 1832 is also striking.[5]

---

[1] See p. 189.

[2] Cf. Bentham to O'Connell, 15 July 1828: *Works*, vol. x, p. 595: 'Mr. Peel is for consolidation in contradistinction to codification; I for codification in contradistinction to consolidation.' Bentham described Peel's object of consolidation as merely 'to lighten the labour employed by learned gentlemen in making use of the index. . . .'.

[3] Macaulay, Minute, 25 June 1835: Dharker, op. cit., pp. 203–4.

[4] Macaulay, speech on the exclusion of judges from the House of Commons, 1 June 1853: *Complete Works*, vol. xii, p. 305: 'Among all his [Bentham's] writings, there is none which I value more than the treatise on Judicial organization.'

[5] See pp. 184–7.

At the outset Macaulay assailed the system of Indian courts, 'a judicial hierarchy of four orders', as he described it. The courts of the *munsif*, the *sadr amin*, the principal *sadr amin*, and the *zila* or district judge, were established on the basis of 'having four classes of judges to try four classes of causes', the causes being classified according to the value of the amount at issue. Macaulay thought the principle 'utterly indefensible', and attacked it with exactly the arguments of Bentham. Often it necessitated a preliminary suit to determine the value of the amount at issue, before the question of right could be tried, 'a most cumbrous machinery . . . susceptible of being abused in the most flagitious manner for purposes of delay and chicane'.[1] There were no grounds for believing that the intricacy and difficulty of a suit depended on the amount in dispute; indeed it was notorious that the difficulty was greater in suits for small sums. As a test of the importance of a suit the pecuniary principle was worthless; and Macaulay did not shrink from an exercise in Bentham's felicific calculus:

The real measure of the importance of a cause evidently is the quantity of pain and pleasure which the decision produces. And the quantity of pain and pleasure depends not on the absolute magnitude of the sum at stake, but on the magnitude of the sum compared with the means of the parties. A hundred rupees may be more to a clerk than a thousand rupees to a writer in the Company's service, or than ten thousand rupees to a Member of Council.[2]

The corollary was to abolish all pecuniary classification of suits and the fourfold hierarchy of courts of original jurisdiction erected upon it. Instead there should be 'one court having original jurisdiction in all civil causes for all amounts and between all parties throughout the mofussil'. This was to be the *sadr amin*'s court, in which the *munsif* was to serve

---

[1] Cf. Bentham, 'Judicial Establishment', *Works*, vol. iv, p. 333: 'Bad as the metaphysical principle of demarcation is, the *pecuniary* is still worse. Why? Because to all the bad qualities of the metaphysical, it adds others of its own. To such a court shall belong the cognizance of such and such sorts of causes, says the metaphysical principle: provided they are not beyond such or such a *value*, subjoins the pecuniary. What follows? That, besides being plagued about the *sort* of cause, you are plagued about the *value*.'

[2] Macaulay, Minute, 25 June 1835: Dharker, op. cit., p. 206. This is the exact argument used by Bentham, 'Codification Proposal', *Works*, vol. iv, p. 541. Cf. also 'Judicial Establishment', ibid., p. 333.

as an assistant and be competent to try all suits referred to him. The office of the principal *sadr amin* would be discontinued, and the *sadr amin*'s position raised in status and emolument. Macaulay's conception, it will be remarked, is exactly that of Bentham and his disciples, Mill and Ross— a single grade of omnicompetent tribunals of original jurisdiction, sufficient in number to make justice near and readily available. Following Bentham again, Macaulay was in favour of making suits transferable among these tribunals to meet the convenience of the parties, a feature which Bentham had termed 'intercommunity of jurisdiction'.[1]

The procedure of these courts remained to be regulated, and once more Bentham was the master. Macaulay advocated oral pleadings and confrontation of the parties, the arguments for which—as for his proverbial schoolboy—were 'familiar to all who have paid any attention to the philosophy of jurisprudence'. The initial plaint could not be dispensed with, but all subsequent pleadings, after the defendant had been informed of the nature of the claim against him, would be oral.[2] Wilful falsehood by any of the parties would be punished equally as if from a witness.[3] Although the general rule should be for the confrontation of parties, Macaulay was prepared to make the same significant exceptions as Bentham to the rules of jurisprudence when these conflicted with local popular prejudice. Persons of high rank, Macaulay asserted, should be examined in their homes if necessary, a suggestion which he seems to have taken directly from Bentham's *Essay on the Influence of Time and Place in Matters of Legislation*.[4] This essay had obviously had a profound influence on Macaulay, and its ideas ran through the whole of his argument in his great parliamentary speech of 10 July 1833 when he dealt with the question of a codified law for India. For his

---

[1] Macaulay, Minute, 25 June 1835; Dharker, op. cit., p. 210. Cf. Bentham, 'Judicial Establishment', *Works*, vol. iv, pp. 329, 335.

[2] Cf. Bentham, 'Principles of Judicial Procedure', *Works*, vol. ii, pp. 76–78, 173.

[3] Ibid., p. 92. Also cf. 'Petition for Justice', *Works*, vol. v, p. 451.

[4] Macaulay, Minute, 25 June 1835; Dharker, op. cit., p. 212. Cf. Bentham, 'Essay on the Influence of Time and Place', *Works*, vol. i, p. 182: 'Among the inhabitants of Hindostan, a man of a certain rank would think himself extremely dishonoured, were he obliged to make his appearance in a court of justice. What does that signify? Persons of that description are always rich: send a special commission to examine them, and make them pay the expense.'

proposals on the law of evidence there was the same debt; it was a subject, Macaulay confessed, 'on which, as indeed on most other parts of the philosophy of jurisprudence, it is not easy to add to what has been said by Mr. Bentham'. The central principle was 'that all evidence should be taken at what it may be worth, that no consideration which has a tendency to produce conviction in a rational mind should be excluded from the consideration of the tribunals'. Like Bentham, Macaulay proposed that the evidence of parties to a suit should be generally admitted, since they were better acquainted with the truth, and their bias more obvious, than any witness.[1] He ended with the hope that echoed the master: 'I cannot but hope that when we have brought justice near to every man's door, when we have made pleading oral, when we have made the law of evidence simple and rational, the number of unjust prosecutions will shrink to a small amount, and that the decisions will generally be just and speedy.'

Having considered the organization and procedure of the court of primary jurisdiction, there remained the process of appeal. Macaulay repeated, in almost the same words, the charge Mill had levelled at this part of the judicial system in his parliamentary evidence in June 1832. There was no part of the jurisprudence of Bengal that was more defective.[2] He outlined the evils—the allowance of two or more appeals, and the hearing of fresh evidence by the appeal court. Appeals naturally divided themselves into two kinds, appeals on matters of law and appeals on matters of fact. Appeals of the first kind should go directly to the *Sadr Diwani Adalat*, the highest tribunal.[3] This Court would be able to decide all such cases by being relieved of trying appeals on matters of fact, and by vesting in a single judge, sitting alone, the whole power of the Court, so obtaining 'the advantage of what has been quaintly but expressively called "single-seated justice"'. Appeals of the second kind, appeals on matters of fact, which were by far the greater proportion, were not strictly

---

[1] Cf. Bentham, 'Rationale of Judicial Evidence', *Works*, vol. vii, pp. 124, 147, 401, 487–9.

[2] Macaulay, Minute 25 June 1835: Dharker, op. cit., p. 216. Cf. James Mill, evidence, 29 June 1832: *P.P.*, 1831–2, vol. xii, p. 122, Qu. 1043.

[3] The same course was advocated by Mill; see p. 185. Cf. also James Mill, evidence, 29 June 1832: ibid., p. 123, Qu. 1048.

allowable. On a question of fact it should not be permissible for a judge who had not heard the evidence to revise the decision of one who had. In Macaulay's mind were the Benthamite criteria for the authenticity of evidence; these provided that not only the logic and consistency of evidence should be taken into consideration, but also the manner in which evidence was orally delivered.[1] Hence a court of appeal, Macaulay declared, was a less competent tribunal in considering evidence on questions of fact than the original court before which the evidence was orally delivered by the parties and witnesses. There was an insuperable objection to the summoning of witnesses for re-examination. 'If the Court of Appeal calls for the witnesses and re-examines them, it ceases to be a Court of Appeal. It tries the cause over again.' When therefore an appeal was lodged on a question of fact, the question should be tried again by the same or another court of original jurisdiction. Now this argument as to the essential distinction between original and appellate jurisdiction is taken, of course, from Bentham and his popularizer, James Mill.[2] And Macaulay, like Mill and Ross, reinforced it by applying to the local circumstances of India that conception of Bentham's which saw appeal as largely a controlling and checking function. Macaulay considered that Europeans should be confined to the work of appeal, and original jurisdiction made over wholly to Indian judges. This to him seemed an excellent division of labour. For determining the probity of oral evidence Indian judges were by far the best qualified; but on account of moral, intellectual, and obvious political reasons, the work of appeal was best done by Europeans. Macaulay, following Bentham and Mill, regarded the appeal judge not merely as the head

[1] Macaulay, Minute, 25 June 1835: Dharker, op. cit., p. 218: '. . . it seems to me most extraordinary that we should suffer a judge who only knows a cause from the depositions to reverse the decision of a judge who has looked the witnesses full in the face, who has noted not merely their words, but the tones in which those words were uttered, who has read the lines of their countenances, who has observed in one the stammering of a man conscious of fraud, in another the suspicious fluency of a man who is repeating a tale learned by rote.' Cf. Bentham, 'Rationale of Judicial Evidence', *Works*, vol. vi, p. 228; vol. vii, pp. 29, 44.

[2] James Mill's *Encyclopaedia Britannica* article 'Jurisprudence', written in 1820 and privately printed together with his other essays, is the best succinct statement of Bentham's doctrines on jurisprudence.

of a superior tribunal, but as an active supervisor and inspector of all the judicial organization subordinate to him. But this involved him in one obvious difficulty. If the only appeal court was to be at the metropolis, close personal supervision of the native judges was impossible. Macaulay, therefore, like Mill, appeared to envisage the district judge as being virtually deprived of his functions as an original or appeal judge, and being given the role of a sort of judicial inspector, 'to inspect and check' the subordinate courts 'at every stage of their proceedings'.[1]

He continued this Minute, the most extensive and most general that he wrote on the law system of India, by a lengthy argument for the abolition of institution fees and all other forms of law taxes. The train of thought was as always his own, but in refuting the theory that fees on the institution of suits checked excessive litigiousness, he could do little but use the arguments of Bentham.[2] To compensate for the loss of revenue Macaulay suggested that in certain instances the losing party should pay a fine to Government in addition to the costs. Finally, he proposed the abolition of the suit *in forma pauperis*, by which poor persons had hitherto been exempted from institution fees and had been provided with legal aid. If the reforms he advocated were effected, justice would be cheap, swift, and accessible, and there would be no need to make an exception in favour of a particular class. Now Bentham had also condemned a special form of justice for the indigent, but he had provided for their needs in a far more comprehensive way than the old suit *in forma pauperis*. On the principle of 'justice to the helpless', there was in his scheme to be a state organization to provide free legal aid.[3] There is a significant pointer here to the sharp gulf that existed between the outlook of Bentham and Macaulay outside the purely technical sphere of law reform. Macaulay stood for an individualism that was tinged with an

---

[1] The district judge under Macaulay's scheme was to hear complaints against denial or delay of justice, a function Bentham had termed 'quasi-appeal' ('Principles of Judicial Procedure', *Works*, vol. ii, pp. 162–4). It should be remembered, of course, that the district judge was also a criminal as well as a civil judge, and his original jurisdiction in this first capacity was not touched by Macaulay's proposals.

[2] Cf. Bentham, 'Protest against Law Taxes', *Works*, vol. ii, pp. 576 et seq.

[3] Cf. Bentham, 'Constitutional Code', *Works*, vol. ix, pp. 577–9.

element of puritanical sternness. He had no use for the bureau-cratic intervention of the state.

We are bound to make a lawsuit as cheap and easy a proceeding as it can be made. But, when we have done this, we are no more bound to relieve a man from the inconveniences which poverty produces in a lawsuit than from the inconveniences which it produces in all the other parts of human life. We are no more bound to find a man a vakil gratis than to find him rice and clothes gratis. Good legal advice may be important to a suitor. But surely it is not more important to him than good medical advice to an invalid. And why the State which suffers its poor subjects to die by thousands for want of good physicians should be bound to find them good advocates, I am unable to comprehend.[1]

Professional advice would not be essential under his pro-posed system of procedure; and even if it were, the plaintiff would always find lawyers to undertake his cause on specula-tion, or money-lenders to advance the fees. But at all events, it was wrong to make a precedent by departing in this matter from the principle of *laissez-faire*: 'These things always adjust themselves when Governments are wise enough to leave them alone. But one departure from sound principles renders other departures necessary.'

There was another significant hint in this Minute of Macaulay that shows the bearing of his thoughts on the more critical questions of political theory. The establishment of the local omnicompetent courts (the *sadr amin* courts) on the scale he envisaged incurred an obvious financial objec-tion. He was eloquent enough in refuting this objection; it was sufficient to answer 'that the administration of justice is the end of government; and that no Government has a moral right to raise twenty crore from a people, and then tell them to put up with injustice because justice costs too much'. But there was one change of administrative system which, he agreed with Ross, might well meet the additional expense and also improve efficiency. This was no less than 'divesting the functionaries engaged in the collec-tion of revenue of all their judicial functions, and thus saving

---

[1] Macaulay, Minute, 25 June 1835: Dharker, op. cit., p. 224. Macaulay's views were later modified (cf. speech on Fielden's Ten Hour Bill, 22 May 1846: *Complete Works*, vol. xii, pp. 199 et seq.; cited G. M. Young, *Victorian England*, pp. 51–53). But in 1835 he was hostile to almost all intervention by the State except in educa-tion; cf. Minute on Indigo Contracts, 13 Nov. 1835: Dharker, op. cit., pp. 276–7.

the whole cost of the machinery which is now required to enable them to perform those functions'. Here, within five years of its formal introduction, the union of the collector and magistrate was already being subject to a powerful attack in Council, and by implication the whole philosophy of rule which lay behind the measure was being assailed. The hollowness of the conflict which Macaulay waged with Prinsep over his proposed law reforms stands exposed. On the fundamental principle of the Cornwallis system, the separation of revenue and judicial powers, there was no disagreement between them.

Prinsep believed, however, that a great issue was at stake. Macaulay had revealed his designs for creating a comprehensive body of rational codes rather than merely composing a set of digests of the existing law. Prinsep objected to such a plan: 'I look upon it as contrary to the spirit and letter of the law [i.e. of the Charter Act] that the whole of what is now in existence, shall first be laid prostrate in the idea that a new system theoretically perfect can readily and with ease be established'.[1] He proposed the immediate enactment of Millett's set of Regulations (which comprised with a few amendments the digest of the existing law of civil procedure) instead of delaying in the hope of a more perfect reform. While he did not deny the eventual need for an entirely new system of civil law, he believed that Millett's work of consolidation provided an immediate measure of relief. A new system, on the other hand, would take several years to fashion, and would have to embrace the whole of British India. And his prejudice was in favour of the existing system: he defended against Macaulay the monetary classification of suits, and the institution and stamp fees on suits. He thought that Macaulay's proposal for a single grade of court to hear all original causes would mean an impossible expense.[2] Over the question of institution fees he was supported by the ill-starred Macnaghten, who advanced the argument of experience that institution fees were necessary to check the

---

[1] H. T. Prinsep, Minute, 11 June 1835: Ind. Leg. Proc., 15 June 1835, No. 2 (Board's Collections, vol. 1555, No. 63507, f. 13).

[2] H. T. Prinsep, Minute, 25 August 1835, paras. 4 et seq.: Ind. Leg. Cons., 3 April 1837, No. 19.

propensity for groundless litigation. In an interesting post-script Macnaghten said that he had been recommended to read Bentham's *Protest against Law Taxes*; and it is significant of the authority which Bentham's name commanded by this time, that Macnaghten dared not dissent from the general doctrines of 'that eminent philosopher', but contented himself with arguing that in this question they were inapplicable to India.[1]

The opposition which Macaulay encountered was doubtless in some measure partisan, and also partly the natural hostility of long-experienced Indian civil servants to the scheme of a transient and brilliant speculative reformer. The opposition hardly reached to any deep difference of principle, but it was sufficient, by merely protracting the discussion, to prevent the carrying into effect of Macaulay's comprehensive plan. His ally, Ross, probably hardened resistance by his recourse to Bentham's authority on every occasion. In answering Prinsep's defence of institution fees and stamp duties on lawsuits, Ross referred to 'Mr. Bentham's celebrated tract on Law Taxes for a complete refutation of every argument that has yet been advanced in favor of them', and he obligingly summarized Bentham's ideas in a Minute advocating the consolidation of the Stamp Laws.[2] A petition 'from the inhabitants of Calcutta' for jury trial to be introduced in the King's Courts brought forth another lecture on the Benthamite dogma. A jury should not be employed in a court of original jurisdiction, although it could be employed in a court of appeal. But it was impossible to give more than a brief indication of the arguments; the members of Council were again referred to the master's writings, in this case Bentham's *Letters to Lord Granville on Scotch Reform*.[3] To such a doctrinaire application of theory even moderate

[1] Macnaghten's opinion is given as a Note to Prinsep's Minute of 25 Aug. 1835. W. H. Macnaghten was at this time Secretary to Government in the Political and Secret Depts., but he was a leading authority on law. He was murdered while acting as Envoy in Afghanistan in Dec. 1841.

[2] A. Ross, Minute, 10 Nov. 1835, para. 17: Ind. Leg. Cons., 3 April 1837, No. 20. Also undated Minute enclosed in above: ibid., No. 23.

[3] A. Ross, Minute, n.d. (enclosed in Minute of 10 Nov. 1835), para. 9: Ind. Leg. Cons., 3 April 1837, No. 22. The Supreme or King's Court had sole jurisdiction over Calcutta (within the Mahratta ditch). Cf. Bentham, 'Letters on Scotch Reform', *Works*, vol. v.

reformers were opposed. T. C. Robertson, later to be Lieutenant-Governor of the North-Western Provinces, voiced
their opinion.[1] Disclaiming any excessive reverence for the
principles of Cornwallis, he thought it wrong to set out with
the assumption—in Mackintosh's words—'that our predecessors have been hitherto toiling to build up an elaborate
system of folly, a stupendous edifice of injustice'. His complaints against the proposed reforms were that they constituted a violent break with the past, and that 'instead of
grafting on the Cornwallis Code what is wanting to supply
its deficiencies, the object now seems to be to level the whole
fabric in the dust, and raise a new edifice upon its ruins'.
Macaulay and Ross had proceeded by '*a priori* reasoning', on
theories and not on facts; and the charge that a few years
previously Macaulay had levelled upon Mill now rebounded
upon him. Robertson quoted Clarendon against him:

> He is a much better Counsellor who by his experience and observa-
> tion of the nature and the humour of the people who are to be governed,
> gives advice what ought to be done, than he who from his speculative
> knowledge of mankind and of the rights of Government and of the
> nature of Equity and Honour attained with much study, would erect an
> engine of Government by the rules of Geometry more infallible than
> experience can ever find out.

Macaulay's scheme had no root in experience, Robertson
declared, but rested on the teachings of a single man. 'For
none of these burly innovations have we the assurance of a
single tried experiment in any quarter of the globe, but in its
stead the authority of a great modern jurist.' There could be
no greater testimony to the strength of Bentham's authority,
and Robertson could pit against it only that of 'the great
father of Political Economy himself' as an advocate of
gradual and moderate reform.

The weight of opinion in favour of the immediate enactment of Millett's draft Regulations was so great as to incline
Auckland to its side,[2] but Macaulay's influence and prestige
was strong enough for the question to be referred to the Law

---

[1] T. C. Robertson, Minute, 3 March 1836: Ind. Leg. Cons., 3 April 1837,
No. 25. Robertson was at this period a member of Council.

[2] Minute of Governor-General, 15 May 1836: Ind. Leg. Cons., 3 April 1837,
No. 26.

Commission, which meant in effect a victory for Macaulay's view. In reviewing the discussion a year after his original Minute of June 1835, he saw no reason to alter his opinions in their essential point.[1] He was still sanguine although more guarded in his forecast of the labours of the Law Commission. He anticipated that the Penal Code would be ready for submission to the Government in the cold weather of 1836–7, that the Code of Criminal Procedure would be completed during the course of 1837, and that by the beginning of 1838 the Law Commission would be ready to commence framing the Code of Civil Procedure. If the Code of Civil Procedure was to be complete within two years, was it then desirable, Macaulay asked, to enact Millett's very imperfect Code for Bengal in 1836; to interrupt the work of the Law Commission on the Penal Code in order to perform for Bengal what would have to be done for the whole of India a short while later?

Unquestionably there was an element of obstinacy in Macaulay's attitude. He was postponing the question of civil procedure to a date when he knew he would probably be no longer in India.[2] In fact, the Bengal Presidency was deprived of the benefit of Millett's very serviceable code of Regulations, and had to wait until the Indian Code of Civil Procedure was passed in 1859 before it received proper relief. He had himself to admit that he would be happy if the Code of Civil Rights were complete by 1850.[3] That grandiose conception of a pyramid of codes, which had inspired him in 1833, had faded into a future he could not control. The scheme of judicial organization and procedure, about which he had been so hopeful in June 1835, was by 1836 tacitly admitted to be impossible of achievement during the years that remained to him in India. The proud confident Minute of 1835, written in the year when his party was carrying the Municipal Reform Bill through Parliament, the immense reforms he had in hand which were to 'make old Bentham jump in his grave',[4] these recorded hopes remained

---

[1] Macaulay, Minute, 6 June 1836: Dharker, op. cit., p. 239.
[2] Already in Dec. 1836 Macaulay was announcing his intention to be in England by the summer of 1838; cf. Trevelyan, *Macaulay*, p. 321.
[3] Macaulay, Minute, 6 June 1836: Dharker, op. cit., p. 240.
[4] Cf. Macaulay to Ellis, 7 June 1835: Macaulay Correspondence, Trinity College Library, Cambridge: 'I have immense reforms in hand such as you Knight

merely as testimony to the strength of his convictions. By the end of 1836 he found that the utmost achievement of the Law Commission during his period of office would be the preparation of the Penal Code, and that he himself would not be present to pass it into legislation.

Even many of the minor reforms which he agreed to except from his general rule of not making 'partial alterations in a judicial system which is about to undergo a thorough revision' failed to be enacted because the Law Commission was unable to cope with the mass of business deluging it. Macaulay had thought the Supreme Court at Calcutta could be usefully remodelled as a pilot experiment for the larger reforms. He tried to introduce oral pleadings when the Court sat as a Court of Equity, and his good understanding with the Chief Justice, Sir Edward Ryan, and with Sir Benjamin Malkin, made him hopeful of success. The Home Authorities had also instructed the Supreme Court to reduce its establishment and to draft a scheme for altering the remuneration of its officers from fees to fixed salaries, a reform in keeping with the Benthamite current of thought.[1] But the practical suspension of the Law Commission through the illness of three of its members delayed the question. The proposal for *viva voce* proceedings was shelved, although the objections to it had never been more than those of detail; and Macaulay reluctantly agreed to what he considered the excessive establishment and salaries proposed by the judges in order to preserve 'that close alliance which at present exists between the Government of India and His Majesty's judges'.[2]

There were, of course, individual and sometimes spectacular triumphs, such as the so-called 'Black Act' (Act XI of 1836). This made Europeans resident outside Calcutta subject to the jurisdiction of the Company's courts in civil causes, and deprived them of their right of appeal to the Supreme Court.[3]

Templars would abhor, but such as would make old Bentham jump in his grave—oral pleadings—examination of parties—single seated justice—no institution fees—and so forth.'

[1] Macaulay, Minute, 16 May 1836: Dharker, op. cit., p. 199. Judicial Despatch to India, 10 June (No. 13) 1835.

[2] Macaulay, Minute, n.d.: Dharker, op. cit., p. 201.

[3] The question is surveyed comprehensively in the Judicial Letter from India (Leg. Dept.), 30 May (No. 6) 1836.

The step had clearly been envisaged by Parliament in its grant of full legislative authority to the Government of India, and had been expressly enjoined in the accompanying Public Despatch of 10 December 1834.[1] The subjection of Europeans to the authority of Indian *sadr amins* aroused opposition from a small group in Calcutta, breathing 'the spirit of an exclusive caste', and Macaulay fought them with all the zest and matchless torrent of argument that he employed on a great parliamentary occasion. It was perhaps the Utilitarian as much as the Liberal in his make-up which prompted him. At least the principle of uniformity, which he had enunciated in his speech on the Charter Bill in 1833, was among his foremost arguments on this issue, and it was a principle whose relevance to India in this respect had been firmly stated by James Mill.

The principle on which we proceeded was that the system ought, as far as possible, to be uniform, that no distinction ought to be made between one class of people and another, except in cases where it could be clearly made out that such a distinction was necessary to the pure and efficient administration of justice.[2]

Yet apart from these individual failures and successes, Macaulay was obliged by 1837 to modify his attitude against piecemeal and partial reforms in order to save something of his ambitious scheme for a new judicial system and procedure. A proposal came from the two courts of *Sadr Diwani Adalat* (at Calcutta and Allahabad) to extend the provisions of Regulation V of 1831, so that the district judge could refer not only regular but also summary appeals to a principal *sadr amin*.[3] As a safeguard, a second or special summary appeal from the orders of the principal *sadr amin* to the district

[1] See p. 194.
[2] Macaulay, Minute, n.d. (Ind. Leg. Cons., 28 March 1836, No. 13): Dharker, op. cit., pp. 176–7. Cf. James Mill, evidence, 21 Feb. 1832: *P.P.*, 1831–2, vol. ix, p. 53, Qu. 373.
[3] Judicial Letter from India (Leg. Dept.), 20 March (No. 3) 1837, paras. 22 et seq. In response to Ross's criticism Regulation V of 1831 had been framed so as to make the decision from all native judges generally appealable to the district judge; see p. 166. A special proviso (Regulation V, 1831, xvi. 2), however, made it possible for the district judge, when his file was so heavy as to cause serious delay, to apply to the *Sadr* Court for permission to refer a specified number of appeals from the decisions of *munsifs* and *sadr amins* to the principal *sadr amin*. Apparently it had become the practice by 1837 to make extensive use of this provision.

judge was suggested. This multiplication of the stages of appeal was naturally assailed by Ross, the disciple of Bentham, again stressing the principle that all appeals should be heard by European judges and that the district judge in consequence be relieved of all original jurisdiction. Macaulay agreed wholeheartedly and his view was adopted officially by the Government. In practice this meant doing away with the monetary limitation which restricted the jurisdiction of principal *sadr amins* to suits of 5,000 rupees in value. The *Sadr* Court at Calcutta, with Rattray at its head, demurred at such sweeping changes; and Macaulay, with ill-concealed contempt, trounced every argument in favour of the pecuniary classification of suits in the best Benthamite manner.[1] On principle he was opposed to giving the principal *sadr amin* any appellate jurisdiction, but there were practical difficulties.

My own wish would be to give the native functionaries original jurisdiction in every case and appellate jurisdiction in no case; I certainly would not give them appellate jurisdiction, in order to relieve the European functionary, until I was satisfied that sufficient relief would not be given by extending the original jurisdiction of the native functionary.[2]

If it was impossible to increase the number of European judges where the pressure of business was so considerable, he would 'very unwillingly grant the new appellate jurisdiction to the Principal *Sadr Amins*'. The final outcome was that by Act XXV of 1837 principal *sadr amins* were given jurisdiction to any amount in original suits, and appeals from their decisions for amounts of more than 5,000 rupees were made to lie directly to the *Sadr* Court. This meant that there would be only a single stage of appeal from the principal *sadr amin*, either to the district judge or directly to the *Sadr* Court. But the absolute distinction which Ross and Macaulay wished to see made between judges of appeal and judges of first instance was not achieved. The district judge was not deprived of his power of original jurisdiction for suits

---

[1] Letter of Registrar, Court of *Sadr Diwani Adalat*, Lower Provinces, 21 April 1837: Ind. Leg. Cons., 21 July 1837 (Board's Collections, vol. 1682, No. 67823, f. 7). Macaulay, Minute, 15 May 1837: Dharker, op. cit., pp. 229–34.

[2] Macaulay, Minute, 6 Feb. 1837: Dharker, op. cit., p. 227.

over 5,000 rupees in value, and the principal *sadr amin* was likewise permitted to exercise both original and appellate jurisdiction.

This was the sum and substance of Macaulay's achievement in reforming the judicial system. It was indeed the palest reflection of his ambitious project. The law of procedure remained unreformed, and all the old faults that Macaulay had inveighed against continued to vitiate the system. There was still a multiplicity of courts of primary jurisdiction—the *munsif*'s, the *sadr amin*'s, the principal *sadr amin*'s, and the district judge's—with their jurisdiction determined by the monetary classification of suits. There was a multiplicity of courts of appeal—the principal *sadr amin*'s, the district judge's, the *Sadr* Court; and appellate and original jurisdiction continued to be exercised by the same persons.

Macaulay's important and lasting achievement was the Penal Code, but before discussing this topic it is convenient to deal briefly with a matter to which it was allied and whose outcome is typical of that general frustration of his attempts at radical reform. In December 1835 Macaulay proposed a committee to inquire into the subject of prison discipline, his argument being that 'the best Criminal Code can be of very little use to the community unless there be a good machinery for the infliction of punishment'.[1] The committee naturally included the members of the Law Commission, Macaulay, Cameron, Anderson, and Macleod. Their Report, which appeared in 1838, was a learned and voluminous affair and was a classic of its kind. It reflects the whole Benthamite cast of mind and the leading principles of the master, although it disclaimed any excessive reverence for Bentham's doctrines.[2] It is sufficient to quote a summary of the committee's findings to realize the debt to his thought.

---

[1] Macaulay, Minute, 14 Dec. 1835: Dharker, op. cit., p. 278. Judicial Letter from India (Leg. Dept.), 29 Feb. (No. 2) 1836, para. 47.

[2] The report is contained in the Collection to Legislative Despatch to India, 30 Oct. (No. 19) 1839. Macaulay dissented from Bentham over the question of transportation, and introduced it for India as an alternative penalty to death. Macaulay's general agreement with the recommendations of the committee can be inferred by the similar views put forward by him in the Notes accompanying the Penal Code; cf. *Complete Works*, vol. xi, p. 26.

The general features of the system of Prison Discipline recommended by the Committee are these viz. that a Penitentiary for all prisoners sentenced to more than one year's imprisonment shall be established in the centre of every 6 or 8 districts, and that a better system for the classification of prisoners shall be adopted: that each prisoner shall have a separate sleeping place: that solitary confinement shall be much resorted to: that monotonous, uninteresting labour within doors shall be enforced upon all prisoners sentenced to labour: that prisoners shall be deprived of every indulgence not absolutely necessary to health, and that the management of each Penitentiary shall be committed to an able trustworthy Superintendent, either European or Native.[1]

Is not this the authentic voice of the new Poor Law, of Chadwick and Southwood Smith? The note is sterner than that of Bentham, but there is an obvious debt to his *Principles of Penal Law* and to his 'Panopticon' plan.[2] Such sweeping changes of system met the same fate as the other plans for judicial reform. The committee and the Bengal Government had modestly proposed that the initial measures should be confined to the erection of an experimental penitentiary for the seven districts adjacent to Calcutta. The Home Authorities gave the Report high commendation, but argued that the principles it urged were untried in Indian conditions and that strong financial objections existed to building even one model penitentiary. It was suggested that existing gaols should be converted in order to provide the necessary segregation of each class of prisoners, and to enable tests to be conducted into the practicability of the system of prison discipline recommended by the committee.[3] Although in later years the Report was to provide the general principles of prison reform, the hopes of immediate and comprehensive measures were therefore blighted.[4]

---

[1] Legislative Despatch to India, 30 Oct. (No. 19) 1839, para. 3.

[2] The general system of prison discipline advocated by Bentham is most succinctly stated in 'Principles of Penal Law', *Works*, vol. i, pp. 420–1, 498–503. Classification of prisoners is discussed, pp. 499–500 (also cf. 'Panopticon', *Works*, vol. iv, pp. 137–41); the use of solitary confinement, vol. i, pp. 425–7.

[3] Legislative Despatch to India, 30 Oct. (No. 19) 1839, paras. 5–9.

[4] Cf. J. S. Mill, *Memorandum of the Improvements in the Administration of India during the Last Thirty Years* (1858), cited Sir G. C. Rankin, *Background to Indian Law*, pp. 215–16. Cf. also J. C. Durai, 'Indian Prisons', *Journal of Comparative Legislation and International Law* (3rd Series), vol. xi, pp. 246–77.

4. *The Penal Code*

To a follower of Bentham the object of an efficient judicial establishment was subordinate to the larger aim. A body of codes, a 'pannomium' as Bentham termed it, was regarded as the master-work for the philosophic reformer. The confusion of law systems in India before the Charter Act of 1833, and the practical need for reform, which was admitted by the most conservative observers, inspired the hope of a great chain of codes for the Indian Empire. Bentham had long recognized the opportunity which India presented, but it was left for Macaulay to make the matter one of practical politics. In his speech on the Charter Bill of 10 July 1833 Macaulay echoed the sentiments which Bentham had expressed half-a-century before, and which Mill had written into his *History*.

As I believe that India stands more in need of a code than any other country in the world, I believe also that there is no country on which that great benefit can more easily be conferred. A Code is almost the only blessing—perhaps it is the only blessing—which absolute governments are better fitted to confer on a nation than popular governments.[1]

This is the language of the legislator conceived, in the manner of Bentham, as the sword-arm of the eighteenth-century despot; it is the authoritarian conception which had led Mill to favour a legislative commission which was to be kept as small as possible and in practice the creature of a single mind. There was opposition from sections of the Court of Directors and in Parliament to a uniform code of laws; and Macaulay had to emphasize the deference that would be paid to native custom and prejudice.

We do not mean that all the people of India should live under the same law; far from it. . . . We know how desirable that object is; but we also know that it is unattainable. We know that respect must be paid to feelings generated by differences of religion, of nation, and of caste. Much, I am persuaded, may be done to assimilate the different systems of law without wounding those feelings. But, whether we assimilate those systems or not, let us ascertain them; let us digest them. We propose no rash innovation; we wish to give no shock to the prejudices of any part of our subjects. Our principle is simply this;

[1] See note S, p. 328.

uniformity where you can have it; diversity where you must have it; but in all cases certainty.[1]

This was exactly the position adopted by Bentham and Mill, and, on the setting-up of the Law Commission in 1835, it was Bentham's methods that Macaulay largely followed. Ross had already elaborated the master's principles of codification at great length, and cited the encomium that 'a high American functionary', in a letter to Bentham, had lavished on him who should be the law-giver of the nineteenth century.[2] The model, Ross said,

had been supplied by Mr. Bentham, and upon that model and upon those principles explained and demonstrated by the great jurist in his writings on Jurisprudence and Legislation . . . an all comprehensive body of laws for our Indian Empire should be executed.[3]

Bentham had considered that the order of composition of the pannomium should logically be the codes of substantive law—the penal, the civil, and the constitutional—and then the codes of adjective law, which would include the code of judicial procedure. It is noticeable, however, that in his own studies he devoted his most intensive labours to the law of procedure and to constitutional law. In practice, as he was ready to admit, the penal code was easiest to compose, and then the code of judicial procedure, together with that portion of the constitutional code which dealt with the organization of the judicial establishment.[4] These were universal in their nature and could be largely framed without reference to conditions in particular countries. Bentham never went beyond the barest outline of what he termed 'the civil law substantive', that is the law which defined and secured the rights of person and property.

Macaulay started from a more practical basis. The digest of the Bengal Regulations by Millett comprised in effect, as Macaulay said, 'what Mr. Bentham would call the civil law

---

[1] Macaulay, speech, 10 July 1833: *Complete Works*, vol. xi, pp. 581–2.

[2] The letter quoted by Ross was printed in Bentham's 'Codification Proposal' (published 1822), *Works*, vol. iv, p. 579. The part quoted begins with the passage: 'What may be called the philosophy of law . . .' and ends with the sentence: 'The utility of such a work would be acknowledged in every part of the civilized world. . . .'

[3] A. Ross, Minute, 30 Dec. 1833, para. 9: Board's Collections, vol. 1555, No. 63507, ff. 39–40.   [4] See note T, p. 328.

adjective of the presidencies of Fort William and Agra'.[1] This was naturally therefore the most suitable point of departure for commencing the codes. Macaulay felt in 1835, in the first flush of optimism, that the Law Commission would 'be able in a few months after the reference to frame a complete Code of Civil Procedure for the whole Indian Empire', or at least for the Bengal and Agra Presidencies. There would be an interval of a few months, however, before the matter could be referred to the Law Commission. What better use could the Commission make of this interval than to frame 'a Criminal Code for the whole Indian Empire?'[2] It was in this rather casual manner that Macaulay took up the work which constitutes, apart from his decisive intervention in the education controversy, the permanent achievement of his Indian years. His belief that the preparation of a penal code presented little difficulty probably rested on the view officially stated by the judges of the Calcutta Supreme Court in 1830. 'Any one intelligent English lawyer', they declared, 'and one of the civil servants employed in the Nizamut Adawlut, with the Reports of that Court recently published, might jointly prepare a Regulation, which would be for all persons throughout India as good a penal code as any now existing in the world.'[3] But undoubtedly the judges had in mind the consolidation of existing law and not the Benthamite code which Macaulay intended.

The Minute by which he introduced the subject followed the best traditions of philosophic radicalism.

One reason for beginning with the Criminal Law is that there is no department of law which so early attracted the attention of philosophers, or which still excites so general an interest among reflecting and reading men. It is more than seventy years since the famous treatise 'Dei delitti e delle pene' acquired an European reputation, and from that time down to the present day a succession of men eminent as practical and as speculative statesmen has been engaged in earnest discussion on

---

[1] Macaulay, Minute, 25 June 1835: Dharker, op. cit., p. 203.

[2] Macaulay, Minute, 4 June 1835: Ind. Judic. Cons., 15 June 1835, No. 1 (Board's Collections, vol. 1555, No. 63507, f. 7). Dharker unfortunately omits this important paper of Macaulay.

[3] 'Some Observations on a Suggestion of the Governor-General in Council as to the Formation of a Code of Laws for the British Territories in the East Indies', Enclosure No. 2, in letter from judges, 13 Sept. 1830: P.P., 1831, vol. vi, p. 582.

the principles of penal jurisprudence. There is perhaps no province of legislation that has been so thoroughly explored in all directions.[1]

The directions which Macaulay suggested for the Law Commission, and which were adopted, instructed it to frame a complete Criminal Code for all parts of the Indian Empire, which should not be a digest of existing law but should embrace all reforms thought desirable. The two great principles on which the Code was to be framed were 'the principle of suppressing crime with the smallest possible infliction of suffering, and the principle of assertaining truth at the smallest possible cost of time and money'. The Code was to be complete. 'Not only ought everything in the Code to be law: but nothing that is not in the Code ought to be law.' The commission was to aim at uniformity as far as was practicable; differences of law for different races or sects were not to be established without a clear and strong reason. Crimes were to be separately defined, and the commission was cautioned against the use of vague terms such as treason and manslaughter.[2] No indictment was to be good that did not follow the words of one of the definitions in the Code, and no conviction was to be imposed on account of an act that did not come distinctly within that definition. Conciseness and perspicuity of language were enjoined, for in general these qualities were not only compatible but identical. The commissioners were directed to append notes to the Code assigning their reasons for all provisions for which the reasons were not obvious. The rule was that 'the Code should be purely imperative; and no argumentative matter whatever should be introduced into it'.

Here broadly expressed are Bentham's principles of punishment and his criteria for a code, which Ross had already quoted:

aptitude for notoriety in respect of its contents, conciseness and clearness in respect of its language, compactness in respect of its form;

---

[1] Macaulay, Minute, 4 June 1835. Macaulay refers to the work *Dei delitti e delle pene* of Beccaria which appeared in 1764.

[2] Cf. Bentham, 'Book of Fallacies', *Works*, vol. ii, p. 456. Macaulay's draft of the Penal Code did, however, use the term 'manslaughter' but defines it strictly; cf. *A Penal Code prepared by the Indian Law Commissioners*, Calcutta, 1837, sections 295–6. The term was dropped in the final version: Act XLV of 1860, sections 299–300.

completeness in respect of its contents; intrinsic usefulness in respect of its character, and justifiedness i.e. manifested usefulness in respect of the body of instruction by which in the form of principles and reasons it ought to be illustrated.[1]

Macaulay had broken completely with any attempt at a code which was a mere consolidation of existing law. Despite the strictures of Prinsep that to draft a completely new code of penal law was going beyond the terms of reference of the Law Commission, Macaulay stood out for the Benthamite ideal.[2] Admittedly the criminal law was the most susceptible of being recast *de novo*, without giving shock to Indian custom and prejudice. By 1835 the Muslim criminal law, which the British had inherited and claimed to administer, had been so overlaid by Regulation law that it was unrecognizable and of negligible effect. The discontinuance in 1832 of the *fatwa*, the written opinion of the Muslim law officer, marked in fact 'the end of the Mahomedan criminal law as a general law applicable to all persons'.[3]

Macaulay had, however, underestimated the difficulties. The Law Commission was inundated with miscellaneous questions arising from the ordinary business of the Government, and in 1836 the toll of illness left Macaulay as the sole active member of the commission. Anderson, who had been concerned with the framing of the Bombay Code of 1827, Macleod, the representative of Madras, and above all Charles Hay Cameron, 'a disciple and ultimately the last disciple of Jeremy Bentham' (as Leslie Stephen described him),[4] were all incapacitated for the latter part of 1836. Millett, the Secretary, was unable through pressure of other duties to render Macaulay much assistance. The latter was

[1] The passage quoted by Ross in his Minute of 30 Dec. 1833, para. 3, is from Bentham's 'Papers on Codification' (published 1817), *Works*, vol. iv, p. 480. Cf. 'Essay on Political Tactics', *Works*, vol. ii, p. 355, where Bentham states the criteria of legislation as: '1. Brevity in the articles. 2. Simplicity in the propositions. 3. The pure expression of will. 4. The complete exhibition of all the clauses.' Cf. also *Works*, vol. iii, pp. 207–9.

[2] H. T. Prinsep, Minute, 11 June 1835: Ind. Leg. Cons., 15 June 1835, No. 2 (Board's Collections, vol. 1555, No. 63507, ff. 13–14).

[3] Rankin, *Background to Indian Law*, p. 180.

[4] *D.N.B.*, vol. iii, p. 741. Also cited Rankin, op. cit., p. 201. For a testimony to Macaulay's labours on the Penal Code, see the evidence of J. R. Macleod: *P.P.*, 1852–3, vol. xxx, p. 300.

to a large extent justified in making a spirited defence of
the Law Commission when the Governor-General formally
inquired as to the causes impeding its progress. But there
was substance in Prinsep's contention, expressed at the outset in June 1835, that the preparation of a body of codes was
a much more protracted task than Macaulay imagined; and
in defending himself Macaulay tacitly admitted he had been
too optimistic.[1] This in no way detracts from his achievement; the drafting of the Penal Code which he effected
almost single-handedly was in itself an impressive intellectual
accomplishment for the work of two years. Perhaps his excess of optimism was constitutional, a facet of that exuberance
of judgement which marks all his writings.[2] His pictorial
imagination, like the Evangelical mind, saw only in terms of
black and white, and knew nothing of half-tones. With his
historical experience rooted in the experience of 1688 and
1832 he found it difficult to conceive of historical change as
other than sudden and total. He had still to discover with
his contemporaries that reform was to be a never-ending
process of piecemeal adjustment instead of a few swift
strokes ushering in a fresh golden age.

Of all his springtide hopes of 1835 the draft of the Penal
Code was the sole durable monument. The Code had to
wait for more than twenty years before it was enacted in 1860
as the general criminal law of India. Despite modifications
it retained the cast Macaulay had given it. That cast was

---

[1] Cf. Macaulay, Minute, n.d. (Trevelyan, *Macaulay*, p. 300, gives it the same
date as that of the Consultation): Ind. Leg. Cons., 2 Jan. 1837, No. 3 (Dharker,
op. cit., p. 253): 'I must say therefore, that even if no allowance be made for the
untoward circumstances which have retarded our progress, that progress cannot be
called slow. People who have never considered the importance and difficulty of the
task in which we are employed are surprised to find that a Code cannot be spoken of
extempore or written like an article in a magazine. I am not ashamed to acknowledge
that there are several chapters in the Code on which I have been employed for months,
of which I have changed the whole plan ten or twelve times, which contain not a
single word as it originally stood and with which I am still very far indeed from
being satisfied. I certainly shall not hurry on my share of the work in order to gratify
the childish impatience of the ignorant. Their censure ought to be a matter of
perfect indifference to men engaged in a task on the right performing of which the
welfare of millions may during a long series of years depend.'

[2] One recalls 'the brave words which form the opening sentence of the first
volume of his History': 'I purpose to write the History of England from the accession
of King James the Second down to a time which is within the memory of men still
living.'

Bentham's, a code of law drawn not from existing practice or from foreign law systems, but created *ex nihilo* by the disinterested philosophic intelligence. In no other of the Indian codes did this idea prevail. When the task of law reform was undertaken afresh after the Mutiny, Bentham's universality of outlook was abandoned. In 1861 all attempt to win the heights of a completely codified law system was given up with the express abandonment of the objective of codifying the Hindu and Muslim substantive civil law; and Bentham's authority served only to achieve a majestic but incomplete series of codes which were for the most part little more than rationalized digests of English law and practice.[1]

It would be idle to draw far-fetched parallels of the details of the Penal Code with the ideas expressed in Bentham's writings, and Macaulay indeed disclaimed taking any particular model for his example. The debt to Bentham is rather to be sought in the design and informing spirit of the Code. Of course, as Macaulay admitted, a sweeping innovation was much more possible in the penal than in the civil law, where vested property rights were involved; and in the conditions of the time there was little alternative to constructing the whole system of penal law entirely anew. In the Bengal and Madras Presidencies the Muslim law had been retained, but had been overlaid by Regulations which differed widely in each Presidency. The effect was that the Muslim law had been 'dis-stated to such an extent as to deprive it of all title to the religious veneration of Mohammedans, yet retaining enough of its original peculiarities to perplex and encumber the administration of justice'.[2] In Bombay the ground work was the Hindu criminal law as amended by the Regulations, which had been digested to form part of the Elphinstone Code of 1827. But this Code had no virtue beyond being a digest of extant law, and perpetuated all its anomalies and omissions. Macaulay's arguments for refusing to take any of the existing Indian criminal law systems as the basis for the Penal Code were consequently strong in face of the wealth of evidence he could marshal of their disparity and chaotic nature.

[1] See note U, p. 329,
[2] Letter from Indian Law Commissioners, 2 May 1837: Dharker, op. cit., p. 261.

He was quite explicit that he took no existing system of law as the groundwork of the Code, and in particular he was firm in rejecting the English criminal law, to which the population of the Presidency towns within the local jurisdiction of Supreme Courts were subject. The population living under the English criminal law were subject, he declared, to a very artificial, complicated, and foreign system, framed without the smallest reference to India, and pronounced by a commission in England so defective that it could only be reformed by being entirely taken to pieces and reconstructed.[1] He acknowledged the assistance he had derived from comparing his work 'with the most celebrated systems of western jurisprudence', and he referred especially to the aid he had derived in this way from the *Code Pénal* of Napoleon and Livingston's *Code of Louisiana*, both of which bear the marks of Bentham's inspiration.[2] But he claimed originality for the production of the Law Commission. It is important to stress this fact, because it has been argued that the Penal Code was of a piece with the other Indian codes; that the method pursued was the same, 'to take the law of England, reform it so far as a small committee of the day working with an absolutely free hand thought that it required reform; then to inquire how far the resultant draft required modification to suit Indian conditions; and finally to clothe the product with the force of an Act of the Indian Legislature'.[3] Undoubtedly the Penal Code is in substance English law; as Whitley Stokes described it: 'Its basis is the law of England, stript of technicality and local peculiarities, shortened, simplified, made intelligible and precise.'[4] But it is quite false to Macaulay's viewpoint to suggest that he approached his work in the attitude adopted by the framers of the later Indian codes, and that his Code was merely an attempt to apply a reformed English law to Indian conditions. The emphatic disclaimer which the Law Commissioners made on the completion of

[1] Letter of Law Commissioners to Governor-General, 14 Oct. 1837: Macaulay, *Complete Works*, vol. xi, pp. 11–12.

[2] For Bentham's connexion with Livingston and Livingston's acknowledgement of his debt to Bentham, see Bentham, *Works*, vol. xi, pp. 23, 35–38, 51.

[3] See note V, p. 329.

[4] Whitley Stokes, *The Anglo-Indian Codes*, vol. i, p. 71, cited Rankin, op. cit., p. 204. Cf. Stephen, *History of the Criminal Law*, vol. iii, p. 300.

the draft code must be taken as genuine: 'the system of penal law which we propose is not a digest of any existing system; and . . . no existing system has furnished us even with a ground-work'.[1] Macaulay's aim was a code that was not derivative from the laws of any creed or country but sprang from the universal science of jurisprudence. And to neglect this universality of outlook, this cast of mind that was of the eighteenth-century *philosophe*, is to lose the historical atmosphere in which the Code took shape. That outlook, which was Bentham's, is to be seen in Macaulay's insistence on the vital interconnexion of the Penal Code with the prospective codes of procedure and substantive civil law, and in his emphasis on the Penal Code as but one portion of the great pannomium.[2] The achievement owed more to English law than his professions warranted, and Macaulay was perhaps too English to be actively aware of this debt, of 'the mine he was working';[3] but this in no way diminishes the importance and directness of Bentham's influence and the distinctiveness with which it invests Macaulay's code.

In the arrangement of the Code, Macaulay abandoned the complex classification of offences which Bentham had suggested in favour of a simpler and looser ordering. Bentham had classified offences in a dual manner: firstly, according to the persons they affected, from whence he derived private, self-regarding, semi-public, and public offences; and secondly, according to their effect, from whence he derived offences against the person, against property, against reputation, and against condition.[4] The first classification was to be the

---

[1] Letter from Indian Law Commissioners, 2 May 1837, para. 4: Dharker, op. cit., p. 260.

[2] Cf. Letter from Indian Law Commissioners, 2 May 1837, para. 4: Dharker, op. cit., pp. 259–60: 'Such is the relation which exists between the different parts of the law that no part can be brought to perfection while the other parts remain rude. The Penal Code cannot be clear and explicit while the substantive civil law and the law of procedure are dark and confused.' This is again stated at greater length in the Notes to the Penal Code, Macaulay, *Complete Works*, vol. xi, pp. 144–5. Cf. Bentham, *Works*, vol. iii, p. 195. Also cf. Whitley Stokes, op. cit., vol. i, p. xi.

[3] Rankin, op. cit., p. 207.

[4] Bentham, 'Principles of Morals and Legislation', *Works*, vol. i, pp. 96 et seq. 'View of a Complete Code of Laws', *Works*, vol. iii, pp. 163 et seq. *Theory of Legislation* (ed. C. K. Ogden), pp. 239 et seq. In a draft plan of a penal code, written much later than these earlier works, Bentham considerably modified his scheme. Self-regarding offences were dropped entirely, and semi-public offences made superfluous;

primary division, and each class would then be further sub-
divided according to the secondary classification. Bentham
had to admit that his method was not perfectly satisfactory,
and that it would be impossible to avoid overlapping of the
classes.[1] In fact he never grappled with the practical difficulties of drafting a code according to his scheme. Macaulay
avoided any attempt at a rigid method,[2] and in practice was
more influenced by the simpler ordering of the French *Code
Pénal*. Offences are not explicitly classed, but in the arrangement of the Indian Code they fall into four broad divisions:
offences against the public, offences against the person (the
human body), offences against property, and offences against
condition and reputation. Bentham had argued that public
offences should follow and not precede private offences. He
claimed that this was the logical order, and later added a
political argument that in a democracy the legislator should
thus symbolically pronounce the rights of the individual to
be his first care.[3] Macaulay chose, however, to adopt the
arrangement of the French Code in this matter, and placed
public offences first. It is not easy to see any strong parallel,
therefore, with Bentham's classification and ordering, but it
is certainly arguable that chapters xx to xxvi of Macaulay's
draft owed something to the discussion of offences against
condition and reputation, carried out in the *Principles of
Morals and Legislation* and in Dumont's collection of the
Traités de Législation. The opening chapters of Macaulay's
work follow the philosophic method of which Bentham had
been an advocate, the first giving definitions and explanations, the second defining punishments, the third comprising
general exceptions (or what Bentham meant under 'grounds

cf. Bentham, 'Penal Code—Table of Contents as shown by Titles of Chapters
and Sections' inserted in 'Constitutional Code' (published 1830), *Works*, vol. ix,
pp. 8–9.

 [1] Bentham, 'Principles of Morals and Legislation', *Works*, vol. i, p. 98 n.

 [2] Letter of Law Commissioners, 2 May 1837, para. 13: Dharker, op. cit., p. 263:
'The arrangement which we have adopted is not scrupulously methodical. We have
indeed attempted to observe method where we saw no reason to depart from it. But
we have never hesitated about departing from it when we thought by doing so we
should make the law more simple. We conceive that it would be mere pedantry to
sacrifice the practical convenience of those who were to study and to administer the
Code for the purpose of preserving minute accuracy of classification.'

 [3] Cf. 'View of a Complete Code of Laws', *Works*, vol. iii, p. 162. 'Letters to
Count Toreno', *Works*, vol. viii, pp. 519–20.

of justification and exemption'), and the fourth dealing with abetment or accessories to an offence.[1] Again the finer details are not those of Bentham, nor is his general influence easy to assess with any accuracy; but that influence is undeniably present.

The form in which the law is stated in Macaulay's Code— a form followed by the later Indian codes—has been described by Fitzjames Stephen as 'an entirely new and original method of legislative expression'.

In the first place the leading idea to be laid down is stated in the most explicit and pointed form which can be devised. Then such expressions in it as are not regarded as being sufficiently explicit are made the subject of definite explanations. This is followed by equally definite exceptions, to which, if necessary, explanations are added, and in order to set the whole in the clearest light the matter thus stated explained and qualified is illustrated by a number of concrete cases.[2]

Now it is true that Macaulay did not adopt Bentham's proposed legislative method in its entirety. The difficulties which he felt in 1835 over attaching reasons to the laws prevented him from using Bentham's device, so strongly urged by Ross, of interweaving a rationale into the statement of the laws.[3] Macaulay contented himself with appending a series of Notes, which explain the grounds for the various leading provisions. These Notes were eventually embodied in the Statement of Objects and Reasons which accompanied Act XLV of 1860 in its passage through the legislature; but they are not an integral part of the Code and do not appear in modern editions of it.[4] Yet, in principle, Macaulay's method of legislative expression (as described by Stephen) is exactly that of Bentham. Bentham had broken down the statement of a law into different parts in order to attain his fourfold criteria of correct legal expression: 'brevity', 'simplicity', 'pure expression of will', and 'completeness'.[5] As usual Bentham's pursuit of the 'exhaustive method' led him into excessive elaboration, but in its simplest form he divided

---

[1] See note W, p. 329.
[2] Stephen, *History of the Criminal Law*, vol. iii, pp. 302–3.
[3] See p. 201.
[4] The Notes are to be found in Macaulay, *Complete Works*, vol. xi, pp. 22 et seq.
[5] Bentham, *Works*, vol. ii, p. 355; vol. iii, pp. 207–9.

the wording of a law into main text, expository matter, and rationale.[1] This was the principle followed by Macaulay, except that he detached the rationale completely. It was to state the law in its initial formulation as a simple brief command, a pure expression of will, stripped completely of all qualifying or explanatory matter. The subsidiary matter followed this bare statement, first in the form of explanations to clarify it, and then in the form of exceptions or modifications to it (or what Bentham termed grounds of justification, exception, aggravation, and extenuation).[2] The actual draftsmanship also was strongly influenced by Bentham's principles of 'nomography'. The Indian Penal Code is indeed remarkable in its drafting when compared with the cumbrous form of the contemporary parliamentary statute. Long before any serious attempt was made to reform the enactments of Parliament of their complicated legal language, their circumlocution, their tautology, their lack of order and facility of reference,[3] Macaulay had introduced into Indian legislation the ordinary, pellucid, and exact English of his country's philosophical tradition. In the Penal Code are to be found most of the improvements which Bentham had advocated, if not originated—the division into chapters and the numbering of paragraphs;[4] the precise definition of a term followed by a constant use of that term to the exclusion of any other;[5] the allocation of a separate paragraph to each distinct idea or proposition;[6] the use of the third person masculine singular

[1] Cf. Bentham, 'Letters to Toreno' (published 1822), *Works*, vol. viii, pp. 532–3. His more elaborate divisions are used in 'Equity Dispatch Court Bill', *Works*, vol. iii, p. 323, and are: 1. Enactive; 2, Instructional; 3. Exemplicative; 4. Ratiocinative; 5. Commentative.

[2] Cf. 'Specimen of a Penal Code', *Works*, vol. i, pp. 164 et seq. Bentham actually used the analogy of a military command; cf. Letter to Wellington, 12 Dec. 1828: *Works*, vol. xi, p. 12. Cf. also 'Essay on Political Tactics', *Works*, vol. ii, p. 356.

[3] The first attempt to reform the drafting of parliamentary enactments was made in Aug. 1838 when Arthur Symonds's proposals were laid before Parliament.

[4] 'View of a Complete Code of Laws', *Works*, vol. iii, p. 208. Cf. 'Nomography', *Works*, vol. iii, pp. 265 et seq.; Bentham coins a watchword that expresses a good deal of the Benthamite atmosphere of the eighteen-thirties: *Denominate, enumerate, tabulate*. . . .

[5] Cf. Bentham, 'View of a Complete Code of Laws', *Works*, vol. iii, p. 209: 'The same ideas, the same words. Never employ other than a single and the same word, for expressing a single and the same idea. . . . The words of the laws ought to be weighed like diamonds.'

[6] Cf. Bentham, 'Nomography', *Works*, vol. iii, p. 264: 'To be perfectly clear to the

to denote a member of either sex or a number of persons; and the use of the 'categorical' rather than the 'hypothetical' form in an enactive clause.[1] The most original feature of Macaulay's Code was the employment of illustrative examples 'to exhibit the law in full action and show what its effects will be on the events of common life'.[2] Traces of this feature are certainly to be found in Bentham, as Whitley Stokes has pointed out,[3] but they are no more than rudimentary, and Macaulay was the first to use the device in practical legislation.

If in the form and drafting of the Code there are signs of Bentham's influence, the actual content also is indebted to his work. There are no specific borrowings, but everywhere there is the mark of Bentham's discussion of the general principles of jurisprudence. Firstly, Macaulay adopted the approach of *The Principles of Morals and Legislation* which was common to the thinkers of the Enlightenment. The nomenclature and classification of offences, which was the whole touchstone of a system of penal law, was on the 'natural' and not the 'technical' system.[4] In company with Bentham Macaulay rejected that technical denomination and arrangement of offences which English law inherited from its historical growth. Treason, malice, felony, tort, misdemeanour, slander, libel—such terms find no place in the Code.[5] Secondly, it is obvious that Macaulay's mind was filled with Bentham's criteria for determining punishment —that punishment should be variable, equable, commensurable, characteristic of the offence, exemplary, frugal, subservient to reformation, popular, simple, remissible, &c.[6] Macaulay refused to fix the absolute amount of fines, except

conception, the judgment, and the memory, every distinguishable proposition must be presented by itself, unconnected with every other.'

[1] See note X, p. 330.

[2] Letter from Law Commissioners, 2 May 1837, para. 19: Dharker, op. cit., p. 265.   [3] See note Y, p. 330.

[4] 'Principles of Morals and Legislation', *Works*, vol. i, p. 96 n.

[5] Cf. Bentham, 'Nomography', *Works*, vol. iii, p. 273: 'The division of the qualities of plants into hot, cold, moist, and dry, was not more compatible with correct, complete and useful conception of the various subjects of the vegetable kingdom, than the still established division of offences into treasons, praemunires, unclergyable felonies, clergyable felonies, and misdemeanours.'

[6] Cf. 'Principles of Morals and Legislation', *Works*, vol. i, pp. 91 et seq.

in less serious offences, and declared they ought to be adjusted to the pecuniary means of the offender; he also held that as part of the criminal law pecuniary satisfaction should be made by the offender to the injured party in addition to suffering the penalty of imprisonment.[1] In Bentham again he found intellectual arguments to support his humanitarian instinct against cruel punishments, against the pillory or flogging or an extensive use of capital punishment.[2] The most striking feature in the content of the Code is, however, the manner in which the mental circumstances involved in a criminal act are carefully distinguished and made use of. Professor Vesey-Fitzgerald claims that: 'The care with which the Indian Penal Code (avoiding the vague term *mens rea*) distinguishes between the various mental states which may be ingredients in crime, is a good example of the influence of this part of Bentham's work.'[3] Here again the debt to Bentham is general rather than specific. The consideration of various mental circumstances gives rise to the most elaborate parts of the Code, the chapter on 'General Exceptions' and the chapter on 'Offences relating to the Body'. The constituent elements of *mens rea*—motive, intention, and consciousness—are certainly held in view, but the clear distinction which Bentham wished to make between motive and intention, in order to avoid the ambiguous term 'voluntary', is not preserved.[4] Over the section on 'Voluntary Culpable Homicide' Macaulay took the greatest pains, and although it has been criticized as the weakest part of the Code, it remains a monument to this form of mental analysis.

There are other parallels with Bentham's ideas. Both Bentham and Macaulay used the term 'defamation' to embrace the offences of libel and slander under English law; both gave a wider meaning to defamation as a criminal

---

[1] Macaulay, Notes to Penal Code, *Complete Works*, vol. xi, pp. 30, 38–41. Cf. Bentham, *Works*, vol. i, pp. 371 et seq.; vol. iii, pp. 360, 426–7.

[2] Macaulay, *Complete Works*, vol. xi, pp. 22–24, 42–46. For Bentham on the pillory: Margery Fry, 'Bentham and English Penal Reform' in *Jeremy Bentham and the Law*, p. 44. For Bentham on flogging: *Works*, vol. i, pp. 413–15; vol. ix, pp. 421–2; vol. x, pp. 71–72. For Bentham on capital punishment: *Works*, vol. i, pp. 525 et seq.

[3] S. G. Vesey-Fitzgerald, 'Bentham and the Indian Codes' in *Jeremy Bentham and the Law*, p. 231.

[4] Cf. Bentham, 'Principles of Morals and Legislation', *Works*, vol. i, p. 40 n.

offence so as to include spoken words;[1] and both admitted in certain cases the plea that the imputation was true, as a means of rebutting the charge of defamation.[2] But it would be wrong to press analogies too closely. Macaulay made no acknowledgements to Bentham. The debt to Bentham lies in the informing spirit of the Code and its general doctrines of jurisprudence rather than in matters of detail. Nevertheless, the Code remains, as all legal historians have recognized, a monument to Bentham's proud boast that he would be the dead legislative of British India.

[1] Cf. Notes to Penal Code, Macaulay, *Complete Works*, vol. xi, pp. 180–2. Cf. Bentham, 'View of a Complete Code of Laws', *Works*, vol. iii, pp. 164–5.

[2] Macaulay, *Complete Works*, vol. xi, pp. 183–93. Draft Penal Code of 1837, para. 470. Cf. Bentham, 'Letters to Toreno', *Works*, vol. viii, pp. 510–11.

IV

THE UTILITARIAN LEGACY

1. *The End of the First Age of Reform*

OUR study of the Benthamite influence after the Charter Act of 1833 has been confined wholly to the sphere in which its effect was most apparent. But a movement of law reform is necessarily part of a wider current of thought even though this be little expressed. In revenue policy the stream of Utilitarian influence had been turned largely into channels of the old paternalism of Munro's school; and the ascendancy of Bird and Thomason in the North-Western Provinces was a triumph for the active assertion of executive government in the ordering of society. But until the eighteen-forties the triumph was no more than local; and in the counsels of the Supreme Government, with the departure of Holt Mackenzie and Bentinck, with Malcolm's retirement from Bombay, and with Metcalfe's lessening influence, a reformed whiggism took hold at Calcutta. Of this policy Macaulay and Ross were the representatives; and for our purposes Ross was the more outspoken and explicit of the two. He acknowledged himself a fervent Benthamite, but he had not looked close enough, or had not cared, to detect how much stronger in Bentham's thought was the principle of authority than the principle of liberty.[1]

Ross had regarded with grave mistrust the judicial and administrative reforms of 1829–31 and the system of revenue settlement embodied in Regulation IX of 1833. To the attempt to unite the Utilitarian programme with the authoritarian paternalism of the Munro tradition he opposed the *laissez-faire* alternative. Under the Cornwallis system this had degenerated into mere passivity and instinctive opposition to change, whether it concerned the form of government or the native systems of law and education. Ross took the doctrine of *laissez-faire* and transformed it, like his contemporaries

---

[1] Cf. Halévy, *Philosophic Radicalism*, p. 74.

in England, into a watchword for radical reform. Although the influence of government in determining the state of a society was acknowledged to be paramount, the new attitude confined the positive intervention of government to two essential functions: removing restrictions on the individual, and securing to him the fruits of his industry. This did not mean that the legislator was of any less importance. For if property was the great instrument of happiness, it was itself, as Bentham had pointed out, no more than a creature of the mind, an 'established expectation', born of the security which the law alone created. Everything therefore hung upon the state of the law and its administration.[1]

With Ross, law was to be the sole instrument of change. The force of this belief transfuses his Minute of 1833 on the need for a panoply of codes for India.[2] To the absence of all the Benthamite criteria in the Indian laws—certainty, promptitude, cheapness, simplicity, accessibility, 'cognoscibility'—and to the regulations restricting trade, could be ascribed the fact 'that the agriculture and manufactures of India have made no advance whatever under our rule'. The administration of the law was not, of course, to be understood as the actions of executive officers vested with discretionary powers, but solely as the operation of the judicial process in the courts. The revolution of Indian society was to be silently and unobtrusively effected. Ross certainly felt less constraint about interfering with indigenous law than Bentham had shown in his *Essay on the Influence of Time and Place*. His view was that a proper system of law 'would ensure to every class the enjoyment of particular laws and usages, so far as these might be deemed unobjectionable and not inconsistent with the prosperity of the country at large'. But the indigenous laws he deemed objectionable were the most fundamental of Indian society. He singled out 'the Hindoo and

---

[1] Cf. Bentham, 'Principles of the Civil Code', *Works*, vol. i, pp. 307–9. Halévy, *Philosophic Radicalism*, p. 46. Cf. Ross, Minute on Draft Regulations for consolidating Stamp Laws, enclosed in Minute, 10 Nov. 1835: Ind. Leg. Cons., 3 April 1837, No. 23: 'That it is only by encouraging Industry that improvement of the people or of the resources of the country can be effected; that security in the enjoyment of its fruits is essential to the encouragement of Industry and that to afford that security is the sole end for which laws are enacted, are positions which cannot be questioned.'

[2] A. Ross, Minute, 30 Dec. 1833, para. 3: Board's Collections, vol. 1555, No. 63507, ff. 26–27.

Mahomedan Laws of Inheritance: the usages observed in the management of joint landed estates, the Regulations enacted by the Government in regard to the protection of such joint estates . . . and also the usages which prevail in regard to the rights and privileges of the Ryots or immediate occupiers and cultivators of the soil'. Ross was in fact advocating a rapid and complete transformation of the complex relationships of Indian society, which were founded on communal ownership and management, and their replacement by the simplified economic structure of individualist, capitalist England. The instrument to work the transformation was to be the Benthamite codes of law administered by an efficient judiciary. If the courts recognized and enforced individual property rights, the tangle of 'feudal' tenures could be reduced to the simple relationship of landlord and tenant. For the same purpose changes were required in the law in order to encourage the partition of joint-estates, to allow a full power of testamentary disposition, and to debar the fixing of subordinate cultivators' rents or other interference between 'landlord and tenant'.[1]

The scheme of administration which Ross deduced from this political philosophy was essentially different, as it has been seen,[2] from that of the paternalist school. His symbol was not the collector or the commissioner but the judge. The constant discretionary interference by the executive officers in settlement operations and questions of landed property was inimical, he believed, to the security and liberty on which alone a free individualist society could flourish. From the eighteen-twenties he had constantly advocated reducing the power of the executive by excluding it entirely from judicial functions and by making the local executive officers firmly subordinate to the judiciary. He wanted to see the post of commissioner abolished, and the collector shorn of the office

---

[1] Cf. p. 116. Ross does not actually mention the power of testamentary disposition. The introduction of wills was an important device for overcoming the Hindu laws of inheritance. It was formally established in Bengal by a decision of the *Sadr* Court in 1831, at a time when Ross was a judge of the Court. Legal authorities assert that such a right is clearly contrary to Hindu law. The importance of the feature is that it frees the individual from the restriction imposed by Hindu law under which 'a coparcener is prohibited from disposing of his own share of the joint ancestral property'. Cf. J. D. Mayne, *Hindu Law and Usage*, 7th edn., chap. xi, sections 353 et seq., 404 et seq.   [2] See pp. 157-9.

of magistrate and reduced to the lowly function his name implied, 'the mere realization of the assessment on land'. He believed that the financial saving to be gained from the reduction of the strength and status of the revenue branch would make possible a great increase in the judicial establishment.[1] Macaulay sympathized with the plan as a means of providing the great network of local omnicompetent courts which he envisaged in his Minute of 25 June 1835; and it suited his natural Whig distaste against combining judicial and revenue functions, 'a blending of Somerset House and the Old Bailey'.[2] There was no question in practice of a wholesale reversal of Bentinck's reforms, but there were to be considerable inroads upon his administrative system.

In 1836 Metcalfe proposed giving powers of criminal jurisdiction to native judges.[3] One of the members of Council, H. Shakespear, in arguing that the measure was unsafe at that time, widened the issue by urging 'that the weakness of the Police and Criminal Administration, which has led to the proposed enactment, may be traced to the union of the offices of Collector and Magistrate, an arrangement often destructive to the efficiency of both departments, and almost always to one'. Macaulay concurred entirely with Shakespear's view.[4] But Auckland, the Governor-General, felt the difficulty of effecting another general change of system, and his disinclination towards further major changes was significant of the lessening ardour for radical reform. The Government contented itself with asking the Home Authorities for discretionary authority to separate the offices of collector and magistrate in Bengal whenever the pressure of business made this necessary. Auckland had made a further proposal for making the police system more effective. This was to relieve the commissioners of revenue of their police functions, and to revive the superintendents of police which Bentinck had abolished in 1829. The Council was unanimous in agreement, and Ross took the opportunity

---

[1] Cf. Ross, Minute, 2 May 1835, paras. 5 et seq.: Ind. Leg. Cons., 3 April 1837, No. 21.

[2] See p. 209.

[3] Judicial Letter from India (Leg. Dept.), 20 March (No. 3) 1837, para. 38.

[4] Notes by Shakespear and Macaulay, 12 Dec. 1836: Ind. Leg. Cons., 19 Dec. 1836, No. 19 (Board's Collections, vol. 1760, No. 72084, f. 13).

once again to urge the abolition of the commissioners of revenue.[1] But there was no support for such a drastic reduction of the power of the executive arm; only the proposal to deprive the commissioners of their police functions was put forward to the Home Authorities. Even this measure encountered opposition in the North-Western Provinces, where Metcalfe was Lieutenant-Governor. He had always championed unified personal rule against departmentalism, and the prestige of the régime in the North-Western Provinces was sufficient by 1839 for the Home Authorities to accept his arguments.[2] The Act which Auckland passed in 1837 to permit the re-establishment of superintendents of police therefore took effect only in Bengal.[3] But the discretionary authority given to the local Government of Bengal to separate the offices of collector and magistrate, where pressure of business appeared to make this necessary, had a much wider effect. By 1845 only in three districts of Orissa did the offices of collector and magistrate remain united.

This success in reviving the Cornwallis form of administration was, however, local and temporary. The separation of the collector and magistrate took place in Bengal alone, and at a time when the Bengal school was losing its power and influence in the counsels of the Governor-General. After 1837 the Governor-General spent much of his time up-country, preoccupied with the political problems of the North-West Frontier. Bengal was left to be administered as best it might by the Governor-General's Council, whose composition was constantly altering. As an administrative influence Bengal was soon outshone by the energy and progress displayed in the Government of the North-Western Provinces under Bird and Thomason. When Dalhousie came to look into the state of neglect into which the senior province had fallen by the fifties, he attributed the cause

[1] Judicial Letter from Bengal, 30 May (No. 18) 1837, para. 12. Minute by Governor-General, 12 June 1837; H. Shakespear, Minute, 14 June 1837, and A. Ross, Minute, 1 July 1837 (Board's Collections, vol. 1682, No. 67823); Macaulay, Minute, 10 July 1837: Dharker, op. cit., p. 248.

[2] Judicial Despatch to India, 1 May (No. 6) 1839, para. 6. In 'Despatches to Bengal and India' (Original Drafts), vol. 20, para. 6 is noted as being added by the Board of Control: 'We concur in the opinion of Sir Charles Metcalfe and consequently object to deprive the Revenue officers of the superintendence of the Police.'

[3] Act XXIV of 1837.

partly to the lack of a separate governor for Bengal, but also to that very separation of the offices of magistrate and collector which Ross and Macaulay had believed so desirable. In 1859 Canning took Dalhousie's advice, against the opposition of the Bengal school, and reunited the offices.[1] They have remained united ever since.

The age of reform had in fact come to its close by 1838. After Bentinck left in 1835 it enjoyed a few expiring triumphs. Relying successfully on Metcalfe's delusions about himself as an apostle of liberalism, Macaulay persuaded him to free the press of its last legal restrictions in the interregnum which followed Bentinck's departure. Ross, acting as Governor of the short-lived Agra Presidency, also took advantage of the occasion. On his own responsibility he decided to abolish the transit duties in his province, and so fulfil the hopes raised by Charles Trevelyan's celebrated *Report on the Town and Transit Duties* (1834), in which their complete extinction had been recommended. Ross's action forced the Supreme Government to follow suit in the Lower Provinces, and by Act XIV of 1836 the town as well as the transit duties were abolished throughout the Bengal Presidency. These measures called down the displeasure of the Home Authorities who were not prepared to acquiesce in such unilateral action in the cause of reform.[2] In January 1838, after seeing his draft Penal Code through the press, Macaulay left India. With him went his brother-in-law, Charles Trevelyan, the heart and soul of all 'improvement'. A few months later Ross retired, the censure of the Court of Directors still ringing in his ears. Auckland, although a Whig, was but a lukewarm reformer. The immediate enactment of Macaulay's Code, to which J. S. Mill gave his philosophic blessing in the *Westminster Review*, would have tested the courage of the most intrepid Governor-General, and it was perhaps natural that Auckland should refer it for

---

[1] Buckland, *Bengal under the Lieutenant-Governors*, Calcutta, 1901, vol. i, pp. xx, 24–25.

[2] Despatch of Court of Directors, 1 Feb. 1837: *P.P.*, 1852, vol. x, p. 812: '. . . such is our sense of the extreme want of judgement manifested by Mr. Ross on this occasion, that supposing he still continued to exercise the functions of Government in the Presidency of Agra, we should have come to the resolution of cancelling his appointment.'

the comments of the judges in each of the Presidencies.[1] But his real attitude emerged when he rejected the opportunity of filling the vacancy on the Law Commission with the Radical James Young. '. . . *between you and me*, I thought that enough of pure Benthamism was already secured to our Code', Auckland wrote to Hobhouse, the former *enfant terrible* of radicalism, but now orthodox and respectable as President of the Board of Control.[2] Whatever Auckland's disposition, his hands were rapidly tied by political and military business. His correspondence with Hobhouse, which opened with questions of internal administration, soon had to devote itself exclusively to the Afghan question; and by 1838 the Indian Government was launched upon a round of war and diplomatic activity that was to last for twenty years.

In 1841 the *Edinburgh Review* lamented the closing of the reform era in India. Because of the press of military and diplomatic questions, matters of the most vital importance had been lying over for years. 'The criminal code, drawn up by Mr. Macaulay and his able colleagues in the law commission, which was laid before the Supreme Government in the latter end of 1837, might as well for any practical purpose, repose in the Record Office in the Tower.'[3] The labour of the Committee on Prison Discipline had likewise been fruitless. This failure to make sufficient progress with the reform of the internal administration of India explained the disappointment of the high hopes held out by the Charter Act of 1833, and was the reason why British capital and settlers had not flowed in once all legal restrictions to their admission had been removed.

The fault, then, lay at the door of the Indian authorities, who because of war and diplomacy had 'no adequate leisure for civil concerns of the utmost importance to the happiness of millions'. This was no doubt the reason why law reform languished until after the Mutiny. But in a larger sense the Benthamite age of reform had come to its natural term.

---

[1] Article, 'Penal Code for India' in *Westminster Review*, vol. xxix (Aug. 1838), p. 393. J. S. Mill's authorship is attested in *Bibliography of Published Writings of John Stuart Mill*, ed. N. MacMinn, J. R. Hainds, and J. M. MacCrimmon, Northwestern University, Evanston, Illinois, 1945, p. 51.

[2] Auckland to Hobhouse, 14 July 1837: Auckland MSS., Add. MS. 37691.

[3] *Edinburgh Review*, vol. lxxiii (1841), p. 457.

Bentham himself had died in 1832; and even more decisive was the death of James Mill in 1836. Utilitarianism as a rigid creed and programme was extinguished. Its clarity and simplicity had been the products of the eighteenth-century Enlightenment, but this intellectual self-confidence was denied to the hazier, more troubled mind of the Victorian period. The younger Mill, upon whom fell the Utilitarian mantle, was the foremost to separate himself from his father's rigid doctrine. In 1837 he was anxious to rid his attitude of the reproach of sectarianism and to form a broad front of all shades of Radical opinion. Explaining to Lytton Bulwer the new principles of philosophic radicalism which he meant to adopt as the new editor of the *Westminster Review*, Mill said his aim was

to soften the harder and sterner features of its Radicalism and Utilitarianism both of which in the form in which they originally appeared in the *Westminster* were part of the inheritance of the eighteenth century. The review ought to represent not Radicalism but Neo-Radicalism, a Radicalism which is not democracy, not a bigoted adherence to any forms of government or of one kind of institutions, and which is to be called Radicalism, inasmuch as it does not palter nor compromise with evils, but cuts at their roots—and a utilitarianism which never makes a peculiar figure as such, nor would ever constitute its followers a sect or school—which fraternises with all who hold the same *axiomata media* (as Bacon has it) whether their just principle is the same or not—and which holds in the highest reverence all which the vulgar notion of utilitarianism represents them to despise—which holds feeling at least as valuable as thought, and Poetry not only on a par with, but the necessary condition of, any true Philosophy.[1]

The old school, said Mill, was now only a remnant, and was dying out. The attempt to create a coherent party of Philosophic Radicals, Mill later confessed in his *Autobiography*, was 'from the first chimerical: partly because the time was unpropitious, the Reform fervour being in its period of ebb, and the Tory influences powerfully rallying; but still more, because, as Austin so truly said, "the country did not contain the men"'.[2] In 1840 Mill recognized the failure and gave up the proprietorship of the *Westminster*.

[1] J. S. Mill to E. Lytton Bulwer, 23 Nov. 1836: *Letters of John Stuart Mill*, ed. H. S. R. Elliot, 1910, vol. i, pp. 103–4.
[2] J. S. Mill, *Autobiography*, ed. H. J. Laski, World's Classics, 1924, pp. 181–2.

Utilitarianism did not of course die out. In G. M. Young's phrase, the Philosophic Radicals vanished as a party to work in widening circles out of sight. But the new eclecticism which John Stuart Mill represented meant that its practical objectives were more uncertain than of old. The unquestioning faith in the power of political institutions to mould human character was lost, and Mill himself placed education before tinkering with political institutions as the great instrument of progress. Utilitarianism survived as a body of thought which provided the intellectual basis of liberalism, J. S. Mill's *Political Economy* (1848) supplying the scientific statement of a free economy, and his *Logic* (1843) the appropriate empirical philosophy and logical method. But it was no longer as a closed system of thought that utilitarianism made its appeal. Rather was it for a certain toughness of mind, a fearless hard-hitting logic, that it was prized by later generations who wished to deal with a few specific problems rather than construct society anew. The diffusion and dilution of the Benthamite spirit meant for India that there could be no return to the extravagant hopes of the Bentinck period, when it seemed to Bentham as if the golden age of British India was lying before him. Never again was the same height of vision to be achieved. Only in a peculiarly acute internal crisis of her history was England prepared to listen to the intellectual nostrums of Bentham and James Mill, or to be bold enough to send out as a legislator a man so inexperienced in the law as Macaulay. The idea of some sudden sweeping transformation of Indian society, of an entirely new system of law to be constructed in the space of a few years, of a new judicial and administrative machinery under which India would be propelled at a bound from feudal darkness into the modern world—this sort of attitude could only flourish in an age brought up to believe in sudden conversion. The Victorians were more sober-minded, still eager and hopeful, but with longer views and more modest pretensions. After James Mill's controlling hand was removed, the unity and concentration of aim directing the reforming impulse was lost to Indian policy. But his succession did not fail. If he lacked a coherent band of disciples, dedicated to every article of the Benthamite plan and imbued with the true reformer's contempt for historical fact and circumstance, his larger conception did not altogether vanish from sight. In the sixties and seventies that conception achieved a measure of success which James Mill might have viewed with a certain dour satisfaction.

2. 'The Dead Legislative of British India'

The decade of wars which followed the opening of the Afghan campaign in 1838, while it effectively halted the progress of further internal reform, did not entirely check the reforming impulse. Indeed, it tended to divert it into other channels. The annexation of Sind in 1843 and the final absorption of the Punjab in 1849 presented an administrative problem of great magnitude. These extensive areas, inhabited by wild and martial peoples, had to be pacified, provided with the elements of a civilized administration, and made to pay their way as rapidly as possible. In Sind Sir Charles Napier showed the large measure of success which could be attained by an entirely despotic, military type of rule. In the Punjab, although the Sind model was not followed and the civil service supplied at least half the corps of administrators, the type of government was also military in form and spirit. Metcalfe's ideal of a completely unitary structure was applied. Indeed, Metcalfe could claim to be one of the founding fathers of the Punjab system, having been its pioneer in the Delhi Territory where John Lawrence received his training. In the Punjab all governmental powers, both administrative and judicial, were kept united in the hands of individual officers who were organized into a closely disciplined and graded hierarchy. The Punjab was divided into divisions and districts, each under a single commissioner and deputy-commissioner. No separate judiciary was established. The deputy-commissioner (i.e. the district officer) acted as collector, magistrate, and civil judge. The system was justified on the grounds of economy and as a means of securing the maximum energy and unity of purpose. But it also realized the fondest hopes of the patriarchalists led by John Lawrence, providing each unit of territory with a recognized head and giving him full powers to govern. It appeared to guarantee a strong, simple, paternal rule, devoted to the welfare of a society of sturdy peasant proprietors. Lawrence was delighted that the separation of the judiciary and executive, which he believed was ruining the North-Western Provinces, was not to be reproduced in the Punjab. When in charge of the Jullundur Doab (annexed in 1846) he expressed his feelings with characteristic force:

> I want no such person as a sessions judge here. I have not a bit too much work, though I have plenty of it. I have a great objection to the civil and revenue work being separated. A regular civil court plays the very devil. Its course of procedure is ruinous to the tenures of the country, for the agriculturists cannot fight their causes in that court. It is ruining the people in the North-West Provinces, and will do the same wherever it is introduced. We are getting on capitally here. This, I think, will prove the pattern district of the North-West and will pay Government famously if you do not let off too many jagheers.'[1]

It would be wrong, however, to think of the Punjab administration solely as one of Old Testament simplicity, fulfilling Lawrence's ideal 'of a country thickly cultivated by a fat, contented yeomanry, each man riding his own horse, sitting under his own fig-tree, and enjoying his rude family comforts'.[2] No doubt that element existed and appealed strongly to the Tory Evangelical strain in the Punjab school. They readily imagined themselves as appointed to lead a people out of bondage into a land flowing with milk and honey, and like judges in Israel to bring it slowly towards the light; and the element of a deep, personal religion coloured all their works. One recalls the familiar images of John Lawrence seen by all praying on his knees in his tent, or offering public prayers before the nobles and citizens of Lahore to 'Almighty God through the mediation of our Lord and Saviour' at the cutting of the first sod of the railway. But the popular notion tends to caricature. There was little of the arbitrary and discretionary rule that might be imagined from the more colourful figures. Nicholson, kicking the volume of government regulations out of his door, fearing God and the face of no man, and 'smiting the Amalekites' before Delhi with terrible ferocity, is not a typical symbol. The most arresting feature of the Punjab

---

[1] Bosworth Smith, *Life of Lord Lawrence*, vol. ii, p. 202.
[2] R. N. Cust, *Pictures of Indian Life*, p. 255.

system was the way in which such powerful personalities acting at a great distance in unsettled country were knit together into a highly disciplined force. Control was achieved on the best Benthamite principles—personal responsibility, accountability, and inspectability. A rigid system of recording and reporting was enforced, in addition to the personal check exercised through the almost military chain of command. The union of all judicial and executive authority in the hands of a single officer might seem to give him well-nigh arbitrary power, but his judicial like his executive functions were controlled through the process of appeal, through the necessity to record all his proceedings, and through the requirement of making a personal report on each case. Finally, he was obliged to adhere to a rough code of criminal and civil law, which had been drafted by Richard Temple.

All this was far from the rule of the strong hand untrammelled by law which the reminiscences of men like Herbert Edwardes tended to suggest. Such writings were all too eagerly read by a generation in England which had fallen in love with heroes, 'when as it seemed, to those who recalled the sordid and sullen past, England was renewing her youth, at Lucknow and Inkerman, with Livingstone in the African desert, with Burton on the road to Mecca, and speaking to the oppressors of Europe in the accents of Cromwell and Pitt'.[1] Of course, the period of the Residency and Council of Regency (1846–8) could be interpreted as a halcyon age: 'What days those were! How Henry Lawrence would send us off to great distances: Edwardes to Bunnoo, Nicholson to Peshawur, Abbot to Hazara, Lumsden to somewhere else, etc., giving us no more helpful directions than these, "Settle the country; make the people happy; and take care there are no rows!" '[2] But once annexation had taken place and the Board of Administration was fairly at work, the system was in fact one of the most closely controlled in India. Fitzjames Stephen (law member 1870–2) was at great pains to clear away popular misconceptions on this point. To say that the Punjab had been ruled without law

[1] G. M. Young, *Victorian England—Portrait of an Age*, pp. 76–77.
[2] *Memorials of Herbert Edwardes*, vol. i, p. 58; cited Thompson and Garratt, *Rise and Fulfilment of British Rule in India*, p. 376.

was to forget the existence of the Punjab Civil and Criminal Code and the Rules for the Administration of Civil and Criminal Justice. John Lawrence's administration afforded the clearest proof, he declared, not only of the necessity of having laws to govern by, but of the superiority of simple and scientific laws over cumbrous ones.[1]

Although ultimately conservative in aim, the Punjab system was militant in character, thrusting with an amazing energy the framework of a civilized state upon a bewildered peasantry. It was this militant aggressive quality which brought the reforming impulse to its side. In the North-Western Provinces, under Bird and Thomason, the paternalist tradition had already shown how it could blend with the authoritarian element of utilitarianism. A similar alliance was now to be effected in the Punjab. Its note can be heard in Robert Cust's eulogy of the Punjab achievement in the decade which followed annexation:

> Order and firm rule were established where there had been none for centuries: . . . an abolition of monopolies, except that of liquor and drugs, an equitable and fixed assessment of the land-tax, a reduction of pensions, and of Assignments of Land-revenue, which wasted the resources of the State, a disbandment of all feudal troops, and the substitution of a strong and disciplined police; a simple, cheap and rapid system of Justice between man and man; a stern protection of life and property from violence and fraud; a levelling of all petty fortresses, a disarmament of the warlike classes; freedom of religion, freedom of trade, freedom of speech and writing, freedom of locomotion; the foundation of a system of national education; the lining-out of roads, the construction of bridges, the demarcation of village-boundaries, the establishment of Posts and Telegraphs; the encouragement of commerce and manufactures by the removal of every possible restriction. When I think of all that was done, when I recall the state of the country before the annexation, and the marvellous change that came over it in the course of so few years, I cannot but regret, that such men are not found for the other dark places of this globe.[2]

The Benthamite note can be detected more precisely in the

---

[1] Minute of J. Fitzjames Stephen on Administration of Justice in India: *Selections from the Records of the Government of India*, No. lxxxix, Calcutta, 1872, p. 8. For the Punjab system of personal control and its elaborate system of reports and returns, see Punjab Administration Report 1849–51, paras. 225–6: *P.P.*, 1854, vol. lxix, p. 527.   [2] R. N. Cust, *Pictures of Indian Life*, p. 247.

first Punjab Administration Report written by the young Temple. The construction of the new central gaol at Lahore was minutely described. It consisted of 'two circles . . . each surrounded by iron palisades, with compartments (also walled), radiating from the centre to the circumference . . . within these compartments are the wards both for male and female prisoners, workshops and solitary cells. At the centre a lofty watch tower rises so as to command a view of all compartments.' The three provincial gaols, at Multan, Rawalpindi, and Ambala, were to be constructed of one circle on a similar model. There was to be no out-work system but only indoor labour, and all prisoners were to be strictly classified. In such an unexpected fashion did Bentham's 'panopticon' idea triumph and his ghost preside as the tutelary deity of the Punjab prison system. His inspiration did not cease at this point, but permeated the whole administration of justice.

The Board [of Administration] desire that substantial justice should be plainly dealt out to simple people, unused to the intricacies of legal proceedings. Their aim is to avoid all technicality, circumlocution, and obscurity, to simplify and abridge every rule, procedure, and process. They would endeavour to form tribunals, which shall not be hedged in with forms unintelligible to the vulgar, and only to be interpreted by professional lawyers, but which shall be open and accessible courts of justice, where every man may plead his own cause, be confronted face to face with his own opponents, may prosecute his own claim, or conduct his own defence.[1]

There was no slavish adherence to the Benthamite judicial system. The disposal of original suits was dealt with according to their monetary value, the deputy-commissioner hearing all suits above 1,000 rupees and his subordinates hearing the remainder. The rapid increase in litigation also led to the establishment of Small Cause Courts, with a special summary type of justice for petty suits. But if Bentham had inveighed against the monetary classification of suits and the provision of a special form of justice for suits of small amount, the general spirit of his ideas was enthusiastically adopted. The highly organized system of regular reports and the collation of all kinds of statistics, bearing fruit in the well-known early

[1] Punjab Administration Report 1849–51, para. 221: *P.P.*, 1854, vol. lxix, p. 526.

Punjab Administration Reports, supply the proper corrective to the Nicholson myth. They represent precisely that form of inspection and control which Bentham had suggested in his *Constitutional Code* as the proper safeguard against the dangers of a concentration of authority in individual officers. The despatch of the Home Authorities commenting upon the first Punjab Administration Report was drafted by J. S. Mill, and there seems an almost personal note in its paean of praise.[1]

The Punjab school grew up under Dalhousie's direction,[2] and he watched over it as over a favourite child. The 'Non-Regulation' system which he established in the Punjab was also employed for his other annexations and conquests, particularly for the Central Provinces, Oudh, and Lower Burma. But Dalhousie was no patriarchalist of the Lawrence mould, with his heart in the immemorial Indian village and the simple values for which it stood. He employed the 'Non-Regulation' system because it gave him a personal control over these territories and because it promised to be more economical, more energetic, and more efficient in securing their rapid development. At the end of his life he felt that the Lawrences had secured too much credit for the Punjab achievement, and believed his own contribution had been neglected. In his hands the Non-Regulation system became an instrument for the rapid modernization of India; and it was doubtless with Dalhousie particularly in mind that Dr. G. M. Young refers to 'the natural alliance between the Tory gentleman and the scientific Benthamite administrator' being achieved in India.[3] Dalhousie was not of the type which gave explicit statements of their deeper political beliefs, but he once admitted himself to be 'a curious compound of despot and radical'. By birth and training his instincts were authoritarian and conservative: the ideal he set before himself as a young man was to be 'a Christian, a gentleman, and a nobleman'. Yet his character and intellect were singularly unlike those of his class. At Oxford he led

---

[1] Despatch of Court of Directors, 26 Oct. 1853: *P.P.*, 1854, vol. lxix, p. 465. For J. S. Mill's authorship of this despatch, see MacMinn, &c. (ed.), *Bibliography of Published Writings of J. S. Mill*, and Home Misc. Ser., vol. 832.

[2] The Marquis of Dalhousie, Governor-General, 1848–56.

[3] G. M. Young, *Victorian England: Portrait of an Age*, p. 54.

a hard-reading, sedentary life' which injured his health. This was in an attempt to win first-class honours, an object which he 'so long laboured for, thought of, talked of, dreamed of, almost solely lived for', but which he had eventually to abandon for family reasons.

When holding office at the Board of Trade he further damaged his constitution by an incredible application to his duties quite remarkable for a titled junior minister at that time. Although a Conservative, he had, like Gladstone, to admit a greater sympathy with Liberal measures.[1] And his state papers reflect the clear, decided mind, the rapid reduction of a question to a few relevant points, the concentrated logical argument, and the firm conclusion, characteristic of the Benthamite administrator at his best. Dalhousie's writing is particularly remarkable. The terse, simple language, free of all qualification or ornament, conveys his meaning with the immediacy and directness of a physical shock. With these qualities Dalhousie may be held, in a certain sense, to stand in the line of the Utilitarian succession; the strong authoritarian reformer, the enlightened despot, which Bentham and James Mill had thought the ideal type for the government of India. His utilitarianism, if such it may be called, was characteristic of his age. It was no longer a fixed programme derived from the texts of Bentham, nor was it a set of intellectual dogmas. It was rather a practical cast of mind, a strong aggressive logic with which a man of affairs could approach specific political issues.

In India Dalhousie's most visible achievement was the expansion of the area under direct British rule. He regarded the Indian states as anachronisms, and held before himself the ultimate ideal of shaping the whole Indian subcontinent into a modern unitary state. This was a good utilitarian attitude, although the generally pacific policy preached by the Utilitarians in foreign affairs, and the severe handling which James Mill had dealt to Wellesley for his annexations, might at first suggest otherwise. But James Mill in his evidence before the Parliamentary Committee of 1832 had

---

[1] *Private Letters of the Marquess of Dalhousie*, ed. J. G. A. Baird, pp. 372, 410, 411–12. W. Lee-Warner, *Life of the Marquess of Dalhousie*, vol. i, pp. 10, 24. G. M. Young, *Victorian England*, p. 54.

put forward remarkably bellicose views with regard to the
Indian states. He thought their government uniformly op-
pressive, and believed they had only been allowed to survive
because English public opinion would not countenance a
further expansion of British territory at the time they were
conquered. The most obvious policy, James Mill declared,
was 'to make war on those states and subdue them'.[1] There
would be little risk in taking over the administration of the
states and pensioning off their rulers 'by judicious means',
but he admitted there would be a very great outcry against
it in England. This was not the first time that the elder Mill
was to find himself in opposition to ordinary Liberal opinion.
There was nothing now, he declared, between the British
and the most desirable frontier but the territory of Ranjit
Singh. He concluded that the best policy was to annex the
Indian states 'according as circumstances would allow', and
the period in which they should be allowed to survive 'ought
to be as short as you can conveniently make it'. Dalhousie's
policy towards the states would certainly have met with
James Mill's hearty approval.

Dalhousie's other great work was to effect a remarkable
expansion in the activities of government in India. The task
of transforming India into a modern state and redeeming the
promise of the 1833 Charter Act presented itself to him in
mainly physical terms. His first concern was the extension
of the area under British administration, and his next care
its organization as a modern political and economic unit using
the agency of modern communications—roads, railways,
ports, posts, and telegraphs. The administrative instrument
he created for this second task was the new 'all-India' department governed by single heads, whose function was to lay
down policy and exercise unified control. The example of
such central agencies was to be found in English bodies such
as the Poor Law Commission and the Railway Board, which
owed much to Bentham's administrative ideas. In India
Dalhousie could be more sweeping. He could insist on individual control and was able to sweep away boards wherever
practicable. 'My own opinion has long been decidedly in
favour of placing a single authority at the head of every

---

[1] Evidence of James Mill, 16 Feb. 1832: *P.P.*, 1831–2, vol. xiv, p. 8, Qu. 49.

public department. In that form only can sustained promptitude of action be maintained and real responsibility enforced.' The Superintendent of Electric Telegraphs, an official in charge of the whole Indian system, was told by Dalhousie to adopt as his guiding principles: 'Uniformity of management and unity of authority.'[1] Were not these the accents of one of Bentham's administrative disciples? The establishment of a central Public Works Department to plan the development of large-scale irrigation schemes, and Dalhousie's personal share in laying down a railway policy and programme, are rightly regarded as among his most notable achievements. His own experience at the Board of Trade in dealing with English railway development enabled him to work confidently and boldly. Freed from the limitations imposed by the parliamentary system he was able to achieve his own ideal of central railway planning and control.

In this vigorous promotion of the agencies of modernization Dalhousie transcended the narrower patriarchal limits of the Punjab school. He succeeded in harmonizing the vigour and efficiency of the paternalist tradition with the Liberal modernizing current. The result was sometimes to give an air of paradox to his actions. At once the most authoritarian and despotic of all governor-generals, he nevertheless actively encouraged the development of his Legislative Council into a parliamentary body, provided it with elaborate rules of procedure taken from the English Parliament, and defended its independence against the assaults of the Home Authorities. He even favoured the admission of Indian members to the Legislative Council, a step which quite bold Liberals like J. S. Mill and Bright were reluctant to suggest. The most striking example of the blending of the paternalist and Liberal traditions was in the field of education. Sir Charles Wood's famous Education Despatch of 1854 stole Dalhousie's thunder (a practice of unacknowledged borrowing of which Dalhousie thought him much too fond). Dalhousie had already suggested a similar policy, although he was, of course, unable to sanction anything like so sweeping a scheme as Wood outlined. The Liberal view on education was founded on the diffusionist theory and was identified

[1] Lee-Warner, op. cit., vol. ii, pp. 183, 189, 193.

with Macaulay's pronouncement of 1835. It concentrated on higher education in English so as to create an English-educated middle class who would be 'interpreters between us and the millions whom we govern'. The paternalists, on the other hand, looked to the welfare of the peasant and wanted mass education at an elementary level. Their principal aim was to furnish the peasant with merely a sufficient degree of literacy to enable him to understand the village land records and to defend himself against the wiles of the money-lender. Little was achieved for the paternalist policy until Thomason, as Lieutenant-Governor of the North-Western Provinces (1843–53), secured permission to levy an educational cess and established a system of *tehsil* schools giving an elementary education in the vernacular. The Despatch of 1854 merely declared the desirability of generalizing Thomason's system for the rest of British India, and integrating it with higher education policy, thus providing the framework of a complete educational system.

No sharp incompatibility was felt in the fifties and sixties between the Liberal and paternalist outlook. The period constituted, in a milder and less ambitious form, a second age of Indian reform. It reflected the buoyancy and confidence of an England in prosperity, with the 'hungry forties' left behind and the value of the Free Trade victory being proved in the leaping figures of British commerce. The Education Despatch of 1854 reiterated the ideals and hopes of the earlier reforming generation:

Nor, while the character of England is deeply concerned in the success of our efforts for the promotion of education, are her material interests altogether unaffected by the advance of European knowledge in India; this knowledge will teach the natives of India the marvellous results of the employment of labor [*sic*] and capital, rouse them to emulate us in the development of the vast resources of their country, guide them in their efforts and gradually, but certainly, confer upon them all the advantages which accompany the healthy increase of wealth and commerce; and, at the same time, secure to us a larger and more certain supply of many articles necessary for our manufactures and extensively consumed by all classes of our population, as well as an almost inexhaustible demand for the produce of British labour.[1]

[1] Education Despatch to India, 19 July 1854, para. 4: *Selections from Educational Records Part II, 1840–59*, ed. J. A. Richey, p. 365.

When Parliament came to consider the renewal of the East India Company's Charter in 1853 there was a general feeling that the work of the 1833 Charter Act had been left unfinished. Most witnesses at the Committees of Inquiry urged that the task of the defunct Law Commission ought to be taken up afresh and the movement of administrative and judicial reform once again set in motion. Charles Trevelyan appeared as the unswerving champion of the liberalism of the earlier reforming period. He still believed that the value of property in India and the facilities for its exchange would be greatly enhanced by 'the improvement of our judicial system, making justice more cheap and speedy, and economical'.[1] He naturally placed great reliance at this time on the benefits to be expected from material progress, from public works, irrigation schemes, roads and, above all, from railways. By means of the railway 'the whole machinery of society will be stimulated', and 'increased intensity' would be given 'to every other improvement whatever, both physical and moral'. Yet he placed his greatest faith, as of old, in the 'progressive education of the natives, by which they will be fitted to co-operate with us in every purpose of improvement, both administrative and social, and by which their attachment to our Government will be increased'. It was fitting that he should hand in for publication in the proceedings of the committee an extract from his treatise of 1838, *On the Education of the People of India*, where he had given the most splendid expression to his faith in the political wisdom of education.[2]

Trevelyan's suggestions for the organization of the Indian Government also fell into line with the ideas of the eighteen-thirties. He envisaged 'a Supreme Government for the whole of India, entirely separated from any local administrative responsibility'; an expanded Legislative Council; and presidencies under governors appointed by the Governor-General and dispensing with executive councils. He also renewed the recommendation, which James Mill and Macaulay had pressed twenty years earlier, for the unification of the *Sadr* and Supreme Courts at the Presidencies and the extension

---

[1] Evidence of Sir Charles Trevelyan, 7 July 1853: *P.P.*, 1852–3, vol. xxviii, p. 495.

[2] See pp. 46–47. Printed in *P.P.*, 1852–3, vol. xviii, pp. 433 et seq.

of the criminal jurisdiction of the Company's courts over Europeans. Finally, Trevelyan gave a clear analysis of what he considered were India's requirements in the field of codified law; firstly, a penal code, with civil and criminal procedure codes applicable to all classes and races; secondly, a common body of civil law, except in the 'extremely limited' number of cases where it was impossible to reconcile this with Hindu and Muslim law; and lastly, a digest of those parts of Hindu and Muslim law which had to be maintained as excepted cases. All this adhered fairly closely to the original Utilitarian programme.

Enlightened paternalists, such as George Campbell,[1] the rising young civilian of the North-Western Provinces, found themselves largely in agreement with this statement of Liberal aims. While looking sceptically on the hopes for a great moral and social revolution to be effected through an educated middle class, they had to admit the necessity of higher education in the interests of India's material progress. Campbell wanted higher education to take the form of professional training, declaring that he 'would without delay provide a free passage to England for the gentlemen who teach Milton in the Hindoo College, and entertain in their place mechanicians and chemists and professors of all manner of useful knowledge'. The paternalists had always disliked the urban products of an exclusively literary English education, and thought the Liberal assertion that they would be zealous supporters of British rule a highly dubious proposition. But there was no reason to anticipate any political danger from such a class at this time.

Bengalese who learn English may become bad subjects and servants, and (if permitted to do so) they may write any amount of treason; but I do not in the least apprehend their acting upon it. The classes most advanced in English education, and who talk like newspapers, are not yet those from whom we have anything to fear; but on the contrary, they are those who have gained *everything* by our rule, and whom neither interest nor inclination leads to deeds of daring involving any personal risk. For a long time to come, if we incur any political danger, it will be from enemies of the original native stamp.

Written four years before the Mutiny this was a remarkably

[1] See Biographical Notes, p. 331.

true forecast. Campbell saw that without a sense of nationalism there was no danger to British rule from such a class. If
in the improbable future such a sense of political unity was
developed, Britain would no doubt have to make concessions
to it, but Campbell certainly did not propose to encourage it
in any fashion. He declared that he saw no object in attempting the political elevation of the natives beyond the limits
of small municipalities.[1] But there was no real practical
question at the time concerning the possibility of representative institutions. Even John Stuart Mill, who in theory contemplated with equanimity the progressive admission of
Indians to high office, and eventually the granting of self-
government to them, did not consider that the time was ripe
in 1853 for the introduction of a single Indian member into
the Legislative Council.[2]

Apart from this difference in sympathies Campbell agreed
generally with Trevelyan's programme. As a paternalist he
naturally favoured a strong central government under the
Governor-General, with the local governments effectively
subordinated to him by placing them all under lieutenant-
governors without councils. He also agreed that if law were
to be simple and efficient, it was necessary to form it into
a proper system of codes; and that if civil justice were to
be well administered, it must be confided to a specialized
judiciary, except that all rent cases ought to be reserved for
the revenue courts, and criminal justice maintained in the
hands of the executive. Despite this harmony of viewpoint
among the leading Indian authorities, the English distaste
for concentrating power in individuals made the new Charter
Act of 1853 a somewhat hesitant affair. The relief of the
Governor-General from the administrative responsibility
for Bengal, Bihar, and Orissa could no longer be postponed;
but the question whether to constitute a separate presidency
under a governor and council, or alternatively, to form a
lieutenant-governorship without a council and more dependent on the authority of the Governor-General, was left un-
decided and optional under the Act. For reasons of economy
and because Calcutta remained the capital of the Supreme

[1] George Campbell, *India As It May Be*, 1853, pp. 105, 404, 410.
[2] Evidence of J. S. Mill, 22 June 1852: *P.P.*, 1852–3, vol. xxx, pp. 318–19.

Government, only a lieutenant-governor without a council was appointed in 1854. This final separation of the Supreme Government from the work of local administration and its emergence as purely a controlling body realized James Mill's ideal, but it was still not quite the unquestioned central authority he had envisaged. James Mill had been a strenuous advocate of the lieutenant-governor system, but in 1853 (as in 1833, or as in 1899, when Curzon made the proposal) the Home Government was not prepared to abolish the presidencies of Madras and Bombay and reduce them to lieutenant-governorships under the immediate authority of the Governor-General. When questioned by the Commons Committee on the point, John Stuart Mill was unable to offer any decided opinion in contrast to the dogmatic certainty of his father twenty years earlier.[1] The 1853 Act further departed from James Mill's axioms by enlarging the Legislative Council to include two judges from the Supreme Court and an official representative each from Bengal, Madras, Bombay, and the North-Western Provinces. The arrangement was abandoned in 1861, not because of Mill's theoretical objection to admitting the judiciary to any share of legislative power, but because of the practical nuisance which the Chief Justice, Sir Barnes Peacock, made of himself. At the same time legislative councils were restored to the Presidencies, and the Governor-General's Legislative Council was made to include European and Indian unofficial members in response to the lessons of the Mutiny. Although the Council was strictly confined to legislative business and its powers were closely shorn to prevent it again assuming parliamentary airs, it had certainly diverged from James Mill's ideal of a small expert body, free from any quasi-representative element; and the restoration of legislative powers to the Presidencies appeared to indicate a loosening of central control. The matter could not be disposed of dogmatically, even from the Utilitarian viewpoint. Bentham had provided for local sub-legislatures in his ideal state, and he was rather the advocate of the logical distribution of power than of an excessive centralization. The authority to legislate for the whole of India was in no way impaired by

[1] Evidence of J. S. Mill, 22 June 1852: *P.P.*, 1852–3, vol. xxx, p. 325.

the Indian Councils Act of 1861, and the Governor-General's assent was required for all acts of the provincial legislatures. In fact Fitzjames Stephen was able to rejoice in the early seventies that legislation for a vast empire could be drawn up by a knot of experts sitting in a small room. The real work of legislation, particularly the drafting of the Indian codes, continued to be performed by the legal member and his staff together with a small committee of the Legislative Council. Where the Indian system of government failed to meet the Benthamite ideal was in its failure to give the Viceroy—as he was known by this time—full executive control over the Governors of Madras and Bombay. Appointed directly by the Home Government from persons outside the Indian Civil Service, they were permitted to conduct a separate correspondence with the Secretary of State, and were provided with executive councils and the apparatus of completely distinct governments. They remained a thorn in the side of any strong Viceroy such as a Lytton or Curzon. It was here that the real flaw in the system persisted from a Benthamite viewpoint. The decentralization measures in relation to finance, initiated by Mayo and carried further under Lytton, tend to give a misleading impression. John Strachey, their chief architect, believed he was strengthening rather than weakening the central authority in India by imparting to the whole system increased efficiency and a better distinction between the executive and controlling functions.[1] The Viceroy's authority was not impaired; but he continued to experience difficulty in his relations with Madras and Bombay, not because of any privileged legal status in comparison with the other provinces, but because of their historical tradition of independence, that 'qualified privilege of insubordination' of which Curzon complained.

This partial triumph for Utilitarian ideas in the organization of Indian government, this achievement which stopped short of final symmetry and logical perfection, was matched by a similar progress in the field of law. The revived or second Law Commission, set up as a result of the Charter

[1] Sir John Strachey, *India*, 1888, pp. 45–48, 68–71. Cf. Sir J. Fitzjames Stephen, letter to *The Times*, 4 Jan. 1878.

Act of 1853, contained many figures of the earlier age of reform: Sir Edward Ryan, now a distinguished Privy Councillor, Cameron and Millett, as well as Sir John Romilly, a Benthamite friend of John Mill in his younger days. But the Report put out by the commission in 1856 was markedly conservative in comparison with the ambitious plans of its predecessor. Admitting the need for a codified body of substantive civil law, the commission nevertheless recommended that its basis should be simplified English law, modified in some instances to suit Indian conditions. Whatever the actual debt to English law of Macaulay's labours on the penal code, he would have resisted fiercely this anglicist approach. The 'over-confident Benthamism of 1833'[1] was abandoned, and the aim of codifying those parts of Hindu and Muslim law which would have to be retained, as exceptions to the general body of substantive civil law, was given up.

What remained and was actually accomplished has always been recognized as the fruit of Bentham's inspiration.[2] At the head of the body of Indian codified law stands the trinity of the three principal codes—the Penal Code, the Code of Civil, and the Code of Criminal Procedure—all of which were enacted between 1859 and 1861. They had long been meditated, but it took the Mutiny to end the twenty years of delay and hesitation and to prompt the Indian Legislature to act with decision and energy. A draft Code of Civil Procedure had been produced by Frederick Millett for the benefit of the first Law Commission in 1835. This had been a digest of the relevant Bengal Regulations, together with certain modifications and improvements. With the superb impatience of the reformer in full career, Macaulay had waved aside the proposed enactment of Millett's draft, urging that a much more perfect work could be rapidly executed by the Law Commission.[3] Macaulay's plans came

---

[1] Sir G. C. Rankin, *Background to Indian Law*, p. 43.

[2] Cf. Sir J. Fitzjames Stephen, 'Review of Hildreth's translation of Bentham's *Theory of Legislation*' in *Horae Sabbaticae*, 1892, vol. iii, p. 219: 'When to this it is added that the Code Napoleon, and the Penal and Civil Codes, by which 130 Millions of people are governed in the East Indies, are founded upon it [Bentham's *Theory of Legislation*] no more need be said as to the results which it has produced.'

[3] See pp. 203, 212–13.

to nothing, and Millett's draft was apparently not unearthed again until some eighteen years later when Dalhousie appointed two special commissioners 'for revising the Code of Civil Procedure'.[1] Their work, printed in 1854, was laid before the new Law Commission sitting in London, who in turn produced a draft code of their own. Amended by Barnes Peacock and a Select Committee of the Indian Legislative Council, this latter draft finally became law as Act VIII of 1859. It was by no means an ideal Code of Civil Procedure, and was subject to much subsequent amendment and re-enactment. Nor was it the perfectly designed instrument which Bentham and James Mill had desired for making justice simple, swift, cheap, and readily accessible. Yet whatever its defects, John Stuart Mill (speaking of the Law Commission's draft) thought it promised to secure 'so far as judicial institutions can secure that blessing, as good and accessible an administration of civil justice as the lights of the age are capable of conferring on it'.[2] Bentham's teachings had made sufficient general headway, and their value had been sufficiently proved in the Non-Regulation provinces for many improvements to be introduced into the elaborate and tedious methods of judicial procedure in force in the rest of British India. The most noteworthy was the general abandonment of written pleadings—the elaborate ritual of the plaint, the reply, the replication, and the rejoinder. These had until this time been required in even the pettiest suits, delaying a decision by at least three months and making the employment of a lawyer indispensable. Written pleadings were for Bentham and his followers one of the pillars of the hated technical, fee-gathering system of justice, and both Macaulay and James Mill had crusaded against them in India. The Code of Civil Procedure now put an end to them in their more objectionable form:

Under the proposed code of procedure, the plaint is to be limited to certain specified particulars; and when the suit has been instituted, no

---

[1] Whitley Stokes, *The Anglo-Indian Codes*, vol. ii, p. 383. Whitley Stokes imagined that the First Law Commission produced a draft Civil Procedure Code, but there is no evidence to suggest that any other than Millett's code was drafted. Stokes was probably referring to this, as Millett was of course a member of the Law Commission.

[2] [J. S. Mill], *Memorandum of the Improvements in the Administration of India during the Last Thirty Years*; cited Rankin, op. cit., p. 30.

written pleadings in the technical sense of the term are to be admitted.
The parties are to be orally examined, and they will be at liberty to
tender, at the first hearing of the suit, written statements, confined,
as much as possible, to a simple narrative of facts. In this way the
question at issue between the litigants will be ascertained by a process
much more simple and expeditious, and better calculated to a satisfactory result than that which now prevails.[1]

The Civil Procedure Code gave instant relief, but its
effect was limited by the failure to shorten the process of
appeal. Bentham had laboured the obvious when he had
demonstrated how the allowance of more than one appeal
made it possible to magnify the duration and expense of a
lawsuit immeasurably. The law as it stood permitted only
one regular appeal, but also allowed a second or special
appeal to the High Court (*Sadr Diwani Adalat*) on grounds
broad enough for it to be extensively employed. The Law
Commission of 1853 had recognized the evil, and had proposed to overcome it by abolishing special appeals and allowing a single regular appeal in all cases above 1,000 rupees to
go direct to the High Court. This was a bold suggestion and
recalls Macaulay's even bolder idea that all appeals on issues
of law should go straight from the *sadr amin* to the High
Court. The difficulties of reorganizing the system of courts
proved too formidable, and the Civil Procedure Code made
no alteration in the law of appeal. Another Benthamite
suggestion, put forward by the Law Commission, was the
abolition of stamp duties and fees on the institution of suits.
James Mill in his *History* had made much of this issue, and
Macaulay had fought for it with glowing conviction, declaring that no question in the whole science of jurisprudence
seemed to him clearer, and very few more important.[2] Yet
the handsome revenue derived from stamp duties, and the
old Indian conviction that they were a salutary check to
irresponsible litigation, prevented the acceptance of this
reform. Heavy duties continued to be imposed.

The most justly famous of the Indian codes was the Penal

---

[1] Despatch of Secretary of State, 12 May 1859, para. 12: *P.P.*, 1859 (2), vol. xxiii,
pp. 195–6. Cf. evidence of James Mill, 29 June 1832: *P.P.*, 1831–2, vol. xii, p. 122,
Qu. 1046.

[2] James Mill, *History*, vol. v, pp. 453–8. Macaulay, Minute, 25 June 1835:
Dharker, op. cit., p. 220.

Code enacted in 1860. Macaulay's draft, published in 1837, survived the ordeal of twenty years of detailed criticism at the hands of a multitude of authorities and emerged remarkably unscathed. Auckland had referred the draft code to the *Sadr* and Supreme Court judges at the three Presidencies, and these had smothered it with a mass of comment which Cameron sifted and answered in two extensive reports of July 1846 and June 1847. Despite Cameron's recommendation that the Code should be passed into law, and the Home Authorities' compliance when the matter was referred to them, the Indian Government took no immediate action. Dalhousie was immersed in the second Sikh War, and his law member, Drinkwater Bethune, was uncompromisingly hostile to the Code. In 1850 the matter came up afresh, when legislation was proposed to place British-born subjects under the criminal jurisdiction of the ordinary courts from which they had hitherto been exempt. Dalhousie readily supported the idea but refused to move until the penal law administered in the Company's courts, which was still a compound of the old Muslim law, had been entirely reformed. He expressed himself determined to get a proper penal code despite Bethune's reluctance, but instead of revising Macaulay's draft Bethune produced a draft of his own. Bethune objected strongly to the Benthamite features introduced by Macaulay, particularly to the novel terminology for crimes and the use of illustrations. Bethune's draft completely altered Macaulay's arrangement and his phraseology followed the orthodox wording of English enactments. Feeling he had no authority to decide between such widely-differing proposals Dalhousie referred the question to London. The Home Authorities in reply simply repeated their previous sanction for the Indian Government to enact such a penal code as it thought fit.[1] Meanwhile the new Law Commission appointed under the 1853 Act had been charged with the duty of drafting a Code of Criminal Procedure, and required to know the general outlines of the particular penal code with which it was to be employed. At last the

---

[1] Evidence of C. H. Cameron, 7 June 1852, and David Hill, 26 June 1852: *P.P.*, 1852–3, vol. xxx, pp. 187, 338. Also evidence of David Hill, 10 March 1853: *P.P.*, 1852–3, vol. xxvii, p. 100.

select committee of the Indian Legislative Council made its decision in favour of Macaulay's draft:

> We have come to the conclusion to recommend to the Council, that the Penal Code, as originally prepared by the Indian Law Commissioners when Mr. Macaulay was the president of that body, should form the basis of the system of penal law to be enacted for India. We are accordingly taking into consideration the various alterations and additions thereto that have been proposed to be made; and we intend to submit to the Legislative Council a revised code embodying such of the proposed alterations and additions as may appear to us to be improvements, and such other amendments as may suggest themselves to us in the course of our revisions. We do not intend to recommend any substantial alteration in the framework or phraseology of the original code.[1]

Although the Code took another six years to enact and did not become law until a year after Macaulay's death, he lived to see the certainty of its triumph. In October 1854 he wrote to his sister:

> I cannot but be pleased to find that, at last, the Code on which I bestowed the labour of two of the best years of my life has had justice done to it. Had this justice been done sixteen years ago, I should probably have given much more attention to legislation, and much less to literature than I have done. I do not know that I should have been either happier or more useful than I have been.[2]

It would be tedious and irrelevant to narrate the alterations and modifications made to Macaulay's draft. As had been promised, there was no substantial alteration in the framework or the phraseology of Macaulay's work, and Macaulay's debt to Bentham has already been recounted.

The Penal Code was followed by the Code of Criminal Procedure, passed in 1861. This also had long been under consideration. Cameron had made a draft before he left India in 1848, and this was used by the new Law Commission in the preparation of their own draft code, published in 1856.[3] Amended by the Indian Legislative Council this draft finally became law as Act XXV of 1861. Like the Civil Procedure Code it was subject to much later amendment and

---

[1] Report of Law Commission, 1856: *P.P.*, 1856, vol. xxv, p. 94.
[2] G. O. Trevelyan, *Life and Letters of Lord Macaulay*, 1908 edn., p. 337.
[3] Whitley Stokes, *Anglo-Indian Codes*, vol. ii, pp. 1–2.

was enacted anew by Whitley Stokes in 1882. It incorporated many Benthamite features whose usefulness had been shown in the Punjab and other Non-Regulation areas. The most important of these was the requirement enforcing *viva voce* proceedings, for which James Mill and Macaulay had loudly appealed. These were ensured by the provision in the Code

that in all trials and inquiries the judge or magistrate shall take down with his own hand the evidence of every witness in the form of a narrative, and shall sign it when taken down, and that the evidence so taken down shall form part of the record. If the magistrate or judge does not take down the evidence in his own hand (which usually happens if it is not given in his own language) it must be taken down in his presence and hearing, and he must, as the evidence is given, make a memorandum of the substance of it.[1]

Previously the evidence of witnesses had been recorded by a low-paid Indian subordinate out of the magistrate's hearing, and was merely read over to the magistrate in the presence of the witness at the time of the trial. This had led to a dependence on written depositions often corrupt and full of irrelevant matter. Under the new system introduced by the Code and earlier adopted in the Non-Regulation provinces, 'the magistrate is compelled to learn the facts of the case from the witnesses themselves, instead of trusting to a deposition of a corrupt omlah in a corner'.[2]

It would be idle to search for specific Benthamite influences in the other Indian codes. Much of Bentham's doctrines had become so generally accepted that it would be difficult to mark off his own influence from the general current of contemporary legal ideas. In England law reform was under way, although it went forward in halting and piecemeal fashion. Reform progressed more quickly in India but it may be regarded as part of the same movement. The Succession Act of 1865 was chiefly remarkable for abolishing the distinction between real and personal property, and for providing that marriage did not *per se* confer any rights of property on husband or wife; measures which had long had Bentham's advocacy. The other acts of this period which

[1] Sir J. Fitzjames Stephen, *History of the Criminal Law of England*, 1883 edn., vol. iii, pp. 333–4.
[2] Moral and Material Progress Report, 1859–60: *P.P.*, 1861, vol. xlvii, p. 151.

qualify for the title of codes were much more definitely simplified digests of English law; such, for instance, as the Contract Act of 1872. Fitzjames Stephen's Evidence Act of 1872 laid greater claim to originality. Although founded on an English basis, Stephen claimed to have 'discarded altogether the phraseology in which the English text writers usually express themselves', and to have 'attempted first to ascertain and then to arrange in their natural order the principles which underlie the numerous cases and fragmentary rules which they have collected together'.[1] The original feature was the attempt to provide positive rules (in addition to the negative rules of exclusion which form the English law on the subject) for testing the relevancy of evidence. Sections 5–11 of the Evidence Act incorporate a theory of relevancy which, as Stephen explained in a separate treatise of his own, *An Introduction to the Evidence Act*, attempted to apply the rules of induction set out in J. S. Mill's *System of Logic*.[2] That the Indian codes are too much digests of English law, that they are incomplete and but a fragment of the grand pannomium of Bentham's dream, that the vast arena of Hindu and Muslim law has been left outside their scope, that they have been almost buried beneath case-law, all these are obvious criticisms which require no elaboration. Yet with all their limitations they stand out as impressive intellectual achievements, making Anglo-Indian law far superior in order, clarity, and system to its English counterpart. They are among the most solid and enduring results of the Utilitarian influence.

The organization of the judiciary was also brought nearer to the Benthamite ideal. In 1861 the High Courts Act ended the anomaly of two competing judiciaries by fusing the *Sadr* with the Supreme Court at each of the Presidencies. The Act also effected 'the fusion of law and equity', not accomplished in England until the Judicature Acts of 1873–5, and, in conjunction with the Civil Procedure Code, assimilated the four different kinds of jurisdiction and pleading —common law, equity, ecclesiastical, and admiralty—which had been reproduced in the Supreme Courts in accordance

---

[1] Sir G. C. Rankin, *Background to Indian Law*, p. 119.
[2] Ibid., p. 124.

with the unreformed English law. In the organization of
the subordinate courts Bentinck's work proved remarkably durable. Almost no alteration was made in the system
he established until 1868, when the office of principal *sadr
amin* was converted into that of subordinate judge, and the
office of the ordinary *sadr amin* was abolished. The powers
of the *munsif* were raised at the same time to enable him to
hear suits up to 1,000 rupees in value. The subordinate
judge was given powers co-ordinate with those of his superior,
the district judge, except that appeals from his decisions in
suits under 5,000 rupees continued to be heard by the
district judge and not the High Court. In 1871 provincial
governments received the power to invest any subordinate
judge with the jurisdiction of a small cause court in suits up
to a value of 500 rupees, and similarly a *munsif* in suits up to
50 rupees. A small cause court proceeded in a summary in-
formal way, and there was no appeal from its decisions. This
was the general system established in Bengal and the North-
Western Provinces in 1868, and between 1865 and 1878
enactments regulating the system of civil courts for the ten
provinces of British India were passed. Although in the
former Non-Regulation provinces of Sind, the Punjab, the
Central Provinces, Oudh, Assam, and Burma, the union of
judicial and executive functions was still maintained, in the
North-Western Provinces, Madras, and Bombay, a substantially uniform system of courts was achieved on the basis
of the Bengal model.[1] From the Benthamite viewpoint many
of the old objections still remained. It was a system based on
the monetary classification of suits. It was a system which
tended to run to technicality and become lawyer-ridden. It
was a system which left original and appellate jurisdiction in
the same hands. The High Courts exercised a local jurisdiction in the Presidency towns, as well as an extraordinary
original jurisdiction throughout their provinces. The district
judge, although in practice confined almost wholly to appeal
work, still had powers to hear original suits, and the subordinate judge commonly heard both types of case. The
establishment of small cause courts, with a special type
of justice in petty suits, was also another measure which

[1] Moral and Material Progress Report, 1882–3: *P.P.*, 1884–5, vol. lx, p. 69,

Bentham had expressly opposed. The law of appeal continued to allow a second or special appeal to the High Court, and in suits above 10,000 rupees a further appeal was allowed to the Privy Council. From the Benthamite standpoint the establishment of uniform legislation for the whole of British India was a distinctive achievement; and the enactment of the Indian codes by the central legislature certainly countered any movement in the opposite direction which might have resulted from the restoration of provincial legislatures in 1861. Yet the multiplication of High Courts had some of the results which James Mill had feared when he had opposed the erection of a separate *Sadr* Court for the North-Western Provinces. The High Courts at Calcutta, Madras, Bombay, Allahabad, and the Chief Court at Lahore, were left without any superior co-ordinating authority, and their judicial interpretations of the Indian codes sometimes differed considerably. Having taken into account all these defects, it is nevertheless true that the administration of justice in India attained a degree of uniformity, system, and disciplined organization quite unknown in England. While much of this arose from the practical necessities of British rule, a good deal, as it has been seen, was shaped by Bentham's ideas. Describing the Indian system on its criminal side, Fitzjames Stephen declared that

the grading of the different classes of magistrates, the extent of their judicial powers, and above all, the minute and elaborate system by which the different courts are subordinated to each other, both in the way of discipline and in the way of appeal, and by which all are superintended in every detail by the High Courts, is characteristically and exclusively Indian. . . . Indian civilians are, for the discharge of their duties, judicial or otherwise, in the position of an elaborately disciplined and organized half-military body.[1]

Many defects of the system, as Stephen urged, were inherent in the British position in India; it was a system founded on foreign principles, worked by imperfect instruments, and set down in a society afflicted by poverty and ignorance. So long as a subordinate judge or *munsif* could be suspected of corruption, or a district judge of legal incompetence, it was necessary to retain the power of special appeal to the

[1] Stephen, *History of the Criminal Law*, vol. iii, p. 344.

High Court. So long as the mass of litigants were ignorant and perjury was regarded with moral indifference; so long as Indian society regarded law as a foreign imposition to be circumvented by superior subtlety, it was to be expected that legal chicane would flourish at the hands of a clever lawyer class. A great deal of the odium incurred by the Indian judicial system has, however, been misplaced, and indeed has arisen because of the extreme efficacy of the system. The celerity with which landed property could be transferred, the certainty surrounding its tenure, the facilities for mortgage, all supported and executed by the courts, were undoubtedly instrumental in the rapid development of peasant indebtedness and the transfer of property titles to the money-lending classes. But to deplore this is not properly to convict the system so much as to convict the assumption on which much of the law rested—the perfect applicability of the principles of classical political economy to India's peasant society. Fitzjames Stephen recognized this in 1876 when he remarked upon the gross fallacy of condemning law and legislation in general because the provisions of one particular law which allowed land to be sold for debt might be open to question.[1] It would be foolish to pretend that Bentham's ideal was in any sense attained, and justice in India remained far from cheap, simple, and expeditious. But this has been equally true of most countries where the rule of law has been established, and Bentham's influence requires to be tested by the extent it has mitigated the evils afflicting the administration of justice rather than the extent to which it instituted a positive system of its own. That so much of Indian law (with the exception of the Hindu and Muslim personal law) was codified, that despite the infusion of English law it was simplified and stripped of much of its technicality, and that the system as a whole was better organized and more logical than its English counterpart, was the sort of result to which the Utilitarian influence contributed. Whether the rule of law in India involves more evils than the rule of personal discretion is perhaps a debatable issue, but from the historical viewpoint the degree of choice open to the British

---

[1] J. Fitzjames Stephen, 'Legislation under Lord Mayo', in W. W. Hunter, *Life of the Earl of Mayo*, 2nd edn., 1876, vol. ii, p. 158.

was extremely limited. And if in some areas the rule of law was possibly forced upon India too rapidly, retreat was out of the question. The rising educated classes were attached to it by every tie of sentiment and interest, and they pressed for its further extension, for the complete separation of judicial executive functions, and for the whittling down of the element of personal discretion wherever it was to be found.

A mere catalogue of legislative enactments gives little indication of the spirit in which they were carried. After the Mutiny this was to be all-important. The immediate response to the Mutiny was to bring the paternalist system of the Punjab to the height of favour in popular British estimation. The Lawrences had become legendary heroes, and the success of the Punjab system in stemming and hurling back the tide of revolt seemed to argue for it an intrinsic superiority over the Regulation pattern of administration. The essence of the Punjab tradition lay in a masterful attempt to prolong the atmosphere of military conquest, and to force, as it were, at one bound, the elements of an advanced civilized government on the stupified and bewildered people. But the imperiousness of the tradition was mitigated by its respect for indigenous custom and by its type of personal and paternal rule, which brought the district officer into intimate contact and understanding with the people. This mitigating feature must be remembered when interpreting the motto of the Punjab school carved under John Lawrence's statue in the Lahore Mall: 'Will you be governed by the pen or by the sword? Choose!' After the Mutiny paternalism appeared to gain a number of important victories. The Rent Act of 1859 gave exclusive jurisdiction over rent suits to the revenue authorities, and in the same year the offices of collector and magistrate were permanently reunited in Bengal. The appointment of John Lawrence as Viceroy in 1864 seemed to herald even greater success. But paternalism could not be translated out of its context. When transferred to the headquarters of government at Calcutta, it tended to become a determined assertion in legislative form of the superiority of English principles, with nothing of the warm sympathy and conservative sentiment which marked it in the Punjab.

In Fitzjames Stephen's words, the Mutiny resulted in 'the breakdown of the old system; the renunciation of the attempt to effect an impossible compromise between the Asiatic and European view of things, legal, military and administrative. The effect of the Mutiny on the Statute-book was unmistakable.'[1] The result was the agressive legislation of the sixties and early seventies, carried through in an entirely different spirit from the age of reform of the thirties. In the Bentinck period the movement of modernization had been regarded as a co-operative effort between the British and a corresponding Indian middle class who were to be 'interpreters between us and the millions whom we govern'. The Punjab school had no use for such a view and forced their reforms at the sword-point, believing that a benighted people had to be compelled towards the light. Now reform was to be carried in the spirit of racial conquest that succeeded the Mutiny, with all the strong-handedness of the Punjab school but with none of its personal kindliness or affection.

The general harmony of immediate objectives that existed between the paternalist and modernizing currents continued into the sixties. It was a buoyant, hopeful period, with the long-delayed harvest of the law codes being gathered in, with the cities of India being rapidly linked by the railway, and an unimagined commercial prosperity dispelling the gloomy fears that India's finances were permanently crippled by the Mutiny debt. But there was a tension which could not long be concealed. Paternalism found itself soon running into an alien world with bureaucratic efficiency and expertise gaining at the expense of simple, personal rule. The paternalists had been prepared to accept a few plain law codes, but grew increasingly uneasy as the spate of legislation mounted under Maine's expert hand, and as a tendency to introduce the more technical refinements of English law became apparent. The Punjab fought hard to retain the complete union of all judicial and executive powers in the hands of the commissioners and deputy-commissioners, but the establishment of the Chief Court at Lahore in 1866 was a sign that circumstances were proving too strong, and that the rising flood

[1] Cited G. O. Trevelyan, *Life and Letters of Lord Macaulay*, p. 302.

of litigation would eventually have to be met by the institution of a separate judicial branch. The attempt to maintain
the paternal system of government was also becoming increasingly difficult at a higher level. In 1866–7 the occurrence
of the Orissa famine raised the whole question of the efficiency of the Lieutenant-Governor system. This had been
first adopted in the North-Western Provinces and later
extended to the Punjab and Bengal. It left the government
of a province in the hands of a lieutenant-governor without
any executive council; and its doughtiest champion was
Lawrence, the Viceroy (1864–9). It was now attacked by
the criticism that if the Lieutenant-Governor of Bengal, Sir
Cecil Beadon, had been surrounded by an executive council,
as were the Governors of Madras and Bombay, his error of
judgement in scouting the possibility of serious famine in
Orissa would have been corrected. Bartle Frere, a member of
the Secretary of State's Council and Lawrence's most powerful opponent, wrote a general minute at the end of 1867 in
which he rang the knell of the Non-Regulation system. It
was altogether erroneous, he declared, to look upon the
autocratic rule of a lieutenant-governor as a permanent form
of government for any civilized and settled portion of India.
Such a rule had succeeded only as a temporary expedient in
a newly conquered province, but it was seldom possible to
give really uncontrolled executive power to any one man
beyond the first ten years after conquest. No man in his
senses would now propose to revert, even in the smallest
province, to the most successful and despotic type of Indian
government, that exercised by Sir Charles Napier in Sind,
where all civil and military authority had been concentrated
in a single hand. There could be no going back or even
standing still. 'Perpetual infancy of civil government is just
as impossible as perpetual reconquest.'[1]

Lawrence would make no retreat from the paternalist
form of rule. He rejected any suggestion for surrounding
the Lieutenant-Governor of Bengal with an executive council,
and showed how out of touch he was by proposing that the
Bengal Legislative Council should be abolished.[2] The best

---

[1] Bartle Frere, Memorandum, 2 Dec. 1867: *P.P.*, 1867–8, vol. xlix, pp. 206–7.
[2] Memorandum of Governor-General, 20 Jan. 1868: ibid., p. 228.

form of government in India was 'personal administration by
a single head, without a Council'. It 'secured the momentum
of improvement, the exaction of responsibility, the exercise
of vigilance, in the highest degree ordinarily obtainable'.
The dispute touched his own position as Viceroy. If Bengal
were placed under a Governor and Council on the model of
the other Presidencies, and if this were later to be repeated in
the other provinces, it implied a devolution of authority from
the centre; for the Viceroy exercised a much greater authority
over a lieutenant-governor than over the Governors of Madras
and Bombay. Lawrence believed that there was 'as strong a
necessity as there possibly could be, for one central absolute
authority in India, to which all other authorities in that
country must entirely defer'. The Viceroy's powers must be
preserved unimpaired; if he were only the head of a loose con-
federation of local governments, the whole British position in
the East would be placed in jeopardy should an emergency arise.

Lawrence found himself opposed by his distinguished
law member, Henry Maine. Maine's concern was simply to
find a form of Indian government capable of dealing effectively with the increasing complexity of the task imposed
upon it as a result of the rapid progress of India towards a
modern commercial society.[1] A modern government, he felt,
could not safely be entrusted to the discretion of one man;
an executive council was a safeguard against error and
possible mediocrity in the governor. He was therefore in
favour of elevating Bengal to the same form of government
as that enjoyed by Madras and Bombay. Similarly he thought
it impossible and undesirable to attempt putting the clock
back by the abolition of the Bengal Legislative Council.
After the furore raised against Canning during the Mutiny
it had been found expedient to grant to European merchants
and planters a voice on the Legislative Council, and a similar
voice had in fairness to be conceded to nominated representatives of the Indian educated class. There was no question
of giving this latter class representative institutions, but it
was 'a very serious matter to withdraw from them a formal
legislature when they once had it, and to subject them to that

[1] Minutes of H. S. Maine, 27 Feb. and 3 March 1868: *P.P.*, 1867–8, vol. xlix,
pp. 250, 258.

concrete form of despotism which consists in the complete blending of executive and legislative power'. Maine was clear in his mind that a government of law set over a society rapidly developing into a modern commercial community could not be constituted on the simple paternalist lines favoured by Lawrence. It was much better to pack the Council undisguisedly than to dispense with its share in legislation. Avoidance of public debate was a positive disadvantage in the more civilized provinces.

So far from its being desirable that we should legislate without giving the reasons for our legislation and without meeting objections to it, it seems to me that the want of power to defend our measures is one great weakness. We stand alone among the Governments of the civilised world, in having no means except the most indirect, of correcting the honest mistakes or exposing the wilful misrepresentations of a completely free press.

No action was taken as a result of this discussion, but it had revealed the cleavage between the legalists and the paternalists. With the Mutiny still vividly in every mind and the class of educated Indians growing in numbers and vociferousness, it was not possible to keep the question entirely free from political considerations. Nevertheless, on the level at which the discussion was kept by Maine, efficiency was the principal object held in view. What was the true line of future development for Indian government in this respect? Up to a certain point the paternalist and modernist view had coincided, but having reached that point the essentially conservative nature of paternalism was exposed. By the sixties the Punjab tradition had lost its radical momentum. Once law and order had been established, property rights in the soil defined, and the land revenue fixed in cash, the main paternalist outlook swung round to defend the village communities from further change threatening their disruption. The situation that had made John Lawrence glad to leave the North-Western Provinces had now to be faced in the Punjab. If the movement for modernization was to go forward, it meant necessarily the adoption of a system which rested individual property rights on an impersonal law, administered by an expert judiciary and independent of the executive. It meant the inevitable dissolution of the joint proprietorship practised in the village communities; and on the whole it meant letting the peasant take his chance in a cash economy with all the risks this might involve. This line of development led unerringly to the slow extinction of personal government by officers armed with judicial as well as executive powers, and its replacement by a system in which judicial, executive, and legislative functions were exercised separately. Here was the issue as old as British rule, for which Cornwallis and Munro had provided their rival solutions. It was the ancient issue between government by law and government by personal discretion, between the rule of the law courts and the rule of executive power.

In the eighteen-thirties the issue had been fought by Ross and Metcalfe with two opposing schemes for the government of the Bengal territories. At that time it had been Holt Mackenzie who had suggested a principle which could reconcile the concentrated energy, unity, and exaction of responsibility, characteristic of paternalism, with the division of powers and rule of law, characteristic of a modern, civilized government. Mackenzie had drunk at the Benthamite fountain, and his ideas on Indian government agreed generally with those of James Mill. As a permanent form of government Mackenzie envisaged a separate judiciary and executive, but for energy and efficiency, and to prevent destructive friction between the two arms, he proposed organizing each into a disciplined hierarchy, and at the provincial level subjecting them to the supervision of a lieutenant-governor. The final safeguard against disunity was the active exercise of legislative power by the Supreme Government, so that the decisions of the courts should not be allowed to conflict with its general policy.

The spirit of this scheme was now to be re-interpreted for the conditions of the new India by one who claimed to stand in the most rigorous Utilitarian tradition. Fitzjames Stephen held the office of law member for only two and a half years (1869–72), a tenure shorter than Macaulay's. Yet he counts as one of the most important figures of British Indian history in the later nineteenth century. As one who, in his brother Leslie Stephen's words, 'had sat at the feet of Bentham and Austin, and had found the most congenial philosophy

in Hobbes', he drew up a review of the Indian judicial
system in a Minute published in 1872.[1] Fitzjames Stephen
was concerned with the issue presented by the two opposing
schools of Indian administration. How was an efficient rule
of law to be attained without losing the unity, energy, and
strength of the Non-Regulation system? Stephen drew his
solution from the philosophy of government to be found in
Bentham and Hobbes, where law was conceived in authoritarian terms as the will and command of the sovereign. In
such a philosophy there was no place, properly speaking, for
any notion of the division of powers. The organs of the
State were regarded merely as separate parts of a single
machine, each part performing its specialized function but
all perfectly co-ordinated and directed to a single end. The
State operated by force or the threat of force; but it was the
whole nature of law to make this operation regular and
deliberate, and free from individual caprice. In this sense
law was the distinguishing feature of a civilized community,
and marked off British rule in India from its predecessors.

There was no *a priori* reason why the rule of law necessitated
a separation of judicial and executive functions; the question
was to be decided solely with regard to practical efficiency.
The Punjab system was as much a rule of law as the Regulation system. 'The question, therefore, is between one kind
of law and legal administration and another, not between
government by law and government without law. The
question, indeed, lies much more between different forms
of administration than different forms of law.'[2] It was desirable to unite all powers in one hand, so long as nothing
was attempted which a single officer could not do; but once
that point was reached, the so-called Non-Regulation system,
if persisted in, became less instead of more efficient than the
regulation system. The man who was popularly supposed to
be a benevolent despot became neither more nor less than
an overworked official burdened with a number of heterogeneous functions. Stephen believed that this situation had

---

[1] Minute by the Hon. J. Fitzjames Stephen on the Administration of Justice in
British India: *Selections from the Records of the Government of India*, No. lxxxix,
Calcutta, 1872. Leslie Stephen, *The Life of Sir James Fitzjames Stephen*, p. 308.

[2] J. Fitzjames Stephen, Minute on the Administration of Justice, op. cit., p. 8.

been reached in the Punjab, and that the continued attempt to combine the exercise of judicial and executive functions had led to a sacrifice of efficiency in the performance of the latter. The time had come, therefore, for the separation of these functions throughout the Non-Regulation provinces.

On the other hand, it was imperative that the executive should not be weakened: 'the maintenance of the position of the District Officers is absolutely essential to the maintenance of British rule in India' and 'any diminution in their influence and authority would be dearly purchased even by an improvement in the administration of justice'. Stephen's solution was to take civil justice out of the hands of executive officers, but to leave them still in exercise of criminal justice. The collector magistrate was to be left intact. The solution was in no sense novel, except in its reassertion by an avowed modernist at this time. Stephen supported his case with Hobbesian arguments. The exercise of criminal jurisdiction was the most distinctive and most easily and generally recognized mark of sovereign power; all the world over the man who could punish was the ruler. It was essential to maintain the strong personal influence of magistrates known to and mixing with the people; otherwise a vastly increased military force would be required. 'In a few words, the administration of criminal justice is the indispensable condition of all government, and the means by which it is in the last resort carried on. But the District Officers are the local governors of the country, therefore the District Officers ought to administer criminal justice.'[1] Stephen was constantly at pains to counter the popular prejudice that strong government and a highly developed law system were incompatible. He had to face—as Maine his predecessor had done—the charge of over-legislation, and of loading the judiciary with a mass of technical law entirely unsuited and deeply harmful to a simple agrarian society. Part of his answer consisted in showing that the bulk of his legislative measures were measures of consolidation and codification, which so far from adding to the burden of written law, had enormously reduced its bulk and made it incomparably easier of reference. But his real concern was to demonstrate that 'the notion that

[1] J. Fitzjames Stephen, Minute on the Administration of Justice, op. cit., p. 30.

there is an opposition in the nature of things between law and executive vigor, rests on a fundamental confusion of ideas and on traditions which are superannuated and ought to be forgotten'. Nothing had struck him more forcibly than this inveterate prejudice in the minds of many district officers that law had an independent existence and character of its own; that it was a sort of mysterious enemy, which if introduced into what were unfortunately called the Non-Regulation provinces, would prevent all energetic executive action. On the contrary, nothing could be more destructive of executive vigour than an uneasy suspicion in the mind of an officer that the course which he intended to take might very probably be illegal. The best possible security for executive vigour was to define precisely, by express law thrown into the clearest and shortest form, the amount of discretionary power to be given to judicial and executive officers, the amount being determined by general considerations of expediency. Men under those circumstances knew the limits of their power and acted within it vigorously. He appealed to the paternalists by drawing the analogy between law and military command. In proportion to the ignorance and simplicity of a people, law came to be a rule rather for the ruler himself than the subject, and its sanction lay in the censure which the former would receive if he transgressed it. The officers who ruled a turbulent and primitive district were in the nature of a highly civilized and carefully selected military force on active service, and the laws which they administered were their orders and articles of war. No one would deny that a highly disciplined military force on active service was the very type of prompt, decisive, efficient action; but no soldier would deny that precise and distinct orders and a well-defined organization were the very first conditions towards the efficiency of such an army. If it could be shown that the laws were intricate and ambiguous, or that they left too little discretion to individuals, by all means let them be altered; but to say that law was out of place in a rough district was the very same absurdity as to say that discipline and distinct and definite orders were out of place on a rough campaign.[1]

[1] J. Fitzjames Stephen, Minute on the Administration of Justice, op. cit., p. 94.

With his deep conviction that strong government and the rule of law could go hand in hand, Stephen proceeded with the work of completing the system of codes generally applicable to the whole of British India, and to reducing to formal law those subjects hitherto left largely under the direction of administrative orders, such as the land revenue. In 1871 the Punjab Land Revenue Act was passed and a similar Act for the North-Western Provinces was drafted, being enacted in 1873. But if the revenue officers were now bound by legislation, it was symptomatic of Stephen's faith in executive action that he should propose (unsuccessfully as it proved) that the record of rights prepared by them be accepted as conclusive evidence of title in the courts. After he left India the pressure of litigation and the need for more specialized judges brought about the acceptance of his arguments for the separation of judicial and executive functions in the Punjab. In 1875 the first step was taken, by the appointment of judicial assistants to relieve the deputy commissioners in twenty-three Punjab districts, *munsifs* likewise being appointed to relieve the *tehsildars*. In 1884 a separate judiciary was organized on the model of Bengal, except that in addition to the *munsif*, the subordinate judge, and the district judge, a divisional judge was also instituted. This measure had already been enacted for Oudh in 1879, but it was to be deferred in the Central Provinces and Burma until the present century.

Stephen claimed himself as a follower of Bentham, but he was a Utilitarian of a later age. As law member his ideas on codification differed radically from those of Bentham and Macaulay. To Stephen codification (as distinct from consolidation) meant no more than 'the reduction for the first time, to a definite written form, of law, which had previously been unwritten, or written only in an unauthoritative form, such as that of text-books and reported cases'.[1] It did not mean the construction of a body of law produced entirely by the philosophic intelligence and owing nothing to any

A large part of the chapter Stephen contributed to Hunter's *Life of Mayo* is taken up with proving how the rule of law, so far from weakening government, could make it infinitely stronger and more effective.

[1] J. Fitzjames Stephen in *Life of Mayo*, vol. ii, p. 177.

historical system. Stephen looked to the Utilitarians for an intellectual method and attitude, and not for a hard and fast set of dogmas in jurisprudence. 'Respect for hard fact, contempt for the mystical and the dreamy; resolute defiance of the *a priori* school who propose to override experience by calling their prejudices intuitions, were the qualities of mind which led him to sympathise so unreservedly with Bentham's legislative theories and with Mill's "Logic".'[1] Respect for hard fact meant for him respect for the results of experience. This gave him a very different attitude to English law from that of Bentham, who had condemned it precisely on the grounds that it was a product of haphazard historical growth. Although the English law was unsystematic, ill-arranged, and superficially wanting in scientific accuracy, it represented for Stephen a body of principles worked out by the rough common sense of successive generations, and requiring only to be tabulated and arranged to become a system of the highest excellence.[2] In this spirit he reviewed the Indian judicial system in his Minute of 1872. Gone was Macaulay's impatience with anything that could not be justified according to Bentham's *Draught of a New Plan for the Organization of the Judicial System in France*. Stephen accepted and praised the general structure that he found, although it offended against certain fundamental Benthamite principles. What he admired was its general order, vigour, and system, which contrasted so favourably with its English counterpart.

. . . In the first place there is hardly any nonsense at all in the system. It is a system carefully and laboriously constructed; superintended with extraordinary watchfulness and care, and worked by men who are paid for it and give their whole attention to it. It is not a heap of institutions, resting upon no principle, formed upon no system, and incapable of being understood except by a long course of historical study. . . . Whatever may have been the defects of Indian government, want of interest in the work done, want of vigilance in superintending the manner in which it is done, want of energy and enterprise in improving the manner of doing it, are not amongst them.[3]

Instead of suggesting an entire reconstruction of the existing structure in the light of certain rigid theoretical principles, as

---

[1] L. Stephen, *Life of Sir J. Fitzjames Stephen*, p. 309.   [2] Ibid., p. 209.
[3] J. Fitzjames Stephen, Minute on the Administration of Justice, op. cit., pp. 106–7.

Macaulay had done, Stephen concentrated on mitigating the practical defects of the system as it stood. He made no proposals like those of James Mill and Macaulay for abolish-the monetary classification of suits, for making a complete separation between original and appellate jurisdiction, or for confiding appeals to a single High Court. To compare Macaulay's Minute of 1835 with Stephen's of 1871 is to pass from idealism to an almost too realistic common sense. Stephen's chief suggestion was to shorten and improve the appeal procedure by abolishing second or special appeals. He proposed to do this by a gradual rearrangement of the inferior courts, but the details were not acted upon and little purpose would be served in describing them. He kept before himself Bentham's objectives—that justice should be swift, cheap, certain, and readily intelligible; but for him it was a question how far the existing system could be modified to bring it nearer these ideals rather than building an entirely new system in its stead. He saw the great Indian administrative and judicial machine as almost complete except in a few particulars. Yet it was still in its infancy, and so far had been worked by European and Indian officers who were not properly trained in law. This had led to some degree of clumsiness, technicality, and stiffness in its working, but Stephen believed these faults would be overcome with better training, with the consolidation and codification of the law into a few volumes, and with some improvements in reporting and procedure. Unlike Macaulay, Stephen accepted the view that the Hindu and Muslim law could not be touched by a British legislature; but for the rest he believed that the statutory law of India could be comprised in four or five octavo volumes, and the essential part of it in five or six acts.

Although like a railroad the system would require constant supervision and frequent repair, the main work of construction was over. It only remained to work the system with energy and perseverance, so that the rule of law might complete its civilizing mission. If he was unwilling to make any far-reaching innovations and was prepared to take the existing structure much as he found it, Stephen was as strong and vehement a believer as any of his radical predecessors in the revolution to be effected by the rule of law. If the distinguishing mark of British rule were government by law, its unique result was the growth of private property rights in land under the protection of the courts and settlement officers. The rule of law had not only displaced the rule of personal discretion and despotic power, but it had also displaced the rule of 'indistinct, ill-understood, and fluctuating customs'. The fact that the creation of private rights and the elimination of custom was leading to the decline of the village communities should not give rise to any false sentiment of regret.

The fact that the institutions of a village community throw light on the institutions of modern Europe, and the fact that village communities have altered but little for many centuries, prove only that society in India has remained for a great number of centuries in a stagnant condition, unfavourable to the growth of wealth, intelligence, political experience, and the moral and intellectual changes which are implied in these processes. The condition of India for centuries past shows what the village communities are really worth. Nothing that deserves the name of a political institution at all can be ruder or less satisfactory in its results. They are, in fact, a crude form of socialism, paralysing the growth of individual energy and all its consequences. The continuation of such a state of society is radically inconsistent with the fundamental principles of our rule both in theory and in practice.[1]

This was the note of an outlook that was still aggressive, at a time when the construction of the system of government envisaged by James Mill had been largely completed. James Mill would not have approved of the details of the judicial system or been satisfied with an incomplete body of codes which were no more than rationalized digests of English law and which left outside their orbit the personal laws of the people. Yet a great administrative machine had been created entirely novel to English experience. It was by Stephen's time being brought to the height of its efficiency. The careful overhaul of the land revenue system in the revised settlements being effected in most of the provinces, the registration of deeds, the census of population, and the compilation of statistics, all these were giving by the seventies

[1] J. Fitzjames Stephen, in Hunter, *Life of Mayo*, vol. ii, pp. 165–6.

a new precision and certainty to the working of the machine.[1] Above all, the telegraph and the steel rail were providing a degree of unity unattainable by mere administrative arrangements alone. The whole effect was the product of government action, and the size and activities of the great Anglo-Indian bureaucracy of the seventies were the nearest realization in English experience of Bentham's vision of the administrative state, so minutely recorded in his *Constitutional Code*. To a lawyer such as Stephen, whose business was with the practical world and yet whose intellect led him to prize logical coherence and system, it was the greatest of English achievements. His message, which he constantly repeated in his speeches and writings, was that the existing system, if properly worked, could provide a strong and yet modern government, reconciling those ideals which the two schools of Indian administration often imagined were totally opposed. The aggressive elements in the Cornwallis and Munro traditions could be harmonized; the strong executive action of individual officers blending with a modern system of law—administered by specialized officers and applied in a belligerent manner—to carry through a social and economic revolution of Indian society. To Stephen it was the working example of a political philosophy in the true strain of liberalism, and on his return to England in 1872 Stephen attempted to give it a general expression in *Liberty, Equality, Fraternity*, where he assailed J. S. Mill's political ideas as a departure from the orthodox Utilitarian tradition.

This attitude, while combining seemingly contradictory elements of the two rival Indian traditions, lost the moderating features of each, as has already been remarked. Paternalism grown bureaucratic tended to lose personal touch with the peasant; liberalism grown efficient tended to lose trust in the Indian middle class. Paternalism had always attracted a radical element, and the influence of this element in the

---

[1] It was from the time that Stephen was in India that a central secretariat was established to collect and disseminate statistical information. The first census of British India was taken in 1872. From this work, headed by W. W. Hunter, there eventually emerged the massive *Imperial Gazetteer of India*. Kipling satirized the Indian passion for statistics in his delightful parody of Swinburne's 'Atalanta in Calydon', entitled 'Chorus of the Crystallised Facts', with which he ends his poem 'The Masque of Plenty' (*Rudyard Kipling's Verse—Definitive Edition*, p. 38).

land revenue systems of Bombay and the North-Western Provinces has been described.[1] Generally it expressed itself as a belief that the truths of political economy should triumph over sentiment, and that only in a system of free exchange and completely free individual property rights could the prosperity of the people be fully secured. It tended therefore to steel itself against the sentimental outcry of the conservative paternalists as the break-up of the village communities and the transfer of land to the money-lender became apparent. When the issue had been discussed in the North-Western Provinces in 1854, it was the young Collector of Moradabad, John Strachey, who had given the most pungent expression to this radical opinion. By Stephen's time John Strachey was the most powerful influence in the Indian Civil Service, the tower of strength upon whom Mayo (1869–72) and Lytton (1876–80) leaned for support.[2] Called to the senior post in the Viceroy's Council, Strachey was recognized by Stephen as a brother in arms, and the two men became close friends. It was to Strachey that *Liberty, Equality, Fraternity* was dedicated, and in his turn Strachey dedicated his own work on India, published in 1888, to Stephen. Together their outlook was expressive of the new dispensation. Sprung from paternalism, it rejected its human warmth between ruler and ruled, whether the attachment of Henry Lawrence for the old aristocracy or the love of John Lawrence for the simple village communities. In doing so it claimed to have the interest of all classes most truly at heart. The paternalism of the Lawrences would have stopped the course of reform in its tracks, and attempted the impossible task of insulating the Indian village from further change. But Stephen and Strachey saw no other solution than to carry it to its logical completion. On the other hand, while standing for the modernization of India, they differed fundamentally from the old Liberal school of Macaulay and Ross. Not merely was this due to their belief in a strong executive, but more profoundly to their failure to accept the premisses of the old liberalism. If they distrusted the sentimental attachment of the paternalists to the Indian peasantry, they shared to the full the paternalists' dislike of the Indian educated classes.

[1] See pp. 118, 122.   [2] For Strachey, see Biographical Notes, p. 332.

Macaulay, Ross, and Trevelyan had looked upon the task of modernization as a co-operative enterprise to be increasingly entrusted to Indian hands. The Indian middle classes were to be interpreters and partners in the great civilizing process. And if doubts were raised as to the ultimate political consequences of Western education and of the progressive admission of Indians into the higher administration, the Liberals of the thirties faced the issue squarely; they did not shrink from proclaiming that in the last resort the process must lead to self-government. That consummation, Macaulay said, would be 'the proudest day in English history'. It would occasion no material loss to Britain, for it meant that in place of the barren and precarious hegemony of the sword there would have grown up a modern India, attached to Britain by a far more durable and beneficial relation: in Trevelyan's words, by 'a strict commercial union between the first manufacturing and the first producing country in the world'.

To this argument Strachey and Stephen, and the school of which they were the spokesmen, were completely opposed. Liberal in the sense of subscribing to free trade, equality before the law, the lifting of all restraints on individual initiative and enterprise, and a rational system of law and government, their liberalism did not extend to a belief in self-government. The British Government in India rested not on consent but force. Its aim and achievement could be summed up in two pregnant words—law and order. To this order and to this law India owed everything; the very existence of property itself and all that was built upon it, India's great commerce, her cities, her roads and railways, her colleges and schools, and the new educated classes which had grown with these things. In few countries in Europe, asserted Strachey, was protection to life and property so complete. Excepting England herself, her colonies, and the United States, there was hardly a country in the world where there was so little needless interference on the part of government with personal liberty, or such freedom in the public expression of opinion in matters of politics and religion. Unbroken tranquillity prevailed, except for occasional fanatical outbursts in disturbances between Muslims and Hindus, which showed what would instantly occur if the strong hand of the British Government were withdrawn. Justice was administered under laws of unequalled excellence and simplicity, and there was no country possessing a civilized administration where taxation was so light or commerce so free. Had not J. S. Mill himself declared that the British Government in India was 'not only the purest in intention, but one of the most beneficent in act, ever known among mankind'? But all this depended on the strong hand of Britain, on the government of foreigners. Admittedly it was not a popular government and could hardly be so. Strachey was prepared to state the paradox—because the Government was so good it could hardly be popular.[1] He and Stephen accepted the fact that, for reasons of economy and good policy, educated Indians had to be admitted extensively to positions in the government service, and consulted over proposed legislation. But there was a line which could not be crossed, and there should be no hypocrisy about it:

When we say that we cannot always, in our government of India, ignore differences of race, this is only another way of saying that the English in India are a handful of foreigners governing 250 millions of people . . .. although I suppose that no foreign government was ever accepted with less repugnance than that with which the British Government is accepted in India, the fact remains that there never was a country, and never will be, in which the government of foreigners is really popular. It will be the beginning of the end of our empire when we forget this elementary fact, and entrust the greater executive powers to the hands of Natives, on the assumption that they will always be faithful and strong supporters of our government. In this there is nothing offensive or disparaging to the Natives of India. It simply means that we are foreigners, and that, not only in our own interests, but because it is our highest duty towards India itself, we intend to maintain our dominion. We cannot foresee the time in which the cessation of our rule would not be the signal for universal anarchy and ruin, and it is clear that the only hope for India is the long continuance of the benevolent but strong government of Englishmen. Let us give to the Natives the largest possible share in the administration. . . . But let there be no hypocrisy about our intention to keep in the hands of our own people those executive posts—and there are not very many of them—on which, and on our political and military power, our actual

[1] Sir John Strachey, *India*, 1888 edn., pp. 364–6.

hold of the country depends. Our Governors of provinces, the chief officers of our army, our magistrates of districts and their principal executive subordinates ought to be Englishmen under all circumstances that we can now foresee.[1]

Here was a view of British rule which stood for cold, aloof impartiality, rejected all idea of winning over particular classes to its support, and almost prided itself on its estrangement from its subjects. Fitzjames Stephen, who relished the statement of bitter truths, put the view in his usual blunt fashion:

If it be asked how the system works in practice, I can only say that it enables a handful of unsympathetic foreigners (I am far from thinking that if they were more sympathetic they would be more efficient) to rule justly and firmly about 200,000,000 persons of many races, languages and creeds, and in many parts of the country, bold, sturdy and warlike. In one of his many curious conversations with native scholars Mr. Monier Williams was addressed by one of them as follows: 'The sahibs do not understand us or like us, but they try to be just, and they do not fear the face of man.' I believe this to be strictly true. The Penal Code, the Code of Criminal Procedure, and the institutions which they regulate, are somewhat grim presents for one people to make to another, and are little calculated to excite affection; but they are eminently well-calculated to protect peaceable men and to beat down wrongdoers, to extort respect, and to enforce obedience.[2]

It was natural for this attitude to adopt a defiant posture. Its leading principle of government was force rather than consent. It had to be maintained in the face of the nascent nationalist movement in India, and felt itself constantly liable to be misunderstood and derided in England. It had to meet a challenge from both the Right and the Left. The recession of trade, the falling sterling value of the rupee, famine in Bihar in 1873–4 and throughout southern India from 1876 to 1878, agrarian riots in the Deccan in 1875, and the mounting hostility of the vernacular press, all these disquieting features made Lytton (1876–80) question the adequacy of Strachey's solution by itself. He wanted to see the effort made to win an active loyalty for British rule, and as a Conservative he thought the answer lay in trying to

[1] Ibid., pp. 359–60.
[2] Sir J. Fitzjames Stephen, *History of the Criminal Law*, vol. iii, pp. 344–5.

attach the Indian princes and aristocracy by a tie of personal loyalty to the Crown.

I am convinced that the fundamental mistake of able and experienced Indian officials is a belief that we can hold India securely by what they call good government; that is to say, by improving the condition of the ryot, strictly administering justice, spending immense sums on irrigation works, etc. Politically speaking, the Indian peasantry is an inert mass. If it ever moves at all, it will move in obedience, not to its British benefactors, but to its native chiefs and princes, however tyrannical they may be. The only political representatives of native opinion are the Baboos, whom we have educated to write semi-seditious articles in the native Press, and who really represent nothing but the social anomaly of their own position. . . . To secure completely, and efficiently utilise, the Indian aristocracy is, I am convinced, the most important problem now before us.[1]

Against such an attempt to cultivate the Indian aristocracy as a political support, Strachey's tradition had always steadily set its face. It had grown up in the strongly anti-aristocratic land revenue systems of the North-Western Provinces and the Punjab, and Strachey had joined wholeheartedly with John Lawrence in resisting the aristocratic settlement of Oudh after the Mutiny. In his book on India he could not conceal his contempt for the government of the Indian states, and warned of the strict limitations to the loyalty of their princes.[2] Nevertheless, there were very few material rewards which the Indian Government could hold out to the aristocratic classes, and the somewhat flamboyant conservatism of Lytton and Disraeli had to be content with the proclamation of the Queen as Empress of India and the Delhi Durbar of 1877, at which the order of the *Kaiser-i-Hind* was formally instituted. To such harmless experiments, which in no way altered the character of British administration, Strachey and Stephen could make little objection; and in face of the much more serious challenge of Radical liberalism they welcomed its attempt to rouse a faith in empire both in England and India. Stephen in fact became personally devoted to Lytton.

The challenge from the Left was of much graver impor-

[1] Lord Lytton to Lord Salisbury, 11 May 1877: Lady Betty Balfour, *The History of Lord Lytton's Indian Administration*, p. 109.   [2] Strachey, *India*, p. 320.

tance and exposed the gathering crisis within the Liberal ranks that was finally to result in open schism over the issue of Irish Home Rule. Talk of eventual self-government for India in Macaulay's time had been a gratuitous form of liberalism, so distant was it from practical reality; but by the seventies words had to be more carefully weighed. Most of the leading lights of Liberal opinion preferred to shirk ultimate issues. But Charles Trevelyan, now nearing the end of his life, was prepared to come before a Parliamentary Committee to restate the ideals of his youth. Appearing before Fawcett's Committee on Indian Finance in 1873, Trevelyan declared that although the work of the Indian Civil Service was admirable and an honour to the nation, it was but 'a provisional temporary arrangement', 'a sort of scaffolding which had been erected until the edifice of our Indian Empire is completed, and as it is completed, that scaffolding should be taken down'.[1] He proposed that there should be quasi-representative councils for each province to deal with taxation, and a system of subordinate local bodies reaching down to the village. The councils should be freed from European official presidents, the very point on which Ripon's local self-government scheme was nearly to be wrecked. The experience gained in these councils 'would be a school of self-government for the whole of India, the largest step yet taken towards teaching its 200,000,000 of people to govern themselves which is the end and object of our connection with that country'. This declaration of faith was all the more important because it came not from a lone, dissident politician such as William Digby, or from a known Radical like Henry Fawcett, the 'Member for India', but from a highly distinguished public servant, who had served as Governor of Madras and Finance Member to the Government of India, and who could be regarded as an authentic voice of the central Liberal tradition.

3. *Utilitarianism and Late-nineteenth-century Imperialism*

It was a Liberal Viceroy's attempt to begin a cautious advance on lines similar to those advocated by Trevelyan

---

[1] Evidence of Sir Charles Trevelyan: *P.P.*, 1873, vol. xii, p. 96; also pp. 99–100.

that showed most clearly the Liberal division on India. The Ilbert Bill of 1883, granting Indian magistrates and judges power to try criminal cases against European British subjects, created a public storm which Fitzjames Stephen employed to voice his disquiet about Ripon's policy as a whole. He had no absolute objection to any specific measure but felt alarmed at their general tendency. Much of the language lately held as to local government, education, and some other subjects filled him with apprehension, he declared in a lengthy and important letter to *The Times*.[1] It appeared that a policy fraught with fearful dangers was being meditated, that of 'shifting the foundations on which the British Government of India rests'. What those foundations were Stephen defined with fearless clarity:

It is essentially an absolute government, founded, not on consent, but on conquest. It does not represent the native principles of life or of government, and it can never do so until it represents heathenism and barbarism. It represents a belligerent civilization, and no anomaly can be more striking or so dangerous, as its administration by men, who being at the head of a Government founded upon conquest, implying at every point the superiority of the conquering race, of their ideas, their institutions, their opinions and their principles, and having no justification for its existence except that superiority, shrink from the open, uncompromising, straightforward assertion of it, seek to apologize for their own position, and refuse, from whatever cause, to uphold and support it. . . .

Stephen laid himself open to misunderstanding. To those who were not acquainted with his use of terms, his language seemed to represent a peculiarly blatant and unpleasant form of jingoism. But his views rested upon a carefully-thought-out political philosophy which he had expressed in his work, *Liberty, Equality, Fraternity*, published in book form in 1874. Sir Ernest Barker has described this work as 'the finest exposition of conservative thought in the latter half of the nineteenth century', and remarked upon the importance of Indian experience in the thought of both Stephen and Maine.[2] Stephen's book was first composed as a series of

[1] Letter of Sir J. Fitzjames Stephen to *The Times*, 1 March 1883.
[2] Sir Ernest Barker, *Political Thought in England, 1848–1914*, Home University Library, 2nd edn., 1928, pp. 167, 172.

articles on the voyage home in 1872, and was dashed off when his mind was white-hot with the truths India had stamped upon it. India had, he said, been 'a sort of second University course' to him! In *Liberty, Equality, Fraternity* Stephen attempted not merely to generalize his convictions about the nature of government and law, which he had recently expressed in his Minute on the Administration of Justice in India, but he also tried to show that John Stuart Mill had perverted the utilitarianism of his father and Bentham by trying to marry it into the household of popular liberalism. Stephen is important because he illustrates how the authoritarian element in utilitarianism, which had found in India so much more congenial a field for its development and which was given a working expression in the machine of the Indian bureaucracy, was carried back into English thought and helped to produce the crisis within English liberalism which occurred in 1886.

The Liberal split was caused, significantly enough, not by a conflict over domestic policy as had been expected, but over the issue of applying the principles of democracy and self-government to the dependent empire. On Irish Home Rule the educated mind of England swung against Gladstone and the type of liberalism for which he stood.[1] Stephen contributed to the outcome of this intellectual crisis of liberalism by coming forward with a political philosophy which generalized and rendered articulate the British middle-class experience of efficient and progressive autocracy in India. In his letter to *The Times* of 1883 which has been quoted, he had already applied this philosophy in blunt and pungent form to castigate Ripon's notion of a Liberal policy for India; and Lytton used Stephen's arguments in the Lords to expose the Liberal dilemma further, by making plain that the logical conclusion to which Ripon's language pointed could be none other than Indian self-government.[2] In 1886

[1] Among the intellectual liberals who deserted Gladstone were men like A. V. Dicey, Seeley, Sidgwick, and St. Loe Strachey. Gladstone admitted to the defection of the educated classes: *Contemporary Review*, vol. liii (March 1888). The whole question is dealt with in an important article which has appeared since this work was written: John Roach, 'Liberalism and the Victorian Intelligentsia', *Cambridge Historical Journal*, vol. xiii, No. 1 (1957).

[2] Speech of Lord Lytton in the House of Lords, 9 April 1883: *Hansard*, 3rd series, vol. 277, p. 1735.

Stephen wrote a further series of letters to *The Times* which attracted considerable public attention and in which he attacked Gladstone's Home Rule measures for Ireland with precisely the same political axioms.[1] In this way the authoritarian element in utilitarianism came not merely to justify the continuance of the British despotism in India, but the compound of Indian experience with the severely logical Benthamite tradition helped to turn the English educated classes from Gladstone's liberalism of the heart, and to provide an important ingredient in the formation of late-nineteenth-century English imperialism. To explain Stephen's political philosophy, and to show the manner in which it diverged from popular liberalism, will require some discussion of abstract theory.

Stephen was a Liberal, and, in a sense, a Utilitarian. But he had seen from the early sixties that liberalism could be divided into two types. There was, he argued, a liberalism of the intellect and a liberalism of sentiment. The latter was the popular Manchester variety, and tended to play down to the 'casual opinions and ineffectual public sentiments' of the half-educated. It adopted a mean, petty-shopkeeper attitude to great affairs of state, and it was connected in his mind with the shifts and pandering to popular prejudice which marked party politics. The intellectual liberal, on the other hand, asked whether a theory was true or false, and wished for statesmanlike reforms such as codification of the law, although they might have no appeal for the ten-pound householder.[2] Stephen was here expressing a view common to men, such as Robert Lowe, who were representative of the educated middle-class liberalism of the 1832 Reform Bill and who now saw it threatened by the extension of the franchise to the artisan class. But he was not merely attacking the crude sentiment and prejudice on which popular liberalism founded its appeal: he was resisting its intellectual foundations which were identified with the old abstract doctrines of liberty and the rights of man, and which had long ago been exploded by Bentham in his *Anarchical*

---

[1] Letters of Sir J. Fitzjames Stephen to *The Times*, 4, 21 Jan., 29 April, 1 May 1886. Discussed by Leslie Stephen, *Life of J. Fitzjames Stephen*, pp. 461-2.

[2] James Mill, *Essay on Government*, ed. E. Barker, 1937, pp. 72-73.

Fallacies. This came out in Stephen's controversy with John Stuart Mill, whom he deliberately selected for attack as the accepted oracle of English liberalism. Up to a point he admitted himself to be 'a devoted disciple and partisan' of Mill, that is, with respect to logic and general notions of philosophy, but he believed that Mill in his later writings on morals and politics had fallen victim to the sentimental school, and had deserted 'the proper principles of rigidity and ferocity in which he was brought up'.[1] Stephen wrote *Liberty, Equality, Fraternity* as a detailed reply to Mill's *Liberty* and allied essays, with the object of showing that Mill's attempt to reconcile utilitarianism with sentimental liberalism had perverted the true doctrine of his father and Bentham.

In his essays *On Liberty, Utilitarianism*, and *Representative Government*, J. S. Mill had certainly appeared to lose sight of the Utilitarian criterion of the greatest happiness of the greatest number, and to adopt liberty as an ultimate principle and goal. In his introduction to *Liberty*, he defined human progress in terms of the contest between the principle of liberty and the principle of authority. Human progress was to be measured by the steady advance of one over the other; this advance marking the slow triumph of mind over matter, of intelligence over blind instinct, of reason and discussion over prejudice, superstition, and physical force. The great strides taken by western Europe in material and scientific progress were the result of permitting the free disinterested play of the intelligence, and Mill asserted that the resort to free inquiry in matters of morals and politics was likely to produce results as fully remarkable. Instead of a state of affairs in which the majority of men were the slaves of collective opinion or the ideas of a ruling class, they would become free, spontaneous individuals leading a life of conscious deliberation and choice. The practical consequences of these assumptions were Mill's advocacy of representative self-government as the 'ideally best polity', his support for the Liberal belief that good government was no substitute for self-government, and his claim for a sphere of activity within which the individual should be sovereign and free from all external interference.

[1] Leslie Stephen, *Life of J. Fitzjames Stephen*, p. 308; also p. 299.

Stephen challenged all of these assumptions of popular liberalism. The passionate advocacy of personal liberty and of the removal of all possible restraint by society over the individual, together with Mill's notion that modern society was progressively dispensing with the law of force and solving its problems by rational discussion and consent, appeared to Stephen to rest on the grossest fallacy. The great truth was 'that power preceded liberty—that liberty from the very nature of things is dependent on power; and that it is only under the protection of a powerful, well-organized government that any liberty can exist at all'.[1] Society was rescued from anarchy by the institution of law, which in its turn gave birth to property. Stephen's background is Hobbes. The state of nature was a state of violent competition or war, bred by the striving of men to command the wills and property of their fellows in pursuit of their insatiable desire for felicity and aversion from pain. Political society was the mitigation of this competition by the enforcement of settled rules to conduct it peaceably. Government determined these rules and enforced them sword in hand. The conflict between men was not ended but only conducted in a more limited and less destructive manner. Parliamentary government was simply a mild and disguised form of compulsion. We agreed to try strength by counting heads instead of breaking heads, but the principle was exactly the same. While a few exceptional men of Mill's temperament might try to decide issues by the light of impartial reason alone, the majority decided them according to the view they took of their own interest. Moral and religious systems, and all prevailing ideas, had become accepted in this manner, and were upheld by their ability to command the personal hopes and fears of the majority of men. The great advance in the world was not the abandonment of force in society but its more efficient regulation. The power of the modern state with respect to its subjects was so nearly irresistible that it had rarely to be employed, and then only in the most sparing manner. Its commands or laws met with instant compliance; but the fact that force was rarely employed directly should not be allowed to disguise the fact that society rested just as

[1] J. Fitzjames Stephen, *Liberty, Equality, Fraternity*, 2nd edn., 1874, p. 183.

much upon force as it had done in the rudest times. Liberty was a negation, the mere absence of a degree of restraint. In a strict sense it did not exist: society either in the form of law or public opinion was continually acting upon the individual, persuading and threatening him. Absolute liberty could only be obtained by the destruction of all power, that is by death. Liberty, as the term was commonly understood, was but an armed truce, an agreement not to invoke law (the public force) in those disputes where the issue admitted of doubt or was of comparative unimportance.

The debt to Hobbes, 'the greatest of English philosophers' as Stephen declared, is obvious; and Stephen supplemented it with the Evangelical inheritance of his upbringing. There is no doubt a whole world of difference between Stephen and the early Utilitarians, but their philosophy of law and government also traced its pedigree back to Hobbes. Law and not liberty was for Bentham as for Hobbes the great instrument of all improvement; Molesworth had brought out the standard edition of Hobbes's English works, and John Austin had expressed Hobbes's notion of sovereignty and the nature of law in his famous lectures on jurisprudence. As early as 1828, in the lectures of which John Stuart Mill made such extensive notes, Austin had denounced the worship of political liberty.

> Political or civil liberty has been erected into an idol, and extolled with extravagant praises by doting and fanatical worshippers. But political or civil liberty is not more worthy of eulogy than political or legal restraint. Political or civil liberty, like political or legal restraint, may be generally useful, or generally pernicious; and it is not as being liberty, but as conducing to the general good, that political or civil liberty is an object deserving applause.[1]

James Mill had given the pithiest expression to the authoritarian current in his *Essay on Government*. He started with Hobbes's premises. That one human being will desire to render the person and property of another subservient to his pleasures, notwithstanding the pain or loss of pleasure which it may occasion to that other individual, was, in James Mill's

---

[1] John Austin, *The Province of Jurisprudence Determined*, ed. H. L. A. Hart, 1954, p. 269.

own words, the foundation of government. The desire of power was 'a grand governing law of human nature', and by power he meant 'security for the conformity between the will of one man and the acts of other men'. The desire for power was boundless in extent and intensity; and the means by which it was most decisively secured was the infliction of pain, in comparison with which pleasure was but 'a feeble instrument'. In political society the sovereign was by definition possessed of absolute power. Sovereignty was indivisible; its will was, in a strict sense, law; and it enforced its commands by the threat of inflicting pain. Unless these conditions were perfectly realized law could not operate effectively, and the security which was its chief end was not fully attained. James Mill's safeguard against the abuse of power was not to attempt to set limits to its operation, as did his son, but to identify the absolute and indivisible sovereign power with the will of the majority through 'the grand discovery of modern times', representative democracy. It was only on the grounds of providing a preventive check, and not on account of any belief in the intrinsic worth of individual spontaneity, that James Mill invoked representative democracy. For him happiness and not liberty remained the end of government.

There was therefore an authentic Utilitarian tradition to which Stephen could appeal in denouncing J. S. Mill's views. But if Stephen had perhaps the best of the logical argument, he certainly stood at one pole of the Utilitarian tradition and John Stuart Mill at the other. Stephen said that Mill appeared to think that 'if men are all freed from restraints and put, as far as possible, on an equal footing, they will naturally treat each other like brothers'. Mill had indeed leaned strongly towards the assumption of the natural and spontaneous identification of human interests, and tended to treat all restraint as evil. Stephen on the contrary emphasized the need of ordinary human nature to be subjected to coercion, believing that fear was a stronger motive than hope, that the gift of government consisted in the repression of men's anarchic instincts, and that force, disciplined and regulated in the form of law, played the leading part in the creation of civilization. Now it is true that both Bentham and James

Mill had adopted the theory that the conflicting egoisms of men could be harmonized only artificially by the legislator, but they were both fired by the optimism of the eighteenth-century Enlightenment. They held before them the vision of a time when, by good government and education, human character would have been indefinitely transformed; when virtue would have become habitual, and all forms of restraint by law or public opinion would scarcely be felt and would have grown superfluous. In this fashion, the early Utilitarians had retained, side by side, both the theory of the natural, and the theory of the artificial, identification of interests, so that their political thought occupied a middle position between the anarchy of Godwin and Paine and the despotism of Hobbes. Stephen inclined, however, towards Hobbes's darker view of human nature and its predicament:

I believe that many men are bad, a vast majority of men indifferent, and many good, and that the great mass of indifferent people sway this way or that according to circumstances. . . . I further believe that between all classes of men there are and always will be real occasions of enmity and strife, and that even good men may be and are often compelled to treat each other as enemies, either by the existence of conflicting interests which bring them into collision, or by their different ways of conceiving goodness.[1]

The intermediate position held by Bentham and James Mill, and the extreme positions occupied by J. S. Mill on the one hand, and Stephen on the other, appeared again in their view of democracy. While possessing no belief in individual liberty for its own sake, as avowed by John Mill, Bentham and James Mill looked upon democracy as a checking device against the abuse of power and ultimately as a means of registering the will of the majority. James Mill admitted in his *Essay on Government* that for the immediate future he expected the majority to accept the leadership of the educated middle classes, but he held forth vague hopes that with the progress of education the majority could participate effectively in controlling the legislature.[2] Stephen, however,

[1] *Liberty, Equality, Fraternity*, p. 280.
[2] James Mill, *Essay on Government*, p. 72. J. S. Mill, *Autobiography*, p. 89.

denied that a democratic electorate could operate as a check
or that it could conduce to efficient government. With his
view of the vast indifferent majority as sensual and in need
of restraint, it was impossible for him to contemplate it ever
itself being a genuine restraining force. And taking the view
that most men's views were confined to the furtherance of
their own interests, he could not believe that the majority
could supply the initiatory and creative impulse to government and legislation. For him government was always the
rule of a gifted minority that by force and persuasion (the
two were scarcely distinguishable) imposed itself and its
own ideal of happiness on the vast indifferent majority. A
creative thinker put forth a new ideal, a strong man took it
up, and together by force and persuasion, appealing to the
hopes and fears—material, mental, and supernatural—of the
bulk of mankind, they won their way to power. Because of
the increase, concentration, and more efficient regulation of
force (in the form of law), the actual employment of physical
violence in the modern state had become rare, and men had
decided that it was less destructive to settle disputes peaceably. But because in the parliamentary form of government
men had chosen to count heads rather than break them, it
was still a gifted minority that always held power. Only
the technique of the struggle for power had altered, and the
demagogue reigned. Government, as it always had done,
rested on a type of consent: even in times when the sanction
of physical force was most frequently employed, there was
needed the consent of numbers of men to put their force at
the disposal of a leader, and the consent of the majority to
submit to superior force. Once in power a ruling class
naturally sought to impose its own ideal of happiness and to
make it prevail. The task of government was to enforce this
ideal effectively, and Stephen conceived of law as the most
efficient and economical means (in terms of the prevailing
ideal of happiness).

Earth resembles heaven in one respect at least. Its kingdom suffereth
violence, and the violent take it by force. That such violence is or
under circumstances may be highly beneficial to the world, is, I think,
abundantly proved by history. The evil and good done by it must in all
cases be measured by the principles laid down above. Was the object

good? Did the means conduce to it? Did they conduce to it at an excessive price?[1]

Stephen admitted that an ideal of happiness might become so generally accepted as to reduce the area of difference between rival parties in a state to very small proportions. Given the common ideal of happiness in nineteenth-century England or America—where the establishment of religious truth was regarded as unimportant, where freedom of contract and freedom of trade had become dominant ideas, and where a high level of material comfort had become the common object—then Bentham's rules of legislation were extremely important as an indication of the most efficient means of enforcing this ideal of happiness. Where Stephen differed was that he refused to believe that the ideal could be established efficiently in a democratic type of government, which in effect meant government in the hands of popular demagogues. For an ideal to be efficiently established required that the force of government, expressed in the form of legislative commands backed by force, should be regulated by a calm, logical mind. And popular democracy framed its legislation in quite opposite conditions.

Finally, there is the question of moral theory. J. S. Mill had spoken eloquently of the capability of the individual for a disinterested love of humanity and for the entire suppression of all selfish motives. Bentham and James Mill had sought to avoid sentimentalism and spoke rather in terms of enlightened self-interest. But even they looked forward to a time when men, having been habituated by a perfect political and educational system to regard social and selfish interests as coincident, would become capable of acting spontaneously on the greatest-happiness principle. Stephen would have none of this. Following his master Hobbes, he was convinced that 'self is each man's centre, from which he can no more displace himself than he can leap off his own shadow'. The desire for other men's happiness was more often than not the desire for power to see one's own ideal of happiness prevail. 'Humanity is only "I" writ large, and zeal for My Notions as to what men should be and how they ought to

---

[1] *Liberty, Equality, Fraternity*, pp. 69–70.

live.'[1] The only genuine form of altruistic feeling was that where the object was connected with a person in definite assignable ways—such as a man's family, his friends, or his country—in which his own self-interest was caught up. The so-called 'love of humanity' was to him unnatural and suspect. Altruism was in a strict sense impossible, since it meant acting from somebody else's motives. Least of all should a man attempt to act upon abstract moral principles which involved a gratuitous limitation of his power. It was fantastic to expect men to surrender their interests unless some self-interested consideration compelled them to do so.

This discussion of academic theory may seem far removed from the practical questions concerned in this work, but it was the distinguishing mark of all Utilitarian thinkers to seek out a view of public affairs that was connected logically with a theory of politics and morals. From Stephen's theory flowed his practical arguments against that denigration of power and force by which John Bright and the Manchester Liberals condemned the very existence of British rule in India. He used it against the notion that Britain had a duty to educate India towards self-government, and against the policy of self-effacement and surrender to abstract moral ideas. Taken together, these arguments provided the educated classes with an intellectual justification for the continuance of autocratic rule in India, and for the maintenance of the political integrity of the Empire. They supplied one of the main intellectual contributions to the faith of English imperialism.

In his essay *On Liberty* John Stuart Mill had carefully stated that its doctrines were only meant to apply to those countries which were sufficiently advanced in civilization to be capable of settling their affairs by rational discussion. He was faithful to his father in holding to the belief that India could still be governed only despotically. But although he himself refused to apply the teachings of *Liberty* or *Representative Government* to India, a few Radical Liberals and a growing body of educated Indians made no such limitations. And Mill never denied the abstract right of India to self-governing institutions when she had made the necessary

---

[1] Leslie Stephen, *Life of J. Fitzjames Stephen*, pp. 334–5.

progress in civilization. It was difficult, of course, to find any reputable Liberal spokesman who would commit himself to anything beyond fostering 'sedulously the small beginnings of independent political life' in local self-government institutions, as Ripon had attempted, and it was rather the logical tendency of such views which Stephen felt himself bound to attack.[1] He singled out John Bright as his opponent. Bright's persistent criticism throughout his long political life—and repeated in a speech at Manchester in December 1877—had been that British rule was founded in violence and crime and was maintained by sheer despotic power. Bright's remedy, while not going so far as to suggest the introduction of a representative element into the Government, consisted in the fragmentation of the Indian Empire into five or six separate political units, each controlled independently from London.[2] That an eminent public man like Bright should seriously propose such a nonsensical scheme was sufficient to rouse Stephen's wrath, but he was particularly incensed because the principle of the scheme was the sentimental Liberal's suspicion of all political power as such. To Stephen, India was the convincing illustration of the great truth that power was the inescapable nature and soul of government. The first function of government was to repress men's anarchic instincts, 'to protect peaceable men and to beat down wrongdoers, to extort respect and to enforce obedience'. And this function was performed undisguisedly in India by law backed with power in the form of the Indian codes and the elaborate judicial organization. These were, he acknowledged, grim presents for one people to give another and little calculated to arouse affection, but they were the indispensable conditions before any more positive benefits could grow up. What those positive benefits were he attempted to indicate in a striking passage of his letter of 4 January 1878 to *The Times*:

> Can any person look with greater pride or exultation on the machinery by which such a system is maintained than would be afforded by the view of an ingenious gallows or a well-contrived

---

[1] Resolution of Government of India on Proposals for Extension of Local Self-Government, 18 May 1882, para. 5: *P.P.*, 1883, vol. li, p. 27.

[2] *Public Addresses by John Bright*, ed. J. E. Thorold Rogers, 1879, p. 433.

apparatus for flogging garroters? I should reply to such questions that I regard India and the task of the English in India in a very different light from this. The British Power in India is like a vast bridge over which an enormous multitude of human beings are passing, and will (I trust) for ages to come continue to pass, from a dreary land, in which brute violence in its roughest form had worked its will for centuries—a land of cruel wars, ghastly superstitions, wasting plague and famine—on their way to a country of which, not being a prophet, I will not try to draw a picture, but which is at least orderly, peaceful, and industrious, and which, for aught we know to the contrary, may be the cradle of changes comparable to those which have formed the imperishable legacy to mankind of the Roman Empire. The bridge was not built without desperate struggles and costly sacrifices. A mere handful of our countrymen guard the entrance to it and keep order among the crowd. If it should fall, woe to those who guard it, woe to those who are on it, woe to those who would lose with it all hopes of access to a better land. Strike away either of its piers and it will fall, and what are they? One of its piers is military power: the other is justice; by which I mean a firm and constant determination on the part of the English to promote impartially and by all lawful means, what they (the English) regard as the lasting good of the natives of India. Neither force nor justice will suffice by itself. Force without justice is the old scourge of India, wielded by a stronger hand than of old. Justice without force is a weak aspiration after an unattainable end. But so long as the masterful will, the stout heart, the active brain, the calm nerves and the strong body which make up military force are directed to the object which I have defined as constituting justice, I should have no fear, for even if we fail after doing our best, we fail with honour, and if we succeed we shall have performed the greatest feat of strength, skill, and courage in the whole history of the world. For my own part, I see no reason why we should fail. . . .[1]

Here, then, was the philosophical groundwork of Strachey's apologetic for British rule. The great British achievement was the establishment of peace 'from Adam's Bridge to Peshawur', and its only historical parallel was the *pax Romana*. This peace was the creation of law, but force was an absolutely essential element of all law whatever. Indeed law, as he had said, was nothing but regulated force subjected to particular conditions and directed towards particular objects.[2] Only under its shelter could the arts of

[1] Letter of Sir J. Fitzjames Stephen to *The Times*, 4 Jan. 1878.
[2] *Liberty, Equality, Fraternity*, p. 239.

civilized life develop. And the mere imposition of law and order was in itself an instrument productive of incalculable change. By merely suppressing violence and intestine war, in a country which had for centuries been the theatre of disorder and war, a revolution was produced just as surely as a lake was produced by damming a river.[1] But the British in India were not confined to a passive role; they were the representatives of a belligerent civilization, and they were committed to the management and guidance of the most extensive and far-reaching revolution ever recorded in history. What was the nature of this revolution? What did Stephen mean by the duty of 'open, uncompromising assertion of superiority' which he advocated in that fierce letter to *The Times* of 1883 on the Ilbert Bill, and for which Sir Arthur Hobhouse, his successor as law member, took him to task in the *Contemporary Review*? Firstly he had to discount the smallest unnecessary interference with the social habits and religious opinions of the people. These would in any case be profoundly affected by the social revolution caused by other aspects of British rule: the simple introduction of peace, law, order, free competition for wealth and honour, with an education to match. Although in *Liberty, Equality, Fraternity* Stephen had been concerned to show how important were religious considerations for a complete political theory, he did not disagree with the Utilitarians in dismissing them for ordinary purposes from the orbit of legislation, and leaving their influence on conduct to the working of public opinion. If this were in keeping with the general notion of happiness that prevailed in England, with greater certainty it followed that in India the British Government should not interfere on behalf of any one religion. But if the law were to be founded solely on considerations of temporal expediency, Stephen could still speak of its ultimate moral influence with all the enthusiasm of Bentham:

. . . the establishment of a system of law which regulates the most important part of the daily life of the people constitutes in itself a moral conquest more striking, more durable, and far more solid, than the physical conquest which rendered it possible. It exercises an influence over the minds of the people in many ways comparable to that of a new

[1] J. Fitzjames Stephen, in Hunter, *Life of Mayo*, vol. ii, pp. 174–5.

religion. . . . Our law is in fact the sum and substance of what we have to teach them. It is, so to speak, the gospel of the English, and it is a compulsory gospel which admits of no dissent and no disobedience.[1]

The British task in India he still regarded with the notions of his Evangelical forefathers, although he was devoid of their religious ambitions. The task was to redeem a people sunk in gross darkness and to raise them in the scale of civilization. James Mill in his time had also shared the aggressive Evangelical conception of the British civilizing mission, while disowning the religious objective. And James Mill had equally been the protagonist of imposing the British solution by power, by the instrument of law, and not seeking to evoke it by educating and co-operating with the Indian mind in accordance with the policy of the ordinary Liberal school. In Stephen's words, the British task was the 'introduction of the essential parts of European civilisation into a country densely peopled, grossly ignorant, steeped in idolatrous superstition, unenergetic, fatalistic, indifferent to most of what we regard as the evils of life, and preferring the repose of submitting to them to the trouble of encountering and trying to remove them'. Now the essential parts of European civilization, its ideal of happiness, were peace, order, the supremacy of law, the prevention of crime, the redress of wrong, the enforcement of contracts, the development and concentration of the military force of the State, the construction of public works, the collection and expenditure of the revenue for these objects in such a way as to promote to the utmost the public interest, interfering as little as possible with the comfort or wealth of the inhabitants, and the improvement of the people. The pursuit of a policy based on these European principles would produce an immense social revolution; and the existing machine of Government had only to be steadily worked to attain this result. Such a policy in its nature ran counter to the feelings and opinions of the vast mass of the population. The suppression of practices like 'suttee' and infanticide, the enforcement of free trade and so forth, comprised what he had meant by the open, uncompromising assertion of superiority, and were

[1] J. Fitzjames Stephen, in Hunter, *Life of Mayo*, vol. ii, p. 169.

bound to be unpopular. From this fact the whole of Stephen's final lesson was drawn. Every progress that had been made in India had been forced upon it as a direct result of British power, and if the task which was still in its infancy were to be carried to a successful result British power had to be maintained unimpaired. This was because the purpose and principles of the great revolution were European and not Indian. However much Indians might be used as servants of the Government, the Government had to remain absolute, and composed in all its principal parts of Europeans. The chief reason for this was that Indians neither understood the principles of British policy, nor so far as they understood it did they like it, nor could they be trusted to carry it out if they both understood and liked it, except under constant and vigilant European superintendence.

The substance of all that I have to say is this—The English in India have been by circumstances committed to an enterprise which is in reality difficult and dangerous to the last degree, though its difficulties and dangers have thus far been concealed by the conspicuous success which has attended their efforts. That enterprise is nothing less than the management and guidance of the most extensive and far-reaching revolution recorded in history. It involves the radical change of the ideas and institutions of a vast population which has already got ideas and institutions to which it is deeply attached. The only method of conducting this revolution to a good end is by unity of action and policy, communicated from a central authority to a small number of picked local officers, the central and local authorities being supported by a military force sufficient to give them practically undisputed executive power, and the whole body being regulated by known laws impartially administered. By these means the tremendous change now in progress may be carried out in a quiet, orderly and gradual way, with what specific results no one can tell, but it may be hoped with good ones, unless the ideas on which all our European civilisation is based are essentially wrong. If, however, the authority of the Government is once materially relaxed, if the essential character of the enterprise is misunderstood and the delusion that it can be carried out by assemblies representing the opinions of the natives is admitted, nothing but failure, anarchy, and ruin can be the result.[1]

Having defended the British power in India against

---

[1] J. Fitzjames Stephen, 'Foundations of the Government of India', *Nineteenth Century*, No. LXXX (Oct. 1883), p. 566.

Bright's persistent denigration, Stephen turned to defend it against the notion that there was a moral duty for the British to introduce representative institutions. This was no easy matter, as he tacitly acknowledged, so firmly was the idea of representative and popular government established in England. But he thought it could be safely asserted that absolute government had its own merits and conveniences, that it was as legitimate a form of government as any other, and that if it existed, there was no reason why those who administered it should seek to substitute for it a representative system, or should feel in any respect ashamed of their position as absolute rulers, or desirous to lay it down. Much of the language used about the British Government in India implied, if it did not exactly state, an *a priori* doctrine which might be called the Divine Right of Representative Institutions, or of the Sovereignty of the People. It seemed to assume that the exercise of absolute power could never be justified except as a temporary expedient used for the purpose of superseding itself, and as a means of educating those whom it affected into a fitness for parliamentary institutions.[1] The moral basis of British rule, he had shown, consisted of the attempt to realize an ideal of happiness that was foreign to the great bulk of the Indian peoples, and simply because this ideal was a foreign one it was impossible to make those whose task it was to enforce it responsible to the will of the majority. It had to be an absolute government or fail in its purpose. What Stephen especially objected to was that the hazardous process of shifting the basis of British rule, which was involved in the development of representative institutions, was entirely gratuitous. Among Indians at large there was no desire at all for such a change, and the only section which had suggested it was a very small group of 'Anglicized Bengalese Baboos' who were totally unrepresentative. It is important not to misunderstand Stephen's position. He was opposed to risking the whole edifice of law and order for the gratuitous satisfaction of certain abstract principles. If, however, these principles acquired real force by commanding any serious support amongst the Indian population at large, then they

---

[1] J. Fitzjames Stephen, 'Foundations of the Government of India', *Nineteenth Century*, No. LXXX (Oct. 1883), p. 551.

would have to be reckoned with and probably gradually conceded. But it was for Indians and not Englishmen to make the demand. This followed directly from Stephen's conception of moral and political ideals. An ideal was nothing unless it could command the support of a large section of 'the vast indifferent majority', that is, until it had fought its way to power. No ordinary man could act from a motive which was not connected with his self-interest; and conversely no man could, in the ordinary way, act from disinterested motives in order to gratify the self-interest of others. A small group of educated Indians demanded representative institutions because the ideal also accorded with what they believed to be their self-interest. But they represented, Stephen thought, no real force in Indian politics. If, of course, like any determined minority they could extend their ideal to command a much wider circle of support, then they would become a force which the British would have to deal with on the basis of their own enlightened self-interest, or, what was identical, their own ideal of happiness.

It was fitting that an extract from this article of Stephen's in the *Nineteenth Century* should form the conclusion to Sir John Strachey's book on India, published in 1888 and a standard authority for more than twenty years. Nothing could illustrate better Stephen's relation to the Indian Civil Service. He was its political philosopher and gave to its prejudices and emotions a reasoned and logical support. He showed how a man could consistently favour every aspect of a free society and yet deny the gift of political freedom itself. In this he was standing in the line of intellectual Liberals whose most distinguished representative had been John Austin, one of the fountain-heads of Stephen's philosophy of law. Undoubtedly in his anti-democratic notions Austin was not representative of the Utilitarians as a whole; but after 1832 it was his type of severe logical mind—which cherished order and rational system, which believed that truth in politics and political economy could only be attained by dispassionate intellectual inquiry, and which was convinced that the science of government could only be mastered by an educated élite—that developed the authoritarian element implicit in utilitarianism. And increasingly this type of mind

x

tended to find its ideal of efficiency realized in an authoritarian and bureaucratic form of state. It altered its outlook, however, in one important respect. The Utilitarian mind moved with logical process through a whole circle of belief with respect to empire. Austin could agree with Bentham and James Mill that colonies were useless and costly appendages. But the Mills had always made an exception of India, and had begun to speak in terms of a mission to raise her in the scale of civilization. With Stephen a fiercely imperialist note was struck. If it were British power that unobtrusively sustained the peace established through the length and breadth of India, and so with it all the arts and comforts of civilized life, then the British power was deserving of the utmost devotion and reverence. Was this not the great Leviathan, the vicegerent of God on earth? On the occasion of the Delhi Durbar of 1877 Stephen actually compared the *pax Britannica* with the universal peace announced at Christ's nativity, when as Milton sang, 'Kings sate still with awful eye, As if they surely knew their sovran Lord was by'. In a letter to Lytton he said that he never heard 'God save the Queen' or saw the Union Jack flying in the heart of India without feeling the tears in his eyes, which were not much used to tears.[1] And he tried to show in *Liberty, Equality, Fraternity* how such an emotion followed logically from this view of the *pax Britannica*:

This peace [the *pax Romana*] actually was, and the more highly educated Romans must have seen that it was about to become, the mother of laws, arts, institutions of all kinds, under which our own characters have been moulded. The Roman law, at that period as clumsy as English law is at present, but nearly as rich, sagacious and vigorous, was taking root in all parts of the world under the protection of Roman armed force, and all the arts of life, literature, philosophy and art were growing by its side. An Englishman must have a cold heart and a dull imagination who cannot understand how the consciousness of this affected a Roman governor. I do not envy the Englishman whose heart does not beat high as he looks at the scarred and shattered walls of Delhi or at the union jack flying from the fort at Lahore. . . .[2]

The genesis of an important part of late-nineteenth-

---

[1] Leslie Stephen, *Life of J. Fitzjames Stephen*, p. 398.
[2] *Liberty, Equality, Fraternity*, pp. 98–99.

century imperialism is illustrated in Stephen's thought. It represented the blending of the Utilitarian zeal for efficiency in government with the Evangelical sense of mission and race. Of course, the Utilitarian legacy had ceased to be radical, no longer aiming at an entire reconstruction of political institutions but simply concerned to make existing institutions work efficiently. And the Evangelical legacy had been even more drastically transformed. It was not so much that Grant's vision of education with political freedom as the dimly descried goal had been replaced by the notion of a revolution imposed by British power and rejecting education for independence. Of much deeper importance was the transference of religious ardour from the end to the means. Stephen explicitly renounced the desire or feasibility of determining the end. For him the whole British purpose was contained and limited within the framework of positive law. He had said: 'Our law is in fact the sum and substance of what we have to teach them. It is, so to speak the gospel of the English.' But what law could effect was merely the establishment of certain conditions; it could not determine the final result:

All that the law can do or ought to try to do is to provide a rational and convenient framework in which the new state of things may grow up; but what the new state of things will ultimately be like, it passes the wit of man to say. The utmost, I think, that European experience justifies us in asserting, is, that the maintenance of peace and order and the supremacy of regular law—of a law that is founded on considerations of temporal expediency, and leaving religious and all other speculations to find their own level—is an indispensable condition of the only kind of benefits which it is in our power to confer upon India.[1]

Stephen invested law with the sanctity of the Ten Commandments; for since the existence of God and a supernatural world was disputable and the fear of divine retribution had lost all force in the modern ideal of happiness, it was necessary to accord to the laws and institutions of this world all possible reverence and awe.[2] It was the special character of imperialism to be imbued with this profound religious sense,

[1] J. Fitzjames Stephen, in Hunter, *Life of Mayo*, vol. ii, pp. 175–6.
[2] J. Fitzjames Stephen, *History of the Criminal Law*, vol. iii, p. 367; cited L. Stephen, *Life of J. Fitzjames Stephen*, pp. 427–8. Also cf. Noel Annan, *Leslie Stephen*, p. 203.

and yet to be, strictly speaking, non-Christian. After going out to India Stephen ceased to attend church, and one may say that he had ceased to be a professing Christian from 1869. But to the end he retained a vague belief in some awful and remote God, like the Biblical Jehovah, whose purposes worked themselves out in the material world, whose hand was visible in the great movement of history, and who rewarded obedience to his Law with power and prosperity and visited disobedience with dearth and defeat. Men could not escape their common clay and its desires; their only hope lay in transmuting and consecrating these desires, by directing them to the service of the concrete institutions and relations in which they found themselves set—their work, their family, their country. This attitude was growing common when Stephen wrote in the eighteen-seventies. Bradley was teaching that 'there is nothing higher than my station and its duties'; and through Bradley and Green, Hegel's immanentist theory of the state was making inroads into contemporary English thought. But there is no need to look outside the English tradition for the origin of these ideas. They were present in Burke, received an Evangelical fierceness from Carlyle's dogma that might is in the long term right and that a man's work is the chief part of his religion; and at the end of the century, when the open disavowal of belief in Christianity took place, they took their final shape in the teaching of Kipling. The key then to the emotionalism of imperialism is the transposition of evangelicalism to wholly secular objects, or alternatively the translation of secular objectives to a religious level. In a strict sense its creed was the consecration of force. Stephen's rejoinder to Bright made the point emphatically:

> . . . I deny that ambition and conquest are crimes; I say that ambition is the great incentive to every manly virtue, and that conquest is the process by which every great State in the world (the United States not excepted) has been built up. North America would be a hunting-ground for savages if the Puritans had not carried guns as well as Bibles, and the United States would be a memory of the past if the North, 13 years ago, had not conquered the South. I for one, feel no shame when I think of the great competitive examination which lasted for just 100 years, and of which the first paper was set upon the

field of Plassey, and the last (for the present) under the walls of Delhi and Lucknow. . . .[1]

The creed is complete with its ancillary characteristics which derived from the Hebraic, Puritan inheritance, and which in secular form had long been preached by Carlyle: the gospel of duty, of work done in silence, of the virtues of self-denial, law, order, and obedience.

These were the military virtues, and it was the military doctrine of efficiency which was to attract the authoritarian element of the Utilitarian mind (the 'liberalism of the intellect') to its side. The waste, the shifts and compromises inherent in the working of parliamentary democracy, its want of a steady pursuit of principle, its surrender to emotional oratory and the pressure of narrow interests, were particularly disliked by those whose intellects delighted in efficiency, logical order, and steady work by expert hands. Stephen was overwhelmingly impressed by the contrast between the methods of legislation used in India and England. Bentham had long before been attracted by the efficiency of military methods, and the six years which John Austin had spent as an army officer left their mark on his theory of jurisprudence. Both went back to Hobbes, the most detested of all names to popular liberalism, and founded their criteria of legislation on the analogy of military commands. The cohesion, discipline, and perfect subordination of a military body, which worked almost in silence with the minimum of discussion and a few crisp commands, appeared to such minds a thing of intellectual beauty.

There were many types of imperialism and they are rarely distinguished. There was the imperialism of mob emotion, of the penny press, and Mafeking. There was another form of imperialism which looked to the closer association of the white dominions in a free partnership founded on common ties of race and history. There was again an imperialism of the dependent empire that was extraordinarily subtle in its approach, eschewing the blunt imposition of foreign rule, and attempting to work indirectly and unobtrusively through indigenous institutions and ruling classes. The latter was the

[1] Letter of Sir J. Fitzjames Stephen to *The Times*, 4 Jan. 1878.

imperialism of Cromer in Egypt, of Swettenham in the Malay States, of Lugard in Nigeria. The special character of Indian imperialism was distinct from all these. It bore the stamp of which Strachey and Stephen were the spokesmen, and its poet was Kipling. It was the tradition of direct rule, of impartial law, of empire resting on power and the Evangelical sense of duty, swerving neither to right nor to left, and rejecting as base the notion of buying support by favour to a particular class. And it accepted with almost a sense of pride the fact that it was unbeloved and out of sympathy with its subjects:

> Take up the White Man's burden—
> No tawdry rule of kings,
> But toil of serf and sweeper—
> The tale of common things.
>
> Take up the White Man's burden—
> And reáp his old reward:
> The blame of those ye better,
> The hate of those ye guard—
> The cry of hosts ye humour
> (Ah, slowly!) towards the light:—
> 'Why brought ye us from bondage,
> Our loved Egyptian night?'

Its fullest and last expression found place in Curzon (1898–1905). Stephen and Strachey's message had been that the machine required only to be strongly and firmly worked to fulfil the British purpose. But from the eighteen-seventies routine had set in, and the machine had grown steadily more ponderous and less adaptable. By the end of the century Curzon found that the Government of India had developed all the characteristics of an elephant, 'very stately, very powerful, with a high standard of intelligence, but with a regal slowness in its gait'.[1] His Viceroyalty was an heroic effort to place the administration once more upon the offensive, to show that British rule still had in it 'the vitality of an unexhausted purpose'. In his school-days at Eton Curzon had been fired with enthusiasm for the British imperial role in India after hearing an address by Fitzjames

[1] Earl of Ronaldshay, *Life of Lord Curzon*, 1928, vol. ii, p. 64.

Stephen to the College Literary Society. There was little that was new in his imperialism. He brought to India the idea, common at the time, that the State should work in close partnership with private enterprise for the exploitation of the country's economic resources. But the substance of his creed was still the old doctrine writ large. 'If I were asked to sum it up in a single word, I would say "Efficiency". That has been our gospel, the keynote of our administration.'[1] The British mission was good government by a handful of foreigners driven solely by their own sense of duty and interest, and neither seeking nor giving sympathy or love. And the justification was the greatest happiness of the greatest number, the secure assumption that the Indian middle classes represented no one but themselves, and that the British Government stood for the interests of 'the Indian poor, the Indian peasant, the patient, humble, silent millions'.

Like Stephen, Curzon had lost faith in Christianity only to find a new religion in the service of empire; even if God no longer thundered from Sinai and his oracles were sometimes reported dumb, it was necessary to 'cling humbly but fervently to the belief that, so long as we are worthy, we may still remain one of the instruments through which He chooses to speak to mankind'.[2] In India the Almighty had set the Englishman's hand to the greatest of His ploughs in whose furrows the nations of the future were germinating and taking shape. It must be his ideal: 'To fight for the right, to abhor the imperfect, the unjust or the mean, to swerve neither to the right hand nor to the left, to care nothing for flattery, odium or abuse . . . never to let your enthusiasm be soured or your courage grow dim.'[3]

It would be wrong to suppose that this tradition went unchallenged or unmodified. When Stephen spoke against efforts to prevent the dissolution of the village communities,[4] he was answering the criticism of another powerful current of ideas which did not so much reject as question the stringent application of the Utilitarian doctrines to India.

[1] *Lord Curzon in India, 1898–1905*, ed. Sir T. Raleigh, 1906, p. 564.
[2] Ronaldshay, *Life of Curzon*, vol. iii, p. 392.
[3] Farewell speech at the Byculla Club, Bombay, 16 Nov. 1905; *Lord Curzon in India*, p. 585. [4] See p. 280.

The new school, which won its spurs in Egypt, originated in India. Cromer, its master, had served his apprenticeship as Northbrook's private secretary (1872–6) and later as Ripon's Finance Member (1880–3), and while in India had formed a kinship of ideas with the philosophic mind of Sir Alfred Lyall.[1] By the end of the century Cromer's was the weightiest name in imperial administration, and Lyall as a member of the India Council in London (1888–1902) and a distinguished figure in the best intellectual society, commanded wide respect. Like so many 'imperialists' they remained intellectual adherents of liberalism, while deserting the Liberal Party over Irish Home Rule. As authoritarian Liberals they adhered to the common tenet of the imperialist creed, which held political power to be the great shaping force of civilization and the main lever by which the mass of mankind was raised to a higher mental and moral plane. And it was this belief which supplied for them the moral justification for the existence and continuance of British rule over subject peoples. Where they differed from the Stephen–Strachey school was in their refusal to accept military force as by itself an adequate basis for political authority, or to believe that Utilitarian principles could be rigorously enforced regardless of their effect on the institutions and beliefs of an oriental society.

Their outlook mirrored in practical terms the profound modification of attitude towards utilitarianism which Maine had effected with the publication of his *Ancient Law* in 1861. Maine was, indeed, another instance of a great formative intellect devoting part of his life to Indian affairs and later drawing his Indian experience into the main current of English thought. His principal achievement was to challenge the dominion exercised by abstract ideas over the English mind; a dominion which he attributed to the abstract analytical method of the Utilitarians. Holding the entire range of Utilitarian dogmas to be the product not of intellectual discovery but of long institutional growth, Maine denied that they were of absolute and universal validity. The Utilitarian postulates in jurisprudence or political economy could never be more than conditional truths, relative to a particular stage

[1] For Lyall, see Biographical Notes, p. 331.

in the development of human society. The fatal intellectual error, which threatened the world with disastrous practical consequences, was the severance of an idea from the limitations of its actual historical origin in an institution or system of law. To transpose an idea in abstract form, from a highly advanced stage of society to a country where society before British rule had not even passed through the feudal stage, required the greatest care and caution if violent consequences were to be avoided. With his assumption of a common racial origin and a common institutional ancestry for the Aryan peoples of Europe and India, Maine did much to promote a less impassioned and prejudiced attitude towards Indian society, and to dispel the militant sense of superiority with which James Mill had infected the English educated mind and which Stephen had inherited from his Evangelical background. But his practical counsel was the need for a curb on the movement which was endeavouring to precipitate Indian society from status to contract at one bound.[1]

Possessing a closer knowledge of the country, Lyall reaffirmed Maine's lesson. He saw the action of Western civilization on Indian society as mainly a 'dissolving force', itself incapable of supplying any compensating bond of social cohesion. British rule worked as a great levelling power, breaking down all local forms of independent political life, draining all authority to a common centre, and pounding down the multifarious races and institutions into one uniform and atomized mass. This tendency, common to all Asian despotisms, had gone much farther in the case of British rule because of its superior strength and efficiency. To Lyall it was a situation full of danger. The British dominion threatened to drift towards 'that condition of over-centralised isolation, with shallow foundations and inadequate support, which renders an empire as top-heavy as an over-built tower, and which is unquestionably an element of political instability'.[2] All Lyall's historical studies pointed to the fact that

[1] Sir Henry Maine, 'The Effects of Observation of India on Modern European Thought', Cambridge Rede Lecture for 1875, in *Village Communities in the East and West*.

[2] [Lyall], 'Government of the Indian Empire', *Edinburgh Review*, No. 325 (Jan. 1884), p. 37; attributed to Lyall, Sir H. M. Durand, *Life of Sir A. C. Lyall*, p. 477.

Asian empires had foundered from this cause.[1] The isolation of the ruling authority was intensified because the British power by its nature could not enjoy the support and control of Indian religions, and because it took upon itself the additional responsibility for famine and plague control, which had always been regarded as the responsibility of the gods. At the same time Western influence was sapping existing faiths and loyalties without being able to substitute anything more than scepticism and a restless materialism. There was the danger of a 'spiritual interregnum' in which the traditional beliefs sustaining social order were discarded, and the new beliefs necessary for a changed society had yet to take hold.[2] In this situation, with the ground already cleared of political and religious obstacles by governmental action, the commercial forces of the West were free to complete the work of social dissolution. It was a process which was bound to supply a material basis to the discontent already felt on other grounds, for it profoundly altered the relations among classes, giving the trading and professional classes of the towns a novel supremacy over the peasantry and the old warrior aristocracy. All local barriers having been levelled and the responsibility of the gods discredited, there was a danger that the separate forces of discontent would gather into a single head and hurl themselves at the one authority which remained—the centralized foreign bureaucracy.

On this reading of the Indian problem, the school of soldier-politicals who placed entire reliance on military force stood convicted of fatal short-sightedness. Looking on all kinds of independent authority as potential sources of danger, they had insisted on destroying every barrier between the central power and the mass of the people, oblivious of the truth that 'supports are useless without some capacity to resist pressure'. They had promoted military operations to secure a 'scientific frontier', and had kept up a large garrison force without regard to the effect of the tax burden on the

---

[1] Cf. Lyall, *The Rise and Expansion of the British Dominion in India*, pp. 62–65, 321–2; 'The Moghul Empire', *Cambridge Modern History*, vol. vi, chap. xv; *Asiatic Studies*, vol. i, chap. vii.

[2] Lyall, *Asiatic Studies*, vol. i, p. 322.

feelings of the people. Yet these feelings were the true baro-meter of the stability of empire. Cromer returned the same answer as Lyall to the military school:

There is truth in the saying, of which perhaps we sometimes hear rather too much, that the maintenance of the Empire depends on the sword; but so little does it depend on the sword alone, that if once we have to draw the sword, not merely to suppress some local effervescence, but to overcome a general upheaval of subject races goaded to action either by deliberate oppression, which is highly improbable, or by unintentional misgovernment, which is far more conceivable, the sword will assuredly be powerless to defend us for long, and the days of our Imperial rule will be numbered.[1]

The great lesson that needed to be learnt was that taught by Maine: the necessity of restraint in pressing Western reforms upon an oriental society, for grave danger lay 'in the prospect of its too rapid disintegration'. Lyall pointed to Maine's method 'of finding a *modus vivendi* and a point of conciliation between ancient and modern ideas'. Policy must be concerned 'to arrest what he called the "trituration of societies" and to retard the dissolution of numerous groups and petty jurisdictions into a vast and incoherent multitude under one overburdened foreign government'.[2] In other words, the tendency towards centralization and uniformity needed to be counteracted. So far from encouraging the melting down of different elements into one formless and dangerous amalgam, they were each to be encouraged to pursue a separate development in the interests of diversity and local autonomy. In this way the pressures generated by British rule might be expected to counteract one another, rather than combine. A policy of decentralization was re-quired, together with measures for granting a legitimate sphere of expression to the separate elements of Indian society, whether the educated middle class, the princes, or the aristocracy. While, therefore, both Cromer and Lyall were convinced supporters of Ripon's local self-government measures of 1883, they were also champions of the autonomy

[1] Cromer, 'The Government of Subject Races', *Edinburgh Review*, Jan. 1908; reprinted *Political and Literary Essays, 1908–13*, p. 5.
[2] [Lyall], 'Life and Speeches of Sir Henry Maine', *Quarterly Review*, vol. 176 (1893), p. 316; attributed to Lyall, Durand, *Life of Lyall*, p. 477.

of the Indian states. On frontier policy they upheld the Lawrence tradition of limiting military commitments and opposed the 'forward' school.[1] The question was bound up with that of the financial burden, and Cromer, in particular, never wearied of repeating Lawrence's doctrine that light taxation was the panacea for foreign rule.[2] Lacking every other bond of affinity a foreign government could secure the ready obedience of a predominantly peasant population only by ensuring its material well-being. If it could succeed in this it had little to fear from the superior classes, for their grievances and ambitions could be effectively insulated. But should grounds for deep-seated discontent among the peasantry be allowed to persist, the religious fanatic or political agitator would be able to carry a superficial nationalist movement down to the core of society.[3] A light land revenue had to be, therefore, the principal object of imperial policy.

This acute and profound analysis of the problems of imperial rule issued, it might appear, in no more than a policy of Machiavellian expediency. The Utilitarian gospel, with its emphasis on efficient centralized bureaucracy, its levelling anti-aristocratic bias, and its physiocratic doctrine of a high tax on rent, was in no way disowned, but simply declared to have been pushed too far for political safety. Hence, it was held necessary that foreign rule should be made less obtrusive, even though this meant some loss of mechanical efficiency. The practical counsels of Cromer and Lyall must have appeared strangely oblique, prepared as they were to advocate both political concessions to the Western-educated classes as well as measures to strengthen the conservative elements of society to be found among the great landowners and Indian princes. A superficial observer might have been excused for mistaking their outlook as one of pure expediency, with no other principle than 'divide and rule'. In fact, their

---

[1] [Lyall], 'Twelve Years of Indian Government', *Edinburgh Review*, No. 271 (Jan. 1895); cf. Durand, p. 478. Cromer, 'Sir Alfred Lyall', *Quarterly Review*, July 1913; reprinted *Political and Literary Essays, 1908–13*, p. 77.

[2] Cromer, 'The Government of Subject Races', *Political and Literary Essays, 1908–13*, p. 44.

[3] Cromer, 'The French in Algeria', *The Spectator*, 31 May 1913; reprinted in *Political and Literary Essays, 1908–13*, p. 254.

political philosophy was as high-minded as any, resting on the conviction that foreign rule was still the indispensable instrument of progress, and constituting what was really the policy of Indirect Rule as designed for a sophisticated and advanced society.

It is difficult to discern any positive success for their cause before the end of the century, unless the halt in aggressive legislation and the almost deliberate inertia which followed after 1885 be reckoned as such. Paradoxically, it was not until Curzon's viceroyalty (1898–1905) when the bureaucratic machine was being retuned to a new pitch of efficiency, that the first signs of fundamental change appeared. They took place, significantly enough, in the field of land revenue policy, where, it will be recalled, the doctrine of a high assessment had taken on a new lease of life from the eighteen-eighties.[1] The freedom from famine and plague, which India had enjoyed since 1880, had come to an end in 1896, and the agrarian problem once more forced itself upon public attention. Curzon was sensitive to the charges made by R. C. Dutt that the weight of the land revenue demand was a cause of the increased frequency and intensity of famine, and he drew up an official apologia on land revenue policy, published in 1902.[2] The potency of the rent theory was still sufficiently strong for him to consider that he had disproved the charges, once he had shown that the assessment absorbed no more than a portion of the rental assets. But in practice his liberal remissions and his measures to graduate enhancements and provide for greater elasticity of payment marked the end of the supremacy of the Utilitarian doctrine of rent. The conception of the land revenue as a portion of rent, although never formally abandoned, was steadily replaced by the notion of it as a tax on agricultural income. English economic thought was, of course, moving in the same direction. The 'single tax' theory of James Mill fell into discredit when it was taken up at the end of the century by Socialists like Hyndman and Henry George. The leading economists

---

[1] See p. 138.
[2] *Land Revenue Policy of the Indian Government.* Published by order of the Governor-General of India in Council, Calcutta, 1902. Cf. R. C. Dutt, *The Economic History of India in the Victorian Age*, Book III, chap. vii.

—Marshall, Nicholson, Edgeworth, Bastable—all condemned any specially severe tax on rent property when they appeared before the Royal Commission on Local Taxation in 1899. Their general notion was that 'taxes are paid by persons, not things', and that the true problem was not 'the distribution of the burden of taxation between different classes of property, but . . . between different classes of persons'. Equity of taxation must be determined by the subjective standard of 'the public conscience', and this inclined towards a system of mixed taxation with a graduated income tax as its central feature.[1] From Curzon's time the fiscal policy of the Indian Government moved in accordance with these ideas. In 1909 the half-assets rule of assessment was broken by an executive ruling requiring special sanction for reassessments which exceeded the previous demand by more than one-third. 'All history teaches', declared the official despatch, 'that with the development of a country a greater degree of permanence must be given to the taxation of land, and the time has come when an increase in revenue in future shall be looked for rather in improving trade and industry than in adding largely to the burden on the land.'[2] The rise in railway receipts and customs revenue facilitated the shift in fiscal policy. Before 1900 the land revenue accounted for two-fifths of the total income of the State; by 1913 the proportion had fallen to a quarter, with railway receipts closely rivalling income from the land.[3]

Curzon's departure in 1905 had marked the end of the undisputed sway of the Anglo-Indian bureaucracy, and the system which it represented. The outbreak of violent nationalist agitation following the partition of Bengal and the defeat of Russia by an oriental power produced a critical situation. Minto, a conservative Viceroy, was as insistent as Morley, the new Secretary of State, that 'cast-iron bureaucracy' could not go on for ever. They turned to the policy long advocated by Lyall, making not only inevitable conces-

---

[1] P.P., 1899, vol. xxxvi, pp. 773 et seq. *Official Papers by Alfred Marshall*, London, 1926, pp. 334 et seq.

[2] Revenue Letter from India (No. 2 of 1909—Land Revenue), 18 March 1909; included in printed 'Land Revenue, File No. 90 of 1909'.

[3] Thompson and Garratt, *Rise and Fulfilment of British Rule in India*, pp. 590–2.

sions to the educated classes by strengthening their voice on the legislative councils, but also setting up a Decentralization Commission to suggest ways of loosening the knot of government now held to be tied too tightly. At the same time Minto strove to free the Indian states from the old tutelage, and to give the princes and great landowners a voice in policy through a proposed Advisory Council. But it took the revolutionary impact of the First World War on Indian politics and British thinking to shift the weight of entrenched tradition. It was not until after 1919 that any substantial measure of devolution was attempted, and then only to be defeated by the centripetal force of Indian nationalism. The federal idea of government which took hold in the minds of Montagu and Simon came in response to a very different political situation, marking a retreat of British power never envisaged by Cromer or Lyall. The revolution in political thinking, which the World War completed, conceded the victory of what Stephen had termed sentimental liberalism, with its notion of popular sentiment as the directive force of government. Although prepared to take such sentiment into account, Cromer and Lyall had lived in the same mental climate as the authoritarian Benthamites. The end of government they took to be neither liberty, nor race, nor religion, but happiness (conceived, doubtless, largely in material terms); and they tolerated self-government, whether in Ireland or India, only so far as it could be reconciled with good government. They assumed there to be, in some sense, a science of politics, even though it were no more than reasoning from experience, which prescribed the appropriate principles of government irrespective of popular prejudice and feeling. Such were the principles of free trade, freedom of contract, and individual property in land.

After 1905 these principles, which had received their scientific statement at the hands of the Utilitarians and which had been embodied in the Indian administrative system, were not jettisoned but allowed to be blunted in their application by the pressure of organized Indian opinion. It has been seen how the pitch of the land revenue assessment had in effect been reduced by the limitation placed on enhancements, and this tendency in land revenue policy was continued in the period after the war.[1] Similarly, Curzon's Punjab Land Alienation Act of 1900, which marked the end of official faith in free trade in land, was followed by efforts to reverse the trend towards individualism and to build up co-operative village enterprises. The fact was, of course, that the movement towards more relative and subjective standards was part of the transformation through which the modern world was passing, and was as much an intellectual as a political phenomenon. At bottom Indian policy was undergoing the sea-change which accompanied the withering of Victorian liberalism in all its facets. So it was that the imperialism of Cromer and Lyall had barely begun to affect Indian policy before it was discarded as outmoded. At all events, after 1900 utilitarianism ceased to transmit any living impulse into the present. Leslie Stephen judged rightly that it was time to write its memorial, and his standard work on the Utilitarians was followed in 1901 by the first of Halévy's fertile and suggestive studies.

The enduring influence of utilitarianism on India must be looked for in the administrative and judicial system, 'the steel frame', which, however obscured in its working by the political struggle, continued to supply the daily framework of State action to the end of British rule and beyond. It was in the realm of authority and not liberty that the Utilitarian work was done. It cannot claim parliamentary self-government as its handiwork. Admittedly, there existed in the eighteen-twenties and eighteen-thirties a number of Liberals who accepted much of the Benthamite doctrine and who would normally have been inclined to favour some measure of representative government for India. James Mill's authority seems to have been decisive in quashing such vague and irresolute hopes, and Macaulay seems to have been sincere when, in his speech to the Commons in 1833, he quoted James Mill's statement that any form of representa-

---

[1] By a Madras ruling of 1924 enhancements were limited to 18¾ per cent. In 1925 the standard of assessment in the United Provinces was limited to 40 per cent. and the term of settlement extended to forty years. Similar measures were taken in the Punjab. *Report of the Indian Taxation Enquiry Committee 1924–25*, Madras, 1926, vol. i, para. 76. *Indian Statutory Commission*, vol. ix, London, 1930, Memorandum submitted by the Government of the United Provinces, para. 81, p. 79.

tive government was utterly out of the question. Consequently, Macaulay accepted Mill's conception of the Indian Legislature as a tiny committee of experts rather than a large and varied body on the old colonial model. At all events, this Liberal group, which included men like Trevelyan, Ross, and James Young, turned its energies to the cause of Western education. Only in Ceylon, under the less authoritarian rule of the Colonial Office, did the Liberal wing of the Utilitarian mind predominate. There, Charles Hay Cameron did not limit his Benthamite zeal to establishing a reformed system of courts and to promoting Western education. In company with his fellow commissioner, Colebrooke, he was successful, in 1833, in arguing for an enlarged legislative council of fifteen members, half of whose unofficial membership of six were to be representatives of the Asian community.[1] In this way Ceylon followed the Colonial Office tradition which permitted a considerable practical measure of local autonomy, while India under the influence of Mill's outlook was drawn ever more tightly under the active supervision and control of London. John Stuart Mill was one with his father in this matter and held high notions of the Home Authorities' powers of control. Not until the Montagu–Chelmsford reforms of 1919 did London begin to relax its grip. Similarly, despite his abstract faith in representative government and his pious hopes of Indians eventually ruling themselves, he was not prepared to grant even a single seat to an Indian on any of the legislative councils. In his essay *On Representative Government* (1861) he declared there to be no other practical alternative to a pure and enlightened despotism. It was no doubt the magnificent opportunity which this form of rule permitted to the philosophic reformer that was allowed to outweigh, in the minds of both the Mills, the tradition of political liberty in which they had been trained. In India, as Lyall saw, government, by its attributes and authority, approached most nearly Hobbes's ideal of the Leviathan, 'that mortal god to whom we owe, under the immortal God,

---

[1] Cf. G. C. Mendis, *The Colebrooke-Cameron Papers*, 2 vols., O.U.P., London, 1956. For the significance of the 1833 reforms in the constitutional development of the non-European Crown Colony, see Martin Wight, *The Development of the Legislative Council*, London, 1946.

our peace and defence'.[1] A scrutiny of this Indian Leviathan, if depicted in the manner of Hobbes's frontispiece, would reveal Bentham's calm philosophic brow and James Mill's stern eyes of authority.

[1] [Lyall], 'Government of the Indian Empire', *Edinburgh Review*, No. 325 (Jan. 1884), p. 34.

NOTES

NOTE A, p. 38. Cf. [Anon.], *Free Trade, or An Inquiry into the Pretensions of the Directors of the East India Company, to the Exclusive Trade of the Indian and China Seas: Addressed to the Great Body of the Merchants and Manufacturers of the United Kingdom*, London, 1812. [India Office Library Tracts, vol. 467]. *The Present System of our East India Government and Commerce Considered. In which are exposed the Fallacy, The Incompatibility and the Injustice of a Political and Despotic Power Possessing a Commercial Situation Also Within the Countries Subject to its Dominion*, 1813 [ascribed to 'Mr. Rickards' in India Office Library Tracts, vol. 116], pp. 35–36. Rickards, an M.P., was one of the fiercest of the Company's opponents.

NOTE B, p. 46. Macaulay to his sister, Margaret, 7 Dec. 1834: Trevelyan, *Lord Macaulay*, p. 279: 'He is quite at the head of that active party among the younger servants of the Company who take the side of improvement. . . . He has no small talk. His mind is full of schemes of moral and political improvement, and his zeal boils over in all his talk. His topics, even in courtship, are steam navigation, the education of the natives, the equalization of the sugar duties, the substitution of the Roman for the Arabic alphabet in the oriental languages. . . . His own religious feelings are ardent, like all his feelings, even to enthusiasm. . . .' Charles Trevelyan married Macaulay's sister, Hannah More Macaulay. Their son was Sir G. O. Trevelyan, and grandson the present historian, Dr. George Macaulay Trevelyan, O.M.

NOTE C, p. 49. J. S. Mill had a record kept of all the despatches he drafted. This record is preserved in the India Office Library as Home Miscellaneous Series, vol. 832. The following summarizes the number of despatches Mill drafted in the various departments. It will be seen that his work consisted almost entirely of dealing with political affairs, and that he did not draft a single Revenue or Judicial Despatch.

Bengal Political Department .	791	Bombay Public Works Department	7
Madras Political Department	96		
Bombay Political Department	610	Bengal Ecclesiastical Department	2
Bengal Foreign Department .	2		
India Foreign Department .	7	Madras Ecclesiastical Department	5
Madras Foreign Department .	15		
Bengal Public Department .	39	Bombay Ecclesiastical Department	1
India Public Department .	10		
Madras Public Department .	19	Bombay Marine Department.	5
Bombay Public Department .	25	Bengal Law Department .	1
India Public Works Department	36	Bengal Commercial Department	2
Madras Public Works Department	5	Prince of Wales' Island General Department .	8

NOTE D, p. 57. Revenue Despatch to Bengal, 18 Feb. 1824: *Selections from Educational Records, Part I, 1781–1839*, p. 92: 'The great end should not have been to teach Hindoo learning or Mahomedan learning, but useful learning. No doubt in teaching useful learning to the Hindoos or Mahomedans, Hindoo *media*, or Mahomedan *media*, as they were found the most effectual, would have been proper to be employed, and Hindoo and Mahomedan prejudices would have needed to be consulted, while everything which was useful in Hindoo or Mahomedan literature it would have been proper to retain. . . .' The despatch is attributed to James Mill: George Smith, *Life of Alexander Duff*, 1879 edn., vol. i, pp. 98–99. As a Revenue rather than a Public Despatch it was almost certainly from his hand.

NOTE E, p. 60. *Bengal Hurkaru*, 4 Jan. 1828 (Editorial). The *Hurkaru* attributed the chief cause of the *Morning Chronicle*'s silence on the subject of the East India Company to the influence exercised by John Stuart Mill over its editor, John Black: 'But this gentleman [James Mill] is only the occasional adviser of the *Morning Chronicle*. The reputation of being the *"conseiller intime"* rests with his co-Secretary the Politician, [the 'political Secretary' referred to earlier, i.e. John Stuart Mill]. He is a zealot without temper or tact. The eager and discreet partizan of power—but only when that power is the Company's power and India is the subject of debate. In every other public question he is said to be equally *acharné* for the side of liberality. . . .' Cf. J. S. Mill, *Autobiography*, ed. Laski, p. 75. In the issue of 20 Sept. 1828 the *Hurkaru* attacked the *Westminster Review* on its silence towards the petition of the Calcutta community against the Stamp Act, and blamed James Mill: 'Mr. James Mill could help us to a solution of this curious problem, and perhaps too, he could also account for the silence of the *Morning Chronicle*!!

> What makes all doctrines plain and clear?
> About two hundred pounds a year.
> And that which prov'd true before
> Prove false again?—Two hundred more.'

It was left for the *Edinburgh* to publish Crawfurd's fierce onslaught on the Company over this question (see p. 130, n. 3).

NOTE F, p. 72. On Montesquieu and the division of the powers; Bentham: Constitutional Code', *Works*, vol. ix, pp. 123 et seq. For Bentham's constitutional ideas, cf. Halévy, *Philosophic Radicalism*, pp. 403 et seq. The English translation omits most of the references by which Halévy supported his arguments: these are to be found in the original work, *La Formation du radicalisme philosophique, III—Le Radicalisme philosophique*, Paris, 1904. Halévy's chief point was to stress the authoritarian elements in Bentham's constitutional and legal thought; cf. *Philosophic Radicalism*, pp. 375–6: 'Bentham had never been a liberal; always impatient of philanthropic reforms, he merely passed from a monarchic authoritarianism to a democratic authoritarianism, without pausing at the intermediary position, which is the position of Anglo-Saxon liberalism.'

NOTE G, p. 74. Cf. Bentham, 'Constitutional Code', *Works*, vol. ix, p. 216: 'That which in the excercise of political functions, constitutes *arbitrary* power is—not the unity of the functionary, but his exemption from control, including the obligations, contemporary or eventual, of assigning *reasons* for his acts.' Cf. 'Principles of Judicial Procedure', *Works*, vol. ii, p. 31: 'Against abuse of power, the only effectual or efficient security, is composed of responsibility: substantial, punitional, and dislocational responsibility, legal and moral.' Cf. 'Letters on Scotch Reform', *Works*, vol. v, p. 17: '. . . comes *single-seated judicature,* and with it a new, and in my view. . . a still more important benefit; viz. *individual responsibility.* A board, my Lord, is a *screen.* The lustre of good desert is obscured by it; ill-desert, slinking behind eludes the eye of censure, wrong is covered by it with a presumption of right, stronger and stronger in proportion to the number of folds. . . .' Cf. 'Principles of Penal Law', chap. xxi, 'General Precautions against the Abuse of Authority', *Works*, vol. i, pp. 570 et seq. Also cf. 'Constitutional Code', *Works*, vol. ix, pp. 214 et seq.

NOTE H, p. 118. Sir George Wingate, Memorandum regarding proposals by the Government of India for the Sale of Waste Lands and Redemption of the Revenue, 2 May 1862; *Selections from the Records of the Bombay Government*, N.S., vol. cli, p. 152. Cited pp. 127–8. Dissent of Mr. Mangles, 3 July 1862: *P.P.*, 1862, vol. xl, p. 869. Mangles had been chairman of the Court of Directors in 1857 and after the abolition of the Company became a Member of the Secretary of State's Council. Letter from J. Strachey, magistrate and collector of Moradabad, 30 Sept. 1859; *P.P.*, 1862, vol. xl, p. 747. Another revenue officer, J. H. Batten, said he need hardly add that Strachey drew 'his inspiration from Mr. J. S. Mill's school of political economy': ibid., p. 757.

NOTE I, p. 150. Sir J. Malcolm, Minute, 10 Nov. 1830, para. 129: printed *P.P.*, 1831–2, vol. xii, p. 520. Elphinstone had proposed to build a panopticon-type penitentiary on Bombay Island, and he was supported by Babington, the President of the Regulation Committee, of whom Elphinstone said: 'If he exceeds in any way, he does so in Benthamising'; see Elphinstone to Strachey, 23 March 1822: Colebrooke, *Elphinstone*, vol. ii, p. 134. Cf. Bentham to Col. James Young, 28 Dec. 1827: *Works*, vol. x, p. 577: 'Mill has, at all times, been a declared, and, I have every reason to think, in this instance, a sincere trumpeter of Panopticon, recommending it within the field of his dominion, and, in particular, Bombay, during the vice-royalty of Elphinstone.'

NOTE J, p. 158. Cf. Bentham, 'Judicial Establishment', *Works*, vol. iv, p. 329: 'Where in the opinion of either party, the superior chance of good justice is worth paying for, by the trouble of going to an immediate court, seated in the capital town of a district, instead of a nearer canton court, he may have it. Under such an arrangement, causes which have anything particular in them, either in the way of difficulty or of importance, will naturally find their way to the district court: while the ordinary run of causes will stay, at least in the first instance, in the cantons. . . . On this consideration is grounded in part my establishment of immediate district courts, and the intercommunity of jurisdiction between every such court and the several parish or canton courts within the district. . . .'

NOTE K, p. 159. Cf. Bentham, op. cit., pp. 348–9: 'May the line of appeal stop in different parts of the kingdom, or must it be carried from all parts to a common centre? To a common centre: and this for two reasons: 1. To get the best public that is to be got; 2. For the sake of uniformity. . . . Simplicity on the part of the law; certainty, facility of being known, understood, obeyed, inspected and improved, all concur in manifesting the importance of uniformity in the constructions put upon it.' Ibid., p. 359 n.: 'I take once more a leaf out of the book of the self-condemning pope. Judico me cremari. I sentence to the flames my department-court of appeal, my district court appeal. . . . Obsequiousness drew me into the snares of complication: reflection has restored me to simplicity.' Bentham took up, however, a compromise position in his later work. In his 'Constitutional Code' (1830) he provided for only one grade of immediate 'judicatory', as distinct from the two in his *Draught for the Organization of a Judicial Establishment*; but he resurrected the District Appellate Judicatory. He believed that the size of the state, and other local circumstances, must influence the decision whether to have the 'appellate judicatories' at the metropolis or distributed throughout the districts. Cf. 'Principles of Judicial Procedure', *Works*, vol. ii, p. 22; and 'Constitutional Code', *Works*, vol. ix, pp. 468, 474, 587–8.

NOTE L, p. 170. Cf. Bentham, 'Constitutional Code', *Works*, vol. ix, p. 62: 'While confidence is minimized, let not power be withheld. For security against breach of trust, the sole apt remedy is,—on the part of trustees not impotence but constant responsibility, and as towards their creators—the authors of their political being—on every occasion, and at all times, the strictest and most absolute dependence. In the first place with powers no otherwise limited, on the part of the Supreme Legislative, the most absolute dependence on the Supreme Constitutive, and thus a chain reaching down to the lowest functionary: each link, through the medium of the several increasing links, in a state of equally perfect dependence on the Supreme Legislative, and by this means on the Supreme Constitutive.'

NOTE M, p. 172. 'Principles of Penal Law', *Works*, vol. i, p. 571 n. Cf. p. 571: 'But it is possible to unite, in certain cases the advantages which result from combination, and those which necessarily belong to the responsibility of an individual. In subordinate councils, there is always an individual who presides and upon whom the principal reliance is placed. Associates are given to him, that he may profit by their advice, and that there may be witnesses against him when he neglects his duty. But it is not necessary, for the accomplishment of this object, that they should be his equals in power, nor that they should have a right of voting; all that is necessary is, that the chief should be obliged to communicate to them all that he does, and that each one should make a declaration in writing respecting each of his acts, testifying his approbation or blame.'

NOTE N, p. 177. Cf. Bentham's opinions on the Declaration of Rights of the French National Assembly: *Works*, vol. ii, p. 522: 'In chemistry there is no room for passion to step in and to confound the understanding—to lead men into error and to shut their eyes against knowledge; in legislation, the circumstances are opposite, and vastly different. What, then, shall we say of that system of government, of which the professed object is to call upon the untaught and unlettered multitude . . . to occupy themselves without ceasing upon all questions of government (legislation and administration included) without exception . . . those that require the greatest measures of science to qualify a man for deciding upon, and in respect of which any want of science and skill are liable to be attended with the most fatal consequences !'

NOTE O, p. 180. Grant was regarded as indolent and unbusinesslike. Cf. J. G. Ravenshaw (Vice-President of Court) to Bentinck, 19 Nov. 1831. Ryan to Bentinck, n.d. (in file for 1832): Bentinck MSS. P. Auber (Secretary to Court) to Bentinck, 24 Nov. 1831: Bentinck MSS. Macaulay became an assistant commissioner of the Board of Control in June 1832 and secretary, in succession to Hyde Villiers, in Dec. 1832. For Macaulay's influence, cf. Philips, *East India Company*, pp. 276, 290, 294. Cf. also Macaulay to his sister, 5 Dec. 1833: G. O. Trevelyan, *Life and Letters of Lord Macaulay* p. 251: 'He [Grant] told me yesterday, with tears in his eyes, that he did not know what the Board would do without me. . . . Grant's is a mind that cannot stand alone. . . . It turns, like ivy, to some support.' Holt Mackenzie became an assistant commissioner in Sept. 1832. For his influence cf. Grant to Bentinck 25 Dec. 1833: Bentinck MSS. (referring to the preparation of the India Bill): 'I have, however, been happy in the assistance which I enjoyed pre-eminently so in Holt Mackenzie and my brother Robert—without these two I could have done nothing.' Hyde Villiers was a friend of James Mill: Bain, *James Mill*, p. 367. Cf. *D.N.B.*, vol. xx, pp. 353–4: 'At Cambridge he [Villiers] mixed with Charles Austin, Edward Strutt, John Romilly, T. B. Macaulay and other young men of ability and advanced opinions, most of whom had adopted the views of Jeremy Bentham.' Villiers was secretary of the Board of Control from 18 May 1831 to his death on 3 Dec. 1832, when he was succeeded by Macaulay.

NOTE P, p. 183. Cf. Charles Grant to Bentinck, 25 Dec. 1833: Bentinck MSS: 'One of the points most contested in the course of the Bill thro' both Houses was the giving Councils to the Governments. The opposition Lords, especially the Duke of Wellington, urged the necessity of Councils most violently; and were in this matter no less strongly supported by Lord Wellesley. With the late Chairs I should probably have been obliged to yield and agree to have local Councils both at Agra and Fort William. But the change of Chairs enabled me to carry the proposals of confining the Councils to Bombay and Madras. For the last observation I allude to what passed after the Bill became Law.' For this question and an account of the passage of the Charter Bill, cf. H. H. Wilson, *History of British India from 1805 to 1835* (1838), vol. iii, pp. 370–94.

NOTE Q, p. 187. Judicial Despatch to Bengal, 20 Dec. (No. 11) 1833, para 10: 'Unless the distinction between the two [original and appellate jurisdiction] be preserved, your new system will be violated in its leading principle, and its failure is to be apprehended. When the parties in an original suit have been required to join issue with precision and simplicity and when the points in dispute have been distinctly ascertained and recorded by the Court of primary jurisdiction, the appellant should not be permitted to refer the whole case for what is virtually a new trial before the appellate tribunal, but should be compelled to specify either the point of law or the point of fact which he may allege to have been wrongfully decided against him by the original tribunal, and to that point only should the attention of the superior Court be directed. The Appellate Court should not try a cause over again on the perusal of evidence, which was produced before the Original Court, but should merely decide the point or points of law or of fact upon which an express appeal has been made to its jurisdiction.'

NOTE R, p. 202. Macaulay, Minute, 17 April 1835: Ind. Judic. Proc., 11 May 1835, No. 12 (Board's Collections, vol. 1555, No. 63502, f. 108). Macaulay objected to the exclusion of rent suits from the jurisdiction of the Court, and to the exemption of houses and lands from the operation of its process of execution. For Bentham's opposition to the distinction made beween real and personal property, cf. 'Principles of Penal Law', *Works*, vol. i, p. 508; 'Rationale of Judicial Evidence', *Works*, vol. vi, pp. 543–5; 'Equity Dispatch Court Bill', *Works*, vol. iii, p. 390. The provision that suits for sums larger than 80 rupees should be taken down in writing on the demand of either party, Macaulay regarded as pointless. He used precisely the same argument as Bentham against any pecuniary classification of suits; para. 9. Cf. Bentham, 'Judicial Establishment', *Works*, vol. iv, p. 333; 'Codification Proposal', ibid., p. 541.

NOTE S, p. 219. Macaulay, Speech, 10 July 1833: *Complete Works*, vol. xi, p. 582. Cf. Bentham (*c.* 1782): Bentham MSS.; cited Prof. Vesey-Fitzgerald, *Jeremy Bentham and the Law*, p. 222, who points out the analogy: 'That a complete and explicit body/code/system of laws . . . is the greatest blessing any country can possess is a truth I suppose there will be no occasion to demonstrate: that the British possessions in Indostan have at present a more particular need of such a system is what your Lordship, I imagine . . . is fully sensible of. . . .' Cf. James Mill, *History of British India*, vol. v, p. 479: 'A system of law, which would really afford the benefits of law to the Indian people, would confer upon them unspeakable benefits. It is perhaps the only great political blessing which they are as yet capable of receiving.' Mill seems the more likely source. It will be remembered that Macaulay in his speech spoke of Mill's *History* as 'the greatest historical work which has appeared in our language since Gibbon'.

NOTE T, p. 220. Bentham, 'View of a Complete Code of Laws', *Works*, vol. iii. Cf. Bentham, 'Papers on Codification', *Works*, vol. iv, pp. 526–7: 'The *penal* is the branch of law, with which in contradistinction to the *civil*, I in a manner took it for granted that it would be deemed most proper to commence. Reasons are obvious and seem conclusive. In the penal branch, for instance, circumstances of universal growth have place in a larger proportion than in that other. On that account it lies, in a more extensive degree, within the competence of a foreign hand. In the penal branch, too, changes to any extent may be made, and—so they be but for the better in other respects—neither danger nor alarm be produced by the change.'

NOTE U, p. 225. Rankin, *Background to Indian Law*, pp. 204–6. But Whitley Stokes, *The Anglo-Indian Codes*, 1887 edn., vol. i, pp. xii–xxii, denied that the idea was abandoned suddenly, and held that the successive Law Commissioners always acknowledged the ideal of a completely codified civil law. The Second Law Commission reported in 1856 against codifying the Muslim and Hindu law; the Third Commission never considered the prospect; and it was only with the Fourth Commission of 1879 headed by Whitley Stokes that the proposal was again actively considered. The Fourth Commission deferred the question, however, in order to codify the law of persons. There the matter rested for the remainder of British rule; cf. B. K. Acharyya, *Codification in British India* (Tagore Law Lectures, 1912), 1914, pp. 65 et seq; cf. also Sir C. Ilbert, *Legislative Methods and Forms*, chap. viii.

NOTE V, p. 226. S. G. Vesey-Fitzgerald, *Jeremy Bentham and the Law*, p. 225. Professor Fitzgerald says that this was the method advocated by Bentham in his 'Essay on the Influence of Time and Place in Matters of Legislation', *Works*, vol. i, pp. 171 et seq. This somewhat misrepresents Bentham. Professor Fitzgerald does not, however, support Fitzjames Stephen and Pollock in their assertion that the Penal Code was substantially the criminal law of England 'freed from all technicalities and ambiguities, systematically arranged and modified in a few particulars'. He concludes happily: 'Is it irreverent to suggest that English Criminal Law "freed from all technicalities and ambiguities and systematically arranged", has undergone such a metamorphosis as to be an entirely new thing?'

NOTE W, p. 229. Cf. Bentham, 'View of a Complete Code of Laws' (published by Dumont in 1802 as part of the *Traités de Législation*), *Works*, vol. iii, p. 174:
'The following is the catalogue of the general titles which ought to be treated of in the penal code:

1. Of persons subject to the Law.
2. Of negative and positive offences.
3. Of principal and accessory offences.
4. Of co-delinquents—that is, associates in committing crimes.
5. Of grounds of justification.
6. Of grounds of aggravation.
7. Of grounds of extenuation.
8. Of grounds of exemption.
9. Of punishments.
10. Of indemnification, and other satisfactions to the party injured.'

Because of the uncertainty of English statute law on the question, Macaulay omitted defining the local and personal extent of the Code; this was added in the final version of 1860. Macaulay dealt with most of the headings given by Bentham and compressed them within four general chapters with which the Code commences.

NOTE X, p. 231. Ibid., p. 265. Whitley Stokes, *Anglo-Indian Codes*, vol. i, pp. xxiii, described the rules of draftsmanship used in the Indian codes. They have an obvious sympathy with Bentham's teachings on the question: . . .'their chief rules have been: that all matter of the same kind should be thrown together: that the simpler proposition should precede the more complex: that procedure should be dealt with according to the chronological order in which ordinary events occur. . . . As to the wording: that each sentence should have only one enacting verb: that the same word should be used to express the same thing: that nouns should be used in preference to pronouns: that technical expressions should not be used unnecessarily: that "shall" should be used only when the law is directory, that "may" should be used only when the law is permissive.'

Note Y, p. 231. Whitley Stokes, op. cit., p. xxiii. Cf. Rankin, op. cit., p. 203: 'Whether much of the clarity of the Code is due to the employment of illustrations—*a device suggested by Bentham*—may be doubted' (my italics). Many other writers repeat this, presumably on Whitley Stokes's authority; cf. Sir Francis Oldfield, *Cambridge History of India*, vol. vi, p. 388; J. Chailley, *Administrative Problems of British India*, 1910, p. 361. Whitley Stokes referred to Bentham, 'Specimen of a Penal Code', *Works*, vol. i, pp. 164 et seq.; but there is no actual use of illustrations in this. Pollock, *Law of Partnership*, ed. J. W. C. Turner, 1947, p. iv, could not find 'in earlier writers, including Bentham, more than slight rudiments of the idea, and its first distinct appearance was certainly in the draught of the Penal Code'. Illlustrations are given in *Principles of Morals and Legislation*, but there is no indication of using them in the text of laws. 'Examples' are mentioned occasionally; cf. 'Papers on Codification', *Works*, vol. iv, pp. 48–49. J. S. Mill gave the whole credit to Macaulay: 'Simple as this contrivance is, it escaped the sagacity of Bentham, so fertile in ingenious combinations of detail': article on Indian Penal Code, *Westminster Review*, vol. xxix (1838), p. 402. For Mill's authorship cf. MacMinn, Hainds, & MacCrimmon, *Bibliography of Published Writings of John Stuart Mill*, p. 51.

BIOGRAPHICAL NOTES

BIRD, ROBERT MERTTINS (1788–1853). Arrived India, 1808. Held sub-ordinate judicial appointments. Appointed Commissioner of Revenue in Gorakhpur Division. Member of Board of Revenue, North-Western Pro-vinces, 1832. In charge of revenue settlement of North-Western Provinces, 1833–41. After retirement in 1842 took active interest in work of Church Missionary Society.

CAMPBELL, SIR GEORGE (1824–92). Various civil appointments in the North-Western Provinces, 1843–51. Furlough in England; published *Modern India* (1852) and appeared before Parliamentary Committee on India, 1851–4. Further service in North-Western Provinces, 1854–7. Second civil commis-sioner, Oudh, 1857–62. Judge of Calcutta High Court, serving on various commissions, including Bengal Famine Inquiry of 1867, 1862–7. Chief Commissioner, Central Provinces, 1867–8. Furlough in England; published *The Irish Land* (1869), and *Tenure of Land in India* (1870) for the Cobden Club, 1868–70. Lieutenant-Governor of Bengal, 1871–4. Liberal M.P. for Kirkaldy, 1875–92.

ELPHINSTONE, HON. MOUNTSTUART (1779–1859). Appointed to Bengal Civil Service, 1796. Assistant to Governor-General's Agent at Peshwa's Court, Poona. Military attaché under Arthur Wellesley at Assaye, 1803. Resident at Nagpur. Led embassy to Shaj Shuja at Kabul, 1808. Resident at Poona, 1810–16. Took prominent part in final Mahratta War and ensuing political settlement, 1817–18. Governor of Bombay, 1819–27.

LYALL, SIR ALRED COMYN (1835–1911). Appointed as assistant at Buland-shahr, North-Western Provinces; and took active part in Mutiny operations, 1856–57. Commissioner of Nagpur, and then of West Berar, 1865–73. Home Secretary to Government of India, 1873–4. Governor-General's Agent in Rajputana, 1874–8. Foreign Secretary to Government of India, 1878–81. Lieutenant-Governor, North-Western Provinces, 1881–7. Member of India Council in London, 1887–1902.

MACKENZIE, HOLT (1787–1876). Educated Haileybury, 1806–7. Arrived in India, 1808. Secretary to Bengal Government in Territorial Department, 1817–31. Returned to England, 1831. Privy Councillor, Commissioner of Board of Control, 1832–4. Charles Grant, as President of Board, would have appointed him to the Council of the newly modelled Government of India, but he was unable to communicate with Mackenzie in time (Grant to Bentinck, 25 Dec. 1833: Bentinck MSS.). Crawfurd (author of *The Indian Archipelago*) thought Mackenzie's evidence before the Select Committee on the subject of the Company's trading functions 'was excellent and as far as the Company is concerned murderous' (E. Ryan to Bentinck, 5 July 1832;

Bentinck MSS.). Grant told Bentinck that the Chairs 'had a violent prejudice and hatred against him' (Grant to Bentinck, 25 Dec. 1833: Bentinck MSS.).

MAINE, SIR HENRY (1822–88). Regius Professor of Civil Law, Cambridge, 1847–54. *Ancient Law*, 1861. Law Member of the Government of India, 1862–9. Appointed member of India Council, London, 1871. Corpus Professor of Jurisprudence, Oxford, 1869–78. *Village Communities*, 1871. *Early History of Institutions*, 1875. Master of Trinity Hall, Cambridge, 1877. *Dissertation on Early Law and Custom*, 1883. *Popular Government*, 1885.

MALCOLM, SIR JOHN (1769–1833). Entered Company's service, 1782. Envoy to Persia, 1799–1801. Private Secretary to Lord Wellesley, 1801–2. Private Secretary to Arthur Wellesley (Wellington) in Mahratta War, 1803–4. On mission to Teheran, 1808–10. On furlough in England, 1812–16. Took part in military action and subsequent diplomatic negotiations of last Mahratta War, 1817–18. In charge of political relations in Central India. Left India, 1821. Governor of Bombay, 1827–30.

METCALFE, CHARLES THEOPHILUS, *1st Baron* (1785–1846). Arrived Bengal, 1801. On Wellesley's personal staff, 1802. Political officer under Lake in Mahratta War, 1804. Assistant to Resident at Delhi, 1806. On special mission to Ranjit Singh, 1808. Resident at Delhi, 1811–19. Resident at Hyderabad, 1820–5. Resident at Delhi, 1825–7. Member of Supreme Council, 1827–34. Lieutenant-Governor of Agra, 1834. Acting Governor-General, 1835–6. Lieutenant-Governor of North-Western Provinces, 1836–8. Governor of Jamaica, 1839–42. Governor-General of Canada, 1843–5.

MUNRO, SIR THOMAS (1761–1827). Arrived Madras, 1780. Served against Hyder Ali, 1780–4. Assisted in forming civil administration of the Baramahal, 1792–9. Principal Collector of the Ceded Districts (ceded by Hyderabad), where he further developed the *ryotwar* system of land revenue settlement, 1800–7. On furlough in England where his views exercised considerable influence on the Home Authorities, 1807–14. Returned to India as head of commission to reorganize judicial and police system of Madras Presidency, 1814. Governor of Madras, 1819–27.

ROSS, ALEXANDER (1777–18??). Arrived in India, 1795–6. Judge of Provincial Court of Appeal at Bareilly, 1811–20. Resident at Delhi, 1820–3. Judge of Sadr Court, 1825–33. Member of Council, 1833–5. Governor of Agra, 1835–6. President of Council and Deputy Governor of Bengal, 1837–8. Retired from service, 1838.

STRACHEY, SIR JOHN (1823–1907). Son of Edward Strachey (see p. 50). Educated Haileybury, 1840. Appointed Bengal Civil Service, 1842. Held various administrative posts in North-Western Provinces, including that of Collector of Moradabad. Judicial Commissioner, Central Provinces, 1862. Chief Commissioner of Oudh, 1866. Member of Viceroy's Council, 1868. Lieutenant-Governor, North-Western Provinces, 1874. Finance Member,

BIOGRAPHICAL NOTES   333

Government of India, 1876. Left India, 1880. Knighted 1872. G.C.S.I., 1878. J. S. Cotton said of Strachey and his brother, Sir Richard: 'By inheritance and education they belonged to the school of philosophic radicalism represented in John Stuart Mill'. (*D.N.B.* 2nd Suppl. vol. iii, p. 438.)

THOMASON, JAMES (1804–53). Son of Indian missionary, Thomas Thomason, and godson of Charles Simeon, the Cambridge Evangelical. Schoolfellow of Macaulay at Little Shelford, near Cambridge. Also Haileybury. Arrived Calcutta, 1822. Magistrate and Collector, Azamgarh, 1832–7. Secretary to Government of North-Western Provinces, 1837–42. Foreign Secretary to Government of India, 1842. Lieutenant-Governor, North-Western Provinces, 1843–53. Cf. Sir R. Temple, *James Thomason*, Oxford, 1893.

TREVELYAN, SIR CHARLES EDWARD (1807–86). Appointed assistant to Metcalfe at Delhi, 1827. Secretary to Government in Political Department, 1831–6. Married Macaulay's sister, Hannah More, 1834. Secretary to Sadr Board of Revenue, 1836–7. Returned to England, 1838. Served in the Treasury, 1840–59. Joint author with Sir Stafford Northcote of report on organization of the permanent Civil Service, 1853. Governor of Madras, 1859–60. Finance Member of Government of India, 1862–5.

WINGATE, SIR GEORGE (1812–79). Educated Addiscombe. Served in Bombay Engineers from 1829. Career spent in Bombay Revenue Survey of which he was Superintendent from 1838. K.C.S.I., 1866.

BIBLIOGRAPHY

(Short titles used in text and notes are placed in brackets)

1. MANUSCRIPTS SOURCES

A. BRITISH MUSEUM, LONDON

Earl of Auckland's papers in Additional Manuscripts (Auckland MSS., Add. MSS.).

B. INDIA OFFICE LIBRARY, COMMONWEALTH RELATIONS OFFICE, LONDON

(All records are 'Board's' Copies unless otherwise stated)

Appendix to Court Minutes, vol. 5.
Bengal Revenue Consultations.
Board's Collections, vols. 1353, 1555, 1559, 1760.
Bombay Despatches, 'Court's Copies'.
Bombay Revenue Consultations.
European Manuscripts. 676 MS. Eur. D.310.
Home Miscellaneous Series (Home Misc. Ser.), vols. 734, 832.
Indian Legislative Consultations or Proceedings (Ind. Leg. Cons./Proc.).
Indian Revenue Consultations (Ind. Rev. Cons.).
Judicial Despatches to Bengal.
Judicial Despatches to India.
Judicial Letters from Bengal.
Judicial Letters from India.
Legislative Despatches to India.
Personal Records.
Revenue Despatches to Bengal.
Revenue Despatches to Bombay.
Revenue Despatches to Madras.
Revenue Letters from Bengal.
Revenue Letters from Bombay.

C. NOTTINGHAM UNIVERSITY LIBRARY

Lord William Bentinck's Papers in the Portland Collection (Bentinck MSS.).

D. TRINITY COLLEGE LIBRARY, CAMBRIDGE

Macaulay Correspondence—(by kind permission of Dr. G. M. Trevelyan, O.M.).

E. UNIVERSITY COLLEGE LIBRARY, LONDON

Bentham's papers (Bentham MSS.).

2. PRINTED OFFICIAL SOURCES

Acts of the Indian Government, 1834–49, with Index. India Office Library.
Administration Report of the N. W. Provinces and Oude, 1882–3.
A Penal Code Prepared by the Indian Law Commissioners, Calcutta, 1837.
Bombay Administration Report, 1882–3.
COLVIN, A., *Memorandum on the Revision of Land Revenue Settlements in the North-Western Provinces, 1860–72,* Calcutta, 1872.
Directions for Revenue Officers in the North-Western Provinces of the Bengal Presidency . . . , Promulgated under the Authority of the Hon. The Lieutenant-Governor, Agra, November 1, 1829, Calcutta, 1850.
DODWELL, E. and MILES, J. C., *List of Hon. East India Company's Bombay Civil Servants,* London, 1839.
East India Register and Directory, especially for 1821.
HASTINGS, LORD, and OTHERS, *Judicial System of India,* Calcutta, 1815.
Land Revenue Policy of the Indian Government, Calcutta, 1902.
MILL, J. S., *Memorandum of the Improvements in the Administration of India during the last Thirty Years,* 1858, published anon., India Office Library Tract, No. 790.
Parliamentary Papers (P.P.).
Report of the Indian Taxation Enquiry Committee, 1924–5, Madras, 1926.
Reports on the Revenue Settlement of the N.W. Provinces under Regulation IX, 1833, 2 vols., Benares, 1862–3.
SHARP, H., and RICHEY, J. (ed.), *Selections from the Educational Records of the Government of India,* 2 vols., Calcutta, 1920–2.
Selections of Papers at the East India House relating to Revenue, Police, and Civil and Criminal Justice under the Company's Government in India, 4 vols., London, 1820–6.
Selections from the Records of the Bombay Government, New Series (N.S.):
   Vol. cli, 'Papers relating to the Revision of the Rates of Assessment on the Expiration of the first Settlement in the Old Indapur, Bhimthari, Pabal, & Haveli Talukas of the Poona Collectorate', Bombay, 1877.
   Vol. dxxxii, 'Papers relating to the Joint Report of 1847', Bombay, 1917.
Selections from the Records of the Madras Government, Old Series (O.S.):
   Vol. liii, 'Papers relating to the General Revenue Survey of the Madras Presidency', Madras, 1858.
   Vol. lxxiv, 'Papers relating to the General Revenue Survey of the Madras Presidency, Vol. II', Madras, 1862.
Selections from the Records of the Government of India, No. lxxxix, 'Minute by the Hon. J. Fitzjames Stephen on the Administration of Justice in British India', Calcutta, 1872.
Selections from the Records of the N.W. Provinces: Mr. Thomason's Despatches, 2 vols., Calcutta, 1856.
Selections from the Revenue Records of the N.W. Provinces, vol. i, *1818–20,* Calcutta, 1866; vol. ii, *1822–33,* Allahabad, 1872.
The Regulations and Laws . . . of . . . the Presidency of . . . Bengal, 1793–1834, 9 vols., Calcutta, 1827–35.

3. OTHER WORKS

ACHARYYA, B. K., *Codification in British India. Tagore Law Lectures, 1912,* 1914.

ANNAN, NOEL, *Leslie Stephen,* London, 1951.

ARBUTHNOT, A. J., *Sir Thomas Munro: Selections from his Minutes and other Official Writings,* 2 vols., London, 1881.

AUSTIN, JOHN, *The Province of Jurisprudence Determined,* ed. H. L. A. HART, London, 1954.

BADEN-POWELL, B. H., *Land Systems of British India,* 3 vols., Oxford, 1892.

BAIN, A., *James Mill,* London, 1882.

BALFOUR, LADY BETTY, *The History of Lord Lytton's Indian Administration, 1876–80,* London, 1899.

BENTHAM, J., *The Works of Jeremy Bentham,* ed. J. BOWRING, 11 vols., London, 1843.

—— *The Theory of Legislation,* ed. C. K. OGDEN, London, 1931. Another edition, ed. C. ATKINSON, London, 1914.

BRIGHT, JOHN, *Public Addresses,* ed. J. E. T. ROGERS, London, 1879.

BUCKLAND, C. T., *Bengal under the Lieutenant-Governors,* Calcutta, 1901.

BURKE, EDMUND, *Works,* 8 vols., London, 1852.

CAMPBELL, SIR GEORGE, *India as it may be,* London, 1853.

—— *Memoirs of my Indian Career,* 2 vols., London, 1893.

CARLYLE, THOMAS, *Reminiscences,* 2 vols., London, 1887.

CAVENAGH, F. A., *James and John Stuart Mill on Education,* London, 1931.

CHAILLEY, J., *Administrative Problems of British India,* London, 1910.

CHOKSEY, R. D., *Economic History of the Bombay Deccan and Karnatak, 1818–65,* 2 vols., Bombay, 1945.

COLEBROOKE, T. E., *Life of Hon. Mountstuart Elphinstone,* 2 vols., London, 1884.

CORNWALLIS, CHARLES, 1ST MARQUIS, *Correspondence of Marquis Cornwallis,* ed. CHARLES ROSS, 2 vols., London, 1859.

CRAWFURD, J., *A View of the Present State and Future Prospects of Free Trade and Colonization of India,* 2nd ed., London, 1829.

CURZON, G. N., 1ST MARQUIS, *Lord Curzon in India, 1898–1905* [Indian Speeches], ed. SIR T. RALEIGH, London, 1906.

CUST, R. N., *Pictures of Indian Life,* London, 1881.

DHARKER, C. D., *Lord Macaulay's Legislative Minutes,* Madras, 1946.

DURAND, SIR H. M., *Life of Sir A. C. Lyall,* London, 1913.

DUTT, R. C., *Economic History of India in the Victorian Age,* 7th edn., London, 1950.

FORREST, G. W., *Selections from the Minutes and other Official Writings of the Hon. Mountstuart Elphinstone,* London, 1884.

—— *Selections from the State Papers of the Governors-General of India: Lord Cornwallis,* 2 vols., Oxford, 1926.

GLEIG, G. R., *Life of Sir Thomas Munro,* 3 vols., London, 1830.

GRANT, C., *Observations on the State of Society among the Asiatic Subjects of Great Britain, particularly with respect to Morals; and on the Means of Improving It.* Written chiefly in the year 1792. Privately printed, London, 1797.

HALÉVY, É., *A History of the English People in the Nineteenth Century*, 3 vols., London, 1926.

—— *The Growth of Philosophic Radicalism*, London, 1934.

HAZLITT, W., *The Plain Speaker* (Everyman Library, No. 814), London, 1928.

HOWSE, E. H., *Saints in Politics*, London, 1952.

HUNTER, SIR W. W., *Life of the Earl of Mayo*, 2 vols., London, 1875.

—— *The Indian Empire*, London, 1892.

ILBERT, SIR C., *The Government of India*, Oxford, 1898.

—— *Legislative Methods and Forms*, Oxford, 1901.

JONES, R., *Essay on the Distribution of Wealth and on the Sources of Taxation, Part I, Rent*, London, 1831.

—— *Literary Remains of Richard Jones*, ed. W. WHEWELL, London, 1859.

KAYE, SIR J. W., *Administration of the East India Company*, London, 1853.

—— *Life and Correspondence of Charles, Lord Metcalfe*, 2 vols., London, 1854.

—— *Selections from the Papers of Lord Metcalfe*, London, 1855.

—— *Life and Correspondence of Sir John Malcolm*, 2 vols., London, 1856.

—— *Christianity in India*, London, 1859.

KEETON, G. W., and SCHWARZENBERGER, G., *Jeremy Bentham and the Law*, London, 1948.

KNORR, K. E., *British Colonial Theories, 1570–1850*, Toronto, 1944.

LAURIE, DAVID, *Hints Regarding the East India Monopoly—Respectfully Submitted to the British Legislature*, Glasgow, 1813.

LESTER, W., *The Happy Era of One Hundred Millions of the Human Race, or the Merchant, Manufacturer, and Englishman's Recognised Right to an Unlimited Trade with India*, London, 1813.

LYALL, SIR A. C., *Asiatic Studies*, 2nd edn., 2 vols., London, 1899.

—— *The Rise and Expansion of the British Dominion in India*, 5th edn., London, 1910.

MACAULAY, T. B., *Miscellaneous Writings and Speeches*, London, 1889.

—— *The Complete Works of Lord Macaulay*, Albany Edition, 12 vols., London, 1898.

MACMINN, N., HAINDS, J. R., and MACCRIMMON, J. M., (ed.) *Bibliography of the Published Writings of John Stuart Mill*, Northwestern University, Evanston, Illinois, 1945.

MAINE, SIR H. S., *Village Communities in the East and West*, 3rd edn., London, 1876.

MALCOLM, SIR J., *Central India*, 2 vols., London, 1823.

—— *The Political History of India*, 2 vols., London, 1826.

—— *The Government of India*, London, 1833.

MALTHUS, T. R., *The Nature and Progress of Rent*, London, 1815.

—— *Principles of Political Economy*, London, 1820.

MAYNE, J. D., *On Hindu Law and Usage*, 7th edn., Madras.

MILL, JAMES, *Commerce Defended*, London, 1808.

—— *The History of British India*, 2nd edn., 6 vols., London, 1820.

—— *The Elements of Political Economy*, London, 1821.

—— *An Essay on Government*, ed. E. BARKER, Cambridge, 1937.

MILL, J. S., *Principles of Political Economy*, ed. W. J. ASHLEY, London, 1909.
—— *Utilitarianism, Liberty, and Representative Government*, Everyman edn., London, 1947.
—— *Autobiography*, ed. H. J. LASKI, World's Classics, repr. 1949.
MORLEY, W. H., *Analytical Digest of Reported Cases in India*, 2 vols., London, 1849.
—— *The Administration of Justice in British India*, London, 1858.
MORRIS, H., *Life of Charles Grant*, London, 1904.
PACKE, M. ST. JOHN, *Life of John Stuart Mill*, London, 1954.
PHILIPS, C. H., *The East India Company, 1784–1834*, London, 1940.
POLLOCK, SIR FREDERICK, *Law of Partnership*, ed. J. W. C. TURNER, London, 1947.
PRINSEP, JOHN, *Suggestions on Freedom of Commerce and Navigation—More Especially in Reference to the East-India Trade*, London, 1823.
RANKIN, SIR G. C., *Background to Indian Law*, Cambridge, 1946.
RICARDO, D., *Principles of Political Economy and Taxation*, London, 1821.
—— *Notes on Malthus*, ed. J. HOLLANDER, London, 1928.
—— *Works*, ed. R. SRAFFA, 10 vols., Cambridge, 1951–2.
RONALDSHAY, EARL OF, *Life of Lord Curzon*, 3 vols., London, 1928.
SMITH, ADAM, *The Wealth of Nations*, ed. E. CANNAN, 2 vols., London, 1904.
SMITH, GEORGE, *Life of Alexander Duff*, 2 vols., London, 1879.
SMITH, R. BOSWORTH, *Life of Lord Lawrence*, 2 vols., London, 1885.
SPEAR, PERCIVAL, *The Nabobs*, London, 1932.
—— *Twilight of the Mughuls*, Cambridge, 1951.
STEPHEN, SIR J. F., *History of the Criminal Law of England*, 3 vols., London, 1883.
—— *Liberty, Equality, Fraternity*, 2nd edn., London, 1874.
STEPHEN, SIR L., *Life of Sir James Fitzjames Stephen*, London, 1895.
—— *The English Utilitarians*, 3 vols., London, 1900.
STOKES, SIR W., *The Anglo-Indian Codes*, 2 vols., Oxford, 1887.
STRACHEY, SIR J., *India*, London, 1888.
THOMPSON, E. J., and GARRATT, G. T., *Rise and Fulfilment of British Rule in India*, London, 1934.
TREVELYAN, C. E., *On the Education of the People of India*, London, 1838.
TREVELYAN, SIR G. O., *The Competition Wallah*, London, 1864.
—— *Life and Letters of Lord Macaulay*, London, 1908.
VENN, H., *The Complete Duty of Man*, 5th edn., London, 1798.
WARNER, SIR WILLIAM LEE-, *Life of the Marquess of Dalhousie*, 2 vols., London, 1904.
WILBERFORCE, R. and S., *Life of William Wilberforce*, 5 vols., London, 1838.
WILSON, H. H., *History of British India from 1805 to 1835*, 3 vols., London, 1838.
YOUNG, GAVIN, *An Inquiry into the Expediency of Applying the Principles of Colonial Policy to the Government of India & of Effecting an Essential Change in its Landed Tenures, &c.*, published anon., London, 1822.
—— *A Further Inquiry into the Expediency ... &c.*, London, 1828.
YOUNG, G. M., *Victorian England: Portrait of an Age*, London, 1936, reprinted 1949.

INDEX

Acts, Indian: IV of 1835, 202; quoted as example of Macaulay's drafting, 202 *n.* 2.
  X of 1835, 197.
  XI of 1836 ('Black Act'), 214.
  XIV of 1836, 239.
  XXIV of 1837, 238.
  XXV of 1837, 216.
  VIII of 1859 (Civil Procedure Code), 259.
  X of 1859, 121, 268.
  XLV of 1860 (Penal Code), 229.
  XXV of 1861 (Criminal Procedure Code), 262.
  Succession, of 1865, 263.
  Punjab Land Revenue, of 1871, 277.
  Evidence, of 1872, 264.
  North Western Provinces Land Revenue, 121, 277.
  Punjab Land Alienation, of 1900, 320.
Acts, Parliamentary: Charter, of 1833, *see* Charter Act of 1833.
  Charter, of 1853, *see* Charter Act of 1853.
  Indian Councils, of 1861, 257.
  Indian High Courts, of 1861, 264.
  Regulating, of 1773, 2.
Afghan War: 1st, 190, 243.
  2nd, 138.
Anderson, E., 217, 223.
Akbar, Emperor, principle of assessment, 95.
Anglicization, policy of: advocated: Evangelicals, 34–36; free-traders, 37–43; Macaulay, 44–46; Trevelyan, 46–47.
  influence on Cornwallis and Munro systems, 26.
  opposed by Hastings, 2, 35–36.
  origins, xiii.
  under Cornwallis, 3–7, 25–26.
  under Wellesley, 7–8.
Assimilation, policy of, *see* Anglicization.
Auckland, Earl of, 129, 130, 237, 238, 261.
  Governor-General, 190.
  lukewarm reformer, 239–40.

Austin, John: authoritarian utilitarianism of, 305, 306, 309.
  quoted, 293.
Baden Powell, B. H., cited, 103, 105.
Bayley, W. B., 150.
  scheme of judicial reform, 152, 155–7, 166–7, 191.
Bengal Code of Regulations (1793), 149, 174.
  Mackenzie on effects of, 161.
  principle of, approved by James Mill, 145.
Bengal Territories: administrative and judicial reform proposals: (Bayley) 152, 155–7, 166–7; (Mackenzie) 151–2, 161–2; (Ross) 156–61, 236–7.
  administrative and judicial reforms (1831), 163–4.
  collector and magistrate united (1831), 163–5.
  collector and magistrate separated, 237–8.
  collector and magistrate permanently reunited (1859), 239, 268.
  divisional commissioners instituted (1829), 151–5.
  early administrative system, 1–8.
  judicial system revised (1868), 265.
  lieutenant-governor system, 255–6, 270–2.
  (N.)W. Provinces separated from, 164.
  revenue system, *see* Bengal Permanent Settlement.
  See also Cornwallis System.
Bentham, Jeremy, xiv, 18, 48, 81, 322.
  administrative centralization, 73, 75, 173, 256.
  administrative theory, 72–74, 148, 170, 172, 173, 250–1, 256, 326 n. L.
  applicability of administrative ideas to India, 75.
  approves governor's power to overrule council, 172, 326 n. M.
  authentication of laws, 194.

Bentham, Jeremy (*contd.*)
  authoritarian bent, 60, 62–63, 72,
    309, 327 n. N.
  condemns boards, 73–74, 148, 162,
    163, 177, 325 n. G.
  death, 241.
  influence on: Bentinck, 51; Campbell,
    52; Dalhousie, 248–51; Elphin-
    stone, 50, 148–50; Fitzjames Ste-
    phen, 273–4, 278, 290, 297, 301;
    Indian administrative system, 155,
    163, 245–8; Indian codes, 219–33,
    259–63, 328 n. T, 330 nn. X, Y;
    Indian judicial system, 166–7, 264–
    7; Indian Legislative Council,
    176–9; Indian prisons, 149–50,
    217–18; Macaulay, 165, 179, 191–
    2, 197, 198–201, 203–9; Macken-
    zie, 95, 162, 170–3, 325 n. I; Penal
    Code, 219–33, 329 n. W, 330 n. Y;
    Ross, 156, 165, 201, 211–12, 220,
    234–6; Young, 51–52, 116, 240.
  inspectability, 74, 152, 170, 188.
  'intercommunity of jurisdiction', 158,
    159, 205, 325 n. J.
  interest in India, 51–52, 140.
  judicial appeal, 74, 156, 160, 166,
    184–5, 187, 188, 206–8, 326 n. K.
  judicial evidence, 206, 207.
  jury, 170, 211.
  law and judicial organization, 70–77,
    146–7, 159, 202.
  law codes for India, 51, 146, 219–20.
  legislative drafting, 198–201, 229–31.
  legislative procedure, 177–8, 194–5.
  omnicompetent courts, 71, 158, 159,
    166, 186, 189, 205.
  opposes law taxes, 166, 167, 202, 208,
    211.
  opposes monetary classification of
    suits, 71, 156, 160, 166, 186, 202,
    204.
  opposes separation of powers, 72, 165,
    324 n. F.
  oral pleadings, 71, 186, 187, 206, 259.
  political theory, 67, 293–5, 297.
  prison discipline, 218.
  quoted on James Mill's ambition
    for India, 147.
  real and personal property, 202,
    328 n. R.
  separates executive from controlling
    functions, 74, 152, 170.

  single-seated judges, 71, 73, 186, 201,
    202.
  Works: *Codification Proposal*, 177,
    201; *Constitutional Code*, 72, 75,
    160, 165, 170, 173, 177, 188, 192,
    248, 281; *Influence of Time and
    Place in . . . Legislation*, 51, 69 n. 2,
    205, 235; *Judicial Establishment*,
    69, 147, 156, 203, 278; *Political
    Tactics*, 194; *Principles of Penal
    Law*, 218; *Principles of Morals and
    Legislation*, 228, 231; *Protest Against
    Law Taxes*, 211; *Rationale of Judi-
    cial Evidence*, 147; *Traités de
    Législation*, 228.
Bentinck, Lord William, 94, 132.
  administrative and judicial reforms,
    151, 154, 163–4, 166–7, 168.
  codification, 189–90.
  education India's panacea, 45.
  Governor-General, 150.
  leaves India, 190, 234, 239.
  Munro's influence on, 165.
  opposes strong centralization, 174.
  revenue administration, 101–3, 106,
    115, 121, 131, 133.
  Utilitarian influence on, 51, 102.
Bethune, J. Drinkwater, 261.
Bird, R. M., 155, 234, 238.
  anti-aristocratic bias, 115.
  assessment method, 105–6.
  biog., 331.
  fixing of rents, 121.
  paternalist influence on, 118.
Boards: in Cornwallis system, 148, 163.
  general issue in India, 162–3.
  opposed by: Bentham, 73–74, 148,
    162, 163, 177, 325 n. G; Dalhousie,
    250–1; Mackenzie, 151, 163; Mal-
    colm, 167–8; James Mill, 162.
  See also Provincial Boards of Revenue.
Bombay, revenue settlement of, 79.
  over-assessment, 134.
  Pringle's settlement, 94, 99–103, 122–
    3, 134.
  revised system, 103–4, 106–8, 122–8.
  system compared with N.W. Pro-
    vinces, 123–6.
  30-year settlements, 117.
Bracken, Thomas, 41.
Bright, John, 131, 251.
  Indian policy attacked by Stephen,
    298, 299, 304, 308.

Buck, Sir E., spokesman of high-revenue-demand school, 138–9.
Burke, Edmund, xvi, 2, 14, 15, 17, 23, 45, 163 n. 2, 308.

Calcutta Civil Finance Committee, 162–3, 169, 173.
Cameron, C. H., 217, 258.
  Ceylon reforms, 321.
  Penal Code, 261.
  'the last disciple of Jeremy Bentham', 223.
Campbell, Sir George, 122.
  biog., 331.
  on Benthamite teaching at Haileybury, 52.
  spokesman of enlightened paternalism, 254–5.
Canning, Earl, 239, 271.
Carlyle, T., 50, 308, 309.
Ceded and Conquered Provinces: administration, 154.
  become Western Provinces, xv n. 1, 97.
  Mackenzie's memo. on revenue settlement (1819), 94–97, 110–13.
  origin, xv.
  revenue settlement, 85–86, 91.
  See also Western Provinces; North-Western Provinces; United Provinces.
Ceded Districts (Madras), Munro's settlement of, 84.
Central Provinces: judiciary, 265.
  revenue system, 109.
  standard of assessment, 137.
Centralization: favoured by: Bentham, 73, 75, 173, 256; Campbell, 255; Curzon, 256; Lawrence, 271; Mackenzie, 170–1; James Mill, 175, 256; Stephen, 257, 303; Strachey, 257; Utilitarians, 25, 318.
  in Charter Act (1833), 25, 180–3.
  in Charter Act (1853), 255–7.
  opposed by: Bentinck, 174; Directors, 182; Elphinstone, 25, 173; Lyall, 318–19; Malcolm, 22, 173; Metcalfe, 173; Munro, 25, 173.
Chadwick, Sir Edwin, 60, 75, 79.
Charter Act of 1833, 64, 168, 169, 190, 240, 250, 253.
  framing, 179–83.

influenced by: Indian proposals, 173, 175; Macaulay, 180, 191, 327 n. O; Mackenzie, 180, 327 n. O; James Mill, 78, 180, 173, 195; Utilitarians, 25, 180, 327 n. O.
  provisions, 182–3.
Charter Act of 1853, provisions, 255–6.
Clapham Sect, xii, 28, 36.
  See also Evangelicals.
Clive, Robert (Lord Clive): administrative policy, 1, 3, 25, 35.
  attitude to India, xii, 54.
Code, Bombay (1827), 149, 174, 225.
Code of Civil Procedure (1859): Benthamite influence on, 259–60.
  drafting and provisions, 258–60.
  Macaulay's plan for, 203, 213, 221.
  Millett's preliminary work on, 189, 203, 220, 258.
Code of Criminal Procedure (1861), 285.
  Benthamite features, 262–3.
  drafting, 261.
  Macaulay's hopes for completion, 213.
Code, Penal: Benthamite influence on, 219–33, 329 n. W, 330 n. Y.
  chaos of unreformed law, 146.
  delay in enacting, 240, 261–2.
  draft published (1837), 239.
  framing of, 219–33.
  influence of English law on, 226–7, 258.
  judges consider a simple task, 63, 221.
  Macaulay's work on, 213, 214, 219–33, 262.
  J. S. Mill's approval of Macaulay's draft, 239.
Code Pénal (French): influence on Indian Penal Code, 226, 228.
Codification: Bentham, 51, 53, 70–71, 177–9, 219–20.
  Bentinck, 189–90.
  Campbell, 255.
  Charter Act (1833), 169, 181–3, 193.
  Elphinstone, 149, 174.
  Hindu law, see Law, Hindu.
  Indian codes, 258–64; see also under separate Codes.
  James Mill, 145, 146.
  Macaulay, 179, 213, 219 ff.
  Muslim law, see Law, Muslim.

Codification (*contd.*)
paternalist view, 173–4.
Second Law Commission, 258, 329
n. U.
Stephen, 275, 277–8.
Trevelyan, 254.
Collector: as district officer, 75, 164,
275.
commissioners established to control,
148, 151–5.
function in Bengal, 7, 83.
jurisdiction in rent cases, 121, 143,
151, 156.
powers under paternalist system,
21–22, 143–4.
separation from magistrate: effected, 7,
237–8; supported by Bengal school,
79; supported by Macaulay, 210;
supported by Ross, 158–8, 236–7.
united with magistrate: Bengal Territories, 102, 163–5, 239, 268;
Bombay, 148; Madras, 143; N.W.
Provinces, 9, 163–5; supported
by Dalhousie, 238–9; supported
by Mackenzie, 161–2; supported by
Stephen, 275; Utilitarian opinion
divided over, 165.
See *diagram*, 142–3.
Commissioners, Divisional: approved
by Metcalfe, 153.
extensive supervisory powers over
judicature proposed, 187–8.
in Mackenzie's administrative scheme,
151–2, 161–3.
instituted: Bengal Territories, 151–
5; Punjab, 243.
opposed by Ross, 159, 236, 238.
relieved of criminal jurisdiction, 163.
significance of, 154–5.
Commissioners of Revenue (and Circuit), see Commissioners, Divisional.
Cornwallis, Marquis: administrative
policy, 3–7, 25–26, 36, 140–1, 174.
See *also* Cornwallis System.
Cornwallis Code, see Bengal Code of
Regulations.
Cornwallis System: check and balance
in, 5, 148, 163.
inefficiency of, 75, 145–6, 151–2, 160.
influence of Evangelicals on, 27.
introduced into Madras, 141.
modified, 150, 164.

opposed by: Mackenzie, 160–1;
James Mill, 145–6; Munro, 141;
paternalists, 9, 14–16, 19–22, 148.
passivity of, 234.
supported by: Bengal school, 150–1;
European merchants, 60–61, 79,
86, 128; Macaulay, 193; Ross, 79,
234–7.
Utilitarian opinion divided over, 78–
80.
See *also* Permanent Settlement of
Bengal.
Crawfurd, John: anglicist attitude, 42.
attacks revenue system, 62, 130.
spokesman of European merchants,
62 n. 4, 324 n. E.
Cromer, Earl of (Sir Evelyn Baring),
policy of, 310, 312, 315–17, 319–
20.
Curzon, G. N., Marquis, 257, 317, 318.
imperialism of, 310–11.
modifies traditional land revenue
policy, 317–18.
Cust, Robert: quoted on Punjab system,
247.

Dalhousie, Marquis of: advocates union
of collector and magistrate, 238–9.
character, 248–9.
Indian codes, 259, 261.
Utilitarian character of his ad-
ministration, 248–51.
Delhi Territory: John Lawrence trained
in, 243.
Metcalfe Resident of, 9, 144.
Metcalfe's paternalist system in, 144,
148, 153, 154, 160.
W. Fraser's assessment method in, 98,
109.
District Officer, see Collector.
Dundas, H. (Lord Melville), 51.
Dutt, R. C., 317.

East India Company: abolition of commercial functions (1833), 40.
change in Indian administration after
1834, 49–50.
commercial policy, 37–38.
institutes first chair of political
economy, 87.
loss of commercial monopoly (1813),
xiv.

policy attacked by: Evangelicals, 35; free traders, 38–40; Adam Smith, xii.

renewal of Charter: (1813), xiv, 18, 33, 34, 37; (1833), 150, 179–80.

Education: controversy of 1835, 45, 57, 196.

Dalhousie's policy, 251–2.

Despatch of 1854, 251–2.

key to Indian problem: Bentinck, 45; Evangelicals, 32–34; Liberals, 45–47, 131, 251–3, 283; Macaulay, 45–46; Trevelyan, 46–47, 253, 283.

James Mill disagrees with Liberal stress on, 56–58.

paternalist policy, 252, 254.

Elphinstone, Hon. Mountstuart: biog., 9, 331.

influence on his administration: of Bentham, 50, 148–50; of Munro, 9, 86, 148.

opposes administrative centralization and uniformity, 24, 25 n. 1, 173–4.

Ellenborough, Earl of, 169.

Empson, William: Benthamite teaching at Haileybury, 52.

Evangelicals (-ism): alliance with commercial interests, 34, 40.

character, 27–31.

connexion with India, xii, 28, 37.

Indian policy, 30–35.

influence on: imperialism, 307–9; liberalism, xiv.

opposed to E. I. Co.'s policy, 35.

Famine Commission (1880), 138.

Fifth Report of 1812, 4, 56, 86.

Fraser, William: net-produce method of assessment, 98, 109.

Free trade(rs), xii, 40, 283.

advocate assimilation, 37.

oppose E. I. Co.'s policy, 38–40.

See also Merchants, European.

Gladstone, W. E., 289, 290.

Goldsmid, H. E., 103, 107, 122–5.

Grant, Charles, xii, xv, 27, 28, 37, 40, 45, 53, 57.

Evangelical attitude to India, 29–35.

Grant, Charles, the Younger (Lord Glenelg): character, 327 n. O.

framing of Charter Bill (1833), 179–82.

president of Board of Control, 179.

turns Whig, 40.

Grey, Sir Charles, 61.

Haileybury: Benthamite teaching at, 52.

Mackintosh, professor, 52.

Malthus, professor, 87.

Hastings, Warren, policy of, xii, 2–3, 25, 35–36, 39, 54.

Hazlitt, William: attacks Utilitarians, 48, 52, 59.

High Courts, Indian, 260, 279.

created, 264.

multiplication of, 266.

powers, 265.

Hill, David, 162, 173.

Hobbes, Thomas: Indian Leviathan, 321–2.

influence on: Stephen, 274, 293, 295, 297; Utilitarians, 293, 309.

Hobhouse, Sir Arthur, 301.

Hobhouse, J. C. (Lord Broughton), 240.

Ibbetson, Sir Denzil, 138–9.

Ilbert Bill, 288, 301.

Imperialism, intellectual origins of, 290, 298.

Johnston, Sir Alexander: advocates representative councils, 65.

advocates codified law, 174.

Joint Report of 1840 (Bombay), 107.

Jones, Richard: on ryot tenure, 135–6.

Jones, Sir William, code of Hindu law, 146, 174.

Judges, District (Bengal Territories): in Macaulay's scheme, 208.

in Mackenzie's scheme, 161–2.

power to refer appeals, 215–17.

reforms of 1829–31, 155, 166–7.

symbol of rule of law (Ross), 160.

under Cornwallis, 7.

See diagram, 142–3.

Kipling, Rudyard, imperialism of, 308.

quoted, 310.

Law Commission, First, 190, 253, 258.
  limited achievement of, 213–14, 223–4.
  Macaulay's over-optimistic pro-
    gramme for, 213, 221.
  Macaulay president, 193.
Law Commission, Second, 257–61,
  329 n. U.
Law, English: extension advocated by
  European merchants, 41.
  influence on: Penal Code, 226–7,
    329 n. V; other Indian codes, 226,
    258, 264.
  introduction of, 3, 145.
  opposed by James Mill, 60–61.
  Stephen's respect for, 278.
Law, Hindu: codification abandoned,
  225, 258, 329 n. U.
  criminal law digested at Bombay, 225.
  Elphinstone unable to codify, 149.
  Evangelical attitude to, 31–32.
  Halhed's translation, 3.
  Sir W. Jones's digest, 146, 174.
  of inheritance set aside at Bombay,
    125.
  power of testamentary disposition
    invades, 236 n. 1.
  Stephen rejects codification, 279.
  threat to, 3.
  Trevelyan advocates codification, 254.
Law, Muslim: basis of unreformed
  penal law, 223, 225, 261.
  codification, see under Law, Hindu.
Lawrence, Sir Henry, 17, 155, 245, 248,
  268, 282.
Lawrence, John (Lord Lawrence):
  anti-aristocratic bias, 17, 286.
  on Indian taxation, 316.
  proposes permanent settlement, 117.
  paternalist policy, 268–72, 282.
  Punjab system of, 155, 243–6, 248.
  Viceroy, 268, 270.
Legislative Council, Indian: advocated
  by: Bentinck, 174; Mackenzie,
    172–3; James Mill, 64, 176–9, 256,
    321.
  Dalhousie's development of, 251.
  despatch on procedure of, 195.
  establishment of (1833–4), 169, 179,
    183, 190.
  expanded, 253, 256–7.
  J. S. Mill unfavourable to Indian
    representation on, 251, 255, 298,
    321.

standing orders drafted by Macaulay,
  197.
Liberal-ism(-s): attitude to India, 40,
  43–47.
  authoritarian: Austin, 293, 305, 309;
    Bentham, 60, 62–63, 72, 234, 309,
    327 n. N; Cromer, 312; Dalhousie,
    248–51; James Mill, 293–4, 302;
    Stephen, 281–5, 288 ff.; Strachey,
    282–8, 300, 305.
  differences with Utilitarianism, 52,
    55 ff.
  early influence on India, xiv–xvi.
  education policy, 45–46, 57–58, 251–
    2.
  English crisis of 1886, 287, 289.
  orthodox: Bentham, 294–5, 297;
    Bright, 298, 299; Macaulay, xiv,
    xvi, 40, 43–46, 65, 191–3, 283, 320–
    1; James Mill, 295, 297; J. S. Mill,
    241–2, 291, 294–5, 297; Ross, 79,
    120, 234–7, 321; Trevelyan, 18,
    46–47, 239, 253–4.
  reconciled with paternalism: Camp-
    bell, 254–5; Mackenzie, 154, 273;
    Stephen, 273 ff., 281 ff.
Lieutenant-governors, system of, 175,
  273.
  advocated by: Campbell, 255; Law-
    rence, 270–1; Mackenzie, 162, 170–
    1; Trevelyan, 253.
  criticized, 270–2.
Livingston, E.: influence on Penal Code,
  226.
Lugard, Lord, 310.
Lyall, Sir Alfred, 312, 321.
  biog., 331.
  policy, 313–14, 315–17, 319–20.
Lytton, Earl of, 257, 282, 306.
  policy, 285–6, 289.
  Viceroy, 282.

Macaulay, T. B. (Lord Macaulay), xi,
  11, 40.
  appointed law member, 179, 184, 190,
    193.
  arrives in India (1834), 190, 196.
  attacks Utilitarians, 59–60, 130,
    191.
  Benthamite influence on, 191–2, 320–
    1.
  Benthamite influence on work as law
    member: attacks law taxes, 208,

210; attacks monetary classification of suits, 166, 204, 210, 328 n. R; authentication of laws, 197; codification, 179, 213, 219 ff.; discards preambles, 198–201; 'intercommunity of jurisdiction', 205; judicial evidence, 206–7; judicial organization and procedure, 203–8; legislative drafting, 199; legislative procedure, 179; omnicompetent courts, 204–5, 210; opposes racial distinctions, 215; oral pleadings, 205, 259, 263; Penal Code, 222–33; prison discipline, 217; 'single-seated justice', 206.

faith in education, 45–46, 57, 283.

influence on Charter Act (1833), 180, 327 n. O.

law commission, over-optimistic hopes for, 213, 221, 224.

leaves India, 239.

liberalism and India, xiv, xvi, 40, 43–46, 65, 191–3, 283, 320–1.

penal code: delay in enacting, 240, 261–2; enacted, 262; framing, 220–33; hopes for completion of, 213, 221; see also Code, Penal.

supports Cornwallis's principle of separating powers, 193, 209–10, 237.

Macaulay, Zachary, 28, 40.

Mackenzie, Holt: biog., 94, 101, 331.

influence on: Charter Act (1833), 180, 327 n. O; divisional commissioner system, 151–5; form of superior government, 169–73, 273; land revenue policy, 94, 101, 109–16, 131.

paternalist influence on, 118.

reconciles paternalist and liberal administrative traditions, 159 ff., 273.

supports lieutenant-governor system, 170, 175.

Utilitarian influence on, 95, 162.

views agree with James Mill's, 95, 101, 109, 110–13, 175.

Mackintosh, Sir James, 52.

Maclagan, Sir E., 137–8.

Macleod, J. R., 217, 223.

McCulloch, J. R.: contempt of classical economy for peasant proprietorship, 126–7.

Macnaghten, Sir W. H., 210, 211.

Madras: administrative system copied in Bombay, 167–8.

Bengal administrative and judicial system introduced into, 140.

district larger than in Bengal, 144.

Munro's administrative and judicial reforms, 141–4.

Munro's revenue system, see Ryotwar system.

revised revenue system, 108–9, 117, 137.

Magistrate, office of, see Collector.

Maine, Sir H. S., xv; biog., 332.

influence of India on his thought, 288.

law member, 269, 271.

modifies utilitarianism, 312–13, 315.

opposes lieutenant-governor system, 271–2.

Malcolm, Sir John, 51, 94.

administrative reforms in Bombay, 167–8.

biog., 9, 234, 332.

character and outlook, 10–11, 16–17, 19, 20.

dispute with Chief Justice of Bombay, 168.

opposes centralization, 22, 173, 182.

supports ryotwar system, 86.

Malkin, Sir B., 214.

Malthus, T. R., 58.

influence on land revenue policy, 87–88, 90, 95, 99, 100, 130, 132.

Mangles, R. D., 118, 131.

Mayo, Earl of, Viceroy, 257, 282.

Merchants, European: claim assessment retards cotton cultivation, 128–32.

oppose ryotwar system, 61–62, 86, 128.

policy for India, 41–43, 120.

support: English education, 46; permanent settlement, 42, 61, 87, 117; separation of powers, 79.

See also Free traders.

Metcalfe, Sir Charles (Lord Metcalfe), 234, 237.

biog., 9, 173, 190, 239, 332.

character and outlook, 9–10, 16–19, 21, 22.

Delhi system, 144, 148, 153, 154, 160.

frees press, 239.

ideal administrative system, 21, 22, 153–5, 157, 160, 238, 273.

Metcalfe, Sir Charles (contd.)
influence on Punjab system, 243.
opposes centralization, 173.
supports: indigenous revenue practice, 128–9; lieutenant-governor
system, 173, 175; permanent settlement, 116, 120; ryotwar system,
86.
Mill, James, 50, 51, 52, 99, 130, 313.
aggressive policy towards Indian
states, 249–50.
appointed: Assistant Examiner, xii,
48, 94; Examiner, 48, 182.
authoritarian bent, 293–4, 302, 322.
death, 188, 201, 241.
differs from orthodox liberalism, 58–
66, 250, 324 n. E.
History of British India, xii, 48, 53,
60–61, 66, 70, 77, 78, 90, 145, 147,
260; quoted, 53, 54, 56, 57, 328
n. S.
influence on judicial and administrative system: advocates codification,
219, 328 n. S; advocates centralized
judiciary, 185, 253, 266; advocates
Panopticon, 149–50; attacks Cornwallis system, 69, 145–6; attacks
law taxes, 260; judicial organization, 70–71, 184; judicial procedure,
70–71, 184–8, 207; opposes boards,
162; oral pleadings, 156, 259, 263;
panacea for law problem, 146–7;
partial realization of administrative
aims, 80, 243, 256–7; separation of
powers, 164–5.
influence on land revenue system:
Bombay, 122–8; drafts despatches,
48, 81, 90; fixing of rents, 121–2;
land tenures, 87, 92, 110, 112, 113,
115, 117; law of rent and taxation
theory, 77, 87–93, 95, 107, 110,
112, 117, 124, 131, 139, 317; net
produce criterion, 93, 100, 101,
102, 109, 122, 129; opposes permanent settlement, 87, 91, 116, 118,
132–3; supports ryotwar system,
60–61, 70, 76, 92, 127.
influence on superior government:
approves Mackenzie's scheme, 175,
273; Charter Act (1833), 78, 173,
180, 195; favours centralization,
63, 175, 256; instructions to new
Government of India, 193–6;

Legislative Council, 64, 176–9, 256,
321; opposes representative government, 65–66, 320–1.
political and moral theory, 24, 52 ff.,
63 ff., 140, 293–4, 295, 297, 298, 302.
views on education, 56–88, 324 n. D.
Mill, J. S., xiv, 177.
career at India House, 48–50.
criticized by Stephen, 281, 291–2.
influence on Indian policy: approves
Civil Procedure Code, 259; approves fixing of rents, 122; approves
Macaulay's penal code, 239; approves Punjab system, 248; approves
settlement system of N.W. Provinces, 115; authority cited against
permanent settlement, 118, 127;
drafts despatches, 49, 323 n. C;
general influence, vii–viii, 49–50;
opposes representative government,
251, 255, 298, 321; upholds
father's taxation theory, 50, 115,
127–8, 135–7, 139.
modifies Utilitarian theory, 241–2,
291–2, 294–5, 297.
Principles of Political Economy, 115,
127, 135.
Millett, F., 223, 258.
digest of Bengal civil procedure law,
189, 203, 210, 220–1, 258.
enactment of digest opposed by
Macaulay, 212–13, 258.
Minto, Earl of, Viceroy, 318–19.
Montagu–Chelmsford Reforms, 319,
321.
Morley, J. (Lord Morley), xiv, 318.
Munro, Sir Thomas:
administrative and judicial system:
adopted by one wing of Utilitarians, 80, 147–8, 165; character,
20–22, 63; influence on Bentinck,
165; reforms (1814–16), 141–4;
powerful instrument for change,
79, 80; supported by Fifth Report
(1812), 86.
biog., 9, 332.
character and outlook, xvi, 12–13,
19–22, 25, 173.
See also Ryotwar system.
Munsifs, 150 n. 3, 217.
after 1831 reforms, 167.
in Macaulay's scheme, 204–5.
in Ross's scheme, 157–8, 166.

instituted in Punjab, 275.
powers raised, 265.
Mutiny, Indian, 114, 134, 138, 225, 240, 254, 256, 272, 286.
   economic causes in N.W. Provinces, 116.
   effect on British policy, 269.
   paternalism ascendant after, 117, 268–9.

Napier, Sir Charles, 243, 270.
Nash, A., 134.
   quoted, 123.
Net-produce method of assessment: advocated by James Mill, 93, 100, 101, 102, 109, 122, 129.
   approved by Home Authorities, 94, 129.
   cause of over-assessment, 100, 134.
   in settlement of Bombay Deccan, 99–101, 122–3.
   in settlement of (N.)W. Provinces, 95–99.
   in revised Madras system, 108–9.
   relinquished in revised Bombay system, 102–3, 105.
   relinquished in revised N.W. Provinces system, 101–2, 105.
North-Western Provinces, xv n. 1.
   administrative and judicial system: character, 80, 238, 244, 272; reforms (1829–31), 102, 151–67; reforms (1868), 265.
   revenue system: compared with Bombay's, 123–6; under Reg. IX, 1833, 103–6, 115–22, 129, 133, 286.
   See also Ceded and Conquered Provinces, Western Provinces, United Provinces.

Paternal-ism (-ists): attitude to law reform, 147–8, 173–4, 255, 269.
   authoritarian Utilitarians merge with, xvii, 79–80, 157, 165, 234, 246.
   character of, xvi, 14–25.
   differences with Utilitarians, 22–25, 173.
   harmonized with liberalism: Campbell, 254–5; Mackenzie, 159, 273; Stephen, 273 ff., 281 ff.
   influence on administration: after

Mutiny, 117, 268; in Delhi under Metcalfe, 144, 148, 153, 154, 160; in Madras under Munro, 20–22, 78, 141–4; in N.W. Provinces, 80, 118–22; in Punjab under Lawrences, 243–6, 268–9; on defensive from '60's, 269–73.
   opposed by Liberal Utilitarians: Ross, 79, 157, 159, 234–7; Macaulay, 193, 209–10, 234.
   opposed to Cornwallis system, 9, 14–16, 19–22, 148.
   opposed to centralization, 22, 25, 173.
   similarity of some aims with Utilitarians, 23, 147–8.
   See also *Ryotwar* system.
Permanent Settlement of Bengal (1793): compared with *ryotwar* system, 81–83.
   litigation resulting from, 146.
   opposed by: James Mill, 69, 87, 115; J. S. Mill, 115; rent theory, 116, 132–3.
   principles, 5–6, 81–83.
   supported by European merchants, 61, 87.
   vexatious tariffs necessitated by (Ross), 116.
   See also Cornwallis system.
Permanent settlement of land revenue: advocated by: Bentinck, 116; European merchants, 42, 61, 87, 117; Lawrence, 117; Metcalfe, 116; Munro, 83, 84, 86.
   finally renounced, 118.
   opposed by: James Mill, 87, 91, 116, 118, 132–3; rent theory, 91, 116, 118, 127–8; Ross, 116–17; Wingate, 118, 127–8.
   principle accepted by Sec. of State, 117.
   refused in Ceded and Conquered Provinces, 86.
   See also Permanent Settlement of Bengal.
Pringle, R. K.: assessment method approved by James Mill, 94, 99, 100.
   failure of settlement, 102, 103.
   over-assessment, 134.
   use of net-produce criterion in Deccan settlement, 99–101, 122–3.
Prinsep, Thoby, 196–8, 210.

Prison Discipline, Report of Committee on, 240.
quoted, 217–18.
Private property in land: advocated by European merchants, 41, 61, 86, 117 n. 3.
fundamental concept of all early revenue systems, 5, 26, 82, 86.
revolutionary importance of, 8, 280.
unrestricted right: not granted, 116–17, 122–3; opposed by Mackenzie, 110–13, 116; opposed by James Mill, 87, 116, 128.
Provincial Boards of Revenue: abolished in Bengal Territories, 151, 154, 163.
in Madras, 5, 75, 144.
See diagram, 142–3.
Provincial Courts of Appeal: in Cornwallis system, 75.
abolished in Bengal Territories, 143, 152, 156–7, 164.
See diagram, 142–3.
Punjab: adoption of commissioner system, 155.
Land Alienation Act (1900), 320.
'Punjab system': Benthamite influence on, 245–8; Dalhousie's influence on, 248, 277; judicial system, 247; Stephen's views on, 245–6, 274–7.
separate judiciary established, 277.
standard of revenue assessment, 137.

Regulations, Bengal: II, 1793; preamble quoted, 6.
XLI, 1793, 198.
VII, 1822, 97, 102, 114, 129, 151.
I, 1829, 154.
V, 1831, 167, 189, 215.
VII, 1831, 163.
IX, 1831, 167.
IX, 1833, 103, 105, 114, 124.
Ricardo, David, 11, 58, 77, 81, 131.
theory of rent and taxation accepted by James Mill, 88–90.
Rickards, R., 65.
Ripon, Earl of, 312.
local self-govt. reforms, 287–8, 289, 299, 315.
Robertson, T. C., 115, 212.
Romilly, Sir J., 258.

Ross, Alexander, 198, 202.
abolishes transit duties, 239.
advocates: abolition of law taxes, 211; Benthamite legislative drafting, 201; codification, 190, 220; separation of powers, 157, 159, 209, 236–7.
biog., 332.
his ideal judicial and administrative system, 156–61, 186, 189, 207, 236–7, 273.
influence on 1831 judicial reforms, 166–7.
opposes: permanent settlement, 116–17; separate chief court for W. Provinces, 156–7, 163, 167, 185.
Liberal Utilitarian political philosophy, 79, 120, 234–7, 321.
Roy, Ram Mohan: Bentham's letter to, quoted, 147.
catechized by Bentham, 52.
Ryan, Sir Edward, 61, 198, 202, 214, 258.
advocates codification, 189.
reforming character, 180 n. 2, 189 n. 3.
quoted on rent theory, 132–3.
Ryotwar system: adopted in Bombay, 9, 148.
advocated by: Fifth Report, 86; James Mill, 60–61, 70, 76, 92, 127; paternalists, 9, 86, 148.
character, 9, 13, 26, 70, 83–84, 92, 111.
Munro's principle of assessment, 84, 95, 108.
opposed by European merchants, 61–62, 86, 128.
radical influence of in Bombay settlement, 76, 126.
revised Madras system, 108.

Sadr amins, 150 n. 3, 215, 217, 260.
abolished (1868), 265.
after 1831 reforms, 167.
in Macaulay's scheme, 204–5, 209.
in Ross's scheme, 157–8, 166.
See diagram, 141–2.
Sadr amins, principal, 217.
become subordinate judges (1868), 265.
Macaulay proposes abolition of, 205.
proposed by Bayley, 166.

powers of, 167.
powers extended, 216.
See diagram, 141–2.
Sadr Diwani and *Nizamat Adalat*,
    Court of, 141, 158.
appeals to go direct to (Macaulay),
    206, 260.
established by Wellesley, 7.
fusion with Supreme Court, 253,
    264.
separate court for W. Provinces:
    established, 156, 163; opposed by
    James Mill, 185, 266; opposed by
    Ross, 156–7, 163, 167, 185.
'single-seated' judges, 167.
special appeals to, 260, 266, 279.
supervisory function of, 188.
See diagram, 141–2.
Saharanpur Rules, 106, 133.
Separation of powers: advocated by:
    Bengal school, 151, 156; Corn-
    wallis, 5–7, 140; Directors, 165–6;
    European merchants, 79; Macau-
    lay, 193, 209–10, 237; Ross, 157,
    159, 209, 236–7; Wellesley, 7–8,
    141.
opposed by: Mackenzie in part, 160;
    paternalists, 21, 80, 143, 153, 157,
    243–4, 269; some Utilitarian opi-
    nion, 63, 72, 74, 324 n. F.
Utilitarian opinion divided over, 79,
    157, 165.
Shore, Sir John (Lord Teignmouth),
    xii, 27, 28, 39, 40.
Sind: administrative system, 243, 270.
Smith, Adam, xii, 20, 37, 58, 77.
Smith, T. Southwood, 60, 75.
Stephen, Sir J. Fitzjames, xiv, 229, 257,
    269.
appointed law member, 273.
attacks: Bright, 298, 299, 304, 308;
    J. S. Mill, 281, 291–2.
authoritarian liberalism, 281–5, 288 ff.
his Evidence Act, 264.
influenced by: Bentham, 273, 274,
    278, 290, 297, 301; Hobbes, 274,
    275, 293, 295, 297.
influence on Curzon, 311.
intellectual basis of imperialism, 290,
    298, 306–11.
Liberty, Equality, Fraternity, 281, 282,
    288, 289, 291, 301, 306.
relations with J. Strachey, 282, 305.

views on: codification, 277–8; Indian
    codes, quoted, 258 n. 2; Indian
    judicial system, 266–7, 274; Punjab
    system, 245–6.
Stephen, Sir Leslie, 223, 320.
Strachey, Sir John: authoritarian
    liberalism of, 282 ff., 300, 305.
biog., 282, 332.
financial decentralization, 257.
influence of J. S. Mill on, 137, 312,
    325 n. H.
radical view on village communities,
    119–20.
uses rent theory to oppose permanent
    settlement, 118.
Stokes, Whitley, 226, 231, 263.
Strachey, Edward, 50, 149.
Sullivan, John, 131.
Supreme Court(s), 141 n. 1.
Calcutta: Macaulay's plan for re-
    modelling, 214; proposal to extend
    jurisdiction, 41, 61; purpose of
    establishment, 2.
fusion with *Sadr* courts, 168–9, 253,
    264.
Indian Govt. given legislative power
    over, 180, 183, 194.
Swettenham, Sir Frank, 310.

Temple, Sir Richard, 245.
Thomason, James, 155, 234, 238.
biog., 332.
Directions to Settlement Officers quoted,
    104–5.
educational policy, 252.
paternalist outlook, 118, 119.
Thompson, George, 130.
Trevelyan, Sir Charles: biog., 333.
*On the Education of the People of
    India*, 253; cited, 46–47.
Report on Town and Transit Duties,
    239.
representative of Liberal attitude to
    India, 18, 46–47, 253–4, 287, 321,
    323 n. B.

United Provinces, 15 n. 1.
standard of assessment in, 137.
See also N.W. Provinces.
Utilitarian-s (-ism), *see* Bentham,
    Jeremy; Mill, James; Mill, J. S.

Villiers, T. Hyde, 180, 327 n. O.

Wellesley, Marquis, 18, 85, 249.
  outlook and policy, xv, 7–8, 9–10, 37, 141.
Western Provinces: administrative and judicial reforms (1829–31), 102, 151–67.
  become Presidency of Agra, xv n. 1, 164.
  effect of Bengal Regulations on (Mackenzie), 161.
  origin, xv n. 1, 97.
  revenue settlement: failure of, 101–2, 151; under Reg. VII, 1822, 70, 95–99, 103, 114, 129; under Reg. IX, 1833, 103.
  separate *Sadr* Court for, 156, 163–4.
  See also Ceded and Conquered Provinces; North-Western Provinces.
Westminster Review, 49, 239.
  J. S. Mill proprietor, 241.
  silence on East India Co., 48, 60, 324 n. E.
Wilberforce, William, xv, 28, 31, 35, 45.

Wingate, Sir George; biog., 333.
  influence of Utilitarian theory of taxation on, 103–4, 107, 118, 122–8, 131, 134, 137.
Wood, Sir Charles (Viscount Halifax): accepts principle of permanent assessment, 117.
  Education Despatch of 1854, 251.
  issues 'half-assets' rule, 133.
  orders net-produce criterion at Madras, 109.
  Secretary of State, 109.

Young, James: quoted, 116.
  rejected for vacancy on Law Commission, 240.
  relations with Bentham and influence on Indian Government, 51–52, 321.
  urges codification, 189.
Young, Gavin, 120.
Young, Dr. G. M., 242.
  quoted, 245, 248.

PRINTED IN GREAT BRITAIN
AT THE UNIVERSITY PRESS, OXFORD
BY VIVIAN RIDLER
PRINTER TO THE UNIVERSITY